A GUIDE TO APOCALYPTIC CINEMA

A GUIDE TO APOCALYPTIC CINEMA

Charles P. Mitchell

GREENWOOD PRESS
Westport, Connecticut • London

Library of Congress Cataloging-in-Publication Data

Mitchell, Charles P., 1949–
    A guide to apocalyptic cinema / Charles P. Mitchell.
        p.   cm.
    Includes index.
    ISBN 0–313–31527–2 (alk. paper)
        1. Science fiction films—History and criticism.   2. Apocalypse in motion pictures.
    I. Title.
    PN1995.9.S26.M575   2001
    791.43′615—dc21   00–061723

British Library Cataloguing in Publication Data is available.

Library of Congress Catalog Card Number: 00–061723
ISBN: 0–313–31527–2

First published in 2001

Greenwood Press, 88 Post Road West, Westport, CT 06881
An imprint of Greenwood Publishing Group, Inc.
www.greenwood.com

Printed in the United States of America

The paper used in this book complies with the
Permanent Paper Standard issued by the National
Information Standards Organization (Z39.48–1984).

10 9 8 7 6 5 4 3 2 1

Copyright Acknowledgments

The author and publisher gratefully acknowledge permission for use of the following material:

Title page illustration by Roberta D. Mitchell. Used with permission.

All photos courtesy of Robert Brosch Archival Photography except Photo 8 which is courtesy of
the Paul Parla collection. Used with permission.

This volume is dedicated to my wife, Roberta,
and our mirthful, four-footed companions,
Max and Bon Bon

Contents

An unnumbered photo essay begins after page 116

Preface

With the end of the millennium, there grew a heightened interest in, and awareness of, the future last days of humankind itself. In motion pictures, however, interest in this topic increased dramatically throughout the second half ixof the twentieth century; consequently, this body of films can be considered a distinct genre. The purpose of this book is to examine this genre by focusing in detail on fifty films that illustrate the variety, range and different categories of apocalyptic cinema. The volume begins with an overview, which provides a basic definition and considers how the genre both relates to and differs from a similar category of films that is sometimes called post-apocalyptic. Seven major types of apocalyptic films are presented with examples, which are later explored in depth. The criteria for the selection of the entries are also considered.

The entries themselves are arranged alphabetically by title. This is followed by a subjective rating by the author, which should be interpreted in the following manner:

*	Poor to Fair
**	Fair to Good
***	Good to Very Good
****	Very Good to Excellent
*****	Top of the Line

No half stars are used in these ratings, which are meant to apply exclusively to apocalyptic films and should not be compared to other general film ratings. The individual threat contained in each film is described in a few words. The next section provides standardized production information including studio, screenwriters, cinematographers, special effects directors, editors, composers, producers and directors. The credits of more recent films are sometimes voluminous. A hundred people may be listed for special effects alone on a picture like *Deep Impact*, so in these cases I try to identify only the supervisor or key group of supervisors. Some films also may have over a dozen producers, associate producers and executive producers. I try to identify the major line producers only, and when I occasionally include an executive producer, such as Stephen Spielberg on *Deep Impact*, I identify him or her as such. The notation "B & W" is included if the film is in black and white; otherwise it may be assumed the film is in color. This section ends with the running length of the film, rounded off to the nearest full minute. If an alternate version of the film exists, then the running time of both versions is included.

The next segment is an annotated cast list. It includes the performer's name, followed in parenthesis by identification or the character name in italics. As far as possible, each cast member is provided with an annotation that describes the part. This list is arranged to make the notations more fluid and logical, and therefore they may not be in the same order as the studio's end credits. The central section of each entry is a detailed synopsis with an emphasis on accuracy. A critique follows, which provides a critical analysis of the film, stressing in particular the apocalyptic elements. A study of the scientific or mythological basis of the plot is included. The technical presentation and performances of the major cast members are also evaluated. Each entry concludes with three to six representative quotes that help to provide the character and flavor of the production. A photo essay is also included that helps convey the atmosphere of these films. Appendix A provides an annotated list of fifty additional examples of apocalyptic cinema. Appendix B is a filmography of representative titles of post-apocalyptic films and serve as a contrast to the films covered in the main body of this volume. Appendix C explores illustrations of the apocalyptic genre on television (largely episodes from anthology programs such as *The Twilight Zone* or *Tales of Tomorrow*). A general index wraps up the book. In the text, I followed the stylistic format of capitalizing "Earth" except when it is preceded by the article "the," when it reverts to the lower case. I also replaced the word "mankind" with the newly preferred "humankind" in most instances.

I wish to thank the following individuals and organizations for their assistance and encouragement in the preparation of this volume: the Bangor Public Library, Claudia Barrett, John Berrien, Jean Byron, Philip Davey, Dr. Ronald Davis, Sandy Descher, Christian Drake, Lucian Endicott, L. M. Garnett, David Hedison, Joe "Phantom of the Movies" Kane, Jean and Dick Norris, Paul and Donna Parla, Bill and Cheryl Pitz, Luz Potter, Robert Rotter, Robert Schmidt, Dr. Ronald and Amelia Schwartz, Aizo and Seiko Shingo, Pamela St. Clair, and the University of Maine's Fogler Library. As indicated in the dedication, this book would not exist without the full cooperation of my wife, Roberta, who watched and commented on each film with me, read and helped craft each entry, assisted in the laborious process of creating the index and researched obscure pieces of information such as the proper way to spell Kartaphilos—or is it Cartiphylos?

Overview: Cinematic Visions
of the Apocalypse

A basic definition of apocalyptic cinema is a motion picture that depicts a cred-ible threat to the continuing existence of humankind as a species or the existence of Earth as a planet capable of supporting human life. The genre of apocalyptic cinema is closely related to, yet distinct from, a similar genre primarily known as post-apocalyptic cinema, which concentrates on survivors of a catastrophic event struggling to reestablish a livable society. In order to be classified as an apocalyptic film, the event threatening the extinction of humanity has to be pre-sented within the story. If this catastrophe occurs prior to the events depicted on the screen, the film is post-apocalyptic. Naturally there can be a blurring of the lines of these two genres, and a number of pictures can legitimately be labeled as both. In *Deluge* (1933), for example, the first half of the story is clearly apoca-lyptic and the second half is post-apocalyptic. The same is true of the television mini-series based on the novel *The Stand* by Stephen King. The first episode is apocalyptic while the remaining three episodes are post-apocalyptic. Two novels by Philip Wylie and Edwin Balmer also serve to illustrate the difference. *When Worlds Collide* is apocalyptic, and *After Worlds Collide* is post-apocalyptic. Unfortunately in general criticism, the distinctions between apocalyptic and post-apocalyptic categories are often been overlooked.

Apocalyptic films can be classified into seven specific categories: Religious or Supernatural; Celestial Collision; Solar or Orbital Disruption; Nuclear War and Radioactive Fallout; Germ Warfare or Pestilence; Alien Device or Invasion; and Scientific Miscalculation. An eighth category, Miscellaneous, is somewhat of a grab bag that required to account for a few oddball titles outside these regular categories. A few films, such as *Virus* (1980), combine elements from several categories. A close examination of each grouping defines the unusual scope and breadth of the apocalyptic genre.

A. Religious or Supernatural: This grouping is intrinsic since all the major religions of the world envision the last days of mankind. The word "apocalypse" comes from the Late Latin word "apocalypsis," meaning a disclosure or unveiling, and the term is commonly applied to the Book of *Revelations*, the last book of the New Testament in the *Bible*. Attributed to St. John, this book describes, in highly symbolic terms, a wondrous vision about the terrible tribulations humanity will face prior to the last judgment. Each succeeding generation of biblical scholars has interpreted and reinterpreted the many abstract and obscure references contained in the vision, usually in terms of their own time. Many of the elements from the Book of *Revelations* have filtered into world culture, such as the four horsemen of the apocalypse, the beast whose number is 666 and the angels with trumpets. Early believers, for example, equated the Antichrist with Nero, the mad Roman emperor who persecuted the Christians. In time, other candidates were put forth by interpreters, including Attila, Frederick II, Muhammad, various popes, Hitler, Stalin and so on. Certainly the image of the Antichrist is one of the most powerful concepts from the Book of *Revelations*, and his portrayal in literature is a recurring one. In apocalyptic cinema, two excellent examples illustrating the influence of the Book of *Revelations* are *Holocaust 2000* (1978) and *The Seventh Sign* (1988). There are representations of other beliefs as well. *The Last Wave* (1977) considers the end of the world as perceived by the Aboriginal tribes of Australia. Alternatively, *Runestone* (1991) uses Ragnarök, the doomsday scenario from Norse mythology, as its basis. Other films employ semireligious or supernatural elements to present their story, as in *The Man Who Could Work Miracles* (1936).

B. Celestial Collision: Scientists have concluded that major celestial collisions have occurred in the past on at least three different occasions, with the most recent one 65 million years ago leading to the extinction of the dinosaurs. It is inevitable that Earth will face future major collisions. and although it is estimated that another extinction level impact should not occur for 100 million years, there is no guarantee that it will not happen next year. The collision of the fragments of comet Shoemaker-Levy with the planet Jupiter in 1994 demonstrated the destructive power of such a cataclysmic event. It increased the level of public awareness and, no doubt, inspired the films *Armageddon* (1998) and *Deep Impact* (1998). The cinema's interest in the realistic threat posed by comets and meteors goes back to the appearance of Haley's comet in 1910, which inspired a number of short films (some of them now lost) portraying catastrophe, such as *The Comet* (1910) and August Blom's *The End of the World* (1916). There is even a satire of this type of film, starring Norma Shearer and Jack Pickford, entitled *Waking Up the Town* (1925), with a *Chicken Little* plot about the mistaken belief that a comet is about to crash into the earth. Other examples of celestial collision in this book include Abel Gance's epic also entitled *The End of the World* (1930/34), *The Day the Sky Exploded* (1958/61) and *Meteor* (1979).

C. **Solar or Orbital Disruption:** The relationship between Earth and the sun is a crucial factor for survival. Any event that might upset this delicate balance would be devastating. Solar flares are explosions caused by a fluctuation of magnetic energy. The result is a wave of increased radiation registering across the electromagnetic scale from radio waves to gamma waves. In the past, solar flares have disabled satellites and burned out power grids on Earth. In 1989, for example, a solar flare shut down Hydro Quebec's power generation system. Solar flares generally occur in eleven year cycles, and changes in these cycles are believed to effect Earth's climate. A period of minimal activity three hundred years ago was considered to be a cause of the "mini-ice age" that happened in the late seventeenth and early eighteenth centuries. Scientist are researching how solar flares might influence earthquakes, magnetic shifts, or life itself in case of a massive increase in solar activity. Films such as *Solar Crisis* (1990) and *Where Have All the People Gone?* (1974) represent the threats posed by solar changes. Earth's orbit is not circular but rather is elliptical. The sun is the major controlling factor in keeping Earth's orbit stable, but other factors also take part, such as the tilt of Earth's axis and the gravitational fluctuations (called perturbations) caused by the other planets in the solar system. While most scientists do not envision any danger of an orbital shift either toward or away from the sun, they admit that problems could arise if something disrupted the celestial mechanics. Advocates of "chaos theory" suggest that an unexpected phenomenon may always occur, such as a dark star or black hole passing nearby that could totally disrupt the solar system. *The Day the Earth Caught Fire* (1961) pictures a catastrophic shift in Earth's orbit.

D. **Nuclear War and Radioactive Fallout:** Since the dropping of the first atomic bomb over Hiroshima in 1945, the world has lived in dread of the possibility of nuclear warfare as well as its deadly aftereffects, especially radioactive fallout. It is natural for this anxiety to be expressed in films, and these pictures have had a greater impact than any other category of apocalyptic film. Numerous types of nuclear films are covered in this book, including mainstream drama such as *On The Beach* (1959), black comedies like *Dr. Strangelove* (1964) and foreign views such as those provided by *The Last War* (1961) from Japan and *One Night Stand* (1984) from Australia. A different type of nuclear film depicts a third party trying to provoke a nuclear conflict, such as the alien invaders in *No Survivors Please* (1964), a film that combines this category with the next one.

E. **Germ Warfare or Pestilence:** Another Japanese production combined this category with the previous one in the storyline of *Virus* (1980). The biological threat of germ warfare is similar to the nuclear threat, but it is even more insidious since the aggressor can hide behind a mask of anonymity. *Moonraker* (1979) provides a scenario of germ warfare at its most sophisticated. The threat of a man-made virus that could destroy the world was fantasy when *The Satan Bug* (1965) was conceived, but by current scholarly estimates, science is now capable of producing a doomsday scourge. A natural disease with the identical terrifying results is also within the realm of possibility. Another film that covers this topic is *No Blade of Grass* (1970), about a green plague that kills all plant life, leaving humankind to face global starvation.

F. Alien Device or Invasion: This category is one of the keystones of modern science fiction, and countless variants of alien creatures invading Earth form the basis of innumerable films. Of course, the basic intent of the aliens determines whether the film is apocalyptic. In some cases, the alien invaders may not want to destroy humankind, only conquer it. These pictures would then fall outside the basic definition of apocalyptic cinema and would not be representative of the apocalyptic genre. Thus films such as *It Came from Outer Space* (1953), *Invasion of the Saucer Men* (1957), *I Married a Monster From Outer Space* (1958), *Atomic Submarine* (1959), *Strange Invaders* (1983) and *The Day the Earth Stood Still* (1951) are not bona fide films of the genre, despite some apocalyptic elements in their plot. Another factor also disqualifies some science fiction films, namely, if the invaders (or invader) lacks the capacity to threaten the existence of humankind as a whole. It comes down to a judgment call whether *The Man from Planet X* (1951), *The Brain from Planet Arous* (1957), *The Invasion of the Animal People* (1962) or *The Beast with a Million Eyes* (1956) represent such a threat. Sometimes it is a borderline decision. Consider one of the most famous of early science fiction classics, *The Thing* (1951). The lone invader seems almost impervious to most weapons, and it is able to "grow" more Things, since it is a plant. Yet, after learning it is vulnerable to electricity, would humankind as a whole be genuinely threatened with extinction by the Thing? In the original novel, the Thing was also a shapeshifter, but in the film itself it was limited to just one form. Would you consider it to be an apocalyptic threat? In any case, there are many films where the menace is obvious, such as *The War of the Worlds* (1953), *Target Earth* (1953). *Kronos* (1957) and the satirical *Mars Attacks!* (1996). Another variant in this category is the appearance of an alien weapon with the capacity to obliterate the human race, as portrayed in *The 27th Day* (1957) and *Star Trek—The Motion Picture* (1978). In *The Lost Missile* (1958), it is never determined if the threat is a weapon from some remote alien that reached Earth by accident instead of design.

G. Scientific Miscalculation: The public at large has mixed feelings about science, which is sometimes worshiped and other times feared. The category of apocalypse due to Scientific Miscalculation contains some of the most imaginative examples in the entire genre. Mutations, usually developed by radiation from nuclear tests, are the most common threat, frequently in the form of gigantic insects, as in *Them!* (1954). Again, the only gray area is whether the mutations represent a legitimate threat to the continued existence of humankind. Many times, the giant threat is only of local concern, such as the giant rabbits in *Night of the Lepus* (1972) or the giant spider in *Tarantula* (1955). Other forms of science gone haywire include *Crack in the World* (1965), where an experiment to penetrate to the magma from the earth's core produces an unforeseen result; *Quiet Earth* (1985), where an electrical project winds up causing a change in the atomic structure of all matter; and *The Magnetic Monster* (1953), where the creation of a new element threatens the stability of the planet.

H. Miscellaneous: Other types of apocalyptic threats are difficult, if not impossible, to pigeonhole, so for the sake of convenience they are be grouped here. These can encompass such varied concepts as vampirism as in *The Last Man on Earth* (1964); a geological anomaly, as in *The Night the World Exploded* (1957); or a freak fire in the sky above the planet as in *Voyage to the Bottom of the Sea* (1961). A large number of various "nature in revolt" scenarios could also be noted here. Future additions of more miscellaneous are only limited by the imagination of the screenwriters.

The fifty films studied in depth were selected to provide as broad as possible a range of the different types of apocalyptic films, including a mixture of quality films, B pictures and low-budget turkeys. It is deliberate that the films that were selected do not represent the finest in the genre. Many excellent films, which could have easily garnered five-star ratings, were not included here so that the entire group would be as well rounded and diverse as possible. Numerous international films are also included from Australia, England, France, Germany, Italy, Japan and New Zealand. A meaningful genre guide needs to be have as wide as possible a scope and include "the good, the bad and the ugly." Noteworthy and impressive recent films such as *Twelve Monkeys* (1995), *Independence Day* (1996), *Starship Troopers* (1997) and *Men in Black* (1997) were not chosen in order to avoid tilting this guide to the entire genre with more contemporary, big-budget blockbusters. Similarly, a number of well-known classics, such as Alfred Hitchcock's *The Birds* (1963) and Don Siegel's *Invasion of the Body Snatchers* (1956) yielded their positions so that other, lesser-known examples could be explored in depth for the first time. Many of these titles are noted in Appendix A, which includes fifty additional titles that illustrate the remarkable spectrum of films representing apocalyptic cinema.

A Guide to Apocalyptic Cinema:
Fifty Films in Depth

The 27th Day (1957)

Rating: ***   **Threat:** Alien weapon

Columbia. Written by John Mantley based on his novel *The 27th Day*; Photographed by Henry Freulich; Special effects (uncredited) by Ray Harryhausen; Edited by Jerome Thomas; Music arranged by Mischa Bakaleinikoff; Produced by Helen Ainsworth & Lewis J. Rachmil (executive); Directed by William Asher. B & W, 75 minutes.

ANNOTATED CAST LIST

Gene Barry (*Jonathan Clark*, LA newspaper reporter); Valerie French (*Eve Wingate*, British tourist); Arnold Moss (alien spokesman); George Voskovec (*Klaus Bechner*, German scientist); Azenath Janti (*Ivan Godofsky*, Soviet soldier); Marie Tsien (*Su Tan*, Chinese peasant); Stefan Schnabel (Soviet premier); Frederick Ledebur (*Dr. Karl Neuhaus*, U.S. nuclear scientist); Ralph Clanton (*Ingram*, U.S. national security advisor); Paul Birch (U.S. admiral and head, Joint Chiefs of Staff); Grandon Rhodes (UN secretary-general); Paul Frees (*Ward Mason*, television broadcaster); Mel Welles (Russian field marshal); Don Spark (*Harry Bellows*, a painter, Eve's friend); David Bond (*Dr. Schmidt*, Bechner's associate); Ed Hinton (commander); Mark Warren (*Pete*, news copyboy); Monty Ash (Soviet prison doctor); Peter Norman (Soviet prison interrogator); Theodore Marcuse (*Gregor*, Soviet colonel); Sigfrid Tor (*Zamke*, Soviet general); Eric Feldary (Russian officer); Weaver Levy (Chinese officer); Robert Forrest (U.S. Air Force general, Joint Chiefs of Staff member); Charles Evans (U.S. Army general, Joint Chiefs of Staff member); John Dodsworth (British broadcaster); Jacques Gallo (French broadcaster); Mark Bennett (*Gorki*, Soviet spy); Arthur Lovejoy (*Bracovich*, Soviet spy); John Bryant (FBI agent assigned to protect Beckner); Michael Harris (younger FBI agent); Walda Winchell (hospital nurse); Tom Daly (*Joe*, bartender in LA); John Mooney (military police captain); Paul Bowker (U.S. Army doctor); Emil Sitka (newspaper hawker); Philip Van Zandt (cab driver).

SYNOPSIS

This modestly budgeted Columbia feature could be basically described as an intellectual cliff-hanger, relying on a strong, well-conceived proposition. There are only a few action scenes in the entire story, but instead of becoming a boring "talking heads" drama, the film is a compelling tale about moral choices, and it generates a fair degree of tension. The apocalyptical threat is fairly unconventional. An alien doomsday weapon, designed as small capsules, is distributed to five earthlings, apparently at random. These weapons will remain active for twenty-seven days and will only destroy human life, leaving animals, buildings and plants unaffected. This premise sets up a well-crafted little thriller.

The film begins with the title displayed in front of a solar eclipse. After the credits, Eve Wingate is shown watching her artist friend Harry Bellows complete his painting on a beach in Cornwall, England. She takes a walk and is lounging in the sand farther down the beach when a shadowy figure appears and addresses her by name. As she looks up, the figure says, "Come with me, please," and she vanishes in an iris of light. A similar abduction is repeated in the newsroom of a Los Angeles paper, in a village being pillaged by soldiers in mainland China, outside a lab at the University of Koblentz in West Germany, and at a military base in the Soviet Union. Five individuals suddenly find themselves seated in a metallic chamber aboard a flying saucer. An alien being, dressed in a glossy jumpsuit and appearing quite human, enters the room and addresses the bewildered group, consisting of Eve Wingate, newsman Jonathan Clark, farm girl Su Tan, Professor Klaus Bechner and Russian soldier Ivan Godofsky. The alien explains that each of them will hear him in their own language. He answers a few basic questions and reveals that they are all traveling in space. The alien has chosen them as representatives of the human race. "We are here to help you save your beautiful planet. Your entire history has been one of self-destruction. If you destroy yourselves, you also destroy the earth. That we cannot permit, for it is needed." The alien explains that the sun near his home world will enter a nova state within thirty-five days. The aliens' moral code will not allow them to invade another world or destroy any form of life. Instead, they will make available to the people of Earth a weapon that can destroy human life but will harm nothing else. The weapons will only be effective for twenty-seven days, after which time they will become harmless.

Jonathan asks what will happen if the weapons are unused after that time. "Your race will live, mine will die," the alien replies calmly. The weapons will be handed over to each individual, to do with as each one chooses. Five small metallic boxes, resembling makeup compacts, are slowly lowered on a floating platform. "Each of the boxes is tuned to the electrical impulses of its owner," the alien discloses. No other force on earth can open them except their owners' mental projection. "Each of you holds in your hands the power of life and death." Inside each box are three capsules. Each one can be activated by removing its spindle and announcing a longitude and latitude whereupon all human life in a radius of three thousand miles from that spot will be eliminated. Anyone can activate the weapon once the box is open. Finally, the alien reveals that the capsules in each box will become harmless if the owner of the box dies. The alien then prepares to send the people back to earth, telling them that no measurable time has passed since he abducted them. As they return to their chairs, Eve turns to Jonathan and asks him his full name and place of employment. He tells her moments before they disappear in a teleportation beam.

Back on the beach in Cornwall, Eve immediately heads toward a cliff and tosses her box with the weapons into the Atlantic. In China, Su Tan heads toward her burned out house, kneels before a statue of Buddha, and kills herself with a knife. The capsules in her box shrivel after she collapses. In Germany, Professor Bechner opens his box and examines one of the capsules. He then returns it and decides to resume his trip to a scientific conference in America. In Russia, Private Godofsky, back at guard duty, is approached by an officer. "I thought I saw something, but I guess I was mistaken," the soldier replies when questioned. In Los Angeles, Jonathan receives a phone call from Eve in Cornwall, who tells him she will be flying to meet with him as soon as possible.

The next day, as Jonathan is eating lunch at a bar, he is startled to watch as the alien suddenly appears on the television screen. He declares that he has interrupted all broadcasts to make an announcement. After introducing himself, he tells the names of the five individuals he contacted, and cryptically adds that they were given information of the most vital importance. Anticipating danger, Jonathan ducks out of the bar and decides to go into hiding. At the same time, Bechner, on his way to his conference, is struck by a car while absentmindedly crossing the street. In the Soviet Union, Godofsky is tracked down and arrested by a troupe of soldiers led by Colonel Gregor.

Television news commentator Ward Mason announces on his show that the alien broadcast has been confirmed as genuine. He reveals that a massive search is on to locate Jonathan Clark, the American identified by the alien. Eve Wingate arrives at the Los Angeles airport and is surprised by Jonathan, who was waiting for her. He quickly guides her to a cab. They decide to hide out until the twenty-seven days pass.

At a hospital, Professor Bechner is suffering from a concussion and unable to speak. Dr. Karl Neuhaus, a nuclear expert, has been summoned by Ingram, who was appointed by the president to manage the crisis. Ingram hands Neuhaus the box, which Beckner was carrying at the time of his accident. Neuhaus is puzzled by the strange container. In the Soviet Union, the premier, dressed in military garb, examines a similar box. He interviews Godofsky, who reveals very little of what the alien told him. The premier orders Gregor to make him talk.

Jonathan decides to hide out at Hollywood Park race track, which is closed for the season. He and Eve fix up a room in one of the stables, arranging separate cots, and settle down to wait. Eve's transistor radio is their only link to the outside world, and they only need to avoid the night watchman on his hourly patrol.

Meanwhile, around the world, news broadcasts alarm the public with wild speculations about the activities of the people who were abducted by the alien. Panics and riots are breaking out worldwide. In the Soviet Union, the premier is furious that no one can open Godofsky's box. The Chinese government has turned over to him the remains of Su Tan's box, now useless. He orders Colonel Gregor to break Godofsky's will but keep him alive. The premier also directs him to try to eliminate Bechner.

In America, the German scientist is recovering at the hospital, but he refuses to reveal any information about the boxes to Ingram. He does relate that the ethics of the aliens eliminates any danger of an invasion. Bechner then has an amiable discussion with Dr. Neuhaus about the impossibility of opening the alien box by any physical force. That night, two Russian agents slip into the hospital and attempt to kill the professor but are themselves killed by federal agents assigned to protect Bechner. Jonathan and Eve are concerned after hearing the report of this assassination attempt on their radio. Jonathan is stunned to hear that a mob killed a man who had been mistakenly identified as him. Jonathan decides to contact the authorities and try to stop the panic. But first, he confesses to Eve that he has fallen in love with her.

Early in the morning, Jonathan builds and lights a bonfire outside the stable. When the police and fire trucks arrive, Jonathan and Eve reveal their presence. In Russia, Godofsky finally talks after being subjected to drugs. He mentally opens his box after the premier presents him with a sentimental letter from his mother. He also tells how the capsules in the box can be used. The Soviet government then boldly announces their breakthrough and attempt to blackmail the world.

Jonathan, Eve and Professor Bechner confer at a White House meeting to discuss their next step. Bechner wants to examine the capsules himself, because he suspects they may have another use. At a meeting with the Joint Chiefs of Staff, Bechner opens his box and explains how the capsules work. Dr. Neuhaus suggests that the weapon must be tested. Ingram says such an experiment is impossible, but the admiral, who is the head of the Joint Chiefs, says he could clear a three-thousand-mile area in the South Atlantic Ocean to conduct a secret test.

The Soviet premier announces his plan to blackmail America into withdrawing all its armed forces back to the continental United States, at which point he could wipe out North American. When the Joint Chiefs and government authorities debate their response to this ultimatum, Dr. Neuhaus reveals that he has subjected himself to a lethal dose of radiation. He insists that he serve as a test subject. Everyone agrees to the experiment, and the military will feign to conduct a foreign pullout. Twelve days remain until the critical and ever ominous twenty-seventh day.

The admiral, Jonathan, Bechner and Eve are stationed on a destroyer at sea, one mile outside the rim of the test area. Dr. Neuhaus is positioned in a raft just inside the test zone. With him on the boat are an assortment of plants and animals. The admiral reads out their latitude and longitude, which will activate one of the capsules. Suddenly Dr. Neuhaus starts to glow, and then his body disappears, leaving his clothes that crumple to the deck of the raft. All the other plants and animals remain unharmed. The onlookers on the destroyer are stunned into silence, and a montage follows showing that the president has indeed ordered all U.S. forces to withdraw.

On the destroyer, Jonathan speculates that the Soviet leader will attack with his capsules just before midnight that very evening, the last of the twenty-seven days. Bechner recalls that the alien originally had said that the capsules had the power of life *and* death, not life *or* death. The admiral agrees to let him study the capsules, and Bechner discovers a message in code imprinted on them. Since one of his capsules was used, the message is incomplete He asks Jonathan to release his capsules so he can interpret the entire message. Clark and the admiral have misgivings but agree to Bechner's request.

Eve and Jonathan watch the ocean from the deck of the ship, speculating whether humankind can possibly survive. Eve is quite pessimistic. Meanwhile, Bechner works on the capsules in a locked stateroom. He then takes out a map of the world, and examines it.

In his Kremlin office, the premier prepares to activate his set of capsules. Many military officers are gathered in his chambers, included a troubled Ivan Godofsky. The premier steps out onto his balcony and begins to name the first coordinates. Godofsky charges at him, knocking the capsules out of his hand and onto the street below. Ivan is shot by one of the officers. "You fool! If he dies, the capsules are useless," the premier screams. Concurrently, Bechner starts to name coordinates before an open porthole on the ship. Jonathan and Eve, hearing his voice, pound on his door trying to stop him, but the professor continues. He finally unlatches his door, explaining that he has blanketed the world with the capsules. They were launched after he altered them based on instructions in the message. In the Soviet Union, the leader collapses on the street as he tries to retrieve his capsules. He clutches his ears, hearing a shrill, piercing noise, and falls down senseless.

Moments later, a news broadcast reveals the effect of Bechner's action. A handful of people were killed, but they were only the dictators, warmongers and criminals, "known enemies of human freedom." Bechner said he instinctively knew the capsules could be used as a force for good. Eve speculates that this positive outcome for humankind also means death for the aliens. Jonathan wonders if the uninhabited parts of earth, such as the Arctic, could be made available to them as a new home. The admiral arranges for the group's return to the mainland.

The next night, a special meeting of the United Nations is convened. The secretary-general announces that an invitation to the aliens has been broadcast all day. He then turns the podium over to Professor Bechner, who asks the aliens to respond. The voice of the alien then fills the Assembly Hall. "People of earth, we accept your invitation," the alien spokesman declares. "We come in gratitude and love, and bring you greetings from thirty thousand intelligent worlds to tell you they are waiting to greet you among the stars."

CRITIQUE

This unique picture seems more geared to an adult than a juvenile audience, which is unusual for a science fiction entry from the 1950s. The brief special effects by Ray Harryhausen showing the alien's spaceship are lifted from another film, *Earth vs. the Flying Saucers* (1956). Much of the dialogue centers on philosophical matters, such as the nature of humanity, ethics, responsibility and good will. The five human representatives (except for Bechner) are unremarkable and ordinary, but when confronted with this dilemma, they all behave, or attempt to behave, in a heroic fashion. The Soviet soldier in particular shows remarkable courage, keeping his secret as long as possible. The nobility of Su Tan and Dr. Neuhaus, who sacrifice themselves to save the human race is also memorable. The implication is also present that a different set of five individuals would have behaved as nobly in the same circumstances. But as a whole, these individuals have a pessimistic opinion of the human race. The plot also bears out this point by focusing on the rioting and lynch mob attitude of humankind as a whole.

The film also reflects the general anticommunist paranoia of the McCarthy era, even though that concept was in total decline by 1957. The Soviet premier seems modeled after Joseph Stalin, who died in 1953, and like Stalin, he has a paternal exterior but possesses a devious and brutal personality. These plot elements in the picture no doubt were developed by the Canadian author John Mantley when he originally wrote his novel *The 27th Day* on which his screenplay was based. Some elements of his original story were eliminated from the film. In the novel, when Bechner activated his capsules, they not only killed the enemies of freedom, they also eliminated the evil tendencies that were present in other individuals who would have become enemies of freedom. It is this factor that makes possible a new, golden age for humanity. However, no one seems to point out that the killing of all the enemies of freedom is itself a form of genocide. Because the targets are all bad humans, their slaughter is greeted with total enthusiasm. This moral paradox is not addressed or even hinted at in the film, a rather pat oversight.

Another fault of the storyline is the complete impracticality of clearing a three-thousand-mile radius of the southern Atlantic in secret within forty-eight hours. This element of the plot is almost ludicrous. One also wonders, with the alien speaks the last line of the film, why none of the other 30,000 intelligent worlds were willing to accept his race on their own planets when the alien sun starts to go nova. Humankind need not have been pushed to the border of extinction if these 30,000 cultures were benign. Nevertheless, these loopholes are minor in this very thoughtful and serious scenario.

The performances are all adequate and in several cases superb. Arnold Moss steals the show as the alien. Moss made relatively few films, but he seemed to be outstanding in each one. His most representative role was as the unctuous and conniving Joseph Fouché, who continually schemes with, and against, Robespierre in *The Reign of Terror/The Black Book* (1949), Anthony Mann's wild and fanciful caricature of the French Revolution. Moss was also well known for his Shakespearean performances, and he was featured in a remarkable *King Lear* with Orson Welles on television in 1954. Years later, he played a Shakespearean actor in an episode of *Star Trek* called "The Conscience of the King." Moss also became the radio host for the New York Philharmonic in their weekly national broadcasts.

Other solid, believable performances were turned in by George Voskovec as the considerate Professor Bechner, Stefan Schnabel as the wily Soviet premiere, Frederick Ledebur as Dr. Neuhaus and Valerie French as Eve Wingate. The leading actor, Gene Barry, is a trifle bland, but even this suits the character of Jonathan, who is supposed to be an unexceptional individual. The director, William Asher, keeps the story on track. Most of Asher's later work was for television, and in 1963 he married actress Elizabeth Montgomery for whom he later created the classic comic television series *Bewitched*, in which she played Samantha, the witch who married an ordinary mortal.

REPRESENTATIVE QUOTES

"You ask us to learn in twenty-seven days what has escaped the world for thousands of years. You ask us to practice peace or die." (Bechner to the alien)

"The Alien . . . all this nonsense about their high morality. It is double talk. They give us a weapon, and they expect us to use it. And yet they give the impression that they hope we won't. Morality! Like they are so full of morals and loving kindness, how come they just happen to have fifteen nice, shiny human exterminators lying around?" (Jonathan to Bechner at the White House meeting)

"Since the first men hit each other with clubs, the human race has spent more time destroying itself than in any other endeavor. The aliens have not tried to judge us. They have merely intensified our choice." (Bechner to Jonathan and Eve at the White House meeting)

Armageddon (1998)

Rating: ***   **Threat:** Meteor collision

Touchstone. Written by Robert Roy Pool based on a story by Jonathan Hensleigh; Photographed by John Schwartzman; Special effects by John Frazier (supervisor); Edited by Mark Goldblatt, Chris Lebenzon & Glen Scantlebury; Music by Harry Gregson-Williams & Trevor Rabin; Produced by Kenny Bates, Michael Bay, Jerry Brockheimer & Jonathan Hensleigh; Directed by Michael Bay. 151 minutes.

ANNOTATED CAST LIST

Bruce Willis (*Harry Stamper*, foremost deep-core drilling expert); Liv Tyler (*Grace*, his daughter); Scarlet Forge (*Grace*, as a child); Billy Bob Thornton (*Dan Truman*, top NASA official); Ben Affleck (*A. J. Frost*, Stamper's top apprentice); Will Patton (*Chick Chapple*, Stamper's right-hand man); Steve Buscemi (*Rockhound*, wayward genius working for Stamper); Owen Wilson (*Oscar Choi*ce, Stamper's geologist); Michael Duncan (*J. Otis Curleen*, rugged driller nicknamed Bear); Ken Campbell (*Max Lennert*, overweight driller); Clark Heathcliffe Brolly (*Freddie Noonan*, somber team member); William Fichtner (*Col. William Sharp*, pilot of *Freedom*); Jessica Steen (*Jennifer Watts*, co-pilot of *Freedom*); Grayson McCouch (*Lt. Gruber*, nuclear payload specialist of *Freedom*); Peter Stormare (*Lev Andropov*, Soviet space station cosmonaut); Keith David (*Gen. Kimsey*, military liaison officer to NASA); Chris Ellis (*Walter Clark*, NASA flight instructor); Jason Isaacs (*Dr. Ronald Quincy*, NASA's top research scientist); Patrick Richwood, Brian Mulligan (nerd scientists); Marshall Teague (*Col. Davis*, pilot of *Independence*); Anthony Guidera (*Tucker*, co-pilot of *Independence*); Greg Collins (*Lt. Halsey*, nuclear payload specialist of *Independence*); J. Patrick McCormack (*Gen. Boffer*, presidential advisor); Ian Quinn (*Pete Shelby*, astronaut killed in *Atlantis* shuttle disaster); John Mahon (*Karl*, astronomer who sights meteor); Grace Zabriskie (*Dottie*, his wife, for whom the meteor is named); Stanley Anderson (U.S. president); Peter White (secretary of defense); James Harper (*Kelso*, admiral); Ellen Cleghorne (*Helga*, NASA technician teased by Rockhound); Shawnee Smith (redhead in bar with Rockhound); Udo Kier (NASA psychologist); John Aylward (*Dr. Banks*, NASA advisor); Harry Humphries (*Chuck Jr.*, Chapple's son); Judith Hoag (*Denise*, Chapple's wife); Sage Allen (Max's mother); Bodhi Elfman (NASA mathematician); Vic Manni (*Vic*, loanshark); Layla Roberts (*Molly Mounds*, stripper who dates Rockhound); Mark Curry (*Stu*, New York taxi driver); Seiko Matsuda (Asian tourist in cab); Eddie Griffin (messenger on bike in New York); Franky (*Little Richard*, his dog); K. C. Liomiti (street vendor selling Godzilla toys); James Fitzpatrick (NORAD technician); John H. Johnson (launch pad director); Dyllab Christopher (*Tommy*); Lawrence Tierney (*Gapp Stamper*);

Judith Drake (Gapp's nurse); Deborah Nishimore, Albert Wong, Jim Ishida (business executives visiting oil rig); Duke Valenti, Michael Taliferro, Billy Devlin (Vegas roughnecks); Alexander Johnson, Kathleen Matthews, J.C. Hayward, Andrew Glassman, Michael Tuck (newscasters); Patrick Lander, Anne Vareze. Fritz Mashimo, Dina Morone, Ruben O'Lague, Wolfgang Muser (foreign newscasters); Christopher Worret, Adam Smith, Stephen Ford, Odile Broulard, Joe Allen, Victor Vinson, Frank Van Keeken, Fred Weller, Jeff Austin, Googy Gress, Matt Malloy, H. Richard Greene, Brian Brophy, Peter Murnik, Brian Hayes Currie, Andrew Heckler, Andy Miller, Michael Kaplan, Charles Stewart (NASA personnel); Charlton Heston (narrator).

SYNOPSIS

Although opening to mixed reviews, *Armageddon* became the largest box office winner in 1998, grossing over $450 million worldwide on a production budget of $140 million. Although impressive on many levels, the picture has numerous flaws and drawbacks that prevent its artistic and entertainment achievements from equaling its financial ones.

The picture begins with a majestic recreation of the meteor strike that wiped out the dinosaurs and 85 percent of all life millions of years ago. The scene then switches to a modern-day shuttle in orbit with a spacewalk in progress. Unexpectedly, a meteor shower strikes, and the shuttle *Atlantis* is destroyed. On Earth, meteors fall from the eastern seaboard of America to Finland, and New York City is the scene of significant damage. An astronomer named Karl has sighted a collision in the asteroid belt caused by a comet, and a 90-mile-wide chunk of an asteroid is headed toward Earth. Karl calls the National Aeronautics and Space Administration (NASA) and names the huge meteor Dottie after his wife, from whom he claims there is no escape. NASA informs the president that Dottie will totally destroy the earth in eighteen days. NASA scientists brainstorm to determine if there is any defense, and their top researcher, Dr. Quincy, claims there is only one practical method: a powerful nuclear bomb must be planted deep under the surface of the meteor and then detonated at the precise moment to ensure that the two resulting halves will miss the earth.

On an oil rig in the South China Sea, Harry Stamper and his crew are overseeing a complicated drilling operation. Harry discovers that A. J. Frost, his brash, young apprentice, is sleeping with Grace, Harry's daughter, and he chases him around the rig with a shotgun. An army helicopter lands on the rig and picks up Stamper on direct orders from the President, and he and his daughter are immediately transported to NASA headquarters. Dan Truman, the top NASA executive, explains about the approaching doom in the form of the giant meteor. Stamper is asked to prep a team of astronauts to drill and plant the bomb on Dottie. Stamper says there is not enough time to train the astronauts and that he must bring his own team of experts if the task is to be done successfully. Truman agrees, Stamper summons his top seven men, and the Federal Bureau of Investigation (FBI) is dispatched to pick them up. These men are: A. J. Frost;

Chick Chapple, a drilling veteran with a fondness for gambling; "Rockhound," a girl-chasing genius who earned a double doctorate from MIT at the age of twenty-two; Oscar Choice, a flaky but brilliant geologist and cowboy; J. Otis Curleen, simply known as "Bear," a powerful black man with tremendous fortitude; Max Lennert, a hefty drill bit expert; and Freddy Noonan, the soft-spoken member of the team. These men are asked to volunteer and they agree to join the endeavor, but each has an unusual favor they want granted. Bear, for example, wants to use the Lincoln bedroom in the White House for the summer, and all want a permanent dispensation from income taxes. The government grants their requests. NASA seems bewildered by this assortment of misfits, but Truman authorizes their use as the only hope to save Earth. The men go through an intense training period, both psychological and physical.

NASA plans to land on the giant asteroid fragment using the X-71, a huge rocket that can carry two shuttles simultaneously. Each shuttle will carry nuclear bombs and drilling equipment adapted by NASA from Stamper's designs. The two spacecrafts will slingshot around the moon and land on the back side of the meteor after it passes the moon. The two crews will act independently, and it is hoped one of them will be able to plant the warhead at sufficient depth. They will take off and detonate the bomb by remote control before the meteor passes the fail-safe point beyond which the earth is doomed. The astronaut team of Colonel Davis, co-pilot Tucker and nuclear payload specialist Lieutenant Halsey will fly the *Independence*, with Frost, Bear, Choice and Noonan as the drill team. Colonel Sharp, co-pilot Jennifer Watts and Lieutenant Gruber (a nuclear expert), will command *Freedom*, with Chapple, Rockhound, Max and Stamper himself as the drilling crew. Two days before blastoff, Stamper asks Truman to give his exhausted men some time off for what may be their last day on Earth. Truman confides in Harry that he wishes he could have been an astronaut himself and earned a mission patch, but his leg brace precluded that possibility.

Chapple visits Denise, his estranged wife, and leaves her a gift, a model space shuttle, to give to his young son. After Chapple leaves, Denise tells the boy their visitor was only a salesman. Frost and Grace Stamper spend the day together, planning their future marriage. Rockhound borrows money from a loan shark and then treats Max and Noonan to a high-class burlesque show, where Rockhound dates Molly Mounds, the star attraction. The guys are arrested after a trio of roughnecks tries to cut in on their good time.

A large meteor fragment hits Shanghai, causing mass destruction. News about the impending disaster finally goes public, and the president makes a speech announcing NASA's plan to save the world. Harry meets with Grace and says goodbye to her, and Grace tells him that she and Frost are engaged. The men suit up for their mission, and General Kimsey, NASA's military liaison, tells Truman he has little confidence in these men. People worldwide watch the preparations for launch. (Oddly enough, it seems to be daylight all over the world at the same moment!) Chapple's son calls to his mother, "That salesman is on TV!" Amazed, she reveals to the boy that the man is his father. The X-70 takes off successfully, and in space both ships dock with the Russian space station for additional refueling. Lev Andropov, a cosmonaut who has been alone on the station for eighteen months, is somewhat "space happy." Something goes wrong during the fuel transfer and a fire breaks out. All crews return safely to their shuttles as the station blows up. Andropov is rescued and taken aboard the *Independence*.

After slingshoting around the moon, both shuttles encounter an unexpected field of small meteors trailing behind Dottie. *Independence* is damaged and crashes, killing most of the crew except Andropov, Bear and Frost. *Freedom* overshoots its target area and lands on a plate of compressed iron ferrite, the worst possible area for drilling. Stamper sets up his drill, which is mounted on a mobile unit the size of a tank that is referred to as an "armadillo." Max commences drilling but finds it is slow going because the drill bits keep breaking.

Frost concludes they must make their way to *Freedom*. They activate the armadillo from *Independence* and drive it like a tank in search of the other shuttle. Andropov helps Bear and Frost operate the controls of the unit. They encounter an enormous canyon, which they attempt to glide across since the meteor's gravity is minimal. Andropov leaves the interior of the armadillo in flight to repair a damaged thruster. When they complete the crossing, Andropov boasts that he is now a genuine Russian hero.

Back on Earth, General Kimsey panics when he learns how slowly the drilling is going. He speaks with the president, and the military is authorized to take over NASA. Kimsey plans to detonate the bomb at once, and it starts counting down as soon as he sends a signal. Truman is outraged and tries to break off communications with *Freedom*. Colonel Sharp is ordered by Stamper to stop the timer, but Sharp informs him that he is under secret orders to act if he thinks the drilling might miss the deadline before the meteor reaches the fail safe point. After a tense confrontation, Stamper convinces him that the only hope for Earth is to complete the drilling. Sharp backs down and shuts down the bomb with Gruber. Stamper broadcasts a defiant message back to NASA saying that he plans to complete the drilling as scheduled without further interference. Rockhound gets space dementia and fires off a rapid-fire gun mounted on a platform, and he has to be tied up so he can not harm anyone. When an unexpected eruption occurs at the site, Max is killed and the armadillo is destroyed. Moments later, Frost, Bear and Andropov arrive with their armadillo. Meanwhile on Earth, another huge chunk of the meteor crashes into Paris, leveling the city in a spectacular sequence.

Frost takes over operation of the drill with only one hour remaining. At a critical moment the drill appears to buckle, but Frost is eager to continue, and Stamper lets him use his best judgment. Frost then breaks through to the proper depth. A cluster of rocks crash at their location, killing Gruber and damaging the remote control trigger on the bomb. One of the men will have to stay behind and manually detonate the device. The men draw lots, and Frost wins. Stamper accompanies him off the shuttle, then cuts Frost's air hose to his space helmet so he has to return to the ship. Harry tells him to take care of Grace.

Freedom launches. Stamper falls after a tremor, but he recovers and detonates the bomb at the last possible moment. The explosion splits Dottie, and both halves miss the earth. Celebrations break out throughout the planet. As *Freedom* prepares to land on Earth, Rockhound convinces the others to keep his crazy episode a secret.

There is general rejoicing at the landing site as the surviving crew members disembark, sliding down a rubber chute. Grace embraces Frost, and Chapple's wife and son greet him, signaling an end to their separation. Even Molly Mounds appears to kiss Rockhound. Frost gives Harry's mission patch to Truman, saying that Stamper wanted him to have it. This is followed by the end credits, featuring scenes of Grace and Frost's wedding ceremony, with all the mission survivors in attendance.

CRITIQUE

Armageddon is a rather curious mixture, one part *Dirty Dozen* (1967) and two parts *Meteor* (1979). In fact, the resemblance to *Meteor* includes a remarkable number of similarities. Both films have a rogue comet strike an asteroid, propelling the largest fragment on a course for Earth; include the destruction of an American spacecraft at the start of the film; feature a helicopter sent to retrieve an "expert" who will save the world; depict a large meteor "huffing" as it travels through space; portray major damage inflicted upon New York City; feature Russian-American cooperation; depict the destruction of a major Asian city midway through the story; include a timely presidential address; involve a general who adversely effects the mission; and finally, rely on off-beat humor as an essential ingredient. The special effects in *Armageddon*, of course, are vastly superior, yet ultimately *Meteor* may be the more entertaining picture. The *Dirty Dozen* elements of the film involve the training of a group of misfits to undertake an important mission.

The film does not hold together smoothly over its two-and-a-half hour duration. Stylistically, the picture jumps from comedy adventure to science fiction to maudlin romance to vulgar buffoonery, and these various elements never really gel. A lot of the problem has to do with the cinematography and editing, which is very jerky, with too many unnecessary close-ups. They manage to distract instead of helping to build essential tension. There are too many cliffhangers that pop up so rapidly that the film's pacing suffers. The continuity is also ragged right from the start, when Harry Stamper tosses his golf club into the ocean and it reappears in his hands seconds later when he intrudes into Frost's room. The montage of scenes around the world is ruined when each locale is presented in broad daylight. The musical soundtrack is dreadful, sounding like someone using the automatic pop rhythm track on an electric keyboard. Only two musical sequences stand out, the patriotic backdrop as the president addresses the world and the dark chorus when the shuttles encounter the dangerous debris shower trailing the meteor. These shortcomings are all serious, but they are largely counterbalanced by sensational, state-of-the-art special effects that are genuinely overwhelming. Sharp dialogue and excellent casting also save the film from being a complete muddle resembling total chaos.

Bruce Willis is a major action star, perhaps best represented in the *Die Hard* film series. Although good, his work in *Armageddon* is not his finest. His character is hampered by a rather unconvincing subplot of his fatherly concern over his daughter's love for Frost, who is basically a younger version of himself. The broad introduction to Harry Stamper as he chases Frost around the oil rig with a gun is quite awkward, and it takes Willis some time to make his character seem real because of this. The rest of his performance is solid until the film's conclusion where Stamper becomes mawkish and corny, especially during his sentimental goodbye to his daughter over a video monitor. Tears fall from only one of his eyes in the artificial and clumsy bit. The most solid presentation in *Armageddon* is that of Billy Bob Thornton as Dan Truman; this is a straight, sincere and very convincing performance with many nuances. Thornton returns the film to credibility whenever it starts to get sidetracked by the rambling plot. Two classic character performances provide the film with its most entertaining moments. Steve Buscemi is magnificent as Rockhound (we never learn his character's real name); his witty delivery and extraordinary timing make his quips the only highlights of the picture that can rival the special effects. Buscemi is a unique actor, whose performances are always remarkable, grotesque, yet varied, as in such films as *Ed and His Dead Mother* (1993), *Trees Lounge* (1996) and *The Big Lebowski* (1998). In *Con Air* (1997), his eerie portrayal of a child murderer recalls the classic *M* (1931), with Buscemi a 1990s equivalent of Peter Lorre. The other great character part is Cosmonaut Lev Andropov as played by Peter Stormare. His wild antics in the film are reminiscent of the colorful Tim Carey, who played Ulysses in *Bayou* (1957), AKA *Poor White Trash*. Stormare was previously teamed with Steve Buscemi as his kidnapping partner in *Fargo* (1996). Other superb cast members include Owen Wilson as Oscar, Ben Affleck as Frost and Will Patton as Chapple. Patton's attempted reunion with is wife is the most heartfelt moment in the picture, being perfectly understated yet dramatically sincere. Michael Duncan is also incredible as Bear, and he went on to great acclaim as the convict with the power to heal in *The Green Mile* (1999). Liv Tyler is a natural screen presence, and she easily held her own working with the others. Her work as Grace completely overcomes the awkward and cliched nature of the part. She makes it look effortless, and it is very fortunate that her character is allowed to remain in the control room after the *Independence* crashes because she adds the perfect edge in those moments. She shines in her scenes with Affleck, particularly when he serenades her with "Leaving on a Jet Plane" and Bear, Rockhound and the others join in.

The storyline is somewhat cast heavy. Two characters almost disappear in their roles, and you wonder why they were included. Freddy Noonan is one of Stamper's essential team members, but the character is then completely overlooked. Gruber also seems forgotten when *Freedom* lands on the meteor, only gaining notice when he is killed in a rock storm. The many vignettes in the film are excellent, such as the opening scenes in New York when a small dog tries to tear into a six-foot inflated Godzilla toy being sold by a street vendor.

The staging of the sequence with the falling meteors in New York City is astonishing. The destruction of Paris is another masterful sequence, technically perfect and well photographed as the gargoyles of Notre Dame appear to anticipate the approaching doom.

Scientifically, as with *Meteor* and other films with collision scenarios, the threat portrayed is not only credible but inevitable. The opening narration sets the issue of the threat clearly enough, although some nitpickers could point out that the continents would have been positioned differently at the time of the dinosaurs. Also, the asteroid that ended the reign of the dinosaurs occurred 65 million years ago, not 55 million as an erroneous title card proclaims at the end of the prologue. The film seems to purposefully avoid naming the threat. Dottie itself is not an asteroid but a massive fragment of an asteroid destroyed in a collision with a comet. In the script it is usually referred to as "the Rock." What is not scientifically sound is the fact that some meteor fragments start to fall eighteen days in advance. Perhaps "the Rock" took an elliptical orbit in its trajectory towards Earth, but this issue is not explained.

It is frustrating when a picture with as many positive elements as *Armageddon* is undermined by sloppy, rapid-fire editing, third-rate music and a padded, derivative storyline. Many avid filmgoers find it more difficult to watch *Armageddon* on videotape, where the cropping makes the film seem even more jumbled. The letterbox format is definitely required to make the film watchable.

REPRESENTATIVE QUOTES

"This is the earth at a time when the dinosaurs roamed a lush and fertile planet. A piece of rock just six miles wide ended all that. It hit with the force of ten thousand nuclear weapons. A trillion tons of dirt and rock hurtled into the atmosphere creating a suffocating blanket of dust the sun was powerless to penetrate for a thousand years. It happened before. It will happen again. It is just a question of when." (Opening narration)

"Damage? Total, sir. It is what we call a global killer, the end of mankind. It doesn't matter where it hits, nothing will survive, not even bacteria." (Dan Truman, answering the president's estimate of damage should Earth be hit by Dottie)

"The United States government just asked us to save the world. Anybody want to say no?" (Stamper to his team at their NASA briefing)

"You know, we are sitting on four million pounds of fuel, one nuclear weapon and a thing that has two hundred and seventy thousand moving parts built by the lowest bidder. Makes you feel good, doesn't it?" (Rockhound to Stamper moments before lift off)

"I say we stay and die . . . but then that's me." (Rockhound's bizarre suggestion as *Independence* tries to take off from the meteor)

Beneath the Planet of the Apes (1970)

Rating: **   **Threat: Doomsday device**

20th Century Fox. Written by Paul Dehn & Mort Abrahams adapted from the novel *Monkey Planet* by Pierre Boulle; Photographed by Milton Krasner; Special effects by L. B. Abbott & Art Cruichshank; Edited by Marion Rothman; Music by Leonard Rosenman; Produced by Arthur P. Jacobs and Mort Abrahams; Directed by Ted Post. 95 minutes.

ANNOTATED CAST LIST

James Franciscus (*John Brent*, astronaut on rescue mission); Charlton Heston (*Col. George Taylor*, astronaut imprisoned by mutants); Linda Harrison (*Nova*, Taylor's companion); Maurice Evans (*Dr. Zaius*, orangutan elder and minister of science); Kim Hunter (*Dr. Zira*, chimpanzee scientist); David Watson (*Dr. Cornelius*, her chimpanzee mate and fellow scientist); James Gregory (*Ursus*, gorilla leader); Eldon Burke (gorilla sergeant); Lou Wagner (*Lucius*, friend of Zira); Paul Richards (*Mendez*, Leader of the mutants); Victor Buono (heavyset mutant); Jeff Corey (*Caspay*, member of the mutant council); Natalie Trundy (*Albina*, mutant woman); Thomas Gomez (mutant minister); Don Pedro Colley (black mutant); Gregory Sierra (*Verger*, first mutant encountered by Brent); Tod Andrews (*Skipper*, astronaut who headed Brent's expedition); Paul Frees (narrator).

SYNOPSIS

The original *Planet of the Apes* (1968) was an extraordinary film, a classic science fiction adventure. Of course, viewers of the film only discovered it was actually post-apocalyptic in the final scene. George Taylor, played by Charlton Heston, led a deep-space mission that somehow passed through a time warp while the crew was in suspended animation. They crashed on a planet where intelligent apes are the dominant species and humans are primitive, brutish creatures, incapable of speech. Taylor is captured by the apes and later is befriended by Zira and Cornelius, chimpanzee scientists, who help Taylor to escape with Nova, another human prisoner, who is in love with him. In the dramatic final scene, Taylor and Nova ride off on horseback down a beach, heading into an area known as the Forbidden Zone, and Taylor is thunderstruck when he comes across the remnants of the Statue of Liberty. He has been on Earth all along. Human civilization was destroyed in a nuclear war, and eventually replaced by the evolving apes. *Planet of the Apes* spawned four sequels, all of which, to some extent, negated the intent of the original film. The first sequel, *Beneath the Planet of the Apes*, which followed quickly on the heels of the original picture, is the purest example of a picture that is simultaneously apocalyptic and post-apocalyptic since the story is set in a world created by a nuclear upheaval, which is then completely destroyed in another cataclysm.

Beneath the Planet of the Apes opens with a reprise of the last five minutes of *Planet of the Apes*. In this scene, Cornelius is played by Roddy McDowall instead of David Watson. In fact, McDowall's voice opens the picture. McDowell would eventually star in the three remaining sequels, but at the time this film was shot, he was preparing to direct his own film film, *Tam Lin* (1971), a bizarre fantasy starring Ava Gardner. The opening credits appear as Taylor and Nova continue on after encountering the Statue of Liberty, and the terrain becomes a parched desert.

The scene shifts to the wreckage of a another spacecraft where astronaut John Brent is tending to his dying comrade, the skipper of the mission. They had encountered the same time warp as Taylor's ship in the first film, and Brent is able to fix the current date as A.D. 3955, but he is unable to determine the location of the planet upon which they have crashed. His friend dies, and Brent buries him. He encounters a woman on horseback who turns out to be Nova, and Brent is amazed when he discovers she is carrying Taylor's identification tag, which she wears on her wrist. Nova cannot speak and is unable to tell Brent that Taylor vanished when they encountered a series of illusions in the desert. Brent mounts the horse with Nova, and she leads him to the outskirts of Ape City.

Ursus, the gorilla general, is making a jingoistic speech calling for the extermination of humankind. He wants to lead a crusade into the Forbidden Zone to wipe out any humans living there. The gorillas applaud him loudly, but the chimpanzees and orangutans remain quiet. They disapprove but lack the power to prevent this excursion. Brent is shot by a gorilla on patrol, and Nova sneaks him into Zira's house, where she and Cornelius are arguing over the invasion plans of the war crazy gorilla military. They tend to Brent's wounds and provide him with a map highlighting the Forbidden Zone, into which Taylor disappeared. Dr. Zaius, the minister of science, visits Cornelius and Zira, and they hide the humans on his arrival. Zaius is convinced that the Forbidden Zone contains a genuine danger that could threaten what he considers the absolute purity and innocence of the ape civilization. Although he does not approve of the campaign, he plans to accompany his army into the Forbidden Zone and learn the nature of the threat. He asks Cornelius and Zira to assume his duties while he is away. After the departure of Zaius, they furnish provisions to Brent and warn him not to speak if he is captured because the gorillas will kill him instantly.

Brent and Nova are picked up outside the city by a gorilla patrol that is collecting humans to be used as target practice for the army. Zira notices them among the prisoners, and she unlocks the cage in the horse-drawn cart that is transporting them to the target range. Brent climbs out and battles the gorilla driver, knocking him off the fast-moving wagon. Then he and Nova unhitch the horses and gallop off, furiously pursued by a gorilla cavalry. Brent notices a cave, and he and Nova abandon their horses and descend into the opening. The cavern leads to a man-made passage, an ancient subway station. When Brent sees a sign proclaiming Queensboro Plaza, he realizes he is on Earth after all.

Ursus leads his army in a parade leaving the city, but a group of chimpanzees blocks their way, staging a protest rally against the war. Zaius warns the general to avoid harshness since that would only create martyrs. Ursus orders them to be removed gently but firmly, and the gorilla army resumes its march.

Meanwhile, Brent and Nova make their way through various underground passages, stumbling across residue and landmarks of New York City, such as the 42nd Street Library and Radio City Music Hall. Brent enters St. Patrick's Cathedral, where he sees a human figure worshiping the image of a nuclear bomb. The man is Verger, a human mutant and member of a small tribe of human descendants who have not only retained their intelligence, but have learned to communicate telepathically. They are horribly disfigured, however, due to their ancestors' exposure to nuclear fallout. The mutants wear masks to maintain a human appearance. Brent is taken before a council of mutants who question his origins and his knowledge of Taylor and of the plans of the apes. The mutants are able to telepathically project pain to Brent when they are not satisfied with his answers. They plan to ward off the ape army using telepathic illusion, but they fear the primitive minds of the apes may not hold the images they project. The mutants regard Brent and Nova as inferiors, and they toy with them, causing Brent to attack and strangle Nova into unconsciousness.

As the troops of Ursus enter the Forbidden Zone, they see a wall of fire and a vision of apes impaled on a field of stakes. The image of the Lawgiver, the central figure of ape culture, appears, bleeding. The army is about to bolt in panic when Dr. Zaius charges into the illusion and it disappears. He announces that it is nothing but a false vision, and the army continues on its way. The mutants, who worship the bomb, hold a religious service, at which they sing, "All creatures great and small, the good bomb made us all." The mutants plan to detonate their bomb, which is actually a doomsday device that will destroy the world. They bring Brent to a jail cell where Taylor is also imprisoned. The two astronauts greet each other, and Brent informs Taylor about the current crisis. One of the mutants uses his mental powers to force Taylor and Brent to fight to the death. Nova escapes from her mutant captor and comes upon the cell with the battling astronauts. Stunned, she manages to yell Taylor's name, the first word she has ever spoken. The mutant controlling their minds is distracted, and the astronauts turn on him and kill him. Nova enters the cell, but the door clangs shut before the humans can escape.

The gorilla army smashes into the underground network and advance, killing numerous mutants. The astronauts finally manage to break out of their cell, planing to disarm the doomsday weapon. Nova is killed by a gorilla soldier, and the slaughter continues until the mutants are wiped out. The last mutant, their leader, arms the weapon when he is struck down. Ursus starts firing bullets at the bomb and orders that it be pulled down with ropes. The weapon begins to steam as the gorillas topple it. Brent and Taylor appear, uncertain what to do. Brent pounds out a warning on the organ to distract Dr. Zaius, who nearly pushes the detonation lever. The gorillas shoot at the humans. Wounded, Taylor staggers to Zaius, gasping, "Doomsday, the end of the world . . . help me."

Zaius rejects his plea, spouting a stream of hatred against humans. After Brent is killed, Taylor mutters, "Bloody bastards," as he himself pushes the detonation lever with his last ounce of strength. The scene fades and the narrator reveals that the earth is now a dead world.

CRITIQUE

The overriding problem with *Beneath the Planet of the Apes* is that its basic premise is faulty. It would be pointless for Brent to be on a rescue mission to retrieve Taylor, based on the original film. During the opening scene of *Planet of the Apes*, Taylor records in his audio log that seven hundred years have passed on Earth already during their journey because they are traveling at such advanced speeds. Why would a rescue mission be sent a year later when Taylor's mission was anticipated to last for centuries? Thus the entire concept of the picture is skewed by this plot twist. Similar problems plague the plots of the later sequels as well, and they all undercut the story of the original film in various ways. There are a total of five films in the *Planet of the Apes* series, as well as a TV series. How is it possible for a series to continue when the entire world is destroyed in the second episode? In the third film, the writers have two of the characters, Cornelius and Zira, repair Brent's spacecraft and travel back in time to our present era. The offspring of Cornelius and Zira grows to develop an ape culture when the humans recruit apes as slave labor in the fourth film. In the fifth film, human and ape forces battle it out, completely undercutting the premise of the first film, that human civilization fell due to a nuclear conflict. Did the journey back in time by Cornelius and Zira alter original history and replace it with a different scenario? The only thing a film historian can conclude is that the four sequels are just sidetracks that break continuity with the original picture.

There are additional problems with the storyline of the film. It is unexplained how Ursus was tipped off to the presence of the mutant colony in the Forbidden Zone. Why would he violate their culture's deepest taboo to penetrate the Forbidden Zone? He states that he wants to reclaim fertile land to grow crops, but the Forbidden Zone seems to be nothing but an arid desert. It seems unlikely that the topography of New York City would be so altered by a remote nuclear blast that it now resembles southern California. The surviving bits and pieces of New York seem very unconvincing. Surely 51st Street would have been near ground zero and faced total destruction. It all seems very artificial, and the mutant religion is another bizarre touch that can only be regarded in a satirical vein.

There are also a number of enjoyable elements in the film. The makeup remains excellent, equal to the Oscar-winning caliber of the original film. The scenes in Ape City are clever and entertaining. The chimpanzee protest is a cagey reference to the Vietnam War protests. The scenes of the gorilla army are also quite well done. The special effects continue to be excellent. The editing is clever, particularly in the scene where Nova and Brent first meet, and scenes of original star Charlton Heston are intercut into the mix. The cinematography is impressive, especially when viewed in letterbox format. The music, although derivative of Jerry Goldsmith's brilliant score for the original film, has some interesting moments, particularly the choral chants for the mutant's religious service. James Franciscus is solid and straightforward as Brent, but his character lacks depth and we never understand what makes him tick. James Gregory, Inspector Luger from the *Barney Miller* TV series, does a good job as the pompous General Ursus, and he gets a chance to deliver some of the best lines in the film. David Watson is superb as Cornelius, and many fans would have a difficult time distinguishing his performance from that of Roddy McDowall. The returning cast members repeating their roles from the original film do a fine job, particularly Kim Hunter and Maurice Evans. Nothing much fresh, however, is added to their performances, except for Nova, who manages to eke out one word before being killed moments later. Charlton Heston was reportedly unhappy with the script proposals for the remake and would only agree to appear in an abbreviated capacity. Still, there is no room for his character in this story. It is unclear what Taylor intends to do in the final scene. At first he wants to save the world, even if for the benefit of the apes, but when he hears Zaius spewing out a litany of hate, he changes his mind and, with his dying gesture, decides to end the world after all. The film originally ended with a shot from space showing the planet exploding. In fact, the shot of the exploding planet is present in some publicity trailers for the video set of the entire series. At some point, however, it was decided to replace the exploding planet with a closing narration instead. The film was originally to be called *Planet of the Men*, but the studio wanted to retain the *Planet of the Apes* link, so the prosaic title *Beneath the Planet of the Apes* was finally chosen.

Although a disappointing film that was rushed to production to capitalize on the original, the concept of the apocalyptic ending is impressive, and Heston's last moments in the film almost make it seem worthwhile. A remake of the film has been considered for some time as a vehicle for Arnold Schwarzenegger. If the remake bases itself on the concepts of the original, there should be ample material there to develop an excellent film.

REPRESENTATIVE QUOTES

"Our great Lawgiver tells us that never will the humans have the ape's divine faculty to distinguish between evil and good. The only good human is a dead human." (Ursus to the Citizen's Council)

"May the blessing of the Bomb Almighty and the fellowship of the Holy Fallout descend on us all this day and forever more." (Closing benediction at the mutant religious ceremony)

"You ask me to help you? Man is evil, capable of nothing but destruction." (Dr. Zaius to Taylor, mocking him, unaware that he is trying to save the world)

"In one of the countless billions of galaxies in the universe lies a medium-sized star, and one of its satellites, a green and insignificant planet, is now dead." (Closing narration)

Crack in the World (1965)

Rating: **   Threat: Fissure in the earth's crust

Paramount. Written by Jon Manchip White & Julian Halevy; Photographed by
Manuel Berenguer; Special effects by Alex Weldon & Eugene Lourie; Edited by
Derek Parsons; Music by John Douglas; Produced by Bernard Glasser & Lester
A. Sansom; Directed by Andrew Marton. 96 minutes

ANNOTATED CAST LIST

Dana Andrews (*Dr. Stephen Sorenson*, director of Project Inner Space); Janette
Scott (*Maggie*, Sorenson's wife); Kieron Moore (*Dr. Ted Rampion*, project geologist & Maggie's former boyfriend); Alexander Knox (*Sir Charles Eggerston*,
head of United Nations scientific commission); Peter Damon (*John Masefield*,
second-in-command of Project Inner Space); Jim Gillen (*Rand*, commission
member); Gary Lasdun (*Markov*, project statistician); Mike Steen (*Steel*, Rampion's assistant); Emilio Carrere (*Bill Evans*, Sorenson's physician); Sydna
Scott (*Angela*, Sorenson's secretary); John Karlson (*Dr. Reynolds*, eccentric
project scientist); Alfred Brown (*Dr. Gupta,* project scientist); Todd Martin
(*Simpson*, engineer at volcano); Ben Tatar (Indian commissioner).

SYNOPSIS

Crack in the World is rooted in a brilliant and imaginative concept, but the
script was never properly developed, so the resulting motion picture is undermined by clumsy plot loopholes. Nevertheless, the film crowds enough quick-
paced action and dazzle to be entertaining, at least for the juvenile audience, for
which it was primarily intended.

The story opens as a jeep convoy winds its way down a road in a remote area
of Tanganyika, traveling to the headquarters of Project Inner Space. This facility
is attempting to drill through the earth's crust to access the magma, which
would give the world a limitless source of thermal energy and an abundance of
new minerals. Central operations is located in the deepest natural shaft in the
world, two miles down. The United Nations (UN) scientific commission is
coming to hear a progress report by Dr. Stephen Sorenson, head of the project.
The drilling has been stymied by an impenetrable mantle deep in the earth. Sorenson has a plan to penetrate the mantle with a ten-megaton nuclear device, and
he needs their approval. Sir Charles Eggerston, the commission's leading member, questions Sorenson about the risk. The doctor mentions that his staff geologist, Dr. Ted Rampion, fears that underground nuclear tests have weakened the
earth's crust and that there is danger of a fissure that would cause a major calamity. The other staff scientists feel the risk is minimal.

Dr. Sorenson is suffering from a strange skin disease, which his physician,

Dr. Evans, is treating with X-ray therapy. His young wife, Maggie, is unaware of the seriousness of the condition. She believes her husband is no longer interested in her. There is a great age difference in the marriage, and Maggie had been previously involved with Ted Rampion before she met Sorenson. The next day Rampion returns from investigating a volcano and is startled to learn that he missed the commission's visit. He confronts Sorenson to complain that he was deliberately kept out of the way of the visiting officials. When he reads a cable from the commission giving their approval, Rampion resigns from the project and plans to approach the commission himself.

The nuclear warhead is attached to a missile that is positioned to fire down into a specially prepared bore hole. Meanwhile, Dr. Evans informs Sorenson that his disease is totally out of control and will prove fatal in a short time. In London, Rampion meets with Sir Charles and convinces him to postpone the launch of the missile. Sir Charles telephones Sorenson, who refuses to take the call since the final countdown is in progress. After the firing, there is a tremendous blast, which erupts from the bore hole. Moments later, a geyser of magma spouts out of the hole, and the scientists cheer loudly. Sorenson then accepts the phone call and informs Sir Charles that his plan has met with complete success. He also tells the commission head that Rampion is needed back at the project and to ask him to return.

The next day, reporters are given a tour of the magma strike site. Sorenson and Maggie welcome Rampion when he arrives. Maggie spots a huge animal stampede in the distance. Examining the cause, they discover that a series of powerful earth tremors has occurred. Another earthquake occurs farther away in a port city, killing thousands. Rampion theorizes that these quakes are along the Masedo fault and that they were triggered by the nuclear explosion. Sorenson sends Rampion to investigate the floor of the Indian Ocean with a mini-sub to determine if there is actually a crack in the world. His photographs reveal the worst, a fissure that is moving at a speed of three miles per hour. Sorenson knows he is responsible for this development, and he is devastated. Dr. Rampion goes to London to brief the commission about the consequences should the crack travel around the world: total destruction of the planet. Rampion is placed in charge of the project with his mission to save the planet. Back at Project Inner Space, Sorenson retreats to his private lab to devise a solution. His wife tries to talk with him, but he rejects her. Rampion later consults with Sorenson, and they determine a second atomic explosion in the path of the moving crack would stop it cold. The geologist calculates that an island volcano along the fault line in the Indian Ocean offers the only opportunity to place the bomb at a sufficient depth. They then devise an improbable shield that will allow the weapon to pass through molten lava. Rampion and Steel, his assistant, wear thermal outfits and personally deposit the bomb in the volcano. Steel is killed when he slips into the crater.

At first, everyone believes the new detonation is successful, but follow-up statistics reveal that the crack has simply reversed direction and is now returning to the original bore hole site at Project Inner Space. Maggie, who had assisted

Rampion at the volcano site, is finally informed by Dr. Evans that her husband will die within a few weeks. She now understands Sorenson's recent behavior, and she rushes to his side at once.

Maggie and Sorenson have a difficult reconciliation, as Sorenson is in a rapid physical decline. Rampion and Maggie then travel to the coast to watch the crack approach the shore. Rampion calculates the direction and issues an evacuation order to try to save lives. In a long sequence they attempt to ward off a passenger train that is heading toward the crack. They chase after it in a jeep, honking the horn, but the engineer just waves them off. The train derails off a trestle in a spectacular crash. Sorenson orders the evacuation of central operations, but he elects to remain himself and monitor what will happen when the two ends of the crack meet. In a spectacle of steam and lava, the crack returns to the bore hole and a huge chunk of the earth flies off into space to become a new moon in the sky. Maggie and Sorenson watch as this phenomenon occurs, and they observe a chipmunk that emerges from his lair moments later, signaling that the earth has been saved and all will return to normal.

CRITIQUE

Much like *The Satan Bug,* another apocalyptic film with Dana Andrews that was released the same year, *Crack in the World* is handicapped by poor editing and muddled development. These problems detract from the many strong, positive elements of the production. One of the weakest points is the scientific basis, which becomes quite ludicrous as the picture reaches its climax. The concept of a traveling crack in the earth's crust is an excellent threat, but all logic disappears when the crack doubles back on itself to spit out a new moon. Earlier in the film, Rampion describes in devastating detail the result that would occur should the crack suck in the ocean water. But at the climax, nothing like that results. A huge chunk of the earth easily floats out into space. The script never considers what happens to the surface or the hole left behind. Losing such as massive volume of land would also effect the rotational spin of the planet, causing worldwide devastation. In this film, however, the earth heals instantly, and the animals are ready to frolic mere seconds after the crack completes its circuit. Even a child would scoff at this foolishness, which is magnified because the film makes forceful attempts to fill in points of scientific rationale earlier in the film. The benefits of thermal energy and access to new minerals are well presented. The script should have at least attempted some justification to explain what was happening and how this development would alter the doomsday consequences. Add to this failure the other plot gaps, such as the mysterious and unexplained disease of Dr. Sorenson and the ridiculous thermal suits that protect scientists from molten lava, and it seems that the scriptwriters simply abandoned any idea of coherence.

The special effects are also largely ineffective. The traveling geyser that represents the moving crack seems more like the exhaust of some underground steam engine than anything else. This entire depiction is rather mediocre, so the film veers off into a pointless sequence about a train heading toward calamity. With the earth in the balance, having our hero waste his time in this chase makes little sense. Perhaps the art director and special effects team told the director that they could stage a great train wreck. This effect is terrific, the best in the film, but it is a complete sidetrack at this point in the story. The effect of the new moon forming is not bad, but it is a complete failure when the result of this upheaval is overlooked as the camera instantly cuts to a chipmunk venturing out of its burrow. The last moments of the film are pitiful, with not a single line of dialogue from either Rampion or Maggie. It is as if the director said, "Let's bring this to a quick finish and get the audience out of the theater before they realize they have been had."

The picture could have been saved with very little effort. Perhaps Dr. Sorenson could have initiated a dangerous process that would have sealed the remaining cavity in the earth. This would have made the conclusion more meaningful. Instead, Sorenson chooses to remain in the doomed lab simply to monitor the joining of the two ends of the crack. His sacrifice is meaningless, but then, of course, he is dying from a mysterious rash, anyway. The missed opportunity to rectify the cracks in the story seems to be just sloppy filmmaking.

One of the film's strongest components is the excellent work of the cast. Screen veteran Dana Andrews is a master craftsman and adds credibility to any role. Here he manages to modestly enhance the character of Dr. Sorenson into a tragic figure, a dying man determined to achieve a major scientific breakthrough in his remaining few days. He chooses to shield his wife from his condition, a cowardly decision, which troubles him. He is also crushed by the enormity of the result of his carelessness and his determination to correct this lapse. Andrews is magnificent in portraying this complex role. Likewise, Kieron Moore is forceful in his narrower role, and he is especially convincing in his briefing to the members of the commission. Janette Scott is impressive as well, playing the troubled young wife trying to understand her older, but insecure, husband. She previously appeared with Kieron Moore in *Day of the Triffids* (1963). *Crack in the World* was her last film. She gave up her acting career to marry Mel Tormé shortly after completing it. Veteran character actor Alexander Knox is quite good as the dedicated Sir Charles Eggerston, a no-nonsense administrator who is able to cut to the chase in any situation. It is a unfortunate that his vibrant charactrer, one of the most interesting in the story, was excluded from the last one-third of the picture.

Other fine aspects of the film include its musical score, cinematography, and set design, which are uniformly excellent. The central operations lab is particularly impressive. With so much going for it, the fact that this film is an overall disappointment must rest principally on the shoulders of director Andrew Marton. Marston should have sharpened and corrected the problems inherent in the final section, certainly not a difficult task. Instead, he simply allowed the picture to get away from him. He just seemed to give up, and the film never lives up to its potential.

REPRESENTATIVE QUOTES

"You'll save the world or you will destroy it! You're mad, Stephen. You want to play God." (Dr. Rampion to Dr. Sorenson)

"If the world is going to come to an end, at least you won't get caught with holes in your socks." (Maggie Sorenson to Rampion, while offering to darn his socks as he packs to leave Project Inner Space)

"Where the land masses split, the oceans will be sucked in, and the colossal pressure generated by the steam will rip the earth apart and destroy it." (Rampion to the commissioners at their final briefing)

The Dawn of the Dead (1978)
AKA *Zombie*

Rating: ****   **Threat:** Zombie plague

Laurel. Written by George A. Romero; Photographed by Michael Gornick; Special effects by Tom Savini; Edited by George A. Romero; Music by The Goblins with Dario Argento & stock music selected by George A. Romero; Produced by Richard P. Rubinstein; Directed by George A. Romero. 126 minutes; European version, 121 minutes.

ANNOTATED CAST LIST

David Emge (*Stephen*, Philadelphia TV station traffic-report helicopter pilot); Gaylen Ross (*Fran*, his girlfriend and studio production assistant); Scott H. Reiniger (*Roger*, Philadelphia SWAT team member); Ken Foree (*Peter*, his friend, a policeman); David Crawford (*Dr. Foster*, scientist interviewed on television); David Earley (*Berman*, talk show host); Howard Smith (TV commentator); Richard France (scientist with eye patch); Daniel Dietrich (*Givens*, studio executive); Fred Baker (SWAT team commander); Jim Baffico (*Wooley*, bigoted SWAT team member); Jese Del Gre (old priest in tenement); Rod Stouffer (cop on roof who plans to escape by boat); George A. Romero (TV studio director); Christine Forrest (his assistant); John Harrison (zombie janitor); Clayton Mc-Kinnon, John Rice (cops in project apartment); Ted Bank, Patrick McCloskey, Randy Kovitz, Joe Pilato (cops at police dock); Pasquale Buba, Tony Buba, David Hawkins, Tom Kapusta, Rudy Ricci, Tom Savini, Mart Schiff, Joe Shelby, Taso Stavrakos, Nick Tallo, Larry Vaira (motorcycle gang members); Sharon Ceccatti, Pam Chatfield, Jim Christopher, Clayton Hill, Donald Rubinstein, Jay Stover (principal zombies).

SYNOPSIS

In 1968, Pittsburgh-based filmmaker George A. Romero made history with his ground-breaking feature *Night of the Living Dead*. The basic story involved a ghoulish onslaught of reanimated corpses, supposedly caused by high-level radiation from a disintegrating deep-space probe. The independent production cost about $115,000, and in time it grossed over $25 million. Romero delayed attempting a follow-up for about six years, and then it took him four additional years to raise the $1.5 million needed to produce the sequel. *Dawn of the Dead* was eventually issued without a rating and became a marketing phenomenon, the biggest cult blockbuster of the decade, earning over $55 million. Even more surprising, the film was a success with critics, who responded to the satirical heart of the picture, the shopping mall mindset of modern society.

The story opens at WGON, a Philadelphia television studio, which is in a state of chaos, trying to report on the story that corpses of the recent dead are reviving and attacking the living with cannibalistic intent. In the three weeks that have passed since the phenomenon began, civilization has started to crumble. Martial law has been declared, and people are no longer allowed to remain in private residences. Half the rescue centers that the station lists in scrawl at the bottom of the screen no longer exist. The director insists on listing them anyway so that people will not tune out. Dr. Foster, a guest being interviewed, is heckled by the crew as he describes the only method that will neutralize the zombies: destroying their brains. Fran, a production assistant, plans to flee the city with Stephen, her boyfriend, who is the traffic-report helicopter pilot. They plan to take the chopper that evening and head to Canada. Stephen's friend Kevin will recruit a fourth individual to join them. Givens, a studio executive, tells them to go ahead, since the emergency networks are planning to take over all broadcast stations at midnight.

Kevin is a member of a SWAT team, who are instructed to clean out a tenement containing a cluster of zombies. Wooley, a racist cop, plans to shoot any resident who breaks out of the building. He starts shooting at random when the building is stormed, and a black officer named Peter shoots him when he goes out of control. The basement of the building is crawling with zombies, and destroying them becomes a bloody melee. Kevin later talks with Peter and invites him to join in their escape. Other officers who are upset by the carnage plan to sneak away in police boats, hoping, to set up a retreat on some offshore island.

Stephen, Fran, Kevin and Peter depart on schedule. They fly over a rural area of Pennsylvania where a militia is exterminating zombies in the woodlands. The helicopter lands at a remote airstrip to refuel, and several zombies show up and attack. Kevin and Peter dispose of them efficiently, but Stephen is unused to firearms and has difficulty, almost shooting Peter at one point. While traveling on, they spot a large mall complex and decide to land on the roof and gather additional supplies. They locate some storerooms that could be set up as living quarters. The men become enchanted with the deserted mall, and when they find the control center, they turn on all the lights, the fountains and the sound system, which broadcasts taped music and promotional announcements. Peter finds the master set of keys to all the gates and stores. The zombies wandering around the mall seem to be replicating dim memories of their former lives. Scouting through the stores, Peter and Kevin have a relatively easy time getting past the zombies, and they load up a cart with assorted goodies from the principal department store. Stephen tangles with a zombie janitor in the maintenance area behind the stores before joining his friends. The zombies pose a more serious threat when the men attempt to return to the upper floor storeroom. A zombie dressed as a Hare Krishna manages to stumble into the storeroom and stalks Fran. Her friends return in time to rescue her and destroy the intruder.

Fran wants to move on, but the men believe the mall will make an ideal sanctuary with incredible bonuses. They learn from the Civil Defense television broadcasts that events are still spiraling downward. Stephen reveals to the others that Fran is pregnant with their child. The men concoct a plan to lock off the mall from the zombies, barricading the entrances with large trucks from a nearby parking lot. The operation turns out to be far more dangerous than they anticipate, and Kevin's leg becomes infected when he is bitten by a zombie. Nevertheless, they succeed in blocking off the mall, and after locking all the doors, they organize a hunt to track down and eliminate the remaining zombies within the shopping complex. Finally, the area is completely cleared, and the remaining zombies are reduced to harmlessly pounding against the blocked doors from the outside.

The group then transforms their storeroom living quarters into a luxury apartment. They also block off and disguise the entrance to their rooms from the main mall so that if looters or zombies later get into the mall, they will remain safely secluded. Each of them enjoys all the amenities of the mall, picking through the stores, playing games in the amusement center, taking money out of the bank, and so forth. Fran asks Stephen to teach her how to fly the helicopter so they can have a backup pilot. Kevin's health starts to deteriorate, and Fran nurses him with supplies from the drugstore. Finally he is forced to rely on morphine, and his days seem numbered. He asks Peter to keep watch over him when he dies. Kevin will attempt to use all his willpower to avoid returning as a zombie, but wishes to be destroyed if he fails. Kevin dies, and Peter watches somberly as the corpse sits up moments later, and he shoots him in the head. The others bury Kevin in a garden display in the middle of the mall.

All radio and television broadcasts cease, but Stephen keeps the television set turned on, hoping they will resume. Civilization has completely vanished, but Stephen, Fran and Peter continue their idyllic and artificial existence. Peter fixes a gourmet meal for his friends at the restaurant. Fran gives her friends haircuts at the beauty parlor. Stephen and Peter play poker using large sums of money from the bank. They all engage in rifle practice in the ice rink, using manikins as targets.

Finally, a motorcycle gang comes across the mall and decides to loot it. The gang members notice the helicopter on the roof and the organized way the entrances are blockaded, so they broadcast a short-wave message threatening the occupants. As night falls, they blast their way into the mall and loot in a wild spree. Stephen and Peter, heavily armed, watch from well concealed places such as air ducts. The gang members appear to have little interest in hunting down the squatters, but Stephen, feeling a proprietary interest in the mall, starts to snipe at the invaders. A shooting war breaks out, and as the combatants battle, the zombies enter the mall and start to devour the wounded bikers. Almost wiped out, the last few bikers escape from the mall. Stephen is shot in the arm, and the blood scent arouses the zombies, who corner him in an elevator.

Peter and Fran wait anxiously at their hideout. Hours pass, and the zombies now fill the mall. A catchy, bouncy tune starts to play over the mall's sound system. One of the zombies brushes against the button summoning the elevator. When the doors open, Stephen emerges, now himself a zombie. He leads the others to the camouflaged passage leading to the storerooms. Peter blasts Stephen in the head as he leads the break-in to their apartment. He tells Fran to start the helicopter and leave, as he plans to stay and die. As the zombies close in on him, he changes his mind and fights his way to the helicopter. They don't have much fuel, but they fly off into the bleak light of dawn. The end credits appear as the zombies shuffle their way around the mall and through the aisles of the stores. The jaunty melody continues to play in an arrangement featuring a xylophone, and the mall clock tolls the hour as the film ends.

CRITIQUE

In spite of the many scenes of zombie carnage, the most memorable image of *Dawn of the Dead* is the finale where the walking dead stumble triumphantly throughout the mall, accompanied by a brilliant and mesmerizing ditty over the loudspeakers. Some zombies even moan along with the tune, making this the ultimate caricature of canned background muzak. This is truly an apocalyptic vision, as the residue of humankind goes through the motions of their former lives. Of course, the zombies are not the only ones addicted to the place; so are the living. Only Fran initially rejects the location, but even she is won over eventually. In fact, Stephen engenders his own destruction when he launches a shooting war with the bikers in the belief that he and his companions own the mall. In all of the mall sequences, there are many layers of satire aimed at consumer culture. When they have the mall to themselves, the main characters still instinctively check the prices of the articles they take. One of them rolls his eyes in disbelief at the cost of a shearling coat. When the bikers loot the stores, the first items they grab are not valuable ones, but cheap, glitzy junk, perhaps reflecting what they would pick up if they had to pay for it.

Romero shot the film's interiors at the Monroeville Mall outside Pittsburgh with the almost total cooperation of the stores on the premises. The split-level location permitted excellent stunts sequences as well as fluid and interesting cinematography. He had to shoot at night after the mall closed at ten until six in the morning. Most of the zombies were played by local volunteers, who showed up in their own costumes for the extended zombie sequences. A handful of lead zombies were paid performers, but sometimes one or two characters are overused. The zombie dressed as nurse, for instance, manages to show up in almost every key shot until she becomes a distraction. The zombies are cliche figures who stagger around stiff armed for most of the film and are often ridiculed. The bikers, for example, throw pies at them for entertainment. Their elimination scenes can be quite gory, but in turn, if they trap a human, the zombies tear their victim to pieces and try to devour the flesh. The movie has extraordinary violence, but it is cartoon violence, unreal and almost always with comic overtones. The creatures are mere targets. They are objects, not people. One becomes deadened to the violence after the brutal scene in the tenement early in the film. Naturally, some viewers are unable to make the mental adjustment and see nothing in the film but a splatterfest. Nowadays, these sequences seem far less shocking, especially alongside the more realistic violence on display during an evening of professional wrestling. *Dawn of the Dead* was marketed without a rating, since an "X" rating by the MPAA would have crippled promotion and confused the film with pornography in the minds of the public at large. In fact, there is practically no sex at all in the film. The advertising states that no one under 17 may be admitted to a showing.

Technically, the film is quite striking. The cinematography is of the highest caliber, and the editing is equally impressive. The makeup and effects devised by Tom Savini are stunning; after this film, Savini's work was in high demand, but limited almost exclusively to the field of horror. The music is by an Italian rock group called Goblin, which was prepared by Italian filmmaker Dario Argento. Romero added additional cues of stock music, including the most famous selection, the jaunty tune that plays over the end credits. The cast of relative unknowns turns in terrific performances. David Emge is exceptional as Stephen, being vulnerable, impulsive and totally believable. Ken Foree's Peter is strong, intelligent, honest, dependable and brutal when the situation calls for it. Scott H. Reiniger as Kevin is efficient, generous, confident, cocky and ultimately too careless when he allows himself to become bitten and infected. Fran is a strong individual who demands an equal voice in decision making and earns the respect of Kevin and Peter. These characters are credible and complex, being both well defined in the script and well portrayed onscreen. Romero himself and his wife, Christine Forest, have cameos as the director and assistant director at the television station. This picture is undoubtedly Romero's masterpiece, although his modern day Arthurian fantasy set around a troupe of motorcyclists, *Knightriders* (1981), is also a remarkable endeavor.

Romero wrote a third film in his zombie cycle but failed to obtain enough financial backing to produce the film he envisioned. Instead, the pared-down *Day of the Dead* (1985) became a claustrophobic tale of a remote underground army base on an island off the coast of Florida. By this time, civilization has completely vanished, but one scientist continues to experiment on zombies in an attempt to learn how to control them. Eventually, zombies overrun the outpost. Lacking the satirical edge of *Dawn of the Dead*, the picture was regarded as a disappointment., unable to match the apocalyptic vision of the earlier picture. Incidentally, Romero filmed two alternate endings to *Dawn of the Dead*, one in which Peter and Fran commit suicide and one in which they escape. The latter alternative played far better, even if the prospects for the two seem very slim as they fly off at the climax. In Europe, the film played under the title *Zombie*, was five minutes shorter and used only the music by the Goblins. Since the closing music chosen by Romero creates such a memorable image, the European edition is undoubtedly weaker and less effective.

REPRESENTATIVE QUOTES

"Every dead body that is not exterminated becomes one of them. It gets up and kills. The people it kills get up and kill. . . . They kill for one reason. They kill for food. They eat their victims. That's what keeps them going. . . . Every dead body must be exterminated, either by destroying the brain or severing the brain from the rest of the body." (Dr. Foster's grisly instructions during his television interview)

"What are they doing? Why do they come here?" (Fran, when she first sees the zombies stumbling through the mall) "It's a kind of instinct, a memory of what they used to do. This was an important place in their lives." (Stephen in reply)

"When there's no more room in hell, the dead will walk the Earth." (Peter recalling the words of his grandfather, a voodoo priest from Trinidad)

The Day the Earth Caught Fire (1961)

Rating: ***** **Threat: Shift in Earth's orbit**

Melina. Written by Wolf Mankowitz & Val Guest; Photographed by Harry Waxman; Special effects by Les Bowie; Edited by Bill Lenny; Music by Stanley Black & Monty Norman; Produced by Val Guest & Frank Sherwin Green (associate); Directed by Val Guest. B & W, 99 minutes.

ANNOTATED CAST LIST

Edward Judd (*Peter Stenning*, London newspaper reporter); Janet Munro (*Jeannie Craig*, telephone operator); Leo McKern (*Bill Maguire*, science editor of *Daily Express*); Arthur Christiansen (*Jefferson*, managing editor of *Daily Express*); Michael Goodliffe (*Decker*, night editor); Bernard Braden (*Davis*, feature editor); Charles Morgan (foreign editor); Reginald Beckwith (*Harry*, pub owner); Gene Anderson (*May*, Harry's wife); Renée Asherson (*Angela*, Stenning's estranged wife); Ian Ellis (*Mike Stenning*, their seven-year-old son); Austin Trevor (*Sir John Kelly*, head of Meteorological Center); Edward Underdown (*Sanderson*, assignment chief); Geoffrey Cather (*Pat Holroyd*, public relations director of Meteorological Center); Jane Aird (Mike's nanny); John Barron, Peter Butterworth (assistant editors at the *Daily Express*); Michael Caine (traffic cop who warns Pete about the rioters).

SYNOPSIS

The Day the Earth Caught Fire is an earnest and thoughtful apocalyptic entry principally geared toward an adult rather than a juvenile audience. Val Guest, a filmmaker with an admirable record in the British film industry, including *The Quatermass Xperiment* (1956), *Abominable Snowman of the Himalayas* (1957) and *Expresso Bongo* (1959), crafted this picture with great care as writer, producer and director. Guest's personal background as a journalist no doubt influenced his decision to view the end of the world through the eyes of a newspaperman, and this helps to give the film a solid, realistic environment from which to examine the last days of humankind.

The story opens as reporter Pete Stenning roams through the deserted, sundrenched streets of London. The office of the *Daily Express* is completely empty, and Pete must telephone to reach a copyeditor to take down his story (which may be the last story he will ever write) about the fate of humanity and a desperate scientific attempt to save the planet. As he speaks, the story flashes back ninety days to when the crisis originated. In the bustling newsroom, overworked science editor Bill Maguire is entrusted to write an article about the recent American nuclear test in Antarctica, the largest explosion ever attempted. The last few days have seen an outbreak of multiple natural disasters, floods, earthquakes and massive sunspot activity. The assignment chief, Sanderson, asks Pete to cover the sunspot story, advising him that he has not been pulling his own weight lately. Pete has been drinking heavily, feeling depressed over the rearing of his son, whom he can only see once a week. The reporter calls the Meteorological Center and picks a fight with the telephone operator when she fails to put him through to the director. Pete heads over to the center, hoping to get their interpretation about the issue. Instead, his friend from public relations is unusually evasive and refuses to cooperate. Pete then encounters the phone operator, Jeannie Craig, who slaps him for his insults.

At the office, Maguire learns from a teletype story that Russia has announced its own nuclear test, which was even larger than the American explosion. Checking the time frame, Maguire determines that both nuclear tests occurred simultaneously on opposite ends of the earth. Pete is late returning to the office, and he, learns that Maguire has already submitted the sunspot story under Pete's byline. The two newsmen stop at Harry's pub, and Pete confides to his friend that his ex-wife is trying to sabotage his relationship with his son, Mike.

The next day Pete is covering an antinuke protest rally when there is an unexpected total eclipse of the sun. He manages to get a picture, and at the paper, Jefferson, the managing editor, is determined that the *Daily Express* must put all the pieces together to learn what is actually going on regarding the series of unusual events and whether the double bomb test is somehow responsible. Sir John Kelly, head of the Meteorological Center, makes a reassuring speech on television explaining away the significance of the eclipse, but Maguire mocks his feeble theory.

The next day, Sunday, brings the start of an unprecedented heat wave. Pete entertains his young son at the Battersea amusement park during his allotted visitation time. Mike particularly enjoys the ghost train ride, a motorized trip through a haunted house. His son's nanny complains that the exhibit will give Mike bad dreams. After she escorts him away, Pete spots Jeannie Craig sunbathing and relaxing. He strikes up a conversation with her and tries to apologize for his insults, when a thick bank of fog suddenly rolls up the Thames and envelopes the amusement park. Jeannie offers to take Pete to her apartment so he can telephone the news to the paper. Pete learns that this is not a true fog but a heat mist, and the view from Jeannie's window is perfectly clear, showing all of London blanketed in a thick white cloud about three stories high. Pete calls Maguire and learns that the paper will treat the story as a major event. The editor calls a conference where he lays out how he wants the story treated. Foreign reports indicate that the mist covers a third of the planet. Maguire theorizes that the polar ice caps must be melting and the influx of cold water into the warmer currents is causing the phenomenon. He thinks Earth itself might have tilted on its axis, and that this may be the cause of the strange climatic events.

When a radio bulletin orders everyone to remain at their present location, Jeannie invites Pete to spend the night at her flat. Pete finds himself attracted to the lovely Jeannie, and they begin a serious relationship. The heat mist is later broken up when London is struck by violent storms and cyclones. As soon as the weather clears in the morning, Pete makes his way to the *Daily Express*, where most of the staff spent the night. He quarrels with Maguire and plans to resign when Jeannie calls with some important news. They meet at Battersea Park, and Jeannie explains that she overheard a disturbing conversation while eavesdropping at the switchboard. She asks Pete to keep it confidential, but he immediately tells Maguire, since the story confirms his theory of an increased tilt in the axis of the plant. Jefferson telephones Sir John Kelly and forces him to make an official statement.

Jeannie is outraged by Pete's deception, and she is placed in "preventative custody" by the government. Pete is shocked by this turn of events, and Jefferson tries to reassure him about Jeannie and promises to hire her as soon as she is released. The prime minister addresses the nation and describes the change as a mere matter of altering the intensity and character of the normal seasons. As he speaks, a montage of disasters from around the world appears on the screen, which completely undercuts his benign assessment of events. At Harry's Pub, Maguire and Pete ridicule the speech as it is delivered.

Weeks pass, and the situation worsens. Fires provide the greatest hazard, and the London docks are set ablaze by the increasing heat. Temperatures average 140 degrees Fahrenheit, and automobiles have to be equipped with a coolant reservoir on the roof of each vehicle. Pete continually worries about Jeannie and is relieved when she is finally released. He learns that the public water supply will be turned off and community washing centers are being organized. Maguire shows Jeannie around the *Daily Express* offices, and she is assigned duties in the clippings library.

Jefferson receives a phone call with devastating news from his Moscow correspondent. Soviet scientists have finally revealed that the actual crisis facing Earth is not the increased axis tilt, but an orbital change. The new orbit is bringing the planet closer to the sun, and with the increased temperatures, Earth will be unable to support life within four months. Jefferson prepares his staff for the next edition, stressing that his reporters should keep the tone of the paper upbeat. Everyone embarks on their assigned tasks, trying to ignore the impact of certain doom. Pete goes to see Jeannie, and they become immediately reconciled, knowing there is no time for any pretense.

Pete goes to Battersea Park to see his son for the last time. His ex-wife and her new husband are there as well, and Pete wishes them well as they head off to a country retreat, which may be safer than London. Mike wants Pete to join them, but he says he has to stay and let people know when the ghost train ride will reopen with the rest of the amusements. That night, the prime minister speaks again and this time reveals the truth about the approaching end. There is one hope, and the nuclear powers will cooperate by detonating four massive explosions side by side in Siberia, considering it the only possibility of correcting the orbit. On his way to visit Jeannie, Peter encounters a gang of young thugs rioting in the streets. They overturn his car in a mad frenzy, spraying scarce supplies of water into the air and at each other. The rioters have also invaded Jeannie's flat, and Pete rescues her, fighting off the rowdy teenagers.

Pete and Jeannie join Maguire at Harry's Pub to await the hour of the detonation of the bombs. The radio, filled with static, relays the countdown. Worldwide, people are listening as each second is sounded off in various languages. A mist of dust is shaken from the ceiling of the bar after zero is reached. Pete heads back to the newspaper, and the film reprises its opening scene.

Pete concludes dictating his story using poetic language about the hopes that humanity may survive. In the machine room, the other members of the newspaper staff wait to learn which banner headline they will use on their next edition: "WORLD SAVED" or "WORLD DOOMED." The time is approaching noon, and the film ends as the camera focuses in on the steeple of St. Paul's Cathedral while the bells toll the hour. The picture fades to darkness without any end titles.

CRITIQUE

The Day the Earth Caught Fire is a film of considerable depth and subtlety, as profound as *On the Beach*. It is extraordinarily well written and well constructed, with many sophisticated touches that can easily be overlooked with only one viewing. Val Guest no doubt poured his heart and soul into this project, and the passion of his vision makes this an exceptional film. Guest's literate screenplay, written with Wolf Mankowitz, has many unusual touches. For instance, the depiction of an untrustworthy government seems more characteristic of a post-Watergate era, and the scene in which the prime minister's words are juxtaposed with scenes of disaster and sarcastic quips by Bill Maguire is stunning. Even the lighter moments are filled with ironic wit, such as when Maguire writes a feature article about the relationship of fat to coronary thrombosis and then celebrates the completion of his task by ordering a thick steak at the pub.

The threat of the apocalypse is presented in a credible manner for the audience. Scientifically, the orbital shift would require far more tonnage than than that of the two nuclear explosions depicted in the film, but for the purposes of the story, the concept works well enough. There are a few minor flaws in the picture. During the final countdown, both India and New York are shown in bright daylight simultaneously, an impossibility since they are half a world apart. After the detonation, Pete leaves Jeannie at Harry's Pub and walks alone to the newspaper. He then calls the switchboard, and Jeannie is there at work. The axis is tilted an additional 11 degree, according to Jefferson's phone call to Sir John Kelly, but then the same 11 degree figure is used to describe the orbital change. This second figure does not make any sense since the orbit is then described as continuing to move closer to the sun. These glitches are trivial and inconsequential, however, and the only issue that stands out is the questionable attempt to correct Earth's orbit by using additional nuclear blasts.

Many commentators believe the conclusion of the film is filled with hope, given Pete's lofty words and the peal of bells, which they assume connotes a celebration. But if one takes into account that the bells are merely tolling the noon hour, the hopeful interpretation may be illusionary. The desperate attempt to correct the problem may indeed again alter the orbit, this time outward, away from the sun. But this would doom the planet as well, propelling it into regions further out until the planet is too cold to sustain life. In truth, this result seems to be the logical consequence, even though this prospect is not addressed. So even if the "WORLD SAVED" banner is used, it may indeed be premature.

Curiously enough, this interpretation is reflected in an episode of *The Twilight Zone* written by Rod Serling. This episode, "The Midnight Sun," aired in November 1961, simultaneous with the film's release in Great Britain. In Serling's version, a woman, played by Lois Nettleton, faces the collapse of civilization in New York City as the earth's orbit is spiraling toward the sun. The scenario turns out to be a dream produced by a fever. When the woman awakens, she learns the truth: that the Earth is doomed because its orbit is spiraling away from the sun. The natural progression of Serling's tale parallels the same progression in *The Day the Earth Caught Fire*.

Another scientific consideration is the effect of a change in the tilt of Earth's axis. Some scientists have speculated that such a shift might have occurred about 10,000 years ago, bringing the downfall of early civilization that is now regarded as mere legend. In *The Day the Earth Caught Fire*, there seems to be no immediately noticeable results after the shift in the axis, an unlikely prospect since immediate large-scale disaster would accompany such an event.

Most of the technical aspects of the film are superb. The cinematography is splendid, as are the editing and direction. Stanley Black's score is modest but effective, and Monty Norman contributed the music for the scenes of the beatnik riots. Much stock footage, mostly from the Blitz, is used, but it is blended very well into the thrust of the story. Of the film's strengths, none is more remarkable that the dynamic and fascinating portrayal of a newspaper at work. The actual offices of the *Daily Express* were used in the film, and the former managing editor of the paper, Arthur Christiansen, served as technical advisor and played the role of Jefferson, the managing editor in the film. Christiansen, without doubt, steals the show in this role. His every tone and inflection rivet the audience. His character's dedication to telling the news is most impressive, considering the terrible news he has to convey. His greatest moment in the picture is after he hears from his Moscow correspondent about the ultimate fate of the world. At first he is stunned and appears totally numb. Then he snaps into action, calls the reporters in for a conference, and starts to lay out how the paper will cover this powerful story. These scenes rate among the most impressive ever shot showing the setting of a newspaper office. This verisimilitude adds immeasurably to the overall power of the story.

The other cast members also deliver some of their finest performances. Janet Munro is absolutely stunning as Jeannie. Her vivaciousness and charm are well captured. There are a number of scenes where she is seen seminude, while dressing or emerging from a bathtub. Scenes like this frequently stick out like a sore thumb in movies, as needless bits of titillation. Here, however, they seem totally natural and unforced, a regular part of the story. Her romance with Pete is well integrated into the story, and not an artificial subplot. The adult nature of her relationship with Pete is refreshing and never seems exploited. Munro was memorable in numerous other films, such as *The Crawling Eye* (1958) and *Darby O'Gill and the Little People* (1959). Munro seemed to be on the verge of major stardom, considering her talent and attractiveness, but a genuine breakthrough role for her never occurred. She died in 1972, reportedly choking to death while drinking tea. Some of her talent and beauty were inherited by her daughter, Caroline Munro, who enjoyed an interesting film career. Australian-born Leo McKern is brilliant as the cantankerous science editor with a heart of gold. His avuncular attitude toward Pete, his troubled colleague, is especially well portrayed. Note how Maguire casually lends his car to Pete throughout the story, for example. This film helped launch McKern as one of England's most popular character actors, appearing in a great variety of roles from a satirical Moriarty in *The Adventure of Sherlock Holmes' Smarter Brother* (1975) to Thomas Cromwell in *A Man for All Seasons* (1966) and Bishop Maigret in *Molokai: The Story of Father Damien* (1999). American audiences know him best as Horace Rumpole in the series *Rumpole of the Bailey* which he played for fourteen years. Edward Judd is also excellent, although he lacks the natural appeal that could have led him to greater fame. He perfectly embodies the disillusionment and despair of Peter Stenning, who finds personal redemption as the world falls to pieces. His scenes with his son, Mike, are excellent, and his final meeting with his ex-wife is handled with exceptional finesse. The remainder of Judd's screen career was run-of-the-mill, and the only other film for which he is generally remembered is *First Men in the Moon* (1964). Director Val Guest remained active in films up through the 1980s, but none of his other projects had the cohesiveness or sophistication of this apocalyptic masterpiece, which is representative of his best work

REPRESENTATIVE QUOTES

"It is exactly thirty minutes since the corrective bombs were detonated. Within the next few hours, the world will know whether this is the end or another beginning, the rebirth of man or his final obituary." (Pete Stenning's dictation to the copyeditor at the start of the film)

"A solar eclipse occurs as a result of the interposition of the moon between the earth and the sun. When one considers the moon is 240,000 miles away and the sun 93 million, it is an extraordinary thing that astronomers can tell with such a degree of accuracy what their movements will be many years ahead. But any deviation is no reason to start searching for wild causes. In this case, many of you will blame the unfortunate concurrence of the two nuclear detonations, but of course this is nonsense. It is certainly nothing to worry about." (Sir John Kelly in his television address to the nation)

"Why don't I just do five hundred steaming words on how mankind is so full of wind, it's about to outblow nature?" (Pete to Maguire as they work to get out a new edition)

"I felt it necessary to speak to you all if only to stop the many wild and irresponsible rumors precipitated by a general lack of facts. There has indeed been a displacement in the direction of the polar axis, but it is not a catastrophe, nor is it the millennium. Geologists and astronomers have long had evidence that the tilt of the Earth has been altered more than once in the history of its evolution, and it has survived them all." (The prime minister addressing the nation)

"Funny how when the chopper falls, everyone just accepts it." (Pete to Maguire after learning of the orbital change)

"If there is a future for man, as insensitive as he is, proud and defiant in his pursuit of power, let him resolve to live it lovingly, for he knows well how to do so. Then he may say once more, 'truly the light is sweet and what a pleasant thing it is for the eyes to see the sun.' " (The conclusion of Pete's dictation)

The Day the Sky Exploded (1958/61) AKA *La Morte Viene Dallo Spazio* (*Death Comes from Outer Space*)

Rating: **   **Threat:** Meteor collision

Excelsior. Written by Marcello Coscia & Alessandro Continenzia based on a story by Virgilio Sabel; Photographed by Mario Bava; Special effects by Mario Bava, Venanzio Biraschi & Oscar Arcangelis; Edited by Otello Colangeli; Music by Carlo Rustichelli; Produced by Guido Giambartolomei & Samuel Z. Arkoff (executive); Directed by Paolo Heusch. B & W, English-language version, 80 minutes; European version, 82 minutes.

ANNOTATED CAST LIST

Paul Hubschmid (*John McLaren*, American scientist and astronaut); Fiorella Mari (*Mary McLaren*, his wife); Massimo Zepperi (*Dennis McLaren*, their son); Madeleine Fischer (*Katy Dandridge*, British mathematician); Ivo Garrani (*Herbert Weisser*, professor in charge of the Space project); Dario Michaelis (*Pierre Leducq*, French scientist); Jean-Jacques Delbo (*Sergei Boetnikov*, leading Russian scientist); Sam Galter (*Randowsky*, Russian scientist and astronaut); Peter Meersman (*General Van Dorf*, military advisor); Giacomo Rossi-Stuart (*Stewart*, British scientist and astronaut); Anne Berval (lab assistant).

SYNOPSIS

Apart from the controversial truncated epic, *End of the World* (1931/35), which had limited distribution, this Italian/French co-production is the earliest in a long line of "celestial collision" apocalyptic films that includes *A Fire in the Sky* (telefilm, 1978), *Meteor* (1979), *Asteroid* (TV mini-series, 1997), *Meteorites* (telefilm, 1998), *Deep Impact* (1998) and *Armageddon* (1998). Unfortunately, the film's budget was so small that it was unable to adequately portray the scope and impact of the story. The script tried to overcome this by concentrating on a small group of characters, scientists on a space project who both propagated the crisis and resolved it. This film only merits serious consideration because of its uncanny foresight.

The story opens with a montage of newspaper headlines from around the world proclaiming the launch of the first manned space flight, which will circumnavigate the moon. A group of international scientists is overseeing the project, based at Cape Shark in Australia. John McLaren, an American scientist, is selected to serve as pilot for the mission over the other two candidates, Stewart from England and Randowsky from Russia. After the successful rocket launch, Professor Weisser leads a celebration at the launch complex and presents Sergei

Boetnikov, the Soviet scientist, with a solid gold model rocket in appreciation of his work as the designer of the spaceship. Scientist Pierre Leducq admits he has become enamored with Katy Dandridge, an aloof but beautiful mathematician who has declined to join the celebration. He bets the others that he will be able to thaw her with a kiss, unaware that Katy is overhears his comments over the intercom system.

Trouble develops with the spacecraft when it tries to leave orbit, and McLaren jettisons the pilot's capsule, which returns to Earth while the rocket heads off wildly into space. McLaren is recovered and is briefly hospitalized. At his debriefing, the astronaut says that he did not shut down the nuclear motor of the rocket, assuming that Boetnikov would handle it from the control center since the control panel in his own capsule had failed. McLaren becomes depressed about the failure of his mission and the fact that a nuclear missile is flying out of control in space.

Mary McLaren is concerned about her husband's depression and his frequent scolding of Dennis, their son. She plans to return with the boy to the United States. Leducq and Dandridge spend the entire night at the control center monitoring some unusual readings from space. Dandridge allows Leducq to kiss her but then slaps him, revealing she is aware of his bet. They overhear a radio news flash announcing that animals all over the world are behaving in a strange manner. A communiqué from the Sydney Observatory reports that a huge explosion has occurred in the asteroid belt in the area where the rocketship vanished. Further study reveals that a mass of objects from that sector is now headed toward Earth.

Weisser releases a report about this unusual event. Other strange celestial sightings have been reported worldwide. For example, in Paris, mysterious balls of light have been observed in the sky. The scientists develop a theory that a cluster of meteors has become magnetized and is heading toward Earth, grouped together as if they were a single object. In five days, this cluster will reach Earth. General Van Dorf, military advisor to the project, advises that this news be kept secret until the United Nations Security Council is informed. The council asks the scientists at Cape Shark to serve as headquarters for a scientific conference on the threat. The consensus from this meeting is that humanity is doomed. The only hope is that the gravity of the moon may deflect enough meteors from the cluster to save the planet. An additional threat is that magnetism from the cluster may create huge tidal waves, so all coastal areas of the planet must be evacuated at once and a worldwide state of emergency is declared.

John McLaren is worried about his wife and child, and he fears they may become lost in the flood of refugees. Dandridge and Leducq are drawn together by the crisis. Boetnikov places his faith in the Almighty to save humankind at its hour of need. Mary McLaren makes her way back to the control center with her son, and there she and John reconcile their differences. John sends Mary and their son to a local shelter, but they encounter a rambling and desperate crowd that blocks their way.

The meteor cluster is completely unaffected by the moon. The Earth is ravaged by floods and fires. At the control center, one of the scientists, Randowsky, goes mad, blaming all his colleagues for the catastrophe. His outburst gives McLaren an idea. If every nation on Earth with nuclear missiles launched its weapons at the cluster simultaneously, their combined strength might disintegrate the meteors. There are only a few hours to program the world's weapons for this last hope to save Earth. Russia, the United States and the other nuclear powers readily agree to participate in this effort, dubbed "Red Moon." Multiple forest fires break out around Cape Shark, and the control center turns on its air conditioning so the staff can continue to work. McLaren heads off to make sure his family has arrived at the shelter but instead finds them trapped on a side street, and he brings them back to the control center. Randowsky seizes a gun and shuts down the air conditioning, and the computers used for calculations are unable to operate in the rising heat. With time running out, the scientists rush at the mad man, and Weisser is shot. Randowsky is electrocuted when he blunders into some electrical equipment. The dying Weisser places Leducq in charge, and he rushes to complete the calculations as soon as the computers become operative again. The vital data is then relayed to all missile bases.

The barrage of nuclear weapons is effective, breaking up the meteor cluster. Most of the meteors are disintegrated or knocked away from the earth, back into deep space. The control center flashes the news to the anxious world. The next morning, the McLarens, Boetnikov and the others observe the breaking dawn with relief and fresh hope. Young Dennis heads off into the field outside the complex with his dog, Geiger, as the picture ends.

CRITIQUE

This film has many original features but is largely hobbled by a static plot, dull characters and an inadequate budget. The American version, two minutes shorter, was prepared three years after the European release. Some of the story's loopholes are the result of a half-hearted dubbing job. For example, the objects from outer space are often described as meteorites in the film, yet a meteor becomes a meteorite only after it has landed. The threat is never clearly explained, and the various unexplained phenomena, such as the strange lights in the sky and magnetic disturbances, are never integrated into the story. The ability of animals to sense the approaching danger while it was still in deep space is also unresolved.

The dark and moody photography, one of the film's strengths, was handled by Mario Bava, who went on to fame as a colorful director of Italian horror films such as *Blood and Black Lace* (1964). Most of the scenes take place in the darkened lab or outside at night, and they are effective. The stock footage is well managed throughout the film. The music, inspired by the electronic score of *Forbidden Planet* (1956), is decent and not too intrusive. The weakness of the film is that almost all the characters, with the exception of Boetnikov, are flat, lifeless and uninteresting. Most of the cast members are veterans from the Italian film industry, such as Giacomo Rossi-Stuart, who also appeared in *The Last*

Man on Earth (1964). The lead player, Paul Hubschmid, is of Swiss background and also performed under the name of Paul Christian. His most famous role for American audiences was as the lead in *The Beast from 20,000 Fathoms* (1953). In the role of John McLaren, he is bland and wooden. In fact, Sam Galter's wild outburst as Randowsky and Ivo Garrani's brief but poetic death scene as Weisser are the only moments with any thespian flair whatsoever. The script is ponderous and slow moving. The only humor in the film arises unintentionally in the dubbing during the three crowd scenes. The background sounds keep repeating a ten-second loop, starting with a loud squawk, which sounds more like a cockatoo than a person, followed by a man shouting, "Get back," then a softer voice saying, "Stop," and concluding with a woman crying, "My baby!" This nonstop loop sounds more hilarious and phony each time it is repeated. Despite these many weaknesses, *The Day the Sky Exploded* deserves a place of honor in the spectrum of apocalyptic films. The concepts of a disturbance in the asteroid belt, international panic after the threat is learned, Russian-American cooperation and a reliance on nuclear weapons as the means of salvation were all trailblazed in this modest production. All these ideas were later refined and rendered commonplace by the late 1990s.

REPRESENTATIVE QUOTES

"Extraordinary phenomena have been reported from many country [*sic*]. Large herds of animal [*sic*] are abandoning the coastal regions and are making their way into the interior at [*sic*] a colossal and surprising migration, which hour by hour assumes ever more alarming proportions. We are informed that out of season migrations of this magnitude have never before been reported. It appears that this unease is affecting not only the wild animal population, it is also being reported from zoos and owners of domesticated animals. Authorities agree the animals' acute instincts has [*sic*] evidently sensed an indefinable menace, but the sources of the cause of this phenomena are for the moment unknown and cannot be explained." (Radio bulletin overheard by Leducq and Dandridge)

"This is the end! This is your own fault and you all deserve it! And each one of you here is guilty. This is the judgment, the day of wrath! It's all over . . . your blasted rocket was just a missile, a destroyer like the rest of them!" (Randowsky, going mad after the meteor cluster passes the moon)

"At this moment, the safety of the human race is entrusted to the very weapons that were created for its own destruction." (Leducq, moments before the missiles are fired)

Day the World Ended (1956)

Rating: ***   **Threat: Nuclear war and fallout**

Golden State Production. Written by Lou Rusoff; Photographed by Jock Feindel; Special effects by Paul Blaisdell; Edited by Ronald Sinclair; Music by Ronald Stein; Produced by Roger Corman & Alex Gordon (executive); Directed by Roger Corman. B & W, 82 minutes.

ANNOTATED CAST LIST

Richard Denning (*Rick*, geologist); Paul Birch (*Jim Maddison*, survivalist); Lori Nelson (*Louise*, Maddison's daughter); Mike "Touch" Connors (*Tony Lamont*, gangster); Adele Jergens (*Ruby*, Tony's girlfriend); Raymond Hatton (*Pete*, elderly prospector); Paul Dubov (*Radek*, man with radiation sickness); Jonathan Haze (dying man seeking food); Paul Blaisdell (mutant).

SYNOPSIS

This film was Roger Corman's first foray into science fiction, and it is a textbook example of how an entertaining film can be produced with a minuscule budget. The picture has elements of the post-apocalyptic genre, but since the continued existence of any survivors is under constant threat, it fits comfortably in the apocalyptic category as well. *The Day the World Ended* was no doubt aimed at a young audience, but a literate script and fine cast allow the picture to also appeal to an adult audience, and unlike many other science fiction films from the 1950s, this one has aged very well and is still quite entertaining.

The picture begins with a short message announcing "The End" as the image of a nuclear blast fills the screen. Former navy captain Jim Maddison has been preparing for this eventuality for ten years, settling in a secluded valley surrounded by hills rich in lead ore, which serves as a natural barrier against radiation. He has gathered rations (but only enough for himself, his daughter, Louise and her fiancé, Tommy) as he waited for the inevitable nuclear war. When the bombs finally fall, however, Tommy is away and unable to return in time. Instead, a number of stragglers find themselves in this natural haven, including Rick, a geologist and Pete, a prospector. A small-time hood named Tony Lamont and his girlfriend, Ruby, were driving nearby when the holocaust began. When these people seek shelter at Maddison's house, he is reluctant to let them in, but Louise insists that they be saved. At first Tony brandishes his gun and tries to push the others around, but Rick disarms him. Rick has also saved Radek, a man covered with radiation burns, who manages to survive despite having received a deadly dose of radiation.

Jim explains that their survival depends on stretching their rations and the hope that no precipitation occurs before the radiation count drops to a safe level. Pete's only concern is for his companion, his burro, Diablo. He and Tony find it hard to comprehend that the rest of the world no longer exists. After Jim learns Rick is a geologist, he starts to confide in him, particularly about his experiences with radioactive mutations among the animals who were exposed to atomic tests. It was his naval experience in the Pacific Ocean monitoring these nuclear tests that turned Jim into a survivalist.

Three weeks pass, and everyone falls into a routine. Radek spends most of his time in the woods, hunting wild game and eating contaminated meat. The others remain in the compound. Louise falls in love with Rick. Pete takes care of his burro. Tony remains cranky, and Ruby has trouble keeping him cooperative. She entertains the others by dancing and describing her old routines as a stripper. Jim discusses the Bible and his future plans. If the radioactive rain holds off, they can start planting using his storehouse of seed. His library is also filled with books of practical knowledge that will insure survival. Tony mocks the idea of becoming a farmer.

Jim determines that a pool near the house is now safe for bathing. When Louise and Ruby go for a dip, Louise panics, suspecting that something strange in the woods is watching her. Jim finds evidence that a large creature, which he fears is a terrible mutation has moved into the valley. Ruby brings extra sugar for Pete's burro, and makes the prospector promise to share his moonshine with her. Tony tries to flirt with Louise, but she finds him repellent. Rick fights Tony when he learns of his advances. Jim proposes that Louise and Rick get married. He also suggests that Ruby and Tony should take the same step. For humankind to survive, both women should strive to have children.

While scouting around, Jim and Rick encounter a newcomer who stumbles into the valley from beyond the ridge. The man, covered with radiation scars, is dying from starvation. He says there are others who are much stronger but that food is becoming scarce. The man dies moments later. Jim examines the corpse, and detects signs of radical mutation. Rick believes there are definite stages of mutation. Radek is stage one; the newcomer is stage two; the stronger ones that the newcomer described are stage three; and stage four, when it evolves, may be invulnerable.

Jim keeps checking his short-wave radio, always hoping to detect signs of other survivors. Radek returns at night to talk with Rick, explaining that he now has an enemy in the woods competing for game. Radek later steals Diablo, taking him into the woods and killing him. As Radek bends over his prey, he himself is slain by a mutant with huge claws. Losing his companion, Pete becomes unbalanced and wanders off over the ridge. When Jim tries to stop him, he becomes exposed to an overdose of radiation. After returning to the house, Jim collapses and is no longer able to stay on his feet. Tony tries to force himself on Louise again, but Ruby intervenes. Tony kills Ruby and throws her body into a gully. He then feigns ignorance about her whereabouts after rejoining the others.

Later, while Louise is in the pool, she hears someone call her name from the woods. She comes to believe that the mutant must be Tommy, her fiancé. That night, the creature summons her and carries her off. The mutant is hideous, with horns on its head and three eyes. After Rick leaves to track the beast, Tony manages to obtain a gun. Louise breaks free and runs into the water, but the mutant seems afraid to follow her. Rick tries to shoot the monster, but it wards off his attack, and Rick is also forced to take refuge in the water.

The ailing Jim tries the radio again and picks up a broadcast in French. A thunderstorm breaks, and Tony obtains a sample of the rainwater, which he brings to the reclining Jim. He tests it and finds that it is completely clear of radiation. At the pool, the mutant collapses when the rainwater soaks him and dies in a vapor of steam. Tony plans to kill Rick the moment he reappears, but Jim shoots him with a gun that was hidden beneath his pillow. When Rick and Louise return, the dying Jim gives them a few words of encouragement about the future and then expires. Believing the rain shower has dissipated the remaining radiation, the young couple heads off to their new life and the end title proclaims "The Beginning" at the fadeout.

CRITIQUE

This film is basically held together by an intriguing concept and an assortment of interesting, if not entirely credible, characters. The script is well written and provides colorful dialogue for each member of the group. Roger Corman marshals his forces well and keeps the film moving at a brisk pace. The sense of nuclear destruction seems real, even though little is actually shown onscreen. Paul Birch's descriptions alone manage to convey the devastation and the slim chances for survival. The threat posed by the mutant is also credible, and the appearance of the monster, designed and played by Paul Blaisdell, is surprisingly effective. In short, *Day the World Ended* accomplishes all a low-budget film can do, by telling a unique story entertainingly in a neat eighty-two-minute package.

The cast is the strongest single factor in the film, and each member shines in his or her role. The likable Richard Denning makes a solid, dependable hero, as usual. After a moderately successful career, Denning retired to Hawaii and occasionally appeared as the governor in *Hawaii Five-O* (1979-89). Paul Birch is ideal as the former navy captain who foresaw the war. Birch was a crusty character actor who excelled in budget films, most memorably *Not of This Earth* (1957) and *Queen of Outer Space* (1958). Mike Connors, best known as the star of the TV series *Mannix* (1967-74) appeared in his early films as Touch Connors, a nickname he earned during his days as a college football star. He is fascinating as Tony and manages to make his rogue likable even when he committing the most terrible deeds. Adele Jergens comes close to stealing the movie as Ruby. Her enthusiastic recreation of her strip routine is one of the highlights of the film, especially with her delivery of asides during the dance. Lori Nelson, the heroine from *Revenge of the Creature* (1955), seems colorless compared to Adele Jergins, but she projects an unfeigned sincerity that is very refreshing. She provides a fine anchor for the film's more colorful figures. Even the minor characters, such as Raymond Hatton's Pete and Paul Dubov's Radek, are fine and perform with zest. The brief cameo by Jonathan Haze is another bright moment.

The only drawback to the picture is its very narrow range, but even this works to an extent because it creates a sense of claustrophobia. The scientific explanation about radiation is totally fanciful, yet it is presented in such a matter-of-fact tone that it seems believable. The deus ex machina conclusion, with pure rainwater killing any mutants, is too pat, and having Rick and Louise head off out of the valley in the belief that one rain shower has completely dispersed the radiation is a bit ludicrous. Corman merely wanted an ending with the two survivors on their way so that he could post the final title saying "The Beginning." The effect is nice, but it jars with the earlier parts of the story. One can imagine the couple collapsing from an overdose somewhere down the road. There are several inside jokes in the production as well. For example, in the photograph of Louise with her fiancé, the man is actually Roger Corman himself.

Larry Buchanan, the renegade Texas filmmaker, attempted a remake of *Day the World Ended* that only accentuated the merits of the original. This remake was called *In The Year 2889* (1968) and featured Paul Petersen. Much of the dialogue was the same, but the ensemble appeal is completely absent. The house used as the setting was completely wrong, and while the budget was as tiny as Corman's, there was none of the magic of the earlier film. Paul Petersen's earnest performance is this version's only redeeming feature.

REPRESENTATIVE QUOTES

"This is TD Day, total destruction by nuclear weapons, and from this hour forward the world as we know it no longer exists, and over all the lands and waters of the Earth hangs the atomic haze of death. Man has done his best to destroy himself, but there is a force more powerful than man, and in His infinite wisdom, He has spared a few." (Opening narration)

"As long as the wind blows and the rain don't come too soon, we may live. That is, if we are not destroyed by other forces. . . . Make no mistake about it. You are not welcome here. This was planned for three people. That's how much food we've got. Divide that among seven of us, and we'll find ourselves walking around with aching bellies." (Jim to his "guests" on their chances for survival)

"We know that even small amounts of radiation produce change. But if, for some reason, a man could live through complete saturation, a thousand generation changes could have taken place. . . . There may be more Radeks, worse than him." (Rick to Jim while examining the contaminated game trapped by Radek)

"There was a voice on the radio while you were gone. There are others out there. There's a future out there for you two. You've got to go and find it." (Jim)

Deep Impact (1998)

Rating: ****   **Threat:** **Collision with a comet**

Paramount/Dreamworks. Written by Bruce Joel & Rubin Michael Tolkin; Photographed by Dietrich Lohmanns; Special effects by Scott Farrar (supervisor); Edited by Paul Cichocki & David Rosenbloom; Music by James Horner; Produced by Richard E. Zanuck, David Brown, Walter Parkes, Joan Bradshaw & Stephen Spielberg (executive); Directed by Mimi Leder. 120 minutes.

ANNOTATED CAST LIST

Robert Duvall (*Spurgeon "Fish" Tanner*, veteran astronaut); Morgan Freeman (*Tom Beck*, U.S. president); Téa Leoni (*Jenny Lerner*, television journalist); Vanessa Redgrave (*Robin Lerner*, her mother); Maximilian Schell (*Jason Lerner*, her father); Rya Kihlstedt (*Chloe Lerner*, Jason's second wife); Elijah Wood (*Leo Biedermann*, amateur teenage astronomer); Richard Schiff (*Don Biedermann*, Leo's father); Betsey Brandtley (*Ellen Biedermann*, Leo's mother); Katie Hagan (*Jane Biedermann*, Leo's sister); Lee Lee Sobieski (*Sarah Hotchner*, Leo's girlfriend); Gary Werntz (*Chuck Hotchner*, her father); Denise Crosby (*Vicky Hotchner*, her mother); Ron Eldard (*Dr. Oren Monash*, mission commander of *The Messiah*); Jennifer Jostyn (*Marietta Monash*, his wife); Jon Favreau (*Dr. Gus Patenza*, medical office of *The Messiah*); Mary McCormick (*Andrea Baker*, pilot of *The Messiah*); Charlie Hartsock (*David Baker*, her husband); Stephanie Patton (*Brittany Baker*, their daughter); Blair Underwood (*Mark Simon*, navigator of *The Messiah*); Kimberly Huie (*Wendy Mogel*, Mark's fiancée); Aleksander Baluyev (*Mikhail Tulchinsky*, Soviet nuclear specialist on *The Messiah*); James Cromwell (*Alan Rittenhouse*, secretary of the treasury who resigns); Hannah Werntz (*Lily Rittenhouse*, his daughter); Laura Innes (*Beth Stanley*, White House television correspondent); Caitlin Fien and Amanda Fien (*Caitlin Stanley*, Beth's young daughter); Dougray Scott (*Eric Vennekor*, MSNBC supervisor); Bruce Weitz (*Stuart Caley*); O'Neal Compton (*Morton Entrekin*, presidential advisor); Joseph Urla (*Ira Moscatel*, MSNBC reporter); Una Damon (*Marianne Duclos*, Rittenhouse's assistant); Mark Moses (*Tim Urbansky*); Derek de Lint (*Theo Van Sertema*); Charles Dumas (*Jeff Worth*); Suzy Nakamura (Jenny's assistant); Alimi Ballard (*Bobby Rhue*); W. Earl Brown (*McCloud*); Jason Dohring (*Harold*); Tucker Smallwood (*Ivan Brodsky*); Merrin Dungey (*Shiela Bradley*); Francis X. McCarthy (*General Scott*, Beck's military advisor); Benjamin Stralka (boy who questions Partenza at lawn party); Cynthia Ettinger (woman who flirts with Tulchinsky); Gerry Griffin (NASA official); Ellen Bry (*Stofsky*); Concetta Tomei (*Patricia Ruiz*); Mike O'Malley (*Mike Perry*, Leo's high school teacher); Rahi Azizi (*Jason Thurman*, wiseguy student at Leo's high school); Kurtwood Smith (*Otis*

Hefter); Don Handfield *(Dwight Tanner*, Fish's son); Jason Frasca *(Steve Tanner*, Fish's son); Fred Whiteman (priest who marries Leo and Sarah); John Ducey (lieutenant who certifies the Biedermann family); Christopher Darga (section leader at the shelter); Kevin La Rosa (MSNBC helicopter pilot); Charles Martin Smith *(Marcus Wolf*, astronomer who dies in car wreck).

SYNOPSIS

Released several months before *Armageddon* (1998), *Deep Impact* tackled a similar story with a completely different approach, sober, somber and stressing the emotional predicaments of the main characters, through whose eyes the story is told. Instead of the braggadocio and quirky humor of its competitor, *Deep Impact* does sink at times into bathos and soap opera, yet it still manages to realistically depicts global cataclysm on a grand scale.

The picture opens in Richmond, Virginia, with a group of young amateur astronomers observing the heavens. One of them, Leo Biedermann, spots an unusual object though his telescope. His girlfriend, Sarah Hotchner, teases him that he is just misidentifying a common star. He takes a picture of the object and transmits it to Dr. Wolf at the Adrian Peak Observatory in Arizona. Wolf learns not only that the object is a new comet, but also that its trajectory will lead to a direct collision with Earth. The astronomer attempts to transmit his data directly to NASA, but his internet service provider is down, so he places the information on a floppy disk. While driving down from the observatory, he is killed when his car, after avoiding a truck, crashes over a cliff.

A full year passes and he scene shifts to a television newsroom in Washington, D.C. The hot topic is the unexpected resignation of the secretary of the treasury, Alan Rittenhouse. Beth Stanley, the White House correspondent for the cable television network MSNBC, assigns ambitious reporter Jenny Lerner to research the story. From a member of Rittenhouse's staff, Jenny uncovers a rumor that the secretary was having an affair with someone named "Ellie." The reporter confronts Rittenhouse, who responds, oddly, that if Jenny knows about "Ellie," she has the biggest story in history. While driving back to her office, Jenny is kidnapped by the FBI, who take her to a basement cafeteria to meet the president, Tom Beck. He makes her promise to keep "Ellie" a secret for forty-eight hours in exchange for the first question at his press conference. While doing research, Jenny learns that "Ellie" is not a person but an acronym, E. L. E., meaning Extinction Level Event, such as the meteor that wiped out the dinosaurs. Jenny rushes off to meet her father and his new bride for dinner. Still stunned by her recent discovery, she starts to laugh uncontrollably when Chloe, her vivacious new stepmother, says, "Life goes on." Jenny urges her father to keep in touch with Robin, her mother, who is all alone in the world.

At the White House news conference, Beth is startled when Jenny is given special treatment and seated front and center. President Beck gives an address in which he describes a new comet, Wolf-Biedermann, that will collide with the earth in one year. For the past eight months, the United States and Russia have been constructing a new spacecraft in outer space called *The Messiah*. In two months, this ship will take off to rendezvous with the comet and alter its course with nuclear weapons. The crew of the mission will consist of: Commander Oren Monash, pilot Andrea Baker, navigator Mark Simon, medical officer Gus Partenza, veteran astronaut Spurgeon "Fish" Tanner and Soviet cosmonaut Mikhail Tulchinsky, a nuclear specialist. The president then recognizes Jenny for his first three questions. Leo Biedermann is stunned while listening to the press briefing, since his name is mentioned by the president, who mistakenly says that both discoverers of the comet were killed in an auto crash. Leo soon becomes an instant celebrity and is featured on the cover of *Time* magazine. When the astronauts socialize at a NASA lawn party, the younger members resent the presence of Fish Tanner in the crew. Tanner's fame goes back to the moon program, and they feel that he was added simply for public relations reasons. Fish tries to reach out to them, but his appeal falls on deaf ears.

Months pass, and *The Messiah* launches as planned. Jenny is promoted to the anchor desk at MSNBC. The ship prepares to rendezvous with the Wolf-Biedermann comet. Fish takes control of the ship for its landing, a dangerous procedure as he weaves his way through a cluster of rocks trailing the comet. He achieves a perfect landing, and the crewmen start to implant the nuclear bombs beneath the surface. They have seven hours to finish before the comet's rotation exposes them to the intense sunlight, which would make further work impossible. They run out of time, unsure whether the bombs were placed deep enough to be effective. Partenza is killed and Monash is blinded while attempting to return to *The Messiah*. When the bombs are exploded, they split the comet into two halves, with the larger chunk now called Wolf and the smaller one named Biedermann. Unfortunately both objects remain on course for Earth. Fish assumes command of *The Messiah*, which was seriously damaged by debris from the explosion.

The president explains several backup plans in a television address. Nuclear missiles will be used against the comets as they approach Earth. If that fails, approximately a million people can be accommodated in a special underground network of caves in Missouri. A computer will randomly select most of the occupants, with a maximum age limit of fifty. The shelters will have two years of supplies, and these people may survive the impact and its aftereffects. Martial law is also proclaimed to preserve order.

Leo Biedermann is informed that he and his family have been preselected for the shelter. Robin Lerner tells Jenny that she finds it liberating to know she will not be selected. She later commits suicide. Leo proposes to Sarah, saying this would guarantee her inclusion in the shelter as his wife. He also promises to use his influence to include her parents as well. A montage of Jenny's television broadcasts is shown, which reveal that civilization is steadily crumbling as the comets near Earth.

Aboard *The Messiah*, Fish reads the novel *Moby Dick* to Dr. Monash. The crew has developed a new respect for Fish after he assumed command. The veteran astronaut develops a plan to destroy the larger comet, Wolf, but it would be a suicide mission. There is a crease in the comet, and if *The Messiah* crashes into this vent and explode the remaining four bombs that they are carrying, it would eliminate Wolf as a threat to Earth. He proposes this to the others, and they agree to make the effort. Since their long-range communications are down, they will only be able to contact Earth when they get close enough to use their short-range transmitter.

When the time comes for the selectees to be transported to the national shelter, the Hotchner family is not included on the list, and Sarah refuses to go without them. There is chaos at the entrance to the shelter as protesters demonstrate at the gates. After seeing that his parents have arrived safely, Leo tells them he is going back to find Sarah. Jenny's father goes to the station to attempt a reconciliation with her. He brings her some photos from her childhood. Jason is now alone since his new wife has returned to stay with her mother.

After the failure of missile attack on the comets, the president announces that the first comet, Biedermann, will crash into the Atlantic Ocean off the East Coast, causing a huge tidal waves that will obliterate the Atlantic coastline of America and Europe for hundreds of miles. Wolf will strike western Canada three hours later, and it will be an extinction level event. He predicts Earth will be clouded in total darkness for two years.

NASA is startled to hear from *The Messiah*, and they provide to the astronauts the needed information to make another attempt to destroy Wolf. Leo returns to Richmond, which is abandoned. He breaks into the Hotchner home to appropriate her father's souped-up motorcycle. He then speeds off in search of Sarah. He comes across their van, and her parents urge her to leave with Leo in a desperate attempt to reach high ground to avoid the tidal wave. Jenny is assigned a seat in the MSNBC evacuation helicopter, which she yields instead to Beth Stanley and her daughter. Jenny then goes to her father's beachfront home to stay with him and await the tidal wave.

Biedermann flames across the sky and crashes into the Atlantic. An enormous tidal wave crashes into New York City, obliterating it in a spectacular sequence. Leo and Sarah take an offroad route and speed up a mountain. In Houston, family members of the crew gather to say goodbye to them before they begin their operation against Wolf. Fish guides *The Messiah* deep into the crevice, and the resulting explosion totally demolishes the comet. On Earth, people everywhere cheer as they see Wolf explode in the sky. Small fragments of Wolf burn up in the atmosphere.

Weeks later, President Beck rededicates the Capitol Building as Washington undergoes reconstruction, He speaks in memory of the heroic astronauts who gave their lives to save the planet and restore to everyone their home.

CRITIQUE

Many critics dubbed *Deep Impact* a "feminist" apocalyptic film, perhaps an unfair swipe at director Mimi Leder and the script's rather emotional tone. This is entirely unmerited, since other films such as *On The Beach* (1959) also focus on the perceptions and reactions of the main characters. The structure of the screenplay, revolving around four different sets of individuals, is sound and well constructed. Leo Biedermann and his circle are average people who discover the threat. Jenny Lerner and her circle uncover the story and how it affects everyone. President Beck and his circle attempt to manage the increasingly deadly situation. Finally, Fish Tanner and his associates directly encounter and overcome the threat. The story is very well balanced among these four groups, and this solid framework is one of the film's best aspects.

Deep Impact includes breathtaking special effects, particularly at the film's dramatic conclusion. It is fascinating to compare the tidal wave destruction of New York City in *Deluge* (1933) with that in *Deep Impact*. Both represent the effects of their era, and both portray complete devastation. The Statue of Liberty is featured prominently in both sequences as the first victim of the crest of destruction. The underwater shot of the head of the statue tumbling between skyscrapers may be the single most fascinating effects shot in *Deep Impact*, although the overhead shot of the water rushing through the cityscape is also exceptional. In the credits, almost a hundred individuals were cited for their work in creating the marvelous effects.

Oddly enough, the worst moments in both *Armageddon* and *Deep Impact* involve recycling an incredibly maudlin scene from *Marooned* (1969), where three American astronauts, who are unable to land their space capsule, bid farewell to their wives and loved ones over a video screen. In *Armageddon*, we have a weeping Bruce Willis saying goodbye to his daughter. *Deep Impact* triples the gush factor as three separate astronauts repeat the process, culminating in the blind Oren Monash sending a greeting to his newborn son. These scenes ring false in both films and are milked shamelessly. Other weak moments in *Deep Impact* involve the artificial "will she or won't she come" gambit involving Leo Biedermann's search for his high school bride Sarah. The scenario becomes preposterous when Leo finally locates her parent's van in the monumental traffic tie-up in the mountains.

The scientific basis for the threat in the film is credible and well presented. The two year time frame from the initial sighting of the comet to impact is somewhat unlikely. The other questionable element is the length of time for which the earth would be uninhabitable due to the impenetrable dust cloud. The picture proposes two years as almost a certainty, but actual opinion varies on this figure, from a low of six months to as long as twenty years. The prologue in *Armageddon* exaggerates the figure to a thousand years. Since much of the subplot of sustaining a million people in a huge shelter relies on this two-year figure, several lines of dialogue questioning this figure would have been advisable. Incidentally, when first considered in *Dr. Strangelove* (1964), the idea of a mammoth underground shelter was considered absurd satire, but in the context of this film, the concept becomes completely practical.

Most of the technical aspects of the film are sensational, including the cinematography, editing and direction. The musical score by James Horner is weak, however, since it is far too maudlin, soupy and predictable. There isn't a moment in the entire film where the music rises above the banal.

The best feature of *Deep Impact* is the overall strength of the cast. Morgan Freeman is outstanding as President Beck. Since few analysts doubt that Colin Powell would have been electable as president in 1996 had he chosen to run, the question of race is no longer a major issue, and it is refreshing that Beck's background is not even mentioned in the course of the film. Freeman's strong, measured performance holds the entire film together, because had his performance been unconvincing, the picture would have fallen apart. He brings many small nuances to the role as well, and it is one of the most effective outings in his distinguished career. Robert Duvall is equally remarkable as a genuine hero, but one who is out of sync with his times. His timing and delivery are exceptional throughout the film, including special moments involving his awkwardness with his grown sons. The scene where he reads Herman Melville to the blind Oren Monash is another priceless moment in the picture. Téa Leoni handles the role of Jenny Lerner with cool aplomb, and her rapprochement with her father, played by Maximilian Schell, carries genuine impact. Their scene on the beach before the monumental tidal wave is magnificent, particularly when compared to the phony "astronauts' farewell" scene. Elijah Wood is likable as Leo, but he lacks the screen presence to make his character truly memorable. Aleksander Baluyev is wonderful as the Russian cosmonaut aboard *The Messiah*. He has one exceptional line in the lawn party sequence, when he states that the engines of the new rocketship were created by the designers of Chernobyl. The other players range from average to exceptional, with the best work turned in by Vanessa Redgrave, Ron Eldard and especially Charles Martin Smith.

Despite its many strengths, some younger viewers found *Deep Impact* unsatisfying. They considered it too frustrating to wade through the human drama while waiting for the special effects payoff. A similar complaint was noted when *Contact* (1997) was released. It would be unfortunate if this segment of the audience causes a studio trend to avoid making literate science fiction films in favor of mindless action ones.

REPRESENTATIVE QUOTES

"Now we get hit all the time by rocks and meteors, some of them the size of cars and some no bigger than your hand. But the comet we discovered is the size of New York City, from the north side of Central Park to the Battery, about seven miles long. To put it another way, this comet is larger than Mount Everest and weighs five hundred billion tons." (President Beck describing the threat at his news conference)

"At some point over the next ten months, all of us will entertain our worst fears and concerns, but I can also promise you this. Life will go on. We will prevail." (The president's response to Jenny's third question)

"Look at the bright side. We'll all have high schools named after us." (Andrea Baker discussing the suicide mission to destroy Wolf)

Deluge (1933)

Rating: **   **Threat: Global earthquakes and floods**

RKO. Written by Warren Duff & John F. Goodrich based on a novel by S. Fowler Wright; Photographed by Norbert Brodine; Special effects by William Williams & Russell Lawson (matte drawings); Edited by Martin G. Cohn & Rose Loewinger; Music by Val Burton & Edward Kilenyi; Produced by Samuel Bishoff, Burt Kelly & William Saal; Directed by Felix Feist. B & W, 70 minutes.

ANNOTATED CAST LIST

Sidney Blackmer (*Martin Webster*, lawyer and survivor); Lois Wilson (*Helen*, his wife); Ronnie Crosby (*Ronnie*, their son); Billy N. Williams (*Mary Ann*, their daughter); Peggy Shannon (*Claire Arlington*, champion swimmer); Fred Kohler (*Jepsen*, brutish survivor who pursues Claire); Ralf Harolde (*Norwood*, Jepsen's partner); Matt Moore (*Tom*, survival community member who befriends Helen); Lane Chandler (*Jack*, community member); Philo McCullough (*Bellamy*, gang leader); Harry Semels (his sidekick); John Elliott (preacher); Samuel S. Hinds (meteorologist); Edward Van Sloan (top astronomer).

SYNOPSIS

For many years *Deluge* was considered lost, known principally for the clip of the tidal wave that obliterates New York City that was recycled as the climax of the serial *King of the Rocketmen* (1949) and other Republic efforts. Then a virtually complete Italian print was located under the title *La Distruzione del Mondo*. The original soundtrack is lost, and this print is dubbed in Italian. It made its way onto video in several versions, primarily as a silent movie, with the Italian dialogue removed, replaced by an ineffectual organ score while the dialogue is related with English subtitles. In this edition, the only occasion when the original soundtrack is heard is during the earthquake and tidal wave destruction of New York City.

The story opens as meteorologists are puzzled by an unusual phenomenon. The barometric pressure is falling to a record low, indicating that an unprecedented tremendous storm is brewing. All aircraft are grounded and all ships are ordered back to port. Claire Arlington, a champion swimmer, is forced to cancel her proposed swim around the island of Manhattan. When an unexpected eclipse occurs, the chief meteorologist goes to consult with the American Astronomical Society. Their leading astronomer reports the conditions are worldwide, and in Europe, a cycle of major earthquakes has started. Panic is breaking out in the general populace. Next, the astronomer receives a report that the entire West Coast has been wiped out by a massive quake, and all means of communication with Europe is lost. Total devastation appears imminent.

At an elegant home in Westchester, just north of New York City, lawyer Martin Webster is listening to the news of world disaster on his radio. He speaks with his wife, Helen, and they decide to take their two children, Ronnie and Mary Ann, and go to a nearby stone quarry for shelter, believing it to be the safest place possible. Scientists at the society learn that earthquakes are spreading eastward across the United States and the Mississippi delta region is sinking. Quakes beneath the oceans are producing massive tidal waves, and the leading astronomer says that escape is no longer possible.

Webster and his wife return to their house to gather additional supplies. Helen is hurt by falling debris and Martin carries her back to their shelter in the quarry, and then again attempts to retrieve the needed provisions. In New York City, all the skyscrapers collapse in an major earthquake. A massive tidal wave breaks and sweeps over the Statue of Liberty, engulfing the remainder of the city. The entire metropolis is leveled as if it never existed. The storms and earthquakes cease, and the waters withdraw leaving only a barren and desolate landscape. Martin Webster awakes in a pool of mud, seeming to be the only survivor in the entire world, and he wanders off aimlessly.

Several months pass. The scene shifts to a log cabin on an island upstate. Two disheveled men, Jepsen and Norwood, discuss their situation. They believe they may be the only people left on Earth. While gathering firewood, Jepsen discovers an unconscious woman and brings her back to the cabin. She is the beautiful swimmer, Claire Arlington. The two men try to nurse her back to health, but Jepsen, a hulking brute of a man, warns Norwood that he intends to own the girl, just as he believes he owns everything else left in the world. When Jepsen catches Norwood trying to kiss Claire, he attacks him and strangles him to death. Claire runs off while they are fighting, Jepsen pursues her, but she leaps into the vast expanse of water that surrounds the island and swims off. It takes her sixteen hours to cross to the other side.

There is another shack across the water, where Martin has settled. He draws a calendar on the wall and carefully keeps track of each passing day. He notices Claire as she stumbles ashore exhausted, and he brings her to his shack. Jepsen has a boat and the brute crosses the water in an attempt to track Claire down. Instead he comes across some roughnecks known as the Bellamy gang. They were recently expelled from a nearby community, which they tried to dominate. They size up Jepsen and conclude he is as tough as they are, so they invite him to join their gang.

Claire awakes after a long sleep and talks with Martin, whom she comes to see as a decent man. She asks him where they are, and Martin says that although the entire landscape has changed, he calculates they are forty miles north of what was once New York City. Claire wants to explore, but Martin warns her that there is a tough gang nearby. She learns from Martin's observations that Jepsen is nearby as well, and she decides to remain with Martin.

The small community that expelled the gang is struggling to survive. Its members live in the ruins of a former resort town in the Catskills. Only small fragments of civilization remain. They have no doctor, only a dentist. Children play with money they found in the ruins of a local bank, and the former town barber now gives haircuts for free. Ronnie, one of the survivors, has welcomed Helen Webster and her children into his home. Helen, of course, wonders if Martin has somehow survived, but Tom tries to convince her that he probably is dead. Members of the community gather and make plans to destroy the Bellamy gang, whose raids continue to threaten them.

Jepsen kidnaps Claire after knocking Martin out, and he brings her to the camp of Bellamy gang. He tells them to raid Martin's shack for his cache of supplies. At night, Martin sneaks into their camp and frees Claire. They hide out in a cave near his shack and make love. At dawn the Bellamy gang raids the area. Martin holds them off from entering the cave using his rifle. Meanwhile, members from the survival community arrive to battle the gang. Jepsen breaks into the cave, and Martin fights him in a hand-to-hand struggle. The brute overpowers Martin and starts to choke him, when Claire kills Jepsen, striking his head with a club. The Bellamy gang is wiped out, and Martin and Claire are invited to join the survival community. At this point, Martin proudly introduces Claire as his wife.

When they reach the town, Martin is stunned when he discovers his family is living there, and Claire is heartbroken as he walks off to join them. Later, he comes to speak with her, saying it is the saddest moment of his life, but he has no choice. Claire sarcastically replies that she was only his companion in the cave. Meanwhile, the members of the community bicker over the goods recovered from the Bellamy gang. Martin suggests that everyone be given a hundred dollars and then bid for the items in an old-fashioned auction. The idea works and everyone is satisfied. A committee approaches Martin to ask him to consider serving as the town leader.

Helen Webster visits Claire so they can speak privately. She tries to be friendly, but Claire resists. The swimmer says that Martin is the only person she has ever loved in her entire life, and if she cannot have him, she would rather die. Helen reveals that Martin loves her, too. Claire begs her to leave when she brings up the issue of the children. The survivors hold a meeting and elect Martin as leader. He accepts and talks about the importance of children. After the meeting, Martin goes to visit Claire but she is not there. Instead, she has returned to the edge of the lake. She takes off her dress, jumps in the water and swims off to die. Martin then appears, but it is too late to save her.

CRITIQUE

Deluge is clearly divided into two halves. The opening, apocalyptic section is intriguing and powerful. Even the special effects, while perhaps cheesy by today's standards, still are very effective given the technology of the time. The post-apocalyptic section, however, just drags along and is a disappointment. Interest revives briefly with the love triangle, but the idea is smothered quickly, before it has a chance to develop.

The drawback to the film is that the cause of the disaster is never explained. The evidence seems to suggest that the earth has somehow strayed from its orbit or shifted in its axis. Either theory would help to explain the unexpected eclipse. the planet-wide earthquakes and the shifting of the seas. During the second half, the planet again becomes stable, yet no one seems to comment on that. There is no attempt at an explanation in the existing version. Whether the original film included an effort to interpret the disaster is unknown but is unlikely, and this lack weakens the overall effect. The only problem with the opening half is that too much of the action is merely heard in reports read off the ticker-tape machine. A more electrifying set of montages could have helped build the tension until the dramatic sweeping away of New York City by earthquake and flood.

The disappointing second half of the film seems like the leftover script of a Western. The locale is reminiscent of many Westerns, as is the storyline. Jepsen seems like a crazed bully, the Bellamy gang seems like the usual pack of desperadoes, and the survival community seems like any emerging town in the wilderness. The only fresh element in the entire story is the character of Claire, a strong, determined woman who is skilled and self-sufficient. She is the one who saves the situation in the formidable battle with Jepsen, killing him when Martin is about to succumb. Yet when the scene shifts to the town, she has become the discarded women. In fact, her situation bears a significant comparison to the valkyrie Brünnhilde in Richard Wagner's cycle of operas called *Der Ring des Nibelungen*. In *Die Walküre*, Brünnhilde is an active, dramatic heroine. By *Götterdämmerung*, the fourth and final entry, she is a pitiful, lackluster character, seemingly rejected by her lover. Both these vital Amazons lose themselves after surrendering their hearts to a man, and both wind up destroyed in the end. Peggy Shannon is extraordinary as Claire and manages to steal the film. She is lovely, vibrant and stunning, and far outshines Lois Wilson as Helen, Martin's lackluster wife. In the early 1930s, Shannon seemed destined for major stardom, but things turned out poorly for her and she died at the age of thirty-three, largely due to alcoholism. Character actor Sidney Blackmer is cast against type as Martin, but he manages to handle the role adequately well. Blackmer had a long and distinguished career dating back to the landmark serial *The Perils of Pauline* (1914). He also played the role of President Theodore Roosevelt in four feature films, starting with *This is my Affair* (1937). He also appeared in *Charlie Chan in Monte Carlo* (1937), *Maryland* (1940) and *The High and the Mighty* (1954). He later appeared in a number of suave character roles, including Roman Castevet, Ruth Gordon's husband, in *Rosemary's Baby* (1968). Veteran character actors Samuel S. Hinds and Edward Van Sloan are largely wasted and simply reduced to reading reports of bad news. The only other character to stand out is Fred Kohler, who is reminiscent of Gibson Gowland as MacTeague in Erich von Stroheim's masterpiece, *Greed* (1925).

The director, Felix Feist, only twenty-seven-years old when he completed *Deluge*, went on to a long career, helming many memorable efforts as the film noir classic *The Devil Thumbs a Ride* (1947), *This Woman is Dangerous* (1952) and *Donovan's Brain* (1953). He concluded his career in television, directing many episodes of *Voyage to the Bottom of the Sea* telelvision series, as well as many other programs. Although flawed, it is fortunate that *Deluge* managed to be saved from extinction, even if the original English language soundtrack is lost. It is a sincere and unusual effort and a rare example of early apocalyptic cinema.

REPRESENTATIVE QUOTES

"Rome, Italy. Barometer still falling. Four days of unending earthquakes. England. Tremors continue. Public alarmed! End of the world at hand? Millions of people terrified!" (Leading astronomer reading the news on tickertape)

"Indescribable disaster is causing havoc everywhere. There is no cause to panic. Shut off all gas items. Stand by!" (Radio broadcast monitored by Martin Webster)

"Great honeymoon! How do you like the wedding guests?" (Claire to Martin after the Bellamy gang starts its raid)

"We were once ruled by laws, some good, some bad. They've been washed away. We can start fresh. We have years of experience." (Martin speaking at the town meeting)

Doomsday Machine (1967/72)
AKA *Escape from Planet Earth*

Rating: *   **Threat:** Doomsday device

First Leisure. Written by Stuart James Byrne; Photographed by Stanley Cortez; Special effects by David L. Hewitt & William C. Davies; Edited by Charles Hammon; Music by S & S Sound Services; Produced by Harry Hope & Oscar L. Nichols (executive); Directed by Lee Sholem & Harry Hope. 83 minutes.

ANNOTATED CAST LIST

Bobby Van (*Lt. Danny Clark*, communications officer and technician); Grant Williams (*Capt. Kurt Mason*, navigator); Ruta Lee (*Dr. Marian Turner*, flight doctor and microbiologist); Mala Powers (*Lt. Katie Carlson*, computer expert and meteorologist); Denny "Scott" Miller (*Col. Don Price*, *Astra* flight commander); Henry Wilcoxon (*Dr. Christopher Perry*, older space scientist); Lorri Scott (*Maj. Georgiana Bronski*, Russian cosmonaut and co-pilot of *Astra*); James Craig (*Dr. Hanes*, leader of the *Astra* project); Essie Lin Chia (Chinese-American spy); Casey Kasem (mission control leader); Mike Farrell (Reporter).

SYNOPSIS

This oddball film is a genuine curiosity item. The original footage was shot in 1967 with a respectable cast, but production was suspended due to financial difficulties and the picture remained incomplete. Five years later, additional footage was added to finish the film, but without the participation of any of the initial cast. The result is a truncated film capped with a totally bizarre ending that makes no sense whatsoever. *Doomsday Machine* is still entertaining in many ways, and film lovers who enjoy "bad" movies will find it a treasure trove.

The picture is set in 1975, which was eight years in the future for the original production but only three years in the future when the picture was released. A beautiful Chinese-American spy infiltrates a secret laboratory facility in Red China. She photographs a new weapon developed by the Chinese Communists. It is set to explode in seventy-two hours. The spy photographs the controlling mechanism of the invention, which is enclosed in a cell and resembles a machine that makes cotton candy. She makes no attempt to disable it, just snaps a picture and leaves. Later, American scientists review these pictures and conclude that the device, if detonated, would set up a chain reaction below the earth's surface which would totally destroy the planet. The president is notified that if the Chinese are not prevented from testing this weapon, humanity is doomed.

A manned space voyage to Venus, a project known as *Astra*, is preparing to be launched. The crew is informed that a military crisis has developed and three members of the mission will be replaced by order of the president. Colonel

Price, flight commander, is startled to learn the three substitutes are women: Marian Turner, a doctor; Katie Carlson, a computer expert and meteorologist; and Georgiana Bronski, a Soviet cosmonaut and pilot. The crew will now consist of four men and three women, and the lift off schedule is accelerated. Captain Mason, the ship's navigator, is outraged that the traditional system checks have been canceled. On the other hand, Lieutenant Danny Clark, flight technician, appears delighted by the female replacements.

The *Astra* blasts off without incident, but Dr. Christopher Perry, the oldest member of the crew, suffers a seizure during launch. Major Bronski gives him oxygen, and the elderly scientist recovers. When the ship is safely on its way, the crew speculates about the military crisis back on Earth. Russia and the United States are cooperating in in efforts to persuade China to abandon the test of their new weapon. Danny arranges to tune into a popular music radio program from home. Suddenly, the broadcast is interrupted by a special bulletin, which is suddenly cut off. Captain Mason focuses the ship's telescope at Earth, and everyone watches in horror as the planet explodes. The *Astra* has to perform emergency maneuvers to avoid the fragments of the planet hurtled into space.

As their journey continues, the members of the crew start to form attachments. Mason and Katie Carlson, Price and Dr. Turner, and Danny and Major Bronski all are drawn to each other. Colonel Price comments, "We've been paired up on a latter day Noah's Ark." Dr. Perry questions Bronski about lost Soviet space missions. Mason starts to become hostile and picks a fight with Danny. Dr. Perry is troubled by the increase in radiation levels and determines that unless the ship increases its speed dramatically, the entire crew will become sterile. He develops a desperate plan to increase speed and outrun the radiation, but there will only be enough fuel left to land with three crew members. Dr. Perry programs the computer to determine who should be the three survivors.

After increasing speed, the *Astra* approaches the orbit of Venus. The results of the computer provoke new hostilities with the selection of Perry, Turner and Carlson. When Katie defies Mason's plan to take over the ship, he pursues her into an air lock. As they struggle, her shoulder accidentally activates a switch that opens the outside hatch, and the two of them are sucked into the vacuum of space. The others watch from the porthole as the bodies float away. Price rejects the computer selection and pledges to manage a landing with all five or die trying. They strip the ship and eject the debris into space.

The outside booster rockets are discovered to be misaligned and must be corrected and fired manually. Danny volunteers to do this, knowing it is a suicide mission. During his spacewalk, he is unable to make the adjustment, and Georgiana comes out to help him. Together they manage to fix the problem, and as they ship speeds off, they are suspended alone in the void. Danny then spots a derelict Soviet spacecraft, and they float over to board the ship. (At this point, two different voices assume the roles of Danny and Georgiana, and different spacesuits are worn by the actors now playing them.) Danny and Georgiana enter the ship and power it up. They manage to contact the *Astra* and inform them that they will follow in their wake down to the surface of Venus.

Out of nowhere a disembodied voice suddenly informs them that the *Astra* has been destroyed. When questioned, the voice claims to be the collective mind of the inhabitants of Venus. It chastises them for having destroyed Earth, and forbids them to land. The voice ends by wishing them well as it tosses their derelict ship beyond the edge of the universe. With this screwball denouement, the film abruptly concludes.

CRITIQUE

To call this film merely awful is an understatement, since it is a total and complete fiasco. Yet the picture does have an elusive charm also found in the entertainingly bad films of Ed Wood and Phil Tucker. It is a genuine apocalyptic film, since the earth is completely destroyed, and the entire cast is killed with the exception of two survivors who instead are flung beyond the edge of the universe (and probably will not survive for long in a ship without power.) Most audience members who watched this picture unquestionably left the theater with their mouths hanging open in disbelief. The conclusion is totally mind-blowing after the absurd, but entertaining, goings-on during the first four-fifths of the film. No doubt, *Doomsday Machine* originally intended to end with the landing of the *Astra* and the derelict Soviet craft on Venus, with the crew pledging to populate this new world. However, the money for the special effects to finish this film was simply not available, and the film slipped into limbo while the producers tried to raise the closing costs. The ultra-cheap and amateurish conclusion tacked on is completely surreal and one of the most ridiculous endings in motion picture history. First, the substitute voices for Danny and Georgiana are so dissimilar that it is jarring. The shadowy scenes in the Soviet spacecraft include long pointless moments with no dialogue, and when there is dialogue it is slow, stilted and almost meaningless. The ending shots bear no relationship to anything earlier in the story. Perhaps the film makers wanted to approximate some of the awe of the conclusion of *2001: A Space Odyssey* (1968), but showing vague shadows in a derelict spacecraft certainly falls far short of the mark and would only bewilder the audience.

Somehow this "Golden Turkey" had escaped notice by the Medved Brothers and other champions of "so bad it's good" cinema. Even the original sections of the picture are filled with hilarious cliches and farcical absurdities. Each time the *Astra* spacecraft is shown, it is a completely different ship, no doubt lifted from alternate films. At one point, Japanese script can be detected on the side of the spacecraft. At other times, the ship changes from a traditional rocket design to that of a rotating spoke. Even a child would find these substitutions laughable. The effects showing the destruction of the planet are just as silly, particularly when a tidal wave sequence is spliced in for no apparent reason.

The camp value of this film is nailed down by the wonderful cameos in the picture, particularly Mike Farrell (prior to his fame as B. J. Hunnicut in *M*A*S*H*) playing an inquisitive reporter at a news conference and Casey Kasem as the head of mission control. The stars of the film are also quite enter-

taining. Bobby Van brings an enormous amount of charm to his meager part.
Van had an interesting film career, giving excellent performances in such varied
and dismal films as the low-budget *Navy vs. the Night Monsters* (1966) or the
big-budgeted musical disaster *Lost Horizon* (1973). No matter how terrible the
material, Van puts it over with a stylish nonchalance that makes it seem delightful. Even his racist comment about "chopstick jockeys" somehow manages to
seem less offensive. Ruta Lee and Mala Powers are refreshing and both bring a
saucy allure to their roles. Grant Williams, forever linked to his performance as
The Incredible Shrinking Man (1957), plays Captain Mason with such intense
arrogance that his character is hated after only a few moments of screen time.
The moment when Mason gets sucked out into space is a gratifying one for the
audience. On the other hand, Wilcoxon and Miller are so bland in their roles,
that they make no impression at all.

   Doomsday Machine has probably been seen more often as a video release than
any other format, using a number various alternative titles such as *Escape from
Planet Earth*, *Armageddon 1975* or simply *Doomsday*. There is little value to
the picture other than as a prime example of high camp. With this forewarning,
a viewing of the film can still be a very entertaining experience.

REPRESENTATIVE QUOTES

"Doomsday? You guys aren't taking him seriously, are you? Those chopstick
jockeys couldn't come up with a planet-buster, could they?" (Danny reacting to
Dr. Perry's theory that the Chinese device could destroy the earth)

"So in case the world did end, they figured a few people like you and me could do
a rerun on Adam and Eve." (Colonel Price to Dr. Turner)

"We have no malice towards you. You have destroyed your place in the universe. Last of man, listen, of this we will tell you. Your journey will continue. Something very strange and very great awaits you beyond the rim of the
universe. And now, last of man, your journey will begin." (Message received
by Danny and Georgiana)

Dr. Strangelove or: How I Learned To Stop Worrying and Love the Bomb (1964)

Rating: *****   Threat: Doomsday device

Columbia. Written by Stanley Kubrick, Terry Southern & Peter George based on the novel *Two Hours to Doom* by Peter George writing as Peter Bryant; Photographed by Gilbert Taylor; Special effects by Wally Veevers; Edited by Anthony Harvey; Music by Laurie Johnson; Produced & directed by Stanley Kubrick. B & W, 93 minutes.

ANNOTATED CAST LIST

Peter Sellers (*Dr. Strangelove*, former Nazi scientist now serving as the president's technical advisor on weapons; *Merkin Muffley*, president of the United States; *Lionel Mandrake*, British exchange officer); George C. Scott (*Gen. Buck Turgidson*, air force advisor to President Muffley); Sterling Hayden (*Gen. Jack D. Ripper*, commander of Burpleson Air Base); Slim Pickens (*Maj. T. J. "King" Kong*, flight commander of the *Leper Colony*); Peter Bull (*Alexei de Sadesky*, Russian ambassador); Keenan Wynn (*Col. "Bat" Guano*, officer who arrests Mandrake); Tracy Reed (*Miss Scott*, Turgidson's secretary and mistress); James Earl Jones (*Lt. Lothar Zogg*, bombardier on the *Leper Colony*); Frank Berry (*Lt. Dietrich*, navigator on the *Leper Colony*); Glenn Beck (*Lt. Kivel*, crew member of the *Leper Colony*); Shane Rimmer (*Capt. Owens*, co-pilot of the *Leper Colony*); Paul Tamarin (*Lt. Goldberg*, communications officer on the *Leper Colony*); Gordon Tanner (*Gen. Faceman*, army chief of staff); Hal Galili, Laurence Herdon, John McCarthy (soldiers at Burpleson Air Base).

SYNOPSIS

Dr. Strangelove is perhaps the best known and most celebrated black comedy dealing with the Cold War and the possibility of nuclear annihilation. One interesting detail is that the picture was originally conceived as a serious thriller, very similar to *Fail Safe* (1964), which was directed by Sidney Lumet and also produced by Columbia. While working on the initial script, Stanley Kubrick found himself unable to take the plot seriously and thought it would be more fresh and effective as a farce. He then invited scriptwriter Terry Southern to join the project, and this absurdist misadventure emerged.

The picture opens with a scrawl that disclaims the possibility of the events depicted in the film actually happening and asserts that all characters are fictitious. A sentimental rendition of "Try a Little Tenderness" is heard over the credits while a bomber is being refueled in flight. The story picks up at Burpleson Air

Base, where General Jack D. Ripper orders a red alert. He instructs Captain Mandrake, a British exchange officer from the RAF who is serving as his executive officer, to transmit "Plan R" to the bombers of the 843rd Wing, which he commands. This is a strike order against the Soviet Union, and Ripper says he received orders to launch the attack. He also orders Burpleson Air Base to be sealed off from any outside contact.

The crew of one of these bombers, the *Leper Colony*, reacts in disbelief when they decode the attack order. The flight commander, Major "King" Kong, is a rustic Texan whose speech is filled with cowboy slang. As the major exhorts his men about their patriotic duty, "When Johnny Comes Marching Home" starts to play on the soundtrack, and this music becomes a motif heard whenever the setting of the film shifts to the bomber.

In Washington, D.C., General Buck Turgidson is phoned at 3 A.M. and alerted that an attack order has been issued to the 843rd Wing. Buck decides to head to the Pentagon, telling his mistress that he will return before she can say, "Blast off!" At Burpleson, Ripper alerts the base to prepare for an attack by soldiers posing as American troops. Mandrake confronts Ripper when he discovers on local radio that everything seems normal. He learns the general has gone insane and is deliberately trying to provoke a nuclear war. Meanwhile, the *Leper Colony* is that all future communication is to be ignored unless a secret prefix code, O-P-E, is used. Their orders list the Soviet missile complex at Laputa as their primary target. Details of the crew's preparation are portrayed in documentary fashion.

An emergency meeting is underway at the War Room of the Pentagon. President Merkin Muffley heads the meeting at a large, oval table with over thirty men. The president is briefed by Buck Turgidson, who tries to explain how General Ripper was able to launch the unauthorized attack. He is stymied because nothing can be done to recall the planes, which will carry out their attack in ninety minutes. Since the general is incommunicado, the president orders the army to take control of Burpleson and learn the prefix code from General Ripper. Muffley then summons the Russian ambassador, Alexei de Sadesky, and attempts to locate the Soviet leader, Premier Dimitri Kissoff, who is vacationing with his mistress. Buck objects to de Sadesky's presence, and they get into a scuffle over a camera that the ambassador is carrying. The president chides them, and a connection is finally made to Kissoff's secret love nest. Muffley has a long conversation with the premier, but only the president's side of the talk is heard onscreen. Kissoff is drunk, and Muffley tries his best to reason with him, offering to share data on the targets of each plane so the Russians can shoot them down. The president also learns about the Russian doomsday machine, an automatic weapon that will destroy all life on Earth if any nuclear explosion occurs within the borders of Russia. This device is so foolproof that it cannot be disengaged once it is activated. Dr. Strangelove, the president's special weapons advisor, is asked about the existence of this device. Strangelove, a former Nazi scientist confined to a wheelchair, is a bizarre individual who wears dark glasses and a black leather glove on his right hand. The doctor rejected the idea of a doomsday machine when he first studied it, and he is confused that the Soviets never revealed its existence, since its only practical purpose for such a device is to let the enemy know you have it. De Sadesky says that Premier Kissoff was saving it for a surprise announcement the following week.

Mandrake tries to worm the secret prefix code out of Ripper, but the general refuses to divulge it, and rants about Soviet conspiracies to pollute the "bodily fluids" of America by fluoridation of the water supply. Meanwhile, army troops attack Burpleson, and Ripper unpacks a large machine gun for the battle. The general's office is shot up by outside gunfire. When the Burpleson defenders surrender after a brief skirmish, Mandrake again presses Ripper to recall the bombers. Instead, the general retires to his washroom and shoots himself. Mandrake studies a page of doodling left by Ripper, where the phrase "Purity of Essence" is stressed, so the British officer guesses the prefix code is a variant of the letters P-O-E.

The *Leper Colony* is almost shot out of the sky by a Soviet missile. It is now losing fuel, and its communications system is knocked out. Although crippled, the plane continues on its mission, and Major Kong chooses a new target since they are no longer capable of reaching their primary objective.

Colonel "Bat" Guano breaks into Ripper's office and arrests Mandrake, whom he calls a "deviated prevert." The British officer tells him he has figured out the recall code and must telephone President Muffley. Regular telephones are still offline, so Mandrake tries to use a pay phone. He does not have enough change for the call, so he orders Guano to shoot open the change box from a soda vending machine. Guano warns him that if he does not get the president on the phone, he will have to answer to the Coca Cola Company. Guano is sprayed by a stream of soda after shooting at the machine.

There is general relief in the War Room after the bombers respond to their recall signal once Mandrake's code has been employed employed. Four planes are reported shot down by the Russians, and the rest are returning. The celebration ceases when the president, on the phone with Kissoff, learns that only three planes are confirmed destroyed. The fourth one was only damaged. This, of course, is the *Leper Colony*. Buck tells the president that he believes that the bomber will be able to get through and drop its nuclear load.

Lieutenant Zogg reports to Major Kong that the bomb doors of the *Leper Colony* are inoperative. When the manual override also fails, Kong himself heads down to the payload chamber. He climbs on top of one of the nuclear bombs to repair a circuit in a damaged ceiling panel. After he splices two wires together, the doors open and the bomb is released. Kong, astride the atomic bomb, waves his hat in the air and shouts out, "Yee-Haw!"

In the War Room, Dr. Strangelove conceives a plan to save many people from the doomsday device by moving them to deep mine shafts for a hundred years. To be practical, he theorizes, there will need to be ten women for every man, and they will need to be selected for maximum physical attractiveness. The possibility stimulates every man in the room. As Strangelove speaks, he loses control of his right arm, which keeps trying to give the Nazi salute to the president. He punches his arm to keep it under control. The Soviet ambassador sneaks to a corner of the room and starts to take pictures of the display board with a hidden camera. Suddenly, Dr. Strangelove manages to come to his feet, whereupon he exclaims, "Mein Führer, I can walk!" At this point, the action abruptly ends, the screen fills with a series of nuclear explosions and the lyrics of an old wartime ballad, "We'll meet again," are sung.

CRITIQUE

Dr. Strangelove was very popular when initially released, although it was also considered to be somewhat controversial, anti-American and leftist in tone. This is partially true, since this British production lacks an American feel in most of the scenes and situations, and Mandrake, the RAF officer, seems to be the only character without a screw loose somewhere. The picture prefigures the type of humor associated with the Monty Python comedy ensemble, displaying a keen sense of British humor. It is only the strong performances of the quartet of American actors, Scott, Hayden, Wynn and Pickens, that saves it from being strictly perceived as a British comedy.

The picture has retained its popularity over the years. Stanley Kubrick undoubtedly made the right decision by transforming it from a straight thriller to a satire. Its competitor, *Fail Safe*, is now regarded as terribly dated and largely forgotten, but *Dr. Strangelove*, on the other hand, still seems vital and engaging, and it is a genuine cult favorite.

There are numerous gaffes in the film, which are usually disregarded. The opening narration about rumors of the doomsday machine is meaningless since no one had even heard of the weapon until it was revealed to the leaders in the War Room. Burpleson, General Ripper's headquarters, is located on American soil and it is in daylight throughout the film, but in Washington, D.C., it is three in the morning, and the action of the film takes place in a strict two-hour framework. The attack on Burpleson is very unconvincing. The only person who appears at Ripper's office is a colonel dressed in combat gear. All the other attacking forces have vanished, and since the primary mission is to put Ripper in contact with the president, this scene is entirely unconvincing and the satirical edge is lost. With the stress on precise military protocol in the scenes aboard the *Leper Colony*, the complete lack of military procedure in the Burpleson attack weakens the film. The abrupt ending is also weak. The film originally concluded with Buck catching de Sadesky photographing the "big board," which led to a food fight by the buffet table. Some critics applauded the removal, but nowadays we often have access to alternate versions of films with all cuts restored. In fact, viewers can judge three separate endings for Alfred Hitchcock's *Topaz* (1969). It would be fascinating to see the original slapstick ending restored. Another reason this section was jettisoned was due to a line by Buck after President Muffley was knocked down by a pie in the face. The comment by the general, that their leader was struck down in his prime, had disturbing overtones considering the picture was released a mere two months after the assassination of John F. Kennedy. Another line remaining in the film was altered. When Slim Pickens reviews the contents of the crew's survival packs, he finds money, condoms, nylon stockings, lipstick, and so on. His original comment was that you could have a good weekend in Dallas with these rations, but a dubover changed the locale to Vegas instead.

The shortcomings, however, are minor compared to the big picture. The editing is crisp and keeps the pace going. The cinematography is excellent, especially the low-key lighting of the scenes in the War Room. One shot of Dr. Strangelove silhouetted against a brightly lit passageway is particularly impressive. The music, particularly Laurie Johnson's unforgettable arrangement of "When Johnny Comes Marching Home," is another major strength. There are many highlights in the script, including many clever asides and inside jokes. The mistress of George C. Scott's character, played by Sir Carol Reed's daughter, is named Scott. Some references are obvious, like General Jack D. Ripper (Jack the Ripper), Alexei de Sadesky (Marquis de Sade) and Major "King" Kong, (an unusual nickname for a Texas cowboy). The connotations of Strangelove, who translated his name literally from Merkwürdigichliebe in German, is unmistakable. President Muffley certainly "muffs" his chance to save the world, and General Turgidson certainly personifies the "bombastic" connotation of the word turgid. Other references are more obscure. General Ripper is obsessed by "bodily fluids," and his executive officer is Mandrake, the same name as the root that in legend derives from the bodily essence of a hanged man. The initial target for the *Leper Colony* was the Russian missile complex at Laputa, a double reference both to the Spanish term for a hooker and the flying island from *Gulliver's Travels*, by the great satirist Jonathan Swift. The twin motifs of sex and food turn up repeatedly throughout the picture. Both Buck and Premier Kissoff are dallying with their mistresses during the film. Ripper makes it clear he refuses to share his "essence" with any woman lest he waste his vitality. Dr. Strangelove's vision of an underground sanctuary where nubile women outnumber men ten to one piques the interest of all those in the War Room. As for food, everyone seems to be constantly snacking in the course of the picture, on the *Leper Colony*, at Burpleson and in the War Room. Perhaps that is why ending with the food fight would have been so appropriate.

The most outstanding feature is the cast. This film made Peter Sellers a major star. His reading of Dr. Strangelove is one of the most brilliant portrayals in cinema. His accent, artificial smile, wild eyes behind shaded glasses and distinctive voice (like a Teutonic Yoda) have become etched into the public's consciousness, becoming a genuine cinematic archetype. This is even more amazing when you consider that his actual onscreen time is rather brief. The character is so distinctive and indelible that it is the apex of the film career of Sellers, even overshadowing his famous turn as Inspector Clouseau. It is no surprise that the entire film is named after this minor character. His portrayal of President Merkin Muffley is quieter, but also exceptional. The opening disclaimer on the film was added largely due to comparisons of the character to Adlai Stevenson, whom Muffley resembles in an extraordinary way both visually and vocally.

The highlights of Sellers as the president include his long, surreal telephone conversations with Premier Kissoff. They resemble some of Bob Newhart's telephone routines, and the comedian's pacing, droll tone of voice and poker-faced exasperation during these scenes are masterful and hilarious. His Mandrake is far less interesting by comparison and seems almost routine. Sellers was also originally slated to play Major Kong as well, but the Texas drawl seemed to elude him in rehearsal, and he felt he could not effectively pull it off. He then hurt his leg, and Kubrick had to find a replacement. His first two choices were John Wayne and Dan Blocker, both of whom objected to the flavor of the film. Slim Pickens made an ideal choice, and some felt he was largely playing himself for most of the scenes. Pickens later had a number of other screen roles in a similar vein, including his cameo in *The Swarm* (1978). George C. Scott considered Buck Turgidson to be his favorite screen role, despite a career full of colorful characters from Maximilien Robespierre in Peter Ustinov's play, *The Empty Chair*, broadcast live on the highly acclaimed *Omnibus* television series, through General George Patton in two feature films, to his William Jennings Bryan clone in *Inherit the Wind* (1999). His reading is filled with bluster and vitality. At one point in the War Room, he slips and does a comic pratfall. In actuality this was a genuine accident, but Scott continued the scene in character, and it looked so good that Kubrick kept the mishap in the film. Sterling Hayden, who played a dour and bellicose character in many a film noir, is ideally suited as the insane General Ripper. The close-ups of him staring resolvedly with a cigar jammed in his mouth are among the most memorable images of the film. Keenan Wynn does not come off as well as the others. It is not until his line about answering to the Coca Cola Company that he starts to shine, but by then his screen time is almost over. *Dr. Strangelove* also served as the screen debut of James Earl Jones, who went on to become one of America's most distinguished and powerful actors. His role as Admiral Greer in the series of Tom Clancy films, starting with *The Hunt for Red October* (1990), is interesting when compared to his debut. Jones has also been masterful in many Shakespearean productions and was memorable as the voice of Darth Vader for the intial *Star Wars* trilogy.

Incidentally, as with most wordy screen titles, the film is almost always referred to by the diminutive *Dr. Strangelove* instead of the full-length version, similar to *The Persecution and Assassination of Jean Paul Marat as Performed by the Inmates of the Asylum at Charenton under the Direction of the Marquis de Sade* (1966), which is simply known as *Marat/Sade*.

REPRESENTATIVE QUOTES

"For more than a year, ominous rumors have been privately circulating among high level Western leaders that the Soviet Union had been at work on what was darkly hinted to be the ultimate weapon, a doomsday device. Intelligence sources traced the site of the top secret Russian project to the perpetually fog-shrouded wasteland below the Arctic peaks of the Zokoff Islands. What they were building, or why it should be located in such a remote and desolate place, no one could say." (Opening narration)

"Now I've been to one world's fair, a picnic and a rodeo, and that's the stupidest thing I ever heard come over a set of earphones." (Major Kong upon hearing the order to attack Russia)

"You can't fight in here, this is the War Room." (President Muffley to the battling Buck Turgidson and Alexei de Sadesky)

"Bafflorium G has a radioactive half life of ninety-three years. If you take, say, fifty H-Bombs in the 100 megaton range and injecting with the Bafflorium G when they are exploded, they will produce a doomsday shroud, a lethal cloud of radioactivity which will encircle the Earth for ninety-three years." (Alexei de Sadesky explaining the doomsday device to the Americans in the War Room)

"My conclusion was that this idea was not a practical deterrent for reasons which at the moment must be all too obvious." (Dr. Strangelove on the concept of a doomsday machine)

The End of the World (1930/34) AKA *Paris after Dark*

Rating: ****   **Threat: Collision with a comet**

L'Ecran D'Art. Written by Abel Gance & H. S. Kraft based on *Omega: Last Days of the World* by Camille Flammarion; Dialogue by Jean Boyer; Photographed by Roger Hubert, Jules Kruger & Nikolas Roudakoff; Edited by F. Salabert; Music by Peter Illyich Tchaikovsky & others; Sound supervised by R. Baudouin; Produced by Harold Auten (U.S. version); Directed by Abel Gance. B & W, Original version, 105 minutes; U.S. version, 54 minutes.

ANNOTATED CAST LIST

Victor Francen (*Martial Novalic*, French astronomer); Jeanne Brindeau (*Madame Novalic*, his wife); Abel Gance (*Jean Novalic*, their son); Georges Colin (*Werster*, astronomer); Dr. Clyde Fisher (curator of astronomy, American Museum of Natural History).

SYNOPSIS

In its present form, this film is an extract, a mere torso of the original work. Like an unfinished sculpture of Michelangelo, this fragment still has a tremendous power and impact. The high rating listed above is more a tribute to Gance and his original vision than an evaluation of the footage that remains. The background of the film needs to be thoroughly examined. Abel Gance was one of the giants of world cinema, and his final silent epic, *Napoleon* (1927), is one of the greatest and most innovative of all films, and certainly the crown jewel of French cinema. Gance conceived his end of the world epic near the close of World War I, after completing the silent version of *J'Accuse* (1917). He initially intended to call the film *The End of the World as Seen, Heard and Rendered by Abel Gance*. It was rather loosely based on an 1894 novel by the French astronomer Camille Flammarion that portrayed the future end of the world due to a collision with a large comet. When the backers of the project began to fear that the length of this film was becoming extravagant, the producers took control of the film away from Gance. Like Erich von Stroheim and *Greed* (1925), a stunning and exceptional vision was hewn down to a traditional length. The picture was released in France as *La Fin du Monde* (1931), at a length of 105 minutes. Disheartened, Abel Gance eventually disclaimed the truncated version. This film was never shown in the United States, and according to most sources, *La Fin du Monde* is considered a lost film today. The next step in the process was even worse. An American distributor, Harold Auten, bought up the rights to the film and trimmed it down to an unbelievable 54 minutes. A new introduction was shot featuring Dr. Clyde Fisher, who mumbles through an opening narration discussing the scientific basis of the picture. The American edition eliminated almost all the dialogue scenes in the film, except a few featuring Victor Francen as Martial Novalic, a French astronomer who sights a comet hurtling toward the earth and tries to warn the world about its impending doom. Abel Gance, as Novalic's son Jean, was the central character of the French version but is now reduced to just several moments in the background. In place of these scenes, The American version created a series of title cards to explain the action, and stitched together all the crowd and group scenes in the picture. The resulting film is a series of montage sequences. No doubt these scenes were among the highlights of the film, but 50 minutes of non-stop montage is a draining experience for any audience. Auten distributed the film like a road show, hyping, "See the End of the World! A sensation beyond your wildest dreams! Most remarkable because it COULD happen!" No doubt, Auten made a fortune hawking this film out in the sticks. This is the version of the film that has survived and is easily available on videotape. The credits in this version are unreliable and rather jumbled. Gance's name is totally removed, and the director is listed as V. Ivanoff. Andre Lang is credited as the writer. Some of the other credits are accurate, while others are misspelled. For example, sound supervisor Baudouin's name is listed as Bandouin.

To properly evaluate this picture, imagine if someone took *Gone with the Wind* (1939) and stitched together the crowd sequences and the action sequences, eliminated Clark Gable and Vivian Leigh's conversational scenes, but retained various bits of dialogue with Thomas Mitchell. This film is then connected by title cards and would run about 54 minutes. With this arrangement, you would no doubt detect a portion of the greatness of *Gone with the Wind*, but it would be totally distorted. This is the exact problem in appraising *The End of the World*. Much of what we see is magnificent yet rather difficult to comprehend.

The film opens with a rather tinny rendition of music from Tchaikovsky's tone poem, *Francesca da Rimini*. Then Clyde Fisher, the head astronomer from the American Museum of Natural History in New York, begins a short, stilted speech in front of a curtain, directly addressing the film audience. He attests to the scientific accuracy of the theory that a meteor or comet could pose a life-eradicating threat to planet Earth, and that craters on the earth and moon demonstrate that such collisions have happened in the past and will no doubt reoccur in the future. He does say, however, that the possibility is remote that this event would occur in our lifetime. He then responds to a few questions posed by unseen members of the audience. When a child asks Fisher what he would do if he knew about an impending collision, the scientist says the question will be answered in the following film. (It is not, of course.)

The story begins as Nobel prize-winning scientist Martial Novalic summons a number of colleagues to the French National Observatory to confirm his calculations. The Lexall comet, last observed in 1770, is now approaching Earth. Its normal trajectory had been deviated by the gravity of Jupiter, and the new orbit will cause it to impact on the earth. Given the enormous size of the comet, such a collision will destroy the planet. The astronomers pour over his findings and confirm his forecast, each in his own language. The precise hour of the calamity will be in thirty days. Newspaper headlines proclaim the tragic news, but except for the scientific community, the world largely ignores the report. Two weeks pass, and Novalic himself makes a dramatic radio broadcast proclaiming the end of the world. Meanwhile, businessmen, stockbrokers and the general public go about their normal routines unperturbed. Jean Novalic, Martial's son, observes this activity in bewilderment. The French government considers their great astronomer a fearmonger and orders his arrest. Novalic and the other scientists go into hiding, and the police arrive with axes and smash the communications equipment in the observatory. A radio bulletin accuses the scientists of the world of banding together in an attempt to seize world power.

Finally, the Lexall comet becomes visible to the naked eye, and a massive panic breaks out when people realize that the warnings are true. Martial law is proclaimed as the general populace appears to go mad, rioting and running off in complete hysteria. Churches become crowded as people seek God's help. Scenes from around the world flash by on the screen, showing the extent of the reaction. In the Middle East, millions of Muslims crowd Mecca in fervent prayer. St. Peter's Square in Rome becomes overwhelmed with worshipers seeking solace from the pope. No one is exempt from the global terror, as African tribesmen, Australian Aborigines and Arctic Eskimos stare at the sky in dread. Even the animals break out in wild stampedes. A voice on the radio intones the deadline as the final hours pass, "Thirty-two hours left to live!" Then, "Twenty hours left to live!" Only in secluded monasteries do a handful of monks accept the coming destruction calmly, with resignation and prayer.

Martial Novalic himself becomes deluded by these events, and he calls a massive political rally for scientists. He harangues them, saying that if any men do survive, it will be up to the scientists to bring about a new world of peace and understanding. Elsewhere, people gather in huge parties, singing, dancing and drinking themselves into oblivion. The camera cuts ever more quickly to contrasting shots worldwide. The soundtrack becomes a jumble as many voices, sirens, bells, snatches of music and screams are layered over each other. The sky becomes filled with the image of the comet growing ever larger. A meteor pushed forward by the comet crashes into the ocean, causing a devastating onslaught.

Unexpectedly, the comet deviates at the last minute, sparing Earth as it passes by. Universal destruction is averted. The film ends with shots of flames, rubble and wreckage from every corner of the planet. One of the last images shows a mother kneeling before an empty crib in the smoldering ruins. The final title card tells of the fragility of life and asserts that we should dedicate our lives to the benefit of humanity.

CRITIQUE

Based on this truncated glimpse, the original film as conceived by Abel Gance must have been powerful and amazing. As it is, many sequences have a distinctive poetry, and some of the individual shots are phenomenal. Many of the intense close-ups are stunning and may be indelible in the mind of many viewers. The camerawork is breathtaking, and the overall technique, just like Gance's masterpiece, *Napoleon*, is innovative and astonishing. There are multilayered shots, novel camera placements and movements, the creative use of shadows, masterful crowd deployments as an element of stagecraft and an invigorating mastery of editing. Even beyond *Napoleon* is his creative use of sound, which is layered like the climax of a tone poem by Charles Ives. However, with the placing of so many montage sequences back-to-back in the American cut, the audience would no doubt experience an aural and visual overload, since there is too much to take in. The pacing as Gance originally intended it would have sharpened and strengthened these scenes. It is easy to understand that the cut was prompted in order to market it as an exploitation product, largely in rural America. Subtitles were not popular, which was why Harold Auten eliminated as much of the dialogue as he could and inserted title cards to explain the unfolding events to the audience. A film lover can be easily outraged that a masterwork was so brutally hacked. However, had this version not been released, perhaps the entire film would be lost today. As it is, we can still experience a fraction of the brilliance of a most powerful film extravaganza.

REPRESENTATIVE QUOTES

"Our Earth has had a beginning, and it surely will have an end. Will the earth grow cold as the sun grows cold and will life disappear as heat is withdrawn? Or will the end of the earth come by a collision with some great heavenly body, perhaps by a huge comet as conceived by Flammarion, the great French astronomer, and shown in this motion picture?" (Dr. Clyde Fisher in his introduction to the American version)

"Terrific meteorite hurtling towards Britain!" (London newspaper headline, which overlooks the point that the impact will destroy the entire world)

"By some supernatural force, the Earth and its people are saved from total oblivion, but in its wake, the fiery torch leaves its warning in swollen rivers, and embers and ashes which once were cities." (Title card at the end of the film)

Five (1951)

Rating: *   **Threat: Nuclear radiation**

Columbia. Written by Arch Oboler; Photographed by Louis Clyde Stoumen; Edited by John Hoffman; Music by Henry Russell; Produced & directed by Arch Oboler. B & W, 93 minutes.

ANNOTATED CAST LIST

William Phipps (*Michael Rogan*, Empire State Building tour guide); Susan Douglas (*Roseanne Rogers*, pregnant woman); James Anderson (*Eric Rohmer*, world explorer); Charles Lampkin (*Charles*, bank guard); Earl Lee (*Oliver P. Barnstaple*, bank cashier).

SYNOPSIS

Five was the first motion picture to deal with the destruction of the world through nuclear warfare. Arch Oboler produced, wrote and directed this film on a shoestring budget. Unfortunately, the film is so ponderous, dreary and dull that only a handful of fans will have the patience to sit through the entire picture.

The film opens with the detonation of a nuclear bomb. It is unclear if there was a nuclear conflict or if a new type of bomb was simply tested, which produced a deadly cloud of radiation that blanketed the world. There are shots showing London, Paris, Moscow and New York City being swallowed by a radioactive cloud, but without any blast damage. An aerial shot eventually zeros in on a lone woman staggering along a dirt highway in the mountains. She looks at a car stopped in the road, observing that the body of the driver is a mere skeleton. She continues to wander until she enters a small town. She calls out, but no one responds. A newspaper posted outside a store bears the headline, "World Annihilation Feared by Scientists, Savant Warns against New Bomb Use."

The woman eventually wanders to a small house perched on a hilltop. A tall, bearded man appears after she enters the structure. They stare at each other in disbelief, and the woman passes out. She remains in shock for several days and is unresponsive to the man, who introduces himself as Michael Rogan. He was at work as a tour guide at the Empire State Building when the radiation enveloped Manhattan. He was knocked unconscious, and when he awoke, he was the only individual left alive in New York City. He traveled to other cities but found only dead people. The woman finally breaks her silence, asking "Where?" as Michael leaves to go hunting. He goes out of habit even though there is nothing to hunt. That night the woman, who is named Roseanne, tells Michael that she was in the X-ray room of a hospital when the radiation annihilated all life in the city. All her other memories are a complete blur. They try to start a new life together, but when Michael tries to embrace her, she rejects him, mentioning that her husband, Stephen, may still be alive back in the city. Michael refuses to go there and search for him, considering it a futile gesture. Suddenly, they both hear a jeep sounding its horn. They follow the noise and discover two men, a dapper but demented old man named Oliver Barnstaple and his companion, Charles, a gentle black man. They honked their horn after spotting the smoke arising from the chimney of the house. The two of them were in a bank vault in Santa Barbara, where they were working at the time the radiation struck. After they emerged, the old man retreated into a fantasy world.

Charles and Michael work at farming, trying to grow some food. Oliver starts to display signs of radiation poisoning developing blotches on his skin. He asks to be taken to the beach. While there, Michael comes to realize that Roseanne is pregnant, and she tells him the baby will be born in three months. They spot another man who has just washed ashore on the beach. He is Eric Rohmer, an adventurer who was attempting to climb Mount Everest when the radiation swept the earth. Crossing Asia, he found no survivors. Eric managed to reach Hawaii by boat, but again only discovered a mountain of dead bodies. Eric tried to pilot a plane to the mainland of America but ran out of gas and had to ditch it in the ocean offshore. Oliver dies after amiably chatting with Charles.

Many weeks pass. Continuing to toil in the field, Michael and Charles resent the newcomer, who never offers to help. At last, their work shows results as a stalk of corn emerges from the soil. Talking with Roseanne, Eric mocks the primitive goals of the others. Michael decides to procure a generator so they can have light and run appliances. That evening, Eric proposes a theory that the reason why each of them has survived is because they are somehow immune to the radiation. They should be able to go anywhere now in safety. Perhaps there are other survivors with the same immunity. He proposes a thorough search, but Michael rejects the proposal as too dangerous and walks off. Charles seconds Michael's opinion, and Eric turns on him with some racist comments. Roseanne orders him to stop, but Eric knocks her out of the way and starts to push Charles around. Michael returns and breaks up the fight as Roseanne goes into labor. After a difficult night, her son is born in the morning.

Michael wants to force Eric to leave, but Charles insists that exiling him would be too cruel. Roseanne refuses to give her baby a name until she knows the fate of her husband. Michael tries to make peace with Eric. He also tries to propose to Roseanne, but she fails to respond to the suggestion. Several nights later, Eric slips in to visit Roseanne in her bedroom and offers to take her to the city to search for her husband. He suggests they simply slip away without telling Michael, who would become upset. She agrees to sneak off with him, bringing her baby. After stealing supplies, Eric kills Charles with a knife.

At dawn they arrive at the city, which appears undamaged. Sirens are heard, but they seem to be only in Roseanne's mind. When Eric stops the jeep to look through a store, Roseanne wanders off with her child in search of Stephen. She locates his office, where he worked as an architect. She looks at his pipe lying on his desk among his papers. She returns to the hospital where she had been when the disaster occurred, and she finds Stephen's skeleton in the adjacent waiting room. Eric meets her back at the jeep and hands her a fortune in jewels. She asks to be driven back to the house, but he says she will never return there. She struggles with him and suddenly notices that his skin is showing signs of radiation poisoning. Eric cries out in disbelief and runs off, jabbering incoherently. Roseanne decides to walk home, and her baby dies during the long journey. She finds Michael hunting as a downpour soaks them both. He buries her baby and returns to work in his field. Roseanne joins him and offers to help as the end titles appear.

CRITIQUE

Arch Oboler was a very talented and innovative writer who is best remembered for his brilliant radio work in the 1940s on such programs as *Lights Out*. Unfortunately, *Five* is a complete misfire. After conceiving a strong premise for this picture, Oboler's script simply rambles on for 90 boring minutes. There are some poetic passages of dialogue, but Oboler seems unsure how to develop his story almost from the start. Even the title *Five* makes little sense, since most of the action occurs around four live people at any one time. (If you count the baby, however, then there is a total of six.)

The script is very unclear about the origin of the disaster that destroyed the earth. Most writers and critics assume there was a nuclear war, but that is never actually stated at any point. The only clue, the newspaper, is also vague about the event, with scientists warning about the effects of a new bomb. We are shown New York City, Paris, London and Moscow, but they seem physically undamaged, as is the city visited by Eric and Roseanne, presumably Los Angeles. If these primary locations are all undamaged, the nuclear war scenario seems unlikely. Only one bomb is ever shown exploding, that during the opening credits. Did this one device alone produce the radioactive cloud that engulfed the earth? Or was there an atomic war fought with some sort of neutron bombs, which created deadly radiation but damaged no buildings. Oboler's lack of explanation weakens the film from the very start.

It is an unbelievable coincidence that the world has only this handful of survivors, who just happened to meet after starting out from Manhattan, Santa Barbara and Mount Everest. Then the characters are both unappealing and clueless. Michael has a Master's degree, but the idea of installing a generator to provide electricity does not occur to him for months. He becomes obsessed with the idea of developing one patch of ground to grow crops that he never considers trying to locate and revive an existing farm. Nor does he think to provide his guest with any easily obtainable amenities. He pigheadedly concentrates on building a storage shed and working his field. He simply wastes his time in such pointless rituals like his daily hunting excursions when there is no game. Charles is a kind and pleasant person, but he has no thoughts of his own and is always content to follow Michael's lead. Eric is reminiscent of a Nazi with his thick accent and racial hatreds, but at least he tries to think and conceive a long range plan. Roseanne wanders through most of the picture like an automaton. Her unlimited naïveté is simply maddening. After she accompanies Eric to the city and ascertains that her husband is truly dead (which she really must have known all along), she decides to walk back. There are cars everywhere, and she could return quickly. Even if she has never driven before, it would be simple matter to figure it out in a world with no traffic. Her decision, of course, costs the life of her child, and I'm sure much of the audience has lost any sympathy for her long before this. The end of the picture brings the story precisely to the point where it was twenty minutes into the film before Charles and Barnstaple appeared. The last seventy minutes of the film is a dead end loop and a waste of time. It is clear that Oboler intended Michael and Roseanne to be the new Adam and Eve, but he consumed a lot of screen time to make this obvious point.

The performances by the actors are lackluster. Earl Lee is the most colorful as the mad, old-fashioned gentleman, but then he has the shortest screen time of any of the characters. Charles Lampkin is likable and easy-going as Charles, and he reminds one of Ossie Davis. The high point of the film is his Biblical recitation while Roseanne is giving birth. His character, however, is too bland to have much impact. James Anderson wastes much of his time as the villain Eric. His mumble-mouthed speech pattern makes his character appear ridiculous. At one point he even refers to the woman as "Rosy Anne." The two leads, William Phipps and Susan Douglas, are vapid and inspire no empathy from the audience. Technically, the film is well done. The photography is good, and the arthouse touches of the opening and closing aerial shots are striking. The music is also pleasing. The house which Michael occupies was Oboler's own home, designed by Frank Lloyd Wright, and it does make an interesting setting. These positive qualities, however, do little to improve this ponderous and pretentious film.

REPRESENTATIVE QUOTES

"All right, I'll tell you. He's dead, they are all dead, everyone! You and I are in a dead world, and I'm glad it's dead, cheap honkytonk of a world." (Michael to Roseanne in an outburst)

"There is something within our bodies, a chemistry which gives a special immunity to that which killed the others. I see the doubtful look on your faces. Then mark this. During the Middle Ages when the Black Plague swept all of Europe, when men died by the hundreds of thousands, why didn't all mankind die? The deadly organisms were there. There was no protection against them, and yet a small percentage of people lived on as we have lived, with the rest of the world of men dropping dead around them. The odds are then, an immunity to the organism, and the odds are here today, an immunity against the radiation." (Eric explaining his theory to the others)

"And I saw a new heaven and a new Earth . . . And there shall be no more death . . . no more sorrow . . . no more tears. Behold! I make all things new!" (Biblical quote on the closing title card)

Holocaust 2000 (1978)
AKA *The Chosen* and *Rain of Fire*
Rating: **   **Threat: Satanic power plant**

Embassy. Written by Alberto De Martino, Sergio Donati and Michael Robson; Photographed by Enrico Menczer; Special effects by Gino De Rossi; Edited by Vincenzo Tomassi; Music by Ennio Morricone; Produced by Demondo Amati; Directed by Alberto De Martino. 105 minutes.

ANNOTATED CAST LIST

Kirk Douglas (*Robert Caine*, international business magnate); Simon Ward (*Angel Caine*, his son and the Antichrist); Virginia McKenna (*Eva Caine*, Robert's wife); Agostina Belli (*Sara Golan*, Robert's girlfriend and journalist); Anthony Quayle (*Dr. Griffith*, scientist working for Robert); Alexander Knox (*Dr. Ernst Meyer*, foremost expert on nuclear technology); Adolfo Celi (*Dr. Kerouac*, asylum administrator); Ivo Garrani (prime minister of a country in the Middle East); Spiros Focas (*Harbin*, his political opponent and successor); Massimo Foschi (assassin who kills Eva Caine); Romolo Valli (*Mon. Charrier*, religious scholar); John Carlin (*Robertson*, Caine employee); Peter Cellier (*Sheckley*, Caine employee); Gerald Hely (*Clarke*, Caine employee); Penelope Horner (Caine's secretary); Caroline Horner (Angel's girlfriend); Jenny Twigg (air flight hostess); Geoffrey Keen (gynecologist); Joanne Dainton (nurse); Alan Hendricks (fanatical demonstrator); Richard Cornish, Denis Lawson, John Bancroft (journalists).

SYNOPSIS

This Italian-British production was largely inspired by *The Omen* (1976), in which Gregory Peck plays the American ambassador to Great Britain who discovers that his young son is actually the Antichrist. *Holocaust 2000* focuses more on the apocalypse, which the *Omen* series does not consider until its third film, *The Final Conflict* (1981). While *The Omen* is classier and had a larger budget, the series itself stumbles with confused timelines that awkwardly attempts to accommodate the growth of the Antichrist from a small child to his early thirties. *Holocaust 2000* avoids this problem by having its Antichrist, Angel Caine, already grown as the story begins.

Robert Caine is a rich developer promoting a radically different nuclear power plant to be constructed in the Middle East. The prime minister of the unnamed country supports Caine's proposal, even though his political opponent, Harbin, plans to use the issue against him in the next election. At a ceremony in the desert, Robert detonates the first charge to level the ground at the site of the project. He then explores a nearby cave with Sara Golan, a press attaché. After she observes the ancient markings inscribed on the walls, the journalist theorizes that the site could possibly be "the cave of the vision," which inspired the Book of *Revelations* in the *Bible*.

Returning to London, Robert is informed by Eva, his wife, that she has decided to opposed building the power plant. Since she controls 51 percent of the company's stock, her decision can kill the project. At a reception for the prime minister, Robert is attacked by an Arab assassin with a knife. As Robert and his son grapple with the man, Eva is stabbed and killed. When Caine visits the intruder after he is confined in the insane asylum, the fanatic breaks free and tries to kill himself, saying: "Fire will destroy the earth. From your seed comes evil!"

Angel proposes some modifications to the project that will produce some incredibly high temperatures, equal to the heat of the sun. Robert is concerned about the growing opposition to the project by the general public. The prime minister is defeated by Harbin, who tells Caine he will do everything he can to prevent the building of the power plant. He prepares a report that claims the plant could actually destroy the world with a nuclear firestorm. To counter this theory, Angel recruits Dr. Meyer, the world's leading expert on nuclear technology. If Robert could present a positive testimonial from Meyer at the upcoming Geneva conference, opposition from Harbin and other world leaders would evaporate. The scientist agrees to help, but only after testing the operation of the plant using a computer model. The key issue becomes the ten independent security systems to be built into the plant. Caine's computer expert, Griffith, tries to confirm the effectiveness of these systems, but the computer spits out a strange, meaningless formula instead.

Robert flies back to the construction site and meets Monsignor Charrier on the jet. The cleric notices that when it is held up to the light, the meaningless formula is inverted and spells out the name Jesus in Latin. He explains that the formula is actually a symbol of the Antichrist. Robert becomes intrigued, and Charrier relates how everything about the career of the Antichrist will resemble that of Jesus Christ, except in an inverted fashion. For example, instead of 12 disciples, he will have 21. He shows Robert several old texts about the apocalypse. The main function of the Antichrist will be to unleash the seven-headed monster that will destroy humankind.

Demonstrators now protest daily in front of the Caine Building, chanting: "What do our children want to be when they grow up? Alive!" Sara meets with Robert to warn him that Harbin is planning to come to London to denounce the nuclear plant. Robert also learns that Meyer has disappeared. A freak accident occurs at the airport, and Harbin is killed by the propeller blade of his helicopter. Robert brings Sara to his remote country retreat, and they become lovers.

Angel runs the company while his father is in seclusion, and he pushes hard to keep all the subcontractors for the project on schedule. Harbin's successor in the Middle East supports the project. Angel surprises his father at his tryst with Sara and lets them know he approves of their romance. At work, Robert closely examines a scale model of the plant, and he is suddenly struck by how much it resembles the legendary "beast" mentioned in the *Bible* in the Book of *Revelations*. It has seven towers containing turbines, just like the seven heads. Each turbine has ten commutators, resembling the horns on the beast's heads. The plant is situated near the sea, and from the distance it appears to rise out of the sea, just like the beast. The analogy begins to haunt Robert.

Meyer reappears and calls Robert, demanding an immediate meeting at a remote beach. When Robert arrives, the nuclear scientist warns him that the plant has the capacity to destroy the world, and it must never be finished. Moments later the sea sweeps in, and Meyer mysteriously vanishes in the water. That night Robert has a terrible vision, a dream in which the plant metamorphoses into the beast of the apocalypse. He consults Dr. Griffith, who tests Robert with an analytical computer scan. Angel tells his father not to worry, as he himself was also scanned.

Sara takes Angel and Robert out to dinner, and tells them that she is pregnant with Robert's child. They are both delighted. Robert is called away by a phone call from Dr. Griffith who tells him some startling news. In reviewing Angel's medical file, the doctor discovers that his son is not human. His brain waves are completely flat. Griffith dies in a freak accident while leaving the computer lab. Becoming desperate, Robert consults Monsignor Charrier whose interpretation is that the Antichrist will be his second son. Robert assumes this to mean his unborn child with Sara, forgetting that Angel had a twin brother who was strangled in the womb by Angel's umbilical cord. He attempts to force Sara to get an abortion, but she flees from Robert and is set up in a hidden retreat by Angel. Robert gives a letter to Monsignor Charrier to bring to the Geneva conference in case anything happens to him. The letter proposes the cancellation of the nuclear project.

Robert's temper rages out of control at his office, and his employees believe he is having a breakdown. They begin to rely more and more on Angel for guidance. He starts to countermand his father's orders when they threaten the nuclear project. At the office, Robert and Angel finally have a verbal showdown, where his son admits he is actually the Antichrist and plans to annihilate the world. Enraged, Robert leaps on his son and tries to strangle him. Others rush into the room to intervene, and the business magnate is subdued and removed to the asylum. The assassin who tried to kill him earlier leads the other inmates in a revolt, attacking Robert who barely manages to fight them off and escape. Meanwhile, at the hospital, Sara gives birth to a daughter. Robert appears, and he and Sara become reconciled. She runs off with him together with her baby when the other infants in the maternity ward start to die due to the mysterious poisoning of the baby formula.

Charrier boards a jet for Geneva, traveling under Robert's name. The plane explodes and everyone assumes Robert Caine is dead. Instead, he finds a safe haven in the Middle East for Sara and his daughter. He then plans to kill his son and his board of directors when they meet in Geneva before the conference.

Angel assumes the role of president of the company and speaks of the loss of his father in a tragic airplane accident. Angel expands the board to 21 members, and sets a deadline for the completion of the nuclear plant in the year 2000, on the occasion of his 33rd birthday. Someone, presumably Robert, is shown packing a suit vest with dynamite and preparing a detonator. A figure enters the conference room and an explosion occurs, superimposed over a close-up of Angel. His visage remains after the explosion passes, and the end credits roll.

CRITIQUE

Holocaust 2000 is a mixed bag. It has a decent basic script, but its concepts are poorly handled and clumsily executed. The end of the film is a perfect example. The directing of the film is heavy-handed and uncertain. The editing and camera angles are so poor that the audience is unsure exactly what is happening onscreen. Is Robert preparing the bomb? Is his attempt successful? The impression, since Angel's image continues after the explosion, suggests that he survived unharmed. But then a closing title quotes scripture that the false prophet shall be tormented day and night, so the actual intent is somewhat open-ended. In *The Omen,* the supernatural events that destroy the child Damian's adversaries seem controlled by an unseen agent, presumably Satan himself. In *Holocaust 2000,* it is unclear who or what is helping Angel, since the events seem more random and unfocused. In the case of the assassination attempt, one could interpret it that Angel took advantage of the situation to kill his mother, since he, in essence, directed the killer's knife. Harbin's death appears like a simple accident. Only Dr. Griffith's death seems as if it was controlled by a supernatural force. But then this force is quite fallible, since it mistakes Monsignor Charrier for Robert Caine simply because he is traveling under Caine's name. The attack of the tides on Dr. Meyer is also a muddle, being poorly staged and unconvincing. It makes Robert, splashing around in a few inches of water, look stupid, and since Meyer himself is never shown, the scientist merely could have strolled away. These mismanaged sequences weaken the thrust of the film which has many strong moments. Robert's dream of the power plant and the beast is excellent, creepy, and very effective. The scenes in which the power plant is portrayed and compared to the biblical beast are also superb. The opening exploration of the cave is well handled, as is the scene where Monsignor Charrier explains elements of the apocalypse. The threat the power plant poses seems credible in the context of the film.

There are additional loose ends that the script could have tightened. Not identifying the name of the Middle Eastern country is pointless, as it seems clear it is supposed to be Israel. The locale changes so frequently that we are never sure if we are in England, Switzerland or the Middle East. The special effects are decent, and the musical score by Ennio Morricone is another plus. The acting on the whole is difficult to judge because the editing undercuts a number of the performances. Kirk Douglas seems to bounce back and forth between being gung ho about the project to being filled with doubts. Although this plant is the core of Robert's future plans, he seems rather ignorant about it at times. Gregory Peck was impressive as the doubting father who was slowly convinced that his son was the Antichrist in *The Omen*, but Douglas is so inconsistent from scene to scene that his performance really fails to convince. Simon Ward, best remembered for his performance as Churchill in *Young Winston* (1972), is completely consistent as Angel Caine. He seems a normal young man, helpful and supportive of his father and totally committed to his ideals. He never lets the mask slip or appears to be anything else than a dedicated son, and this utter blandness, while intriguing, adds little interest to the film. When Angel finally comes clean with Robert, his revelation seems so matter-of-fact that it is anticlimatic. Agostina Belli is charming and appealing as Sara, and she and Douglas have a few genuinely fine scenes together, especially in the cave. Her feeling of betrayal when Robert suggests an abortion is particularly well played. Anthony Quayle and Alexander Knox, both screen veterans, provide excellent supporting roles as Dr. Griffith and Dr. Meyer. The most impressive cast member is Romolo Valli, who as Monsignor Charrier endows the film with depth and a sense of purpose. Valli was a character actor of genuine esteem whose career included roles in *Five Branded Women* (1960) and *Boccaccio '70* (1962). Tragically, Valli died in a traffic accident a year after his role in *Holocaust 2000*.

The image of the power plant/beast is a potent one, and it manages to stick with the viewer for some time. It is a disappointment that Alberto De Martino was unable to deliver on his promising script with a better film. The dream sequence, nevertheless, remains one of the most impressive moments in apocalyptic cinema.

REPRESENTATIVE QUOTES

"It speaks of a monster with seven heads and ten horns, and on the ten horns ten crowns. It rises from the sea and destroys mankind." (Sara, explaining the apocalypse while exploring the cave)

"People should understand that scientific progress today is like a truck without brakes hurtling downhill. It is stupid to think of stopping it." (Robert speaking to the prime minister)

"Stop talking like a ridiculous prophet of the apocalypse. The world can only save itself through new uses of energy, thermonuclear energy. That's exactly what I'm trying to give it." (Robert to Meyer on the beach before the water sweeps in and swallows up the scientist)

"It is better to run towards the great holocaust. It will purify everything." (Angel to his father)

The Horn Blows at Midnight (1945)

Rating: ***   **Threat:** The doomsday trumpet

Warner Brothers. Written by Sam Hellman & James V. Kern based on an idea by Aubrey Wisberg; Photographed by Sid Hickox; Special effects by Lawrence Butler; Edited by Irene Morra; Music by Franz Waxman; Produced by Mark Hellinger; Directed by Raoul Walsh. B & W, 78 minutes.

ANNOTATED CAST LIST

Jack Benny (*Athanael*, angel assigned to blow the doomsday trumpet); Alexis Smith (*Elizabeth*, his celestial girlfriend); Reginald Gardiner (*Archie Dexter*, suave jewel thief); Dolores Moran (*Fran Blackstone*, Dexter's accomplice); Allyn Joslyn (*Osidro*, fallen angel); John Alexander (*Doremus*, fallen angel); Guy Kibbee (head of the Department of Small Planet Management); Franklin Pangborn (*Sloan*, hotel detective); Margaret Dumont (*Miss Rodholler*, wealthy woman at Cliffside Park); John Brown (*Lew Pulplinsky*, waiter who takes Athanael's trumpet); Bobby Blake (*Junior Pulplinsky*, his son); Ethel Griffies (*Lady Stover*, wealthy hotel guest); Paul Harvey (hotel manager); Mike Mazurki (*Humphrey*, thug working for Archie); Truman Bradley (radio announcer for Paradise Coffee); Murray Alper (*Tony*, bellboy); Oliver Blake (photographer in heaven); James Burke (policeman); Jack Norton (drunk); Patrick O'Moore (hotel clerk); Richard Lane (bridge expert); Francis Pierlot (*Mecurius*, heavenly personnel manager); Monte Blue (restaurant cook); Earl Hodgins (barker at Cliffside Park); Sidney Miller (horn player in Tom-Cats band); Edward Mortimer (hotel guest); Dudley Dickerson (hotel employee).

SYNOPSIS

For over twenty years, Jack Benny had a running gag on his television and radio programs about this film, his last starring role in feature films. He would recall it with a wistful smile, which would set up Eddie Anderson (Rochester), Fred Allen or another guest star to deliver a hilarious crack ridiculing the picture. Posters for the film would appear in Benny's closet, and for his best dinnerware he would use leftover doorprizes promoting the film. Benny got hundreds of laughs making fun of the picture, but in fact it is a fairly amusing, offbeat comedy, and quite out of the ordinary, a far cry from what one would expect from only hearing of the film in Benny's clever jokes.

Like *The Wizard of Oz* (1939) and many other fantasies, *The Horn Blows at Midnight* has a short wraparound segment that casts most of the picture as a dream. Jack Benny is cast as a musician who plays third trumpet in a radio orchestra. He has been awake all night learning a new composition, and as the *Paradise Coffee Program* begins, Jack is lulled into sleep by the soothing tones of Truman Bradley, the persuasive radio announcer.

The scene switches to heaven where a grandiose celestial orchestra and chorus are playing a stellar symphony. One of the trumpeters, an angel named Athanael, is summoned by the Department of Small Planet Management. Elizabeth, Athanael's sweetheart, is the receptionist for the department. The deputy chief gives Athanael an assignment: to sound the doomsday trumpet on planet Earth. Orders have come from "the front office" that the people of Earth have ignored too many warnings to mend their ways. Athanael is to be transported down to Earth, and at precisely midnight he is to play the first four notes of the *Judgment Day Overture*, which will cause the immediate destruction of the planet. If he blows the horn at any other time, however, nothing will happen.

Athanael has his picture taken as he prepares for his mission. He is shown a wall full of portraits of angels who went out on assignments but never returned, becoming fallen angels. The last two angels sent to Earth, Osidro and Doremus, both failed in their mission and are still on Earth. It is arranged for Athanael to be transported to Earth via an elevator at the luxurious Hotel Universe in New York City.

On Earth, wealthy Lady Stover is upset that the express elevator to the roof and penthouse seems to have vanished. Sloan, the house detective, is ordered to locate the missing elevator, and he questions Archie Dexter, an elegant master thief. Archie knows nothing about it but promises to distract Lady Stover. The elevator suddenly reappears and Athanael emerges. After determining the time is 11:15 P.M., the angel decides to pass his time observing the dancers in the ballroom. The two fallen angels spot Athanael and deduce his mission. They scheme to stop him, because at the hour of destruction they will be sent to hell. On the dance floor, Archie attempts to steal Lady Stover's pearls by slipping them to a cigarette girl, Fran Blackstone, who is his accomplice. Athanael interferes, however, and returns the pearls to Lady Stover. After being chewed out by Archie, Fran becomes terribly upset and heads to the roof. Osidro and Doremus approach Athanael and try to distract him from blowing his horn. They take him to a party and describe the temptations of wine, women and song. Athanael resists and goes to the roof to sound the notes of doom. He sees Fran, who is planning to jump, and suggests she merely wait a few more moments. He tries to hold her, but they both topple over the side and wind up clinging to the ledge. The clock tolls, and by the time they regain their footing, midnight has passed and it is too late to sound the trumpet.

In heaven, celestial orchestra members gossip about Athanael's failure. Elizabeth pleads with the chief about the matter. On Earth, Osidro and Doremus explain the consequences of being a fallen angel to Athanael. For instance, they get uncontrollable attacks of "twinges" every hour. They get him a job with a dance band, but he finds the jitterbug style incomprehensible, and he is fired. He orders a meal he cannot pay for in a restaurant, and they confiscate his trumpet until the bill is paid.

Elizabeth descends to Earth to inform her sweetheart that he will be given a second chance at midnight. After she leaves the elevator, she runs across a radio quiz show being broadcast in the hotel lobby. By accident she correctly answers a bridge question and wins a cash prize. She finds Athanael and gives him the good news. He sets out to reclaim his trumpet with the money Elizabeth has won. But the waiter has lent the instrument to his son, who took it with him to a picnic at Cliffside Park, New Jersey. Athanael tracks the boy down to the amusement park, but the lad refuses to hand over the trumpet so Athanael simply snatches it. A wild chase develops as the angel is chased by a gang of kids and a wealthy woman who saw the theft. Athanael finally escapes after being shot out of a canon, landing in a hay wagon miles down the road.

Osidro and Doremus learn that the destruction of Earth has been rescheduled for that evening, and they offer Archie $10,000 to steal the trumpet of doom. With Humphrey, his lumbering sidekick, Archie fashions an elaborate scheme. He gains the confidence of Elizabeth, posing as a symphonic conductor. He also reconciles with Fran and uses her to distract Athanael. Humphrey takes the trumpet when the angel is not looking. The deputy chief himself, concerned over Elizabeth and Athanael, also comes to Earth to supervise its destruction. Sloan tries to question him about the disappearing and reappearing elevator.

Archie hands the trumpet over to Osidro and Doremus at their penthouse apartment. Athanael sneaks in and retrieves it. Humphrey chases him, and the angel topples off the balcony, falling into a giant mechanical signboard advertising Paradise Coffee. He lands in the giant coffee pot and then is poured into a giant cup. The hour of midnight is approaching, and Athanael is determined not to miss the right moment again. The deputy chief and Elizabeth call to him, warning of the time. He perches on the side of the cup as the clock starts to toll, but a giant spoon knocks him off and he falls tumbling to the street below.

Jack awakens as the radio announcer finishes his commercial for Paradise Coffee. Jack notices that the entire orchestra has also drifted off. He topples off the stage, and the announcer wakes everyone up. The orchestra resumes playing as the film concludes.

CRITIQUE

Despite the dream structure of the story, *The Horn Blows at Midnight* merits consideration since the entire basis of the film is its apocalyptic nature. The dream foundation served as a safety valve for Warner Brothers in case their secularized vision of heaven produced criticism. All religious references are largely avoided. Indeed, the dialogue is largely sanitized and couched in vague, satirical terms. God himself is alluded to as "the front office" and the Archangel Gabriel is called "the chief demolition expert." The only saint mentioned is St. Vitus, in a throwaway gag referring to popular dancing. The only other residents of heaven to be mentioned are Methuselah, George Washington and Julius Caesar. The scenes set in heaven are whimsical, as everything seems to operate along the lines of a huge business firm. The special effects are grandiose, particularly those of the heavenly orchestra, which appears to have a thousand members. Everyone is dressed in white robes and, apparently, relationships are not much different there than anywhere else. Earth, however, is a thorn in the side of the Department of Small Planet Management. It seems to be too wicked a place, unworthy of further investment of time and effort. It is unclear how Osidro and Doremus became fallen angels, but given the large number of pictures displayed by the heavenly personnel officer, mission failure seems to be rather common. The hook of the story, the trumpet of doom that signals destruction, is fairly intriguing and cleverly conceived. The source of the concept is the *Bible* in the Book of *Revelations*, which describes how seven angels will blow seven horns at the end time. It is the sounding of the seventh trumpet through which God's will is revealed. Archangel Gabriel, God's messenger, is traditionally portrayed as the seventh angel, and in medieval art Gabriel is usually portrayed bearing a trumpet. Having Jack Benny substitute for Gabriel is an audacious concept, and nothing else in the film equals the boldness of this idea, which was dreamed up by Aubrey Wisberg.

Unfortunately, most of the material of the film is not very well suited to Jack Benny. Harold Lloyd would have been more ideally cast in the role. There is too much slapstick and physical humor in the story for it to be a great Benny vehicle. He is hilarious in the scenes where his timing, word inflections and smug air are required. He is also exceptional in the scene where he functions as a complete innocent. Benny, more than any other comedian, is the absolute master of the comedy of character. He is unequaled in the scenes where the two fallen angels try to tempt him. Athanael is tempted but tries very hard not to show it. Benny shines brilliantly at such moments, but pratfalls, tottering on the edge of buildings and chase scenes are simply not his forte. The first scene on the roof with Dolores Moran and Benny alone does not work and seems very awkward. The second ledge scene at the climax is far better constructed and genuinely funny. Part of this sequence was later restaged, as a tribute, at the conclusion of *It's a Mad, Mad, Mad, Mad World* (1963), a picture in which Benny had a cameo as well. The giant coffee pot and cup gags are brilliant. The odd thing is that the audience is on Benny's side, hoping he gets a chance to blow the horn and complete his mission, even though it means the end of the world. This may be the only apocalyptic film that has the audience pulling for total annihilation. The film manages to set usual audience loyalty on its head, an unusual development.

The other cast members deliver mixed performances. Most of them also appear in the brief wraparound segment as orchestra members or other broadcast personnel. This component of the film does not work very well or seem to be fully integrated into the main story. We never learn, for example, the actual name of Jack Benny's character is when he is awake. We know he is a disgruntled composer, but is he frustrated enough to want the entire world to end? Alexis Smith is ethereal and charming, but her role is really a thankless one. Dolores Moran is miscast and unconvincing. The scene where Fran throws herself at Athanael should be hilarious. Benny is excellent in the scene, but Moran seems forced, which drains some of the humor from the situation. The talented Margaret Dumont is wasted as the interloping society woman in Cliffside Park, but she is far more successful in the wraparound as the pompous operatic singer. Reginald Gardiner is superb as Archie Dexter. The various scenes where he fakes conducting Tchaikovsky's *Fourth Symphony* are priceless. Allyn Joslyn and John Alexander are excellent foils as the fallen angels. The portly Alexander was excellent in comedy and is best remembered as Teddy Roosevelt impersonator of the Brewster clan in *Arsenic and Old Lace* (1944) and as the killer in the film noir classic *Night Has a Thousand Eyes* (1948). Other exceptional bits are performed by Franklin Pangborn (as the hotel detective) who gives a great double take every time he questions someone who emerges from the elevator borrowed by heaven. Bobby Blake is splendid as the spoiled son of the waiter. Blake grew up to be an exceptional performer in such widely varied projects as *In Cold Blood* (1967), *Lost Highway* (1997) and the TV series *Baretta*. Kudos are also well deserved by Guy Kibbee, for his avuncular performance as the deputy chief and by Ethel Griffies, as Lady Stover. Griffies was the memorable Madame Saturnia in *Castle in the Desert* (1942), Fox's last Charlie Chan effort.

Director Raoul Walsh manages to keep the film moving briskly, but one senses his heart was not truly in the effort. The wrapup of the film is too quick, and the last line, in which Benny says he had a wild dream, which would not be believed if seen in the movies, seems a very odd way to close the picture. But then, many aspects of this film are strange and unusual.

REPRESENTATIVE QUOTES

"Planet number 339-001 has gotten completely out of hand. . . . Persecution and hatred everywhere. Goodness knows the front office has warned them often enough. Quakes, floods, volcanic eruptions, droughts, plagues, everything. They pay no attention." (Deputy chief of Small Planet Management to Athanael)

"Are you staying the night, sir?" (Hotel clerk to Athanael) "No, and neither are you." (His reply)

"As Methuselah remarked to me one day, you should live so long." (Athanael to Archie after hearing his boasts of future musical triumphs)

Kronos (1957)

Rating: *** **Threat: Alien device**

Twentieth Century Fox. Written by Lawrence L. Goldman & Jack Rabin based on a story by Irving Block; Photographed by Karl Struss; Special effects by Irving Block, Louis DeWitt, William Reinhold, Gene Warren, Menrad von Mulldorfer & Jack Rabin; Edited by Jodie Copelan; Music by Paul Sawtell & Bert Shefter; Produced & directed by Kurt Neumann. B & W, 78 minutes.

ANNOTATED CAST LIST

Jeff Morrow (*Dr. Leslie Gaskell*, astronomer at Lab Central); Barbara Lawrence (*Vera Hunter*, his assistant and girlfriend); John Emery (*Dr. Hubbell Eliot*, head of Lab Central); George O'Hanlon (*Dr. Arnie Culver*, computer expert); Morris Ankrum (*Dr. Albert Stern*, neuropsychiatrist treating Eliot); Marjorie Stapp (Eliot's nurse); Kenneth Alton (*Sam McCrary*, truck driver possessed by an alien); John Parrish (*Gen. Perry*, officer in charge of Kronos crisis); José Gonzales Gonzales (*Manuel Ramirez*, fisherman hosting the science team in Mexico); Robert Shayne (air force general); Robert Forrest (television newscaster); Richard Harrison (pilot); Don Eitner (military meteorologist); John Halloran (Lab Central security guard).

SYNOPSIS

An imaginative, low-budget feature, *Kronos* is a textbook example of 1950s science fiction. The production makes the most of its small resources. Of course, the special effects are primitive, mostly accomplished by a combination of drawn animation synthesized with models. Its story has a number of fresh concepts and can be appreciated by both a juvenile and an adult audience. When watched on television, *Kronos* is less impressive unless viewed in the letterbox format, which adds considerably to the film's impact. In the traditional television print, for example, the newspaper headlines are truncated so "ASTEROID HEADING FOR EARTH" comes out as "OID HEADING FOR E."

The picture opens as a five-mile-wide, saucer-shaped spaceship approaches Earth. A small, glowing ball emerges from the ship and heads toward the planet. Truck driver Sam McCrary is driving down a desert road, whistling along with "Something's Got to Give" on his radio. His motor seems to stall, and as he inspects it, the glowing ball enters his head and possesses him. He is able to start the truck and heads to Lab Central, a restricted secret base. McCrary breaks in and goes to the office of the director, Hubbell Eliot. The luminous entity flashes into the body of Eliot, and the truck driver crumples to the floor. Security men cart the dead body away, and Eliot starts to examine his restricted files.

Elsewhere at Lab Central, Dr. Leslie Gaskell is plotting the course of asteroid

M-47 (actually the alien spacecraft), which he is tracking. His data indicates that M-47 has made some inexplicable directional changes. Gaskell is afraid the asteroid will hit the Earth, causing enormous damage. Les asks Dr. Arnie Culver to verify his theory with SUSIE (short for Synchro Unifying Sinometric Integrating Equitensor), his master computer. The machine goes haywire as Dr. Eliot enters the computer lab. Les explains the odd behavior of the asteroid, but Eliot dismisses his concerns. Arnie says it will take hours for him to bring SUSIE back online, so Les decides to take his assistant, Vera Hunter, to the movies. When they reaches the car, Les changes his mind and decides to contact other astronomers to get their readings on the asteroid. Good-natured Vera is used to such disappointments, however. Arnie gets the projections from SUSIE, confirming that Earth is in critical danger. Arnie and Les force Eliot to contact the military, and they plan to fire a nuclear missile to destroy M-47.

The nuclear explosion has an unexpected result. Eliot collapses at the moment of impact, and M-47 veers into a new course, landing in the Pacific Ocean off the coast of Mexico. Eliot is removed to the hospital, and Les becomes acting head of Lab Central until his return. Convinced that M-47 is controlled by an alien intelligence, he plans an immediate expedition to Mexico with Arnie to investigate the strange asteroid. Vera later follows them with some scientific equipment that was not packed in their kit. Actually, Vera uses this as an excuse to join the expedition. Manuel Ramirez, a poor fisherman, allows them to use his house as their base of operations.

At the hospital, Dr. Albert Stern is treating Dr. Eliot, who lapses in and out of a coma, mumbling deliriously about an alien existence. Eliot is treated with electric shock therapy, which temporarily allows the scientist to regain his senses and explain to Stern that he is possessed by an alien. At night, the alien regains control of Eliot's mind, which focuses entirely on the alien ship as it undergoing a metamorphosis under the waters of the Pacific Ocean. Finally, a colossal alien robot emerges from the ocean. It stands hundreds of feet high, its body consisting of two huge metallic cubes supported on four metallic pillars. A window-like globe and two huge antennae crown the upper cube. Les, Vera and Arnie fly by helicopter to the top of the robot for a close-up inspection. The alien device, which Les dubs "Kronos" after the legendary Titan in Greek mythology, is dormant, but it becomes active after they land on it. News of this phenomenon soon spreads worldwide.

Eliot, in a lucid moment, tells Stern that the alien machine is a great energy storehouse called an accumulator. It is under the control of the alien possessing him. If it proves successful, other devices will be summoned which will drain the Earth dry of all resources. The alien force assumes total control of Eliot and directs him to kill Dr. Stern and destroy his files. He then makes it look like an electrical accident. Dr. Eliot is later released and returns to Lab Central. He studies his files on Mexico and sends a telepathic message to Kronos to begin its attack. He informs it of the location of all nearby power plants. The monstrous device starts to maneuver, with its four pillars moving up and down like pistons, and it travels quickly, destroying everything in its wake. The Mexican Air Force attacks, but Kronos merely seems to absorb the weapons hurled against it. A powerful force field eliminates the attacking planes.

Returning to Lab Central, Les and his team are startled to learn that Eliot has recommended to the military that an atomic bomb be used against Kronos. When Eliot later assaults Vera, Les pushes him away, sending him crashing into an electronic control panel. After this jolt of electricity, Eliot's real personality emerges to warn Les that a series of giant accumulator robots will arrive on Earth unless Kronos is stopped. He advises him to find a way to reverse the process by which Kronos absorbs energy. Eliot seals himself in a lead-shielded chamber and destroys the apparatus that controls the vault-like door. Eliot then kills himself, apparently with a lethal dose of radiation. The alien parasite leaves his body, but it, too, is injured and now appears in a liquid state. The entity sizzles and sparks before finally perishing.

Les phones the air force to halt the nuclear attack. The general tries to recall the plane, but it is drawn uncontrollably toward Kronos, which positions itself into a single, impenetrable box-like formation. The nuclear bomb explodes as the plane crashes into Kronos. Then the mushroom cloud reverses itself and is completely absorbed by Kronos, as it glows and doubles in size. No longer directed by the alien, the giant robot continues on automatic pilot, accumulating energy and causing general havoc.

Arnie programs SUSIE to suggest methods of dealing with Kronos. An overload of data almost causes SUSIE to crash, and Les wonders if they could use the same technique on the monster. He theorizes that it might cause a change of polarity in the antennae atop Kronos. This would induce the device to feed upon itself, setting up a cycle of destruction.

Panic breaks out as Kronos approaches Los Angeles and a mass evacuation is ordered. The military undertakes the plan recommended by Les. A solitary plane dumps a shower of "omega particles" over Kronos, and the chain reaction envisioned by Les reduces the machine to a small pile of rubble. If other accumulators ever arrive, Les concludes, they will know how to dispose of them.

CRITIQUE

Overall, *Kronos* is a fairly successful film, which could have been even better had more thought and clarity had been used to establish the main characters and their relationships. Enough information is imparted about Kronos. (Cronos, incidentally, is the traditional spelling of this mythological name, whereas Kronos is the German spelling.) Hubbell Eliot's struggle with the alien invader, a key element of the plot and one of the most interesting aspects of the story, is not very well presented. John Emory, a superb actor similar to Arnold Moss, does a fine job, but the editing and script make it unclear exactly what is happening. Eliot's heroic vanquishing of the alien, at the cost of his own life, is awkwardly staged, and the director lets the audience down by not making this dramatic scene more coherent. The intercutting with the nuclear attack sequence is dramatic, but not really related. The exact relationship of the alien and the accumulator is also unclear. By the time of the alien's demise, Kronos seems able to function on its own. The identity of the alien is another mystery. In a lucid moment, Dr. Eliot says that it "commands the stars." At another point, it is stated that this alien dominates its planet telepathically. So this elusive alien ball of energy could be either a dictator or merely an engineer who monitors Kronos to make sure it functions properly. The distinction is never made clear, but it is apparent that there is only one alien. Another plot loophole involves the alien's activity. When it leaves its spacecraft, it heads directly to the vicinity of Lab Central, so Eliot must have been its target. It had to monitor Earth in advance to plot this course of action. It is also strange, with all the photos that Les Gaskell had available of M-47, that he never seems to realize it is shaped like a flying saucer. One can only assume the "effect" of the saucer was created after the main footage was already in the can as an explanation for this gaffe. Otherwise, it makes Les, Arnie and Vera appear rather deficient in their observations.

The action scenes with Kronos, although primitive by contemporary standards, work rather well and are impressive. The only flaw in the design of the monstrous robot is that its antennae resembles the "rabbit ears" on an old television set. The cinematography is good, but the editing and direction are ponderous at times. The cast works well. Jeff Morrow made a mark as the alien Exetor in *This Island Earth* (1955), an apocalyptic film involving the destruction of an alien world called Metalluna. Morrow has an easy-going, natural appeal. onscreen. In his career, Morrow has battled Richard Burton in an epic swordfight in *The Robe* (1953), the Gill-Man in *The Creature Walks among Us* (1956) and an absurd monstrous bird from another dimension in *The Giant Claw* (1957). (The giant bird is undoubtedly the most hilarious big screen monster ever devised.) George O'Hanlon, Morrow's sidekick, is also an appealing character. O'Hanlon is best remembered as Joe McDoakes in a series of well-liked short subjects, and he also provided the voice of George Jetson for the popular television cartoon series *The Jetsons*. John Emery, who was noted for his suave cultured voice, played many memorable character parts in such films as *The Woman in White* (1948) and *The Mad Magician* (1954). He was married for a time to Tullulah Bankhead. Heroine Barbara Lawrence is pleasant as Vera, but not very memorable. The cast also includes screen veterans Morris Ankrum as Dr. Stern and Robert Shayne as an air force general. Their presence in many 1950s genre films made them fan favorites.

In conclusion, *Kronos* has far more pluses than minuses on its scorecard and is decidedly far better than average. The picture has additional impact when viewed in letterbox format. Additional scenes with Eliot and his staff, set prior to his possession by the alien, would have strengthened the film and improved it. Initially, the script envisioned a film somewhat longer than the actual 78 minutes, so the screenplay was trimmed before filming. The completed film no doubt was hurt by this paring down, particularly since the deleted scenes involved character development, an ingredient which definitely would have improved the picture.

REPRESENTATIVE QUOTES

"You and I saw M-47 swerve in its path, take a course impossible to explain by natural physical laws, didn't we? Any mass ten times its size and density should have been pulverized by that atomic barrage, but it wasn't. Instead it changed its path again, struck downward towards the Earth like a wounded animal lashing out at its tormentor. What does all this add up to?" (Dr. Les Gaskell to Arnie and Vera)

"The patient is convinced that he is possessed by a demon, an incubus which dominates his actions and makes him carry out its will. Through this demon he is telepathic, dominating at a distance the inhabitants of some undisclosed world who subsist on pure electrical or atomic energy. Finding their planet depleted, they are scourging the universe for fresh supplies." (Dr. Stern, recording an entry for Eliot's medical file)

"Gaskell, here on Earth we have learned only one half the nuclear secret. We can transform matter into energy. Up there, they have the other half. They transmute energy into matter. They know how to create the basic elements of matter, electrically and atomically." (Eliot to Les, after an electric shock allows him to speak freely)

The Last Man on Earth (1964)

Rating: ***   Threat: Vampirism

American International. Written by Richard Matheson & William P. Leicester based on the novel *I Am Legend* by Richard Matheson; Photographed by Franco Delli Collis; Edited by Gene Ruggiero; Music by Paul Sawtell & Bert Shefter; Produced by Robert L. Lippert & Harold E. Knox; Directed by Sidney Salkow & Ubaldo Ragona. B & W, 86 minutes.

ANNOTATED CAST LIST

Vincent Price (*Dr. Robert Morgan*, scientist who is the last human in a world of vampires); Franca Bettoia (*Ruth Collins*, woman he tries to cure); Giacomo Rossi-Stuart (*Ben Cortman*, leader of a pack of vampires); Emma Danieli (*Virginia*, Morgan's wife); Christi Courtland (*Kathy*, their daughter); Umberto Rau (*Dr. Mercer*, head of research lab); Antonio Corevi (California governor); Hector Ribotta (soldier).

SYNOPSIS

This film is one of the most unusual entries of apocalyptic cinema, combining elements of traditional gothic horror with science fiction. The basic idea was conceived by writer Richard Matheson in his powerful novel, *I Am Legend*, which depicted a world overrun by vampires, largely in the traditional mold, hiding from the sun by day and seeking blood but lacking any hypnotic powers or the ability to change their forms into bats. In fact, these vampires have little reasoning ability beyond their instinct for survival They can be easily destroyed during the day by the standard stake through the heart. This vampirism, however, has a scientific basis, and the hero of the book is a scientist who discovers that the vampirism is brought on by a virus, which could be cured if an effective serum could be developed. *The Last Man on Earth* meticulously follows the book for the first three-quarters of the story, since Matheson himself was one of the screenwriters, using the pseudonym of Logan Swanson. Unfortunately the production was shot in Italy, and this foreign location was a very unconvincing substitute for the American setting of the story.

The picture begins as dawn breaks over a desolate and abandoned city. A number of corpses are scattered throughout the streets and parking lots. The display sign of a church bears the final message, "The End Has Come." The camera pans through the inside of a house and settles on a man, Robert Morgan, asleep in his bed. An alarm clock sounds, waking him, and as he gets up, the credits appear. His thoughts are heard aloud on the soundtrack as he begins his daily routine, checking his electric generator, inspecting the outer defenses of his house, and replacing the garlic and mirrors that he uses to ward off the vampires that approach his home at night. In front of his garage, he examines the dead bodies of "weak ones," who were drained by the stronger vampires for nourishment. The man collects these bodies and drives them to a huge, fiery pit into which he tosses the corpses. His most gruesome task is his search for the vampires in the buildings of the city. Morgan methodically explores a different area of the city each day, destroying as many vampires as possible with a large supply of hand-crafted wooden stakes. After three years, he has yet to cover half the city in his battle for survival. It is a nightmarish existence, but the weary Morgan is relentless in carrying out his daily schedule. He refuels his station wagon from a tanker truck and continues his grisly routine. Sometimes his victims regain consciousness before he can destroy them, but during the day they can only put up a token resistance. At night Morgan retreats into the safety of his barricaded home as the vampires revive and start their vigil, tossing rocks against his house and pounding at the building.

One of the vampires was once Morgan's best friend. Now Ben Cortman is the ringleader, who taunts him every night and shouts for him to come out. Morgan drowns out these sounds by playing jazz records loudly on his phonograph. When that does not work he drinks himself into oblivion. The next morning, he begins the process all over again. This day, however, Morgan decides to visit his wife's mausoleum at the cemetery. He thinks back to their life together before the plague of vampirism erupted. He falls asleep, and it is already dark when he awakes. Dashing to his car, he has to fight off the vampires, who are starting to appear. They shuffle as they walk, and he is able to elude them and drives off. The vampires have already ringed his house, and he uses a mirror, which the creatures fear, to make his way to the entrance.

Upset by his lapse in judgment, Morgan watches some home movies of his wife and daughter. An extended flashback recreates these happy days with his family. His friend and fellow scientist, Ben Cortman, brings Morgan's attention to a strange plague emerging in Eastern Europe. There are rumors that victims killed by the disease revive as vampires. Morgan, a specialist at a top research lab, mocks this rumor. He is puzzled by the unusual virus, which cannot be killed by any traditional method. As the days pass the plague reaches America, and the Mercer Institute of Chemical Research works day and night to try and find a cure. Ben starts to believe in the vampire theory, and he abandons his job. The governor orders that huge pits be dug where the bodies of all those killed by the disease can be burned. Civilization starts to collapse almost overnight. Morgan himself sinks into fear when his daughter becomes infected. When he returns to the Mercer Institute, he is startled to find it totally abandoned except for Dr. Mercer himself, who is still hopeful about a breakthrough. When Morgan reaches home that evening, he finds his daughter's body being taken away to one of the conflagration pits. He pursues the truck and watches in horror as the bodies are burned. Next, his wife perishes from the disease, but Morgan refuses to contact the authorities to remove the body. Instead, he buries her himself in a homemade grave. That night, however, she returns as a vampire and tries to attack her startled husband. Morgan presumably destroys his wife with a stake and places her remains in the mausoleum, as the flashback ends.

Outside, Ben and the other vampires destroy the station wagon. The next morning Morgan heads to an auto showroom to choose a new vehicle. Driving home, he spots a black poodle wandering about in the sunlight. He is startled to find any living survivor, and he chases after it. Morgan then comes across the bodies of vampires killed with iron spears, a technique he himself never used, and he is puzzled by this new discovery. Back home, he broadcasts a message on his home radio station. Soon the poodle reappears and Morgan takes it in, but when he tests the dog's blood, he finds that it is infected. Sadly, he must destroy his new friend with a stake in the heart.

While he is burying the dog, Morgan sees a woman, who runs away in fear. Morgan catches her and brings her home. She calls herself Ruth Collins, and she has survived by hiding each night and scavaging by day. She reacts when Morgan tests her response to garlic, and he believes that she must also be infected. Ruth questions Morgan as to why he is not infected. Years before in Central America, Morgan had been bitten by a vampire bat, and he believes this gave him immunity. Ruth retreats into another room and tries to give herself an injection when Morgan is not watching. When he catches her in the act, she drops the syringe. Ruth then reveals that she is part of a community of infected people who have learned to suppress the vampirism with a daily injection of blood and vaccine. She was sent by the group to learn if Morgan had developed a better vaccine.

The new society plans to kill off the untreated vampires and begin a new civilization. They also plan to destroy Morgan, the last man on Earth, whom they regard as unnatural. They see him as a monster and tell legends about this man who walks in daylight. They plan to attack that very night. Unable to take her injection, Ruth collapses. Morgan tries to save her by giving her a transfusion of his own blood. Remarkably, this process destroys her infection as well and she is completely cured of the vampirism. Moreover, Morgan now believes the antibodies in his blood could cure the others as well.

Several jeeps full of soldiers arrive at Morgan's house and begin to kill the vampires with iron spears. Ruth urges Morgan to run. The men, dressed in black uniforms, slaughter their opponents easily. Ben Cortman climbs on top of a nearby building, and the troops shoot at him until he loses his balance and falls to the ground. Ruth tries to tell them about the cure, but the soldiers rush off in pursuit of Morgan, who runs down the street. After an elaborate chase, they corner him in a church. As a dozen soldiers approach, Morgan struggles up to the altar and proclaims his defiance. Wounded by a spear, he collapses. Ruth rushes to him and cradles him as he dies while repeating in bewilderment, "They were afraid of me."

CRITIQUE

Vincent Price himself thought highly of *The Last Man on Earth* but agreed that the scenery of Rome made a very unconvincing Los Angeles and that the production was very limited in its outdoor footage, which could have made the film more realistic. There are also numerous loopholes that weaken the end of the story. The plot of the "new society" is somewhat confusing. Up until this point, everyone on Earth seems to have died and bodies that were not burned were revived as vampires. Then we learn about a new society of semi-vampires, whom Ruth describes as people who have been infected but have not died. This blurs the concept of the entire film, since the citizens of this new society are simply smarter vampires who can occasionally go out into the sun due to their special serum. Yet Ruth says she will become a mindless vampire without the injection. What exactly does this mean? Would this formula then work on the untreated vampires or does it work on those not killed by the disease? However, since the disease was reported as being 100 percent fatal, there is a good deal of confusion about the attributes of this community. Up until the appearance of the new society vampires, the film is brilliant and convincing. As soon as they appear, however, most of film's power and integrity evaporates. The original novel handed the presentation and explanation of this group far better. The concept that a normal man would be seen as a monster by this new society is a valid and powerful theme as well, but it is totally mishandled in the search and chase finale, which is the weakest section of the picture. Perhaps the last segment was penned by Leicester instead of Matheson, who reportedly was unsatisfied by the end result of this film, or maybe the film crew simply wrapped up the picture too hurriedly.

There are other illogical details that mar the conclusion. Ruth had been sent as a spy to determine if Morgan had any fresh insights about the disease. As it turns out, he stumbled onto a cure at the very end, but how would Ruth make her report if her people simply intended to march in and eradicate him? Her spying mission makes no sense, since no one is interested in anything she has to disclose. All is not lost for the community, since Ruth herself would be able to save them with her own blood, which is now uncontaminated. Also, since Morgan was just killed, his blood could still be used as a serum. But Ruth no longer seem to care about any of this.

Potentially, this picture could have been a great apocalyptic film, and on many levels it is indeed extraordinary. The cinematography is moody and effective, and the haunting score by Paul Sawtell and Bert Shefter is genuinely first rate. The vampires for the most part are believable; an ingenious mix of elements of traditional lore with science fiction trappings, seeming like archetypical images from nightmares. These shuffling, undead creatures are undoubtedly the direct inspiration for the shuffling zombies in George Romero's *Night of the Living Dead* (1968) and other films. The acting of Vincent Price is both convincing and remarkable. Price takes some chances along the way. Few actors would dare to tackle the scene where Morgan watches the home movies and mixes laughter and tears in an extended take. Price is marvelous in conveying the world weariness of his character, and his voice-over narration is a perfect film noir touch. The picture is essentially a one-man show (except for the long flashback), which is just as well since the rest of the cast is unimpressive. A second director, Ubaldo Ragona, handled the Italian cast with little success. Franca Bettoia is simply not given time to develop a cohesive character, and her role as played in the film makes little sense. Giacomo Rossi-Stuart, who went on to appear in many gladiator films, also directed under the name Jack Stuart. His performance is adequate but lacks any nuances. An Italian-language version of the film was released as *L'Ultimo Uomo Della Terra*, but it is unclear if this version differs from the American print in any way.

Seven years later, the picture was remade with a fairly large budget as *The Omega Man* (1971), with Charlton Heston assuming the lead. The concept was retooled, downplaying and eliminating the gothic elements as much as possible. The picture became pure science fiction, with the virus the result of a germ warfare experiment. The vampires became a craftier bunch, led by Anthony Zerbe, and they seem more like a funky cult instead of an inhuman flock. Rosalind Cash was inserted as the Ruth equivalent. She is introduced far earlier in the story and also becomes Heston's love interest. Additional survivors, children, are added to the plot, and in the film's denouement, Heston's blood is saved for their use as a cure. There is nothing at all frightening or genuinely imaginative in the remake. Although an interesting film in many ways, *The Omega Man* is a more traditional and predictable product. It strays too far from the original concept and seems reminiscent of a number of other films instead of being strikingly unique like *The Last Man on Earth*.

REPRESENTATIVE QUOTES

"December, 1965. Is that all it has been since I inherited the world, only three years? It seems like a hundred million." (Morgan's thoughts as he marks off the calender written on the walls of his kitchen)

"What's going to happen, Dr. Mercer? Is everybody in the world going to die before someone finds the answer?" (Morgan to his employer during the flashback sequence)

"Your new society sounds charming." (Morgan's sarcastic comment to Ruth as she describes the genocide planned by her community)

"You are freaks, all of you, mutations! You are freaks! I am a man, the last man." (Morgan's final outcry as the vampires attack him)

The Last War (1961)
AKA *Sekai Daisenso*

Rating: ****   **Threat:** **Nuclear war**

Toho. Written by Takeshi Kimura & Toshio Yazumi; Photographed by Ro-kuro Nishigaki; Special effects by Eiji Tsuburaya (supervisor); Edited by Koichi Iwashita & Kenneth Wannberg (U.S. version); Music by Ikuma Dan; Produced by Sanezumi Fujimoto & Tomoyuki Tanaka; Directed by Shuei Matsubayashi. Original version, 110 minutes; U.S. version, 80 minutes.

ANNOTATED CAST LIST

Akira Takarada (*Takano*, communications officer of the *Kasagi Maru*); Yuriko Hoshi (*Seiko*, his fiancée); Frankie Sakai (*Mokichi Tamura*, Sieko's father and chauffeur for the Tokyo Press Club); Nobuko Otawa (*Yoshi*, Seiko's mother); Chishu Ryu (*Ebara*, ship's cook on the *Kasagi Maru*); Yumi Shirakawa (*Sanae*, Ebara's daughter and kindergarten teacher); Eijirô Tono (captain of the *Kasagi Maru*); Masao Oda (sweet potato vendor); John F. Kennedy (closing narrator); Hank Brown, Harold Conway, Daniel Jones, Harold Larson (American military officers); Hans Horneff, Roy Leonard, Osman Yusuf (Soviet military officers); Toshihiko Furuta, Shigeki Ishida, Jerry Ito, Seizaburô Kawazu, Nadao Kirino, Chieko Nakakita, Nobuo Nakamura, Toshiko Nakano, Kôzo Nomura, Yutaka Oka, Wataru Omae, Minoru Takada, Ken Uehara, Koji Uno, Sô Yamamura.

SYNOPSIS

In the early 1960s, two similar Japanese films were released within a few months of each other. The first picture was *Dai Sanji Sekai Taisen* or *The Final War* (1960) and the second one was known as *Sekai Daisenso or The Last War*. Both films portray a nuclear conflict between the Western forces, led by America, and the Eastern bloc, led by the Soviet Union. The entire world is destroyed in both films, either by an initial blast or by the fallout, which blankets the planet. Both also present their stories on two levels, through the eyes of officials and military leaders as well as through the eyes of ordinary people, such as a reporter and his fiancée in *The Final War*, and a naval officer and his finacée's family in *The Last War*. *The Final War* was shot in black and white, played briefly in U.S. theaters, and then largely disappeared. *The Last War* never played in America theatrically, but it has played extensively on television and is relatively accessible. *The Last War* is considered the finer of the two films, although the English-language version is significantly shorter than the Japanese print.

The Last War begins at sea as the captain of the freighter *Kasagi Maru* outlines the current options available to the crew. The last war is over, having resulted in mutual destruction. They might journey to a remote area of the planet, hoping to avoid their eventual contamination through radioactive fallout, or they could proceed directly to Tokyo and face their doom in their homeland. The crew choses to return to Tokyo, and the captain issues those instructions as his last order. Takano, the communications officer, reflects on his fianéee, Seiko Tamura and her family, and an extended flashback begins, depicting his memories.

Tokyo has risen from the rubble at the end of World War II to become a vibrant, thriving city filled with industrious individuals such as Mokichi Tamura, the chauffeur of the Tokyo Press Club. Mokichi and his wife, Yoshi, have three children, and Takano is deeply in love with Seiko, their eldest daughter. Since his own family perished during World War II, Takano regards them as his surrogate family, and he boards with them when not at sea. Mokichi is a pleasant, well-meaning man who always does his best for his wife and children, and he tries to present a cheerful front, which is difficult when the world situation seems headed toward disaster. The news is filled with tensions that have arisen from the latest war games held in the South Atlantic, where a Soviet spy sub was destroyed while monitoring the activities of the combined naval forces of the Western powers. This crisis is the latest in a series of international incidents and provocations. The Japanese government holds an emergency council meeting to consider ways to defuse the situation after a NATO plane is shot down over the Mediterranean.

Scenes of the home life of the Tamura family show them to be an average family, fairly happy but with occasional small squabbles. Seiko and her father disagree about world affairs. Seiko supports the Anti-Nuclear Bomb Society, but her father finds it foolish, only causing additional worry and fear for the general public. The elderly sweet potato vendor, who drops by every evening, is dedicated like Seiko to the cause of world peace, and he donates 10 percent of his earnings to the society. Takano calls Seiko at work when his ship docks in Yokohama and tells her he will meet her at home after he visits Ebara, the ship's cook, who missed the last voyage due to illness. Ebara's daughter Sanae is a kindergarten teacher, and Ebara enjoys helping her watch over the youngsters while they are at recess. Ebara says he will be able to resume his duties as cook for the next voyage of the *Kasagi Maru*. When he reaches the Tamura home, Takano discusses the wedding plans with Seiko. She has already informed her mother, who is delighted with the news, but Takano is still nervous about approaching her father.

At an American military base, Lieutenant Mack is placed in charge of preparing six new nuclear missiles in their launching silos so they can be made operational. The base is buzzed by spy planes who report the presence of the new missiles to a Soviet base, which in turn readies their own missiles for possible launch. A narrator describes how, in this atmosphere of heightened tension, an accidental launch could easily occur.

Takano and Seiko rehearse the best way for him to approach her father about their engagement. Unknowingly, Mokichi himself overhears their conversation. When he enters, Seiko's father puts them at ease by saying her mother already told him of their plans. He scratches his head and says, "Can you imagine that?" He hems and haws slightly but then gives his wholehearted blessing, especially when his wife comes in and describes how Mokichi himself had proposed to her. Mokichi then breaks out in laughter when Takano starts to call him Father. The next day the betrothed couple stroll past the fountains in a city park as they plan their wedding, which will occur after Takano's next tour of duty. At home, Yoshi buys and plants some tulip bulbs. Mokichi helps her in their garden, and they recall how they had a single tulip on the window sill outside their apartment window when they first got married. Yoshi feels ill, and her husband completes the planting for her. When the tulips bloom next summer, they plan to give one to Seiko and Takano, a symbol of their own marriage tulip. They wonder how soon it will be before they are grandparents.

A false signal to launch missiles is received at the American missile base. When they initiate the firing sequence, the commanding general calls. He says that no attack order had been given and orders that the launching be aborted immediately. The sequence is barely halted in time, with only two seconds remaining in the countdown. But at another location, a tank column and an air squadron exchange fire, and a nuclear explosion occurs. Japan desperately calls for a world summit. At the kindergarten school, Sanae leads the children in singing a badly dubbed version of "It's a Small World" while her father, Ebara, prepares to resume his duties on the *Kasagi Maru*.

In Siberia, a Soviet base is preparing a test missile firing when the base is buried by an avalanche. The armed warhead is activated, and the commander puts his own life at risk as he faces a radiation overdose while disarming the warhead. Seiko accompanies Takano to Yokohama, and they spend the night together. Yoshi had encouraged her daughter to take this step, and even Mokichi had few objections after voicing some old-fashioned comments about modern-day morality. The unspoken reason behind Yoshi's encouragement of the young couple is the world crisis.

A midair collision between a fighter and a drone over the Arctic precipitates another shooting skirmish involving nuclear weapons. The United Nations demands an immediate cease-fire. Japan's west coast is also strafed and bombed with napalm. The radio urges the evacuation of Tokyo as a potential nuclear target. A full-scale war appears inevitable. Seiko returns home just as panic hits the city. Many parents storm Sanae's kindergarten school to retrieve their children. Mokichi decides that it is pointless to flee, saying, "Where do you suppose ninety million Japanese people would hide? Our family is not running." Yoshi prepares a large, festive dinner, and they settle down to a traditional family meal together, trying to ignore the dire news bulletins on the radio. The family goes out to the garden and observes that the tulips have started to sprout. Seiko starts to sob, saying that nobody will survive to watch them grow. Mokichi walks off alone to the balcony overlooking Tokyo and starts to cry, feeling useless since he is unable to protect his family.

Missiles are launched from bases worldwide. A Japanese radar station reports that one of the missiles is headed towards Tokyo. At the kindergarten, Sanae sits alone after having put the remaining children to bed. The missile approaches the city, exploding in an enormous nuclear blast, and many well-known Tokyo landmarks are shown bursting into flames in a spectacular sequence. The ground itself spews out molten lava, which oozes over the remains of Tokyo until nothing appears to remain. The Pacific Ocean is also rocked by the fury of the blast, and a huge tidal wave almost swamps the *Kasagi Maru,* far out at sea. This is followed by a quick montage showing that each of the world's major cities are also in the midst of total destruction. With these images, Takano's flashback ends, and he stares numbly out over the ocean waters while the soundtrack reprises "It's a Small World." The picture ends with the voice of John F. Kennedy, proclaiming that since nuclear warfare has the capacity to destroy mankind, then mankind must put an end to these weapons before they put an end to all mankind.

CRITIQUE

This film has an extraordinary power, and despite a few mediocre effects showing the missiles in silos being prepared, the destruction of Tokyo is devastating, with remarkable detail and impact. This may very well be the most remarkable portrayal of a nuclear explosion in cinema. The other technical aspects of the film are also good, particularly the editing, as events flip back and forth between the world situation and the day-to-day events of the Tamura family. The editing of the English language print had a subtle change in tone from the original Japanese version, which portrayed the United States as more of an equal instigator of the conflict. Still, even the original stressed the outbreak of war as a series of accidental missteps rather than any calculation. Other changes in the American print included the addition of the song "It's a Small World," which sounds rather hokey at the finale. The ending would have been more effective without it. The use of President Kennedy's comments, on the other hand, is masterful and very appropriate.

The cast on the whole does an excellent job, although some of the subtleties are lost in the translation. Frankie Sakai usually is cast in comic parts, and here he is masterful as the well-meaning Mokichi. Nabuko Otawa is also impressive as his wife, and her attempts to smooth the way for her daughter's marriage are a delight to watch. Yuriko Hoshi is quite charming as Seiko, a young woman in love but with a mind of her own. Akira Takarada is a wash as Takano, and he fails to make as substantial an impression as the other leads. The scene of the Tamura family's last supper is extraordinarily well handled. The emotion is underplayed, but no doubt this sequence would bring tears to the eyes of many viewers. In summary, this is a first-rate production, with a genuine visual payoff when the missiles are finally launched at the end of the film. One could almost consider this film as a companion piece to *On the Beach* (1959), as both films could seamlessly flow into each other, with *The Last War* being the perfect curtain-raiser.

REPRESENTATIVE QUOTES

"The world press began headlining each new development. The military canceled all leaves. There were daily councils of war. Events were rapidly approaching the point of no return." (Takano's narration during the flashback)

"If we all get blown up, it would mean that there is no God. People, minding their own business, living for their future with their dreams, prayers and hopes, and then, BOOM, and everything is gone. No, I refuse to believe it." (Mokichi to Seiko)

"I don't want my family to die. Who has the right to take our lives anyhow? Who? Why must I be so helpless now?" (Last scene of the stunned Mokichi on the balcony)

"Today every inhabitant of this planet must contemplate the day when this planet may no longer be habitable. Every man, woman and child lives under a nuclear sword of Damocles hanging by the slenderest of threads, capable of being cut at any moment by accident or miscalculation or madness. Mankind must put an end to war or war will put an end to mankind." (John F. Kennedy's voiceover at the close of the film, culled from his address to the United Nations on September 25, 1961)

The Last Wave (1977)

Rating: ***** Threat: End of a dreamtime cycle

World Northal. Written by Peter Weir, Petru Popescu & Tony Morphett; Photographed by Russell Boyd; Special effects by Mont Fieguth & Bob Hilditch; Edited by Max Lemon; Music by Charles Wain; Produced by Hal & Jim McElroy; Directed by Peter Weir. 106 minutes.

ANNOTATED CAST LIST

Richard Chamberlain (*David Burton*, corporate tax lawyer); Olivia Hamnett (*Annie*, his wife); Katrina Sedgewick (*Sophie*, their daughter); Ingrid Weir (*Grace*, their daughter); David Gulpilil (*Chris Lee*, Aboriginal man accused of murder and David's dream guide); Nandjiwarra Amagula (*Charlie*, tribal holy man); Frederick Parslow (*Rev. Burton*, David's stepfather); Vivean Gray (*Dr. Whitburn*, folklore expert); Peter Carroll (*Michael Zeadler*, Barrister working with David); Walter Amagula (*Gerry Lee*, brother of Chris and defendant); Roy Bara (*Larry*, defendant); Cedric LaLara (*Lindsey*, defendant); Morris LaLara (*Jacko*, defendant); Jennifer de Greenlaw (Zeadler's secretary); John Frawley (policeman); Athol Compton (*Billy Corman*, murder victim); Hedley Cullen (judge); Richard Henderson (prosecutor); Michael Duffield (*Andrew Porter*, man at party); Wallace Eaton (morgue doctor); John Measher (morgue attendant); Merv Lilly (pub operator); Jo England (babysitter); Guido Rametta (*Guido*, parking lot attendant); Malcolm Robertson (*Don Fishbunn*, Legal Aid administrator); Penny Leach (schoolteacher in the outback).

SYNOPSIS

The Last Wave and *Picnic at Hanging Rock* (1975) helped to establish Peter Weir as a major director, and both are extraordinarily rich, thought-provoking films dealing with dreams, mystical occurrences and unexplainable phenomena. They are open to widely varying critical interpretations. Both films are a tour de force, a celebration of the highest cinematic craftsmanship. *The Last Wave* is the darker and more strenuous of the two pictures, but it is still utterly fascinating. It is the most metaphysical of the apocalyptic films profiled in this book.

The credits depict the Aboriginal holy man known as Charlie painting mysterious symbols on the wall of a cave. The scene shifts to a one-room schoolhouse in the arid Australian outback. Children are at recess in the playground when they hear ominous rolling thunder. They look up perplexed, as there are no clouds and the sky is pure blue. Their teacher summons them inside, and softball-size hail starts to fall, smashing the school's windows. The teacher watches the landscape in disbelief, since the sky is still blue.

In Sydney, corporate lawyer David Burton drives home through a downpour, listening to news of the freak hailstorm in Central Australia. When he arrives home for supper, a flood cascades down the stairs from an overflowing bathtub. Neither his wife, Annie, nor his young children, Sophie and Grace, can explain it. That night, David has a dream in which he sees an Aboriginal man summoning him. His stepfather, a minister, visits the next day, and David talks about his unsettling series of dreams. His stepfather reveals he had a similar series when he was very young.

That night, an Aboriginal man named Billy Corman sneaks into a secret cave beneath the storm drains of Sydney and removes an object. Another Aborigine observes him as he leaves, and shouts, "You Die!" Billy heads to a pub, but five other men confront him and pursue him out into the street. The police are summoned and find Billy lying dead in a puddle. They arrest the five men who were standing around the body. At the morgue, the coroner finds it difficult to pinpoint the exact cause of death except that the man's heart simply stopped beating.

Legal Aid asks David to handle the case of the five Aboriginal men accused of manslaughter. He meets four of the five men at the office of Don Fishbunn of Legal Aid. They tell David they did not murder Billy—he simply died. They provide him with very little information. That night, when David steps out of his house, he notices that frogs are falling from the sky with the rain. He then falls asleep and the Aboriginal man from his dreams reappears, holding a stone with some unusual designs.

David questions the owner of the pub, who claims that Billy boasted he was going to get rich by stealing some taboo artifacts and selling them. Michael Zeadler, the barrister advising David, urges that he cuts a deal and plead his clients guilty in exchange for a light sentence. (In Britain and Australia, a barrister is a lawyer who specializes in arguing cases before the court.) David consults with his clients and is startled when he meets Chris, who is the man who appears in his dreams. David asks Chris to come to his house for supper that night. When Chris arrives, he brings Charlie, a painter who speaks no English. Annie asks if they are tribal people, but Chris gives the standard reply that there are no tribal people in the city. Through Chris, Charlie asks David some unusual questions about his background, and he confides in them about his dreams. Chris warns him that his dreams concern tribal secrets and are dangerous for him.

In a conference with Michael, David suggests that the death of Billy was a tribal killing subject to tribal law, but the barrister suggests that would be foolhardy strategy and a mistake. Michael then agrees to drop out and let David handle the complete case himself. David questions Chris about Charlie and learns he is a holy man who possesses great powers. Chris also believes that his lawyer is a *Mokural*, a special individual from another tribe, "across the sea from sunrise," who is significant to their beliefs. David consults with Dr. Whitburn, a folklore specialist at the museum. She explains that a *Mokural* is an individual capable of prophetic dreams that occur just before a major apocalypse and the end of a cycle of life.

Another shower arrives, this time with black rain. David seeks out Charlie, who lives in a simple room without furniture. "Sometimes I speak English, sometimes I do not," the holy man says after David arrives. He motions for the lawyer to sit on the floor and repeatedly asks, "Who are you?" David slips into a trance as Charlie starts to hum a chant. Finally, Charlie asks, "Are you a Mokural?" and David whispers, "Yes." Charlie then dismisses him, telling him to go speak in court. David is very pensive as he leaves in his car, and he suddenly has a vision of the city street completely flooded with the bodies of pedestrians floating by, lifeless. When he arrives home, he asks his wife to take the children and leave the city at once. He embraces her, saying is frightened by his latest vision.

At the trial of the Aborigines, David presents his evidence that the men were following tribal law. Chris finds it impossible to talk about secret matters. Charlie is observing the trial, but then he mysteriously vanishes, as if by magic. Chris refuses to testify any further, saying that Billy merely got drunk and died after a fight. The men are found guilty of manslaughter, and David is crushed, feeling he let them down. He visits his stepfather to discuss the mysteries that are troubling him. He is told that the cycle of dreams he had as a small child, leading to the death of his mother, all came true. David returns home, and water seems to be coming in from all sides as a storm whips around the house, breaking windows.

Chris suddenly appears to David, bearing a sacred stone. "I'll take you now," he says. Chris leads David far down into the storm drains beneath Sydney, and they slip through a crevice into a natural cave. The Aborigine reveals that this cave was a sacred place long before the arrival of the white man, and by bringing him here he is breaking the law, but his dream is forcing him to do it. He hands David the sacred stone and says, "Down there you will find what you are looking for." With his flashlight, David descends into a cavern whose walls are covered with symbols and pictographs. Some of these images David has already seen in his dreams. He believes he sees himself in the images, as well as recent events such as the hailstorm and the black rain. He then sees a series of monumental waves portrayed, sweeping everything in its path. Charlie appears in tribal makeup, chanting plaintively. A second native also appears, this one threatening, and then both Aboriginal men vanish. David takes a final look at the walls and then returns to the surface. The door up out of the stormdrain is locked, so David walks to the end of the drain, which emerges at the beach. He kneels at the edge of the water and watches impassively as a giant wave of immense proportions starts to form and prepares to sweep ashore. It is unclear whether this is another vision or reality.

CRITIQUE

This film is a masterpiece of mood and style, although devotees of clear-cut story lines will find it too surreal and impressionistic for their tastes. Like *Picnic at Hanging Rock*, the film can accommodate radically different assessments. The events could be seen as merely the mental collapse of an overworked corporate lawyer. It could be viewed metaphorically as the destruction of the Aboriginal culture by overbearing Western civilization. At the other extreme, the film could portend the destruction of either Sydney, the continent of Australia or all humankind. It is clear the cataclysm that David foresees involves water. Weir brilliant exploits the water motif, both visually and in terms of dialogue, throughout the story. What event could trigger this apocalypse? The picture fails to spell this out, but a large meteor fall is suggested by the sacred stones, which appear identical to certain meteorites well known to astronomers. A strike of considerable size in the ocean south of Australia would no doubt have the capacity to destroy either Sydney, all Australia or the entire world. The myths related by Dr. Whitburn suggest a rebirth, but what if this cataclysm is indeed the "last" wave, the final blow to finish humanity? The Aborigines believe they would continue in the dreamtime and perhaps be transferred back to an earlier golden age of Aboriginal culture. Some lines to this effect near the end of the film suggest that Chris, Charlie and the others believe they have the ability to travel outside of linear time, back to the age when their culture was unchallenged and supreme. However, this option does not exist for David or any of his people.

There is another analytical line that can be explored. David seems to believe that he can disrupt the approaching apocalypse if he wins his case defending Chris and his four companions. If this is true, the Aborigines themselves choose not to prevent the destruction. After Charlie dematerializes from the courtroom, Chris loses heart and refuses to speak further about tribal matters or beliefs, and resorts to the white man's version of events. Both David and Chris seem trapped between two worlds and are linked by their dreams. It is these dreams that permit Chris to lead David to the taboo cave, apparently with Charlie's consent. Charlie is actually investigating David, somewhat surprised that a white man would have the spiritual depth to be a *Mokural*. Dr. Whitburn clearly states that a white man could have the capacity to serve as one, in the judgment of any tribal believer. Yet David, for better or worse, serves as the Cassandra for this apocalypse, suggesting clearly that this cataclysm will entirely obliterate Western civilization. These are just a few avenues of interpretation, and there are many more, which serve to illustrate the richness and scope of the story.

The technical aspects of the film are excellent. The dark, murky cinematography serves to compliment the story. The music, relying on primitive instruments, also advances the special tone and mood of the film. The special effects of the final wave are a little disappointing and artificial, which makes this wave seem to be a vision instead of reality at this point. The shadow that crosses David's face a moment before the appearance of the wave resembles a similar shadow that crossed his face before the vision of the city street underwater. The effects in this scene are genuinely first rate, and subtly suggested by the scene early in the film when David reaches into the overflowing tub and feels toy cars blocking the plug.

Richard Chamberlain is masterful as David, one of the finest roles he was ever offered in feature films. After this point, Chamberlain found a niche in the genre of the television mini-series, where he excelled in such quality productions as

Shogun (1980), *Wallenberg* (1980) and *The Thorn Birds* (1983). David Gulpilil and Nandjiwarra Amagula are compelling and utterly believable in their performances. The other actors make little impression in their roles with the exception of Vivean Gray as Dr. Whitburn, who delivers some of the best lines in the picture with estimable style. Gray was also featured in *Picnic at Hanging Rock* as the teacher who disappeared with the three students. Peter Weir's daughter Ingrid appears briefly as one of David's daughters. Weir himself went on to a solid career of mainstream Hollywood films such as *Witness* (1985), *Dead Poets Society* (1989) and *The Truman Show* (1998), all of which testify to his exceptional talent that was first revealed in films such as *The Last Wave*.

REPRESENTATIVE QUOTES

"A dream is a shadow of something real." (Chris to David while discussing his dream)

"Aborigines believe in two forms of time, two parallel streams of activity. One is the daily object and activity to which you and I are confined. The other is an infinite spiritual cycle called the dreamtime, more real than reality itself. Whatever happens in the dreamtime establishes the values, symbols and laws of Aboriginal society. Some people with unusual spiritual powers have contact with the dreamtime." (Dr. Whitburn to David)

"*Mokural* . . . is the name given to a race of spirits who came from the rising sun bringing sacred objects with them. . . . A *Mokural* has incredible premonitory dreams. They usually appear at the end of a cycle when nature has to renew itself. Primitive culture see life in cycles. Each cycle ends with an apocalypse." (Dr. Whitburn in answer to David's question about the meaning of *Mokural*)

The Last Woman on Earth (1960)

Rating: ** ** Threat: Worldwide oxygen shortage

Filmgroup. Written by Robert Towne Photographed by Jacques Marquette; Edited by Anthony Carras; Music by Ronald Stein; Produced & directed by Roger Corman. B & W, 71 minutes.

ANNOTATED CAST LIST

Antony Carbone (*Harold Gern*, corrupt businessman); Betsy Jones-Moreland (*Evelyn Gern*, Harold's wife who becomes the last woman on Earth); Robert Towne (*Martin Joyce*, Harold's lawyer).

SYNOPSIS

Shot on a shoestring budget in Puerto Rico, this Roger Corman picture manages to provide 71 minutes of modest entertainment. As with most of his efforts, there are flashes of quirky brilliance mixed together with pure schlock and packaged with genuine flair. If you are familiar with Corman, this picture is representative of his usual work. No matter how cheaply made, each film displays enough talent and energy to make it worth watching.

The Last Woman on Earth starts in typical exploitation style with a glamorous nude serving as backdrop to the credits. The story begins at a cockfight arena in Puerto Rico. Harold and Evelyn Gern are vacationing, but Harold's itinerary is proving very boring to his wife. Martin Joyce, Harold's attorney, arrives with news that Gern has been indicted by the federal government for his role in a housing scandal. Gern is more interested in gambling and promises to review the details of the case the following day, after a morning boat excursion for some scuba diving. During the dive, the three explore some wrecks on the sea bed and encounter a manta ray. When they surface, they are unable to breathe the air for some mysterious reason. Continuing to use their airtanks, they return to the ship and find the dead body of Manuel, their pilot. There still is not enough oxygen in the air to breathe, and they switch to their backup tanks. Gern is unable to start the ship's motor, and they go ashore in a row boat. When their tanks empty, they almost pass out while moving through the jungle. With typical B-movie logic, Harold then lights up a cigarette, and Martin remarks that the oxygen must have returned since his match was able to ignite. He guesses that the plants are renewing the oxygen supply.

When they reach town, they see a number of bodies, all dead of suffocation. After they return to their hotel, Martin tries in vain to make a phone call. They come to the conclusion that some catastrophic event temporarily disrupted the oxygen supply—either an act of God or an unknown weapon. The odor from the bodies would soon make it impossible to remain in town, and Gern suggests they withdraw to his friend's villa at the tip of the island and consider their plans. They fill a truck with supplies and head to the house as their new base of operations.

The next day, the impact of these momentous events push Evelyn and Martin into a stupor, and they believe they are the last people on earth. Gern, however, seemed stimulated by the enormous challenge. He begins to worry that the insect population may explode beyond control from feeding off the dead bodies of animals and people. They may eventually need to go north to Canada to avoid tropical disease. They will need to learn to navigate and fish. They can also carry out a search for other survivors. Harold's strategy helps focus the others, and they begin to make systematic plans. Gern also begins to monitor the radio regularly to check for any signs of human activity.

Later, Gern warns his former lawyer that the "two men, one woman situation" is dangerous, and Martin will just have to learn to live with it. Martin finds the body of a woman washed up on the beach. Both he and Evelyn become increasingly resentful of Gern's authoritarian manner. The days drag by, and Evelyn and Martin spend one afternoon together while Gern is fishing. They wonder if they will both be alive ten years from now. Martin teaches her some Lewis Carroll verse, and Evelyn starts a playful fight, throwing sand at Martin. Eventually, the couple embrace. When Gern returns from fishing, he notices a distinct change in their demeanor.

The next time the two men go fishing, they start to quarrel. After Gern strikes Martin, an all-out fight develops. They fall out of the rowboat and continue flailing away until they reach the shore. After hitting Martin on the side of his head with a shell, Harold orders him to leave the villa. Evelyn is upset and, after arguing with her husband, decides to leave with Martin. They take a car, but they drive into a tree when Evelyn sees a body in the road. Gern follows them in a truck. Now on foot, Martin leaves Evelyn at a church, and decides to confront Harold. The men resume their battle, eventually ending up in the old Spanish fortress overlooking the harbor. Gern easily gets the better of the mild-mannered lawyer. After his beating, Martin stumbles back to the church, but the blows to his head have caused him to go blind. Following him, Gern is moved by Martin's declaration that anything they do now is entirely futile. Martin dies in Evelyn's arms. Somberly, Gern escorts his wife out of the church. He makes some trite remark asking her help to decide if they, or the human race, have any future left.

CRITIQUE

This colorful and diverting product was conceived after the success of *The World, the Flesh and the Devil* (1959), which presented the similar story of two men and one woman as the last survivors on earth. The background story behind the Corman film, however, is far more inventive than any of the actual footage on the screen. The picture was largely developed as it was being filmed. Roger Corman commissioned the screenplay from Robert Towne, but the writer worked so slowly that his script was not ready. The only way Roger could afford to bring Towne along to Puerto Rico was to have him assume one of the three major parts in the film, that of Martin Joyce. Towne agreed, and performed the role under the pseudonym of Edward Wain. Roger and his crew resided at the Caribe Hilton Hotel, which they also used for scenes in the film. He also rented a waterfront villa for the other scenes in the picture. Towne worked night and day to provide the dialogue, which at times is highly poetic. Roger produced an additional film, *Battle of Blood Island,* while Towne continued to write and scout locations. Then, after completing *Last Woman on Earth*, Corman improvised a new third film, which he called *Creature from the Haunted Sea*. He drafted the cast of *Last Woman on Earth* for this additional film, and eventually the budget-conscious Corman wound up finishing the three films in five weeks.

The major weak point of the picture is the unexplained premise for the dissipation of the oxygen in the atmosphere. There is some speculation that it may have been the unintended result of a nuclear attack or some natural disaster, but that idea is disposed of quickly. In reality, there would be many more survivors if the oxygen supply on earth were displaced for an hour. All crews aboard submarines or flying in pressurized aircraft would survive, as would anyone else who had access to an oxygen tank. No effort at all is expended to justify this scenario, and without this background, the events in the picture lack a foundation. Another oddity of the story is that both men are shallow, unlikable characters. Harold Gern is a self-centered and arrogant figure, who sees the people around him as mere objects for his use. But as offensive as Gern is, he still is a thinking individual who is trying to work things out. He is motivated, while Martin Joyce becomes a pure nihilist. When Evelyn decides to leave with him, he coldly rejects her idea of having children, which is also a rejection of the human race. He is an impersonal, empty shell of a man, lacking in any positive ideas whatsoever. His only redeeming features are his wayward sense of humor and his fondness for quoting silly bits of poetry. This leaves Evelyn as the only sympathetic character, and it is doubtful by the end of the plot if she will be able to continue to live with her husband, even if he is the last man on earth. The conclusion of the story is a depressing, another unusual development for Corman, because there seems to be no possible future for Harold and Evelyn. The performances by the cast are adequate, but not exceptional. The heroine, Betsy Jones-Moreland, is appealing as the last woman. After this picture, she had a minimal acting career and only found a niche for herself as the courtroom judge in a series of Perry Mason telefilms in the early 1990s. Antony Carbone gives a straightforward reading, and his character is believable. Robert Towne, drafted into the role of Martin Joyce, performs well, but it is interesting to speculate what a more polished actor could have done with this part. Towne went on to become a major screenwriting talent, capturing an Academy Award for his screenplay for *Chinatown* (1974). He also worked uncredited on the script for another apocalyptic film, *Armageddon* (1998).

Other contributors to the film did excellent work. The cinematography of Jack Marquette is exceptional. The framing of the final visuals in the church is breathtaking. The music of Ron Stein is particularly strong, especially in the last ten minutes of the film, where action dominates. In summary, this film is enjoyable, but it somehow lacks the funky and wayward charm of some of Corman's other efforts. This may be partially due by the limited cast which fails to present any picturesque cameos by Corman stalwarts such as Dick Miller, Bruno Ve Sota or Jonathan Haze. This missing factor weakens the offbeat flavor of the film, one of the usual strong points in Corman's usual work.

REPRESENTATIVE QUOTES

"Maybe we can go back to New York?" (Martin's suggestion) "And see seven million bodies stinking up the streets? No thanks." (Harold's reply)

"All right, we're in a rotten situation, an unprecedented one. But I am not going to fall apart, and neither is anyone else as long as I can help it." (Harold to his wife)

"Your marriage certificate means about as much here as your money." (Martin to Gern discussing Evelyn)

Lifeforce (1985)

Rating: ****   **Threat: Alien vampires**

Cannon. Written by Don Jakoby & Dan O'Bannon based on the novel *The Space Vampires* by Colin Wilson; Photographed by Alan Hume; Special effects by John Dykstra & Robert Shepherd; Edited by John Grover; Music by Henry Mancini & Michael Kamen; Produced by Yoram Globus & Menahem Golan; Directed by Tobe Hooper. Original version, 116 minutes; U.S. version, 106 minutes.

ANNOTATED CAST LIST

Steve Railsback (*Tom Carlsen*, American astronaut and the only survivor from the *Churchill*); Peter Firth (*Col. Colin Caine*, British security officer in charge of the case); Frank Finlay (*Hans Fallada*, professor of biochemistry); Mathilda May (female space vampire); Christopher Jagger, Bill Malin (male space vampires); Patrick Stewart (*Dr. Armstrong*, director of Thurlstone Asylum); Michael Gothard (*Dr. Bukovsky*, head of European Research Center); Nancy Paul (*Ellen Donaldson*, woman possessed by the space vampire); Aubrey Morris (*Sir Percy Hazeltine*, British home secretary); Peter Porteous (British prime minister); Katherine Schofield (*Miss Haversham*, secretary to prime minister); John Keegan (security guard and first revived victim); Jerome Willis (pathologist attacked by revived guard); Derek Benfield (physician); John Woodnutt (metallurgist); James Forbes-Robertson (minister); Owen Holder (scientist); John Hallam (*Lamson*, asylum orderly); Nicholas Ball (*Derebridge*, Carlsen's friend aboard the *Churchill*); Jamie Roberts (*Rawlings*, *Churchill* radio officer); Russell Sommers (*Churchill* navigation officer); Patrick Connor, Sidney Kean, Paul Cooper (guards); Chris Sullivan (*Kelly*, Caine's aide); Milton Cadman, Rupert Baker (soldiers); Gary Hildreth (police surgeon); Nicholas Donnelly (police inspector); Peter Louistrom, Julian Firth (witnesses in park); Carl Rigg, Elizabeth Morgan (radio technicians); Geoffrey Frederick (*Churchill* communications officer); Richard Oldfield (*Churchill* commander); Christopher Barr (*Churchill* trajectory officer); David English, Emma Jacobs, Michael John Paliotti, Brian Carroll (*Churchill* crew members); Burnell Tucker, Thom Booker, Michael Fitzpatrick (NASA officials); Richard Sharpe (rescue ship crewman); John Golightly (colonel); William Lindsay (His aide); Sydney Livingstone (*Ned Price*, white Volvo driver); Ken Parry (*Jeffrey Sykes*, mental patient); John Edmunds (BBC broadcaster); Haydn Wood (helicopter pilot).

SYNOPSIS

This frenetic picture takes the audience on a wild roller coaster ride through various genres before settling down into the apocalyptic mode. Director Tobe Hooper, who launched his career with *The Texas Chainsaw Massacre* (1974), is noted for his hard-edged and sometimes violent films. *Lifeforce*, although containing a few bloody sequences, is far closer to an art film than a splatter film. It is a brilliant but eccentric adaptation of Colin Wilson's novel *The Space Vampires*, and for audience members who can keep pace with the film's feverish plot, a rewarding viewing experience.

The story opens in deep space aboard the space shuttle *Churchill*, an Anglo-American joint venture named after Sir Winston Churchill, the illustrious British prime minister whose mother was American. As the shuttle nears Haley's comet to collect scientific data, the astronauts are startled to discover an alien space vessel two miles long hidden in the head of the comet. Since communication with Earth is impossible, the mission commander orders that this spacecraft be explored. The astronauts discover that this derelict ship is carrying thousands of dead aliens, bat-like creatures in various states of decay. The startling thing is that three human figures, two men and one woman, are located, apparently in suspended animation, positioned in transparent plastic modules. They decide to remove these three units back to the *Churchill*.

Several months later, the *Churchill* has resumed orbiting Earth but fails to communicate with Mission Control. *Columbia* rendezvous with the shuttle and finds it derelict, the interior ravaged by fire. The three hibernating bodies, however, are unharmed, and *Columbia* brings them back to Earth, depositing them at the European Research Center in London. When a guard touches the body of the woman, her eyes open and she embraces the man. As she kisses him, his energy drains away and he collapses, totally desiccated. Dr. Bukovsky, head of the project, watches in amazement, as the woman, totally nude, smiles and reaches out to him. Professor Fallada arrives, finding Bukovsky weakened and unable to stand. The vampire woman next attacks the guards in the lobby, sweeping them aside with a wave of her arm, and escapes into the streets of London.

Colonel Caine of the Special Air Service is assigned to the case. Fallada warns him that the woman is an alien life form, a type of vampire capable of draining the lifeforce from her victims. The two male vampires also revive, but the guards fire machine guns at them and the aliens are apparently destroyed. The guard killed by the woman revives during his autopsy and drains the lifeforce from one of the doctors. Fallada orders the guard and his victim to be placed isolation cells. Fallada theorizes that the victims revive and become predators in two-hour cycles, a dangerous pattern which could quickly get out of control. Caine notifies Sir Percy Hazeltine, the British home secretary, about the emergency. After two hours, the guard and his victim both die, after undergoing seizures during which they desperately tried to reach out for other victims. Their bodies disintegrate into dust, and the home secretary arrives in time to witness their bizarre destruction. Caine is informed that another casualty of the space vampire, a woman, has been discovered in Hyde Park. Her body is strapped to a table, and it also revives after two hours. Unable to secure a victim, the revived corpse explodes. Fallada concludes, "Within days, we could all be doomed."

The escape pod from the *Churchill* lands in Texas, and the surviving astronaut, Colonel Tom Carlsen, is brought to London to help with the crisis. The astronaut recounts how the *Churchill* discovered the bodies and how the crew began to die one by one on the journey home, all drained of life. He tried to burn the *Churchill* so Earth would not be exposed to their infection, and he ejected in the escape pod. He concluded that he must have been bewitched by the queen vampire, who killed all his friends, but he found it almost impossible to leave her. That night, the woman visits Carlsen in his dreams and he discovers there is still a bond between them. Meanwhile, NASA learns that the alien spacecraft described by Carlsen has left Haley's comet and is now approaching Earth.

Fallada hypnotizes Carlsen to see if he can provide a clue to the queen vampire's current whereabouts. They learn that she has the power to transfer from body to body. She is now in the body of Ellen Donaldson, a hitchhiker. A man driving a white Volvo gives her a lift, and she drains the life from him, but not enough to kill him. Caine tracks the man down through the license number, revealed by Carlsen under hypnosis. They discover that Ellen is a nurse at Thurlstone Asylum for the Criminally Insane. Caine heads there at once with Sir Percy and Carlsen, and they interview the director, Dr. Armstrong. Carlsen meets with Ellen and determines that she is no longer the vampire's host. They ask Dr. Armstrong to take them to the cell of one of the inmates, a notorious child murderer. A tranquilizer shot is prepared, but on reaching the cell, Caine injects Dr. Armstrong instead, since Carlsen sensed that he is the current host. Under influence of the drug, the vampire speaks and tells Carlsen that she took her human shape from his concept of the ideal woman in his subconscious mind. He also learns that the two male vampires were not killed, but merely transferred their essence to the security guards. When the vampire queen tries to emerge from Armstrong's body, objects levitate and swirl around the room, and Sir Percy is killed.

A chain reaction of victims initiated by the other two vampires has started to spread across London. Caine and Carlsen fly back to the city by helicopter. They radio Fallada and learn that he has killed one of the vampires who attacked him in the guise of a soldier. Fallada employed "the old way," with a metal stake piercing through the energy center just below the heart. The female vampire finally escapes from Armstrong's body and is free once again. Carlsen admits to Caine that it was he who first awakened the queen vampire on the *Churchill*, and that she shared some of her lifeforce with him so that he could survive the return journey. He says the vampire ship had traveled to numerous worlds which they totally destroyed, and Earth is their next target.

A radio bulletin reports that London is in a frenzy, and much of the city is in flames. The number of victims of the space vampire disease is increasing by the hour. Caine goes immediately to see the prime minister, but discovers the leader himself is affected when Caine oversees him draining the life from his executive secretary. Returning to the helicopter, Caine and Carlsen escape and land at an unaffected NATO military base. Here they learn that the "sterilization" of London by nuclear bombs is being considered to stop the vampire plague. The alien spacecraft has assumed a position in the skies directly over London. A beam of light containing the lifeforce of thousands of victims is being focused upward from the city to the ship. Carlsen believes that only the queen vampire can do this because she must project this beam through her original body. Also, she is summoning him, wanting back the lifeforce she shared with him.

After Carlsen leaves, compelled to answer her summons, Caine follows by car in a desperate attempt to destroy her. The streets of London are like a living nightmare, with people running about wildly, chased by ravenous, infected beings. The origin of the beam of light is St. Paul's Cathedral, where the vampire's original body has been revived along with her essence. At the European Research Center, Caine encounters Fallada, who is now infected. He kills Fallada and takes an ornamental sword from his office to use as a weapon. Caine struggles through the raging mobs to reach the location where he encounters the remaining male vampire. He runs him through with the sword, and the creature reverts to his true appearance, a giant, winged bat, before dying. In the next chamber, Carlsen and the vampire are embracing in the base of the glowing beam. Caine hands Carlsen the sword, and he impales both himself and the queen vampire with it. They disintegrate into light, and the beam vanishes upward toward the alien spacecraft. The ship turns around and flies back to Haley's comet as the end credits roll.

CRITIQUE

Mixing various genres, *Lifeforce* gathers steam as it proceeds, and the climax is remarkably intense. The nighttime shots of London going mad call to mind images from the paintings of Hieronymus Bosch. It is a remarkable portrayal of pandemonium. These scenes alone make the picture a directorial triumph for Tobe Hooper. The other technical achievements in the film are praiseworthy, including the taut editing and moody cinematography. The musical score by Henry Mancini is thrilling, and quite unlike his other work. Michael Kamen, who later developed into a major screen composer, composed some alternate cues used only in the American print. The special effects are commendable, and while not state-of-the-art, they have a vibrant imagination. The alien spacecraft, for example, is ingenious, and foreshadows the magnificent Vorlon ships depicted in *Babylon Five*. The giant bat-like creature revealed when the male vampire is impaled with the sword is another exceptional moment and a powerful image.

There are some weaknesses as well. The scientific technology is too advanced for a picture set in the near future. The mission is portrayed as a British/American joint venture, but the British are depicted as the senior partners, an unlikely scenario. The ending is too abrupt, although the open-ended fate of Carlsen and the vampire is well conceived. The script does leave a number of dangling loose ends throughout the plot. Some of this is due to Colin Wilson's original novel, but the film prefers to leave things murky rather than clear. We know that the vampires have wiped out other planets and civilizations, but they have also visited Earth before. Why was the planet not destroyed at that time? The relationship between Carlsen and the queen vampire is a major theme of the story, but it seems to go through various phases that do not clearly mesh. The events of the disastrous home voyage of the *Churchill* are never rendered understandable, and this segment could have been improved. Another shortcoming is that the cast is weak overall. Only Frank Finlay and Patrick Stewart really deliver excellent performances. Finlay's role calls to mind his decisive performance as Dr. Van Helsing in the PBS version of *Dracula* with Louis Jourdan. Stewart shows exceptional charisma, and this film may have been an important factor in his selection to play Jean-Luc Picard in the series *Star Trek: The Next Generation,* which went into production in 1987. Steve Railsback fails to ignite much interest as Tom Carlsen. Peter Firth also makes little impression and is far too bland as Caine. French actress Mathilda May is gorgeous as the queen vampire, and she appears nude during the entire production. She is unable, however, to fully captivate the audience when compared to Nancy Paul as Ellen, who is possessed by the vampire midway through the story. Other performers, such as Aubrey Morris who plays the home secretary, are simply wrong for their parts. None of these performances actually hurt the picture, but they represent a missed opportunity. The original print, available on video, runs 116 minutes. The version originally released to theaters in the United States was shorter, with some graphic violence and erotic scenes of the naked queen vampire edited. *Lifeforce* garnered both enthusiastic and mixed reviews, and a number of critics found the characters distant. Some of this distance was no doubt deliberate, since a number of the main characters act as if they are in a stupor. Since the life had been drained from some of them, this seems to reflect the situation quite well. This also is in contrast to the energy level of the picture itself, which is dynamic and spirited. Overall, *Lifeforce* is too unorthodox for most tastes, yet its dramatic, apocalyptical vision of London in its death throes is a unique and unforgettable vision seldom equaled on the screen.

REPRESENTATIVE QUOTES

"Our viewers may be interested to know that comets were once considered to be harbingers of evil, and that one of the earliest words for comet was disaster, which in Latin means evil star." (London newscaster)

"It is my belief that the vampires of legend came from creatures such as these, perhaps even from these very creatures." (Dr. Fallada to Caine and Carlsen)

"It was always intended that you should find us and bring us to Earth. The web of destiny carries your blood and soul back to the genesis of my life form. Come. Be with me." (The queen vampire to Carlsen at St. Paul's Cathedral)

DAILY PLANET SPECIAL

★★★★

PLANET, Inc.

Vol. 15 No. 16   Emergency Number   EN ROUTE BY TRUCK   4 Pages

DELUGE Hits NEW YORK

(Story on Page TWO)

EXTRA

(BULLETIN:) **Prof. Carlysle of the National Broadcast Forecasting Laboratory now concedes earth will perish!!!**

WORLD DOOMED

OCEAN IN FURY OVERWHELMS ONCE SUPREME CITY!

(Photograph from Airplane by *DAILY PLANET'S* Staff Photographer)

Mock newspaper headline announces the end of the world in *Deluge*.

The Statue of Liberty gets swept away by a tidal wave in *Deluge.*

Vincent Price faces life as the only human in a world of vampires in *Last Man on Earth*.

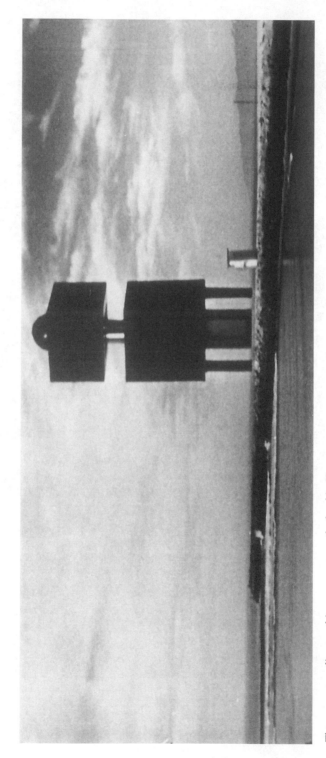

The enormous alien machine sweeps over the land in *Kronos*.

George O'Hanlon, Barbara Lawrence, and Jeff Morrow inspect Kronos after landing atop the giant device.

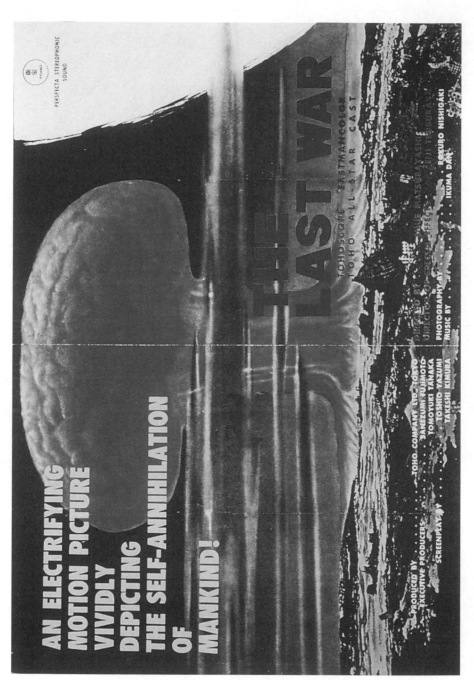

Lobby card for the Japanese apocalyptic thriller *The Last War*.

The imaginative alien spacecraft of the space vampires in *Lifeforce*.

Robert Loggia, dying from exposure to radiation, configures the atomic warhead in the rocket capsule in the climax of *The Lost Missile*. Note Loggia's autograph.

Lobby card for *The Magnetic Monster*, one of the cleverest apocalyptic thrillers of the Fifties.

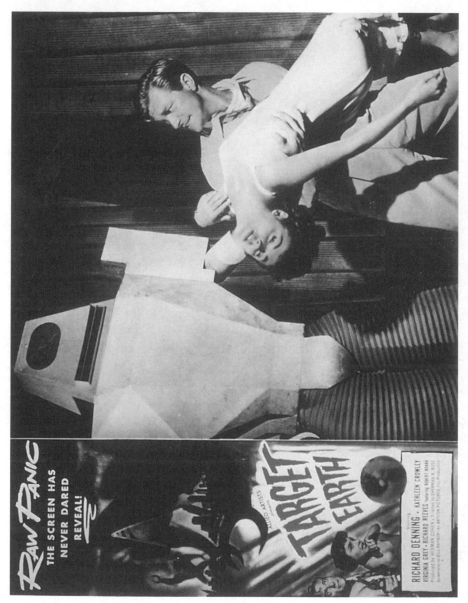

Ludicrous design for the invading robots dispel the screen magic created during the first half of *Target Earth.*

Peter Lorre as Commodore Emory in *Voyage to the Bottom of the Sea*. After Lorre's death, his character was not replaced when the show was developed into a TV series.

New York as portrayed in the post-apocalyptic film *Captive Women.*

Them!

Robot Monster.

The Lost Missile (1958)

Rating: *   **Threat: Heat from a runaway missile**

United Artists. Written by John McPartland & Jerome Bixby based on a story by Lester William Berke; Photographed by Kenneth Peach; Special effects by Jack R. Glass; Edited by Everett Sutherland; Music by Gerald Fried; Produced by Lee Gordon & William Berke; Directed by William Berke & Lester William Berke. B & W, 70 minutes.

ANNOTATED CAST LIST

Robert Loggia (*Dr. David Loring*, Havenbrook scientist); Ellen Parker (*Joan Woods*, his assistant and fiancée); Phillip Pine (*Dr. Joe Freed*, Havenbrook scientist); Marilee Earle (*Ella*, Joe's pregnant wife); Kitty Kelly (Ella's mother); Larry Kerr (*Gen. Barr*, head of Havenbrook Nuclear Laboratory); Bill Bradley (*Bill Bradley*, television announcer); Selmer Jackson (U.S. secretary of state); Thomas E. Jackson (mayor of New York City); J. Anthony Hughes (governor of New York); Fred Engelberg (TV folk singer); Joe Hyams (*Young*, reporter); Peggy Stewart (mother outside schoolbus); Stanley Fafara (blond student in schoolbus); Lawrence Dobkin (narrator); Hari Rhodes, Robert Busch, Myron Cook, Mark Dunhill, Cecil Elliott, Viola Harris, Jack Holland, John McNamara, Don Pethley, Shirley Shawn, Mike Steele.

SYNOPSIS

This poverty row-film had a novel viewpoint, depicting a mysterious, runaway missile from outer space that posed an unintended threat to humankind. Unfortunately, the fifty-five-year-old producer and director of the film, William Berke, had a heart attack and died during the first day of production, a tragic development from which the film never recovered. His son, Lester William Berke, upon whose idea the film was based, stepped in to complete the shooting, which only lasted a week. The end product seemed more like a minimalist sketch of a motion picture than a legitimate film, but since the underlying concept is so unique, *The Lost Missile* does have moments of genuine interest, even if much of its potential is unrealized.

The opening credits show a missile from deep space approaching the earth. It comes in over the Soviet Union, and an explosion from one of their defensive missiles knocks it into a perpetual orbit. At first, the Soviets plan to launch an attack on America, suspecting the missile is of American origin, but data from their computer reveals that the missile is actually of extraterrestrial origin. Since the missile projects enormous temperatures in its wake, it scorches and destroys everything below as it passes. All life will be eliminated as the missile's shifting orbit will eventually reach every part of the earth, down to the very last acre, leaving nothing but charred and smoldering ruins.

Havenbrook Atomic Laboratory in suburban New York (presumably Long Island) is the military's top nuclear research center. One of their projects is Jove, a solid fuel rocket built to carry a nuclear warhead; it is the mightiest weapon in the world, but as yet incomplete. Dr. David Loring is responsible for designing and finishing work on the hydrogen warhead. That day, David is planning to marry his assistant, Joan Woods, during a mid-day break from their work. Their intended best man, Dr. Joe Freed, says he is unable to get away to make their ceremony since the military is pressuring them to complete Jove as soon as possible. Joe's wife is also expecting a baby at any time, and he wants to stay by the phone. David and Joan rush off before they encounter any further delays.

Continental Air Defense Command (CONAD) detects the approach of the missile in Alaska. They send a jet to intercept the UFO as it nears the DEW (Distant Early Warning) radar line. They determine the strange missile is traveling over 4,000 miles per hour with a heat blast in its wake approaching a million degrees Fahrenheit. (The temperature of the interior of the sun is estimated to be 27 million degrees.) Nothing can approach the missile without melting, and weapons fired at it disintegrate in the heat.

Joan fusses over her selection of a ring at a jewelry counter. The design she chooses will take several hours to be properly sized, and she and David quarrel about the time away from the lab. Joan walks away, saying the wedding is off. When David returns to Havenbrook, he is summoned by General Barr to an urgent meeting of the entire staff, where they are shown a picture of the lost missile. David says the structure of the craft is beyond all known design, employing a hydrogen motor. He says it probably has a high-order magnetic field that protects the missile itself from the heat. Barr orders the staff to evacuate at once to safety in special transport crafts. With Joan's help, Dr. Freed attempts to call his wife, but Joan is able to speak with her for only a few seconds before the telephone line is cut off.

The Joint Chiefs of Staff meet to review the known facts and advise the president. The present course of the runaway missile will bring it over Ottawa, Canada in fifty-seven minutes and New York City seven minutes later. An evacuation of the city is ordered immediately, with a priority to the transporting of all school children to safe zones. The Soviet premier calls the president to inform him that the origin of the missile is completely unknown. The secretary of state cancels his press conference, and Young, a television reporter who wants to spread a doomsday alarm, is urged only to report news that is officially authorized. A series of vignettes portray how average people learn about the threat from neighbors, friends and civil defense.

David tells General Barr that he could prepare a mini-hydrogen warhead in twenty minutes and implant it in the Jove rocket, the only device capable of enough speed to withstand the heat of the lost missile. Barr agrees it is their only chance to save the world. Barr gives Joe Freed clearance to go to his wife, and the scientist suggests that the missile may contain passengers from outer space who are attempting to visit Earth.

Ottawa is placed on red alert and all citizens scatter into fallout shelters. Canadian planes attack the missile and are destroyed. The governor of New York makes an emergency broadcast declaring martial law. David assembles the warhead and inserts the plutonium in a protected chamber using robot arms. David, Joan and the warhead travel to the Jove launching site in a two-jeep convoy. While traveling, David and Joan debate the origins of the lost missile. If his calculations are correct, David says, Jove will rendezvous with the alien rocket over Lake Champlain. The second jeep gets into an accident with a white convertible, but General Barr signals for David not to stop and help the injured. Joe's wife, Ella, heads to the basement of her apartment building where her neighbors have gathered. She gives birth while reclining on a cot. Joe Freed finally arrives and comforts his wife, hoping that his newborn son will have more than just a few minutes of life.

Four miles from the missile base, a juvenile gang blocks the road, overpowers David and Joan, and steals their jeep. Another driver gives them a lift, and they find the jeep a mile down the road. The gang had opened the metal case in the back seat, exposing the plutonium, which killed them instantly. David, using his jacket as a shield, puts the cover back on the metal case, but in doing so he absorbs a fatal dose of radiation. He warns Joan to keep back and drives the jeep to the base.

The missile passes over Ottawa, totally incinerating the city and leaving no survivors. David drives up next to the rocket and boards a cherrypicker, which lifts him to the top of Jove so he can insert the hydrogen warhead. The countdown is at three minutes to zero as David positions the warhead inside the capsule atop the rocket. He closes the hatch and collapses, his body sprawled on the descending cherrypicker. Jove launches, and the picture ends with a nuclear blast over Lake Champlain. The all-clear-signal sounds in New York City as the film comes to an abrupt close.

CRITIQUE

The Lost Missile derives over half its length from military and Civil Defense training footage, so the film is a patchwork quilt stitched together by almost non-stop narration. Yet at the end of the picture, the narrator is silent, and the hurried finale leaves a considerable number of questions and issues unresolved. No doubt William Berke would have brought in a tauter, more coherent film. Berke was a credible director of over seventy films, including *Minesweeper* (1943), *Dick Tracy, Detective* (1945), *Jungle Jim* (1948) and *Cop Hater* (1957), an exceptional film noir. His son, Lester William Berke, appeared as Baby Lester in *Gun Grit* (1936), one of his father's first films. Lester apparently lacked his father's flair, and *The Lost Missile* was his only directorial effort. As it stands, the picture could have been modestly successful if it were not for the brush-off ending. None of the other technical personnel is deserving of any praise with the exception of composer Gerald Fried, who always delivered a good, effective musical score. The script is largely to blame for the most disappointing aspects of the film, along with the second-rate direction by Berke's son, Lester.

The audience is never provided with any meaningful clues to the purpose or intent behind the lost missile. Was it an interstellar probe sending greetings from a distant civilization or a lost weapon from a distant interplanetary war that blundered into Earth by accident? It might also be from another dimension, an experiment from the future sent back through time, a crippled space craft or any of a dozen other possibilities. The script of the film remains silent, with only Dr. Freed briefly raising the last possibility as an afterthought. The entire production is considerably weakened by the script's refusal to indicate any of the options. What would have occurred if the Soviet rocket did not knock the missile into orbit? Would it have exploded, destroying the earth, or could it have been programed to land? The basic tenet is not bad, but without any follow-through, the idea is basically hollow. Other elements of the story are rather foolish. Can one imagine an evacuation of the entire school population in New York City being accomplished in sixty-three minutes, from the conception of the idea to complete execution? It is a logistical impossibility! Then how long would it take for the heat trail left by the missile to destroy the world? The film suggests a few days, but with a path of destruction only five miles wide, this would indeed require much more time. Since its orbit is also random, there is little doubt that much of the globe would remain unaffected, especially since the missile's path never seems to dip below the equator. Finally, the workaholic madness of the Havenbrook Lab is truly berserk. These scientists would have cracked under the unending pressure, which is displayed long before the threat of the missile becomes a factor.

There are also a few surprisingly good points to the story. The final chase to the missile base is fairly exciting, even if the scenery fails to correspond in any way to the greater New York area. Having some punks steal the jeep and explore the container with the warhead is an interesting development. This twist forces David to sacrifice his life to save the world. Very seldom in 1950s films does a leading man lose his life in such a credible manner. In fact, the entire subplot of David and Joan's romance works very well, perhaps due to the capable acting of Robert Loggia and Ellen Parker. Their performances are straightforward and sincere. The timing of some of their dialogue is unintentionally hilarious. Loggia fondles an oversize model of Jove when discussing his marriage plans with Joan, a wonderful visual absurdity. Robert Loggia was discovered by Berke for the lead in *Cop Hater*, and his career later blossomed in such films as *Jagged Edge* (1985), *Prizzi's Honor* (1985) and *Independence Day* (1996). Ellen Parker is equally fine, even while wearing an outlandish hat as she hunts for a wedding ring. Her finest scene, a heartfelt moment, occurs after Loggia drives away in the jeep after receiving a radiation overdose. It is a sublime moment for Parker, one a lesser actress might have overplayed. Veteran Selmer Jackson has a nice vignette as the secretaryof state. Phillip Pine is excellent in the part of Joe Freed, the close friend of David and Joan. A veteran actor, Pine never landed a role that brought him any real recognition, although *Star Trek* fans always remember him as the treacherous Colonel Green in "The Savage Curtain," the Abraham Lincoln episode from the original *Star Trek* series. Most of the large cast is difficult to identify since there are so many brief vignettes in the film. One character, Bill Bradley, was a little know TV broadcaster, unrelated to the well known basketball star and senator.

REPRESENTATIVE QUOTES

"The world is one minute away from the start of a hydrogen war. At 12:01 North Europe Time, a blazing, unidentified missile-like object appears on a foreign sky search TV screen, origin unknown. Countdown on their Hunter-type rocket . . . this rocket is designed to track, find, destroy. The terrible object has been diverted into an orbit by the explosion. It streaks across the northern curve of the Earth at an altitude of only five miles. A wild missile loose on the surface of the Earth burning a track five miles wide below it." (Opening narration)

"I'd rather have a wedding than lunch any day." (Joan to David Loring, when he suggests waiting to have a traditional ceremony)

"We decide to miss lunch and get married, fine, but all you can think about is a hydrogen warhead." (Joan to David, calling off their wedding)

"The monster will not fall. It will go on and on until the entire Earth is burned off like an apple being pealed. It will be over Great Britain on its 14th revolution. That means in three days London will be in ashes; Stockholm, one day; Paris, one day; Rome, two days; Moscow, four days." (Narration describing the future if Jove fails)

The Magnetic Monster   (1953)
AKA *Crack of Doom*
Rating: ****   Threat: Orbital shift

United Artists. Written by Curt Siodmak & Ivan Tors; Photographed by Charles Van Enger; Special effects by Harry Redmond Jr. & Jack Glass; Edited by Herbert L. Strock; Music by Blaine Sanford; Produced by Ivan Tors & George Van Marter; Directed by Curt Siodmak. B & W, 76 minutes.

ANNOTATED CAST LIST

Richard Carlson (*Jeff Stewart*, research specialist at OSI); Jean Byron (*Connie Stewart*, his wife); King Donovan (*Dan Forbes*, OSI investigator); Harry Ellerbe (*Dr. Allard*, director of OSI); Leo Britt (*Dr. Benton*, developer of the Deltatron); Leonard Mudie (*Howard Denker*, scientist who creates the new element); Byron Foulger (*Simon*, hardware store owner); Michael Fox (*Dr. Serny*, state university scientist); Jarma Lewis (stewardess); John Zaremba (*Watson*, chief engineer of LA Power and Light); Frank Gerstle (*Col. Willis*, army liaison to OSI); John Vosper (*Captain Dyer*, Department of Civilian Defense official); William Benedict (*Albert*, hardware store employee); Elizabeth Root (*Joy*, hardware store employee); Kathleen Freeman (*Nellie*, OSI switchboard operator); Lee Phelps (city engineer); Roy Engle (general); Watson Downs (Los Angeles mayor); John Dodsworth (*Cartwright*, operator of the Deltatron); Charlie Williams (Cab driver); Michael Granger (*Kenneth Smith*, Los Angeles Airport manager); Douglas Evans (pilot); Strother Martin (co-pilot); Juney Ellis (hay fever sufferer on airplane).

SYNOPSIS

This intelligent entry was conceived by Curt Siodmak, screenwriter of numerous genre films such as *I Walked with a Zombie* (1943) and *The Beast with Five Fingers* (1946) and brother of noted director Robert Siodmak. Both launched their film careers in their native Germany, and Curt decided to tailor his screenplay around a few minutes of remarkable footage from *Gold* (1933), a German feature with Hans Albers and Brigitte Helm. These scenes center on a huge, fantastic, electronic contraption that bombards base metal and turns it into gold. This machine crackles, shoots huge bolts of electricity and eventually explodes. The film also has a number of impressive crowd scenes of factory workers and a futuristic subway car. Together with the Hungarian writer and producer Ivan Tors (who later created *Sea Hunt* and *Flipper*), Siodmak expertly wove this impressive footage into a riveting climax for *The Magnetic Monster*. For the backstory, they conjured up the most imaginative "monster" ever developed, a new, unstable element that doubles in size every eleven hours and creates a powerful magnetic field. Eventually this monster will cause the earth itself to spiral out of orbit and doom all life. *The Magnet Monster*, Curt Siodmak's second directorial effort, was an imaginative accomplishment that he never again equaled.

The story opens with narration by Richard Carlson as protagonist Dr. Jeff Stewart, a key member of a new government agency called the Office of Scientific Investigation (OSI). This group was created to explore phenomena that might threaten public safety. One morning, Jeff and his friend Dan Forbes are assigned to investigate Simon's Hardware Store in Los Angeles, which reports that the entire store seems plagued by an inexplicable magnetic force. With a Geiger counter, they determine that the epicenter of the problem emanates from the apartment above the store. They suit up in special protective clothing and explore the upstairs. The rooms, converted into an electronics lab by a scientist named Denker, are filled with high levels of radiation. They also find a dead body and an empty, lead-lined cylinder normally used to transport isotopes. Whatever element that caused the magnetism and radiation has been moved, and Jeff contacts the police to alert them about the danger.

Radio bulletins alert the public to report any unusual magnetism they might encounter. OSI submits trace elements from beneath the fingernails of the corpse to their master computer to identify the element. But the Mathematical Analyzing Numerical Integrator and Computer (MANIAC) only reveals that the element is completely unknown. A cab driver calls to describe how his taxi conked out at the airport after he dropped off an elderly man carrying an odd briefcase. Jeff and Dan rush to the airport to warn the manager about the danger to any aircraft transporting the mystery element. Dan, using a Geiger counter, tries to discover a clue about which flight is carrying the element. A flight insurance vending machine tests positive, and the flight is identified on a receipt Denker signed. Then the flight is contacted to return at once. Jeff predicts the element will interfere with the plane's engines. He instructs the pilot by radio to place the briefcase as far back toward the tail as possible. One engine fails, but the plane manages to land.

Denker has become seriously ill due to radiation sickness. As he lapses into unconsciousness, the old scientist explains how he created the unstable element, by bombarding a harmless sample of a rare substance called serenium with alpha particles for 200 hours. The new element has become unipolar, which accounts for its magnetism, and it needs to be continually fed electricity to be kept under control. When his assistant died from radioactivity, Denker panicked and tried to transport the element to a safe place, but as he eventually discovers, nowhere on Earth would be a safe place. After the elderly scientist expires, Jeff directs the decontamination team to package the element and transport it to the state university lab.

Jeff returns home and teases his pregnant wife, Connie, that she is too thin. They discuss their future plans, including the purchase of a new home in the suburbs. Jeff receives an emergency phone call that there has been a deadly accident at the state university. The element has caused the laboratory to collapse by imploding, magnetically forcing the structure to crush inward. Grown in size, the magnetic monster is moved to OSI, and Jeff is placed in charge of dealing with it.

After intense research, Jeff discovers that a crisis will occur with the element every eleven hours, at which point it must be fed a huge jolt of electricity or it will implode, absorbing any metal in its vicinity through magnetic power. The amount of power required to feed it is also doubled on each occasion. Unless this cycle can be broken, the Earth is doomed because the growing element will cause the planet to shift its orbit into the void of outer space. Jeff consults MANIAC and concludes that the only chance of doing this is to bombard it with an immense dosage of electricity that would force it to divide into two harmless stable elements. Only one generator in the world is powerful enough to accomplish this, the Deltatron: a super-generator located in an underwater lab off the coast of Nova Scotia. When the eleventh hour approaches, they "feed" the monster by blacking out Los Angeles and directing all the power to OSI. The air force races Jeff, Dan and the element to the Deltatron.

Dr. Benton, the developer of the Deltatron, resists Jeff's use of his invention. He has spent eleven years of his life overseeing its construction. When he reviews MANIAC's projection of the power required to neutralize, he knows that his machine will be destroyed. Benton calls the Canadian defense minister in protest, but he is instructed that Jeff has been given total authority to do as he sees fit. Jeff plans to set the generator to its maximum limit and then abandon it. He and the other workers will hide behind flood gates that were installed in case the Deltatron ever went out of control. Jeff pushes Deltatron's settings to maximum. Benton, unwilling to see his work destroyed, sabotages the flood gates to prevent them from closing. He figures this will compel Jeff to disengage the generator. Instead, Jeff climbs up into the housing over the flood gates and forces them to close manually by cutting the cables. He himself manages to escape before the large metal doors seal shut. The Deltatron puts on a dazzling electrical display before exploding. At first, the operation seems a failure because several tools become magnetized and stick to the flood gates. However, they fall to the ground moments later, indicating that the element has finally split into safe and harmless components. Jeff returns home to Los Angeles, and he and his wife move into their new home as the end credits roll.

CRITIQUE

Although a modest endeavor, *The Magnetic Monster* retains a colorful vitality and freshness when viewed almost fifty years later. Some of this is due to the novel storyline as well as the special care lavished on the production by the three key principals, Curt Siodmak, Richard Carlson and Ivan Tors. In fact, they considered developing a television series based on the activities of the OSI. Then Carlson became involved in another project the same year, a series called *I Led Three Lives,* based on the true-life adventures of Herbert A. Philbrick, who worked as an undercover agent for the FBI while posing as a member of the Communist underground movement. This show became one of the most popular of the independent, syndicated shows, and 117 episodes were produced. By that time, Siodmak and Tors had moved on to other projects, and the OSI series was unfortunately abandoned. Many commentators note the similarity in style and narration between the first half of *The Magnetic Monster* and *Dragnet*, the popular series produced by, and starring, Jack Webb. Carlson's voice in the picture seems patterned on the famous dry, matter-of-fact style that Webb used so well in *Dragnet*.

The highpoint of the film is the exciting special effects lifted from *Gold* and expertly edited into the film. Carlson and Leo Britt match perfectly with the two German actors in the original film in all the long shots involving the Deltatron. Sometimes they resort to a little trickery, such as when Carlson dons an old fashioned cap merely to wander up to the control booth atop the Deltatron. He does this simply to match up with the German actor who appears in the original film. The blending of the footage is, for the most part, extraordinarily smooth and clever. Video collectors who track down *Gold* can fully appreciate how well the sequence is crafted in *The Magnetic Monster*. Other stock footage is also cunningly employed for the jet flight to Nova Scotia, with even the in-air refueling blended into the story.

Another clever device borrowed from *Dragnet* is the use of eccentric characters to populate the story, such as Simon the shop owner, Nellie the switchboard operator and the cabbie who phones in an essential lead. Screen veterans like Byron Foulger and Kathleen Freeman shine in these cameos. A number of subtle, humorous touches are well placed in the script. For instance, John Zaremba, the chief engineer of the power company, is named Watson (a pun on the word watts). When the military commander first hears about the master computer, he creates a laugh when he blurts out, "Who's the maniac?" The film also has genuine human touches. Jean Byron as Carlson's wife is only peripherally involved in the story, but the charming banter between her and her husband makes these brief scenes memorable. In a recent interview[1] between Byron and the author, she commented on how the diet Carlson prescribed for her—eggs, sausage, and white bread—now would be regarded as anything but healthy. But these small casual scenes help the plot seem more realistic.

The scientific basis for the film is completely outlandish. The possibility for such an element to exist—or to interfere with Earth's orbit—seems like pure fantasy, but enough technical jargon is used correctly to give the threat an aura of believability. This comes through clearly when the scientists, military and government officials brainstorm the options of dealing with the problem. For instance, someone suggests that they fire the element into outer space, but the military realistically concedes that it lacks the technology to do it. It is also rare when scenes of scientists observing monitors or looking through microscopes can be rendered exciting, but this film manages to succeed in doing just that. The picture also has some scenes of genuine awe, such as when the air raid sirens sound to alert Los Angeles that the city is blacking out in order to feed the

---

[1] See *Screen Sirens Scream* (McFarland, 2000) pp. 21-34.

magnetic monster. The craftsmanship is clear as all the elements fit together well enough to make the film a textbook example of pure entertainment on a small budget.

REPRESENTATIVE QUOTES

"The operatives of OSI are called A-Men. A-Men sounds like the final words of a prayer. It's not. A stands for atom. Atom stands for power, power that man has unleashed but has not yet learned to control. . . . A Men are detectives with degrees in science. The criminals we seek are sometimes invisible to the human eye like radiation from outer space or particles held prisoner deep in the heart of the atom, infinitesimal, yet within this tiny molecule there's a tremendous force that once unlocked could create or destroy planets. Our Earth is a planet." (Opening narration)

"It's hungry. It has to be fed constantly, or it will reach out its magnetic arm and grab at anything within its reach and kill it. It's monstrous, Stewart, monstrous! It grows bigger. . . . Other scientists will have to find the solution. My contribution is finished. I know this, in nuclear research, there is no place for lone wolves." (Denker's dying words to Jeff)

"As long as the earth remains in equilibrium, nothing will change. But very soon, this element is going to make the earth eccentric. It is going to fly out of its orbit into space." (Jeff to the mayor of Los Angeles, explaining the need to keep the element under control)

"Dr. Benton, our only hope is that she will break that element before she breaks herself." (Jeff to Benton upon the sacrifice of the Deltatron)

The Man Who Could Work Miracles (1936)

Rating: *****   **Threat: Halting of Earth's rotation**

London Film Production. Written by H. G. Wells; Photographed by Harold Rosson; Special effects by Ned Mann; Edited by Philip Charlot; Music by Michael Spolianski; Produced by Alexander Korda; Directed by Lothar Mendes. B & W, 82 minutes.

ANNOTATED CAST LIST

Roland Young (*George McWhirter Fotheringay*, man given the power to work miracles); Edward Chapman (*Major Grigsby*, store owner); Ernest Thesiger (*Rev. Simon Maydig*, Baptist minister); Ralph Richardson (*Col. Winstanley*, Maydig's pompous neighbor); Joan Gardner (*Ada Price*, employee at Grigsby & Blott); Robert Cochran (*Bill Stoker*, her boyfriend and clerk at Grigsby & Blott); Sophie Stewart (*Maggie Hooper*, store clerk with sprained arm); Lady Tree (Grigsby's housekeeper); Laurence Hanray (*Bamfylde*, banker); George Zucco (*Moody*, Winstanley's butler); Wally Lupino (*Bobby Winch*, policeman sent to hell); Joan Hickson (*Effie Brickman*, store clerk with freckles); Wally Patch (*Inspector Smithells*, head of police in Essex); Bernard Nedell (American reporter); Ben Weldon (American reporter); Mark Daly (*Toddy Branish*, pub patron); Una Owen (*Miss Maybridge*, barmaid); Bruce Winston (*Cox*, pub owner); Michael Rennie (bystander in the Great Hall); George Sanders (*Indifference*, semi-divine spirit); Ivan Brandt (*Player*, semi-divine spirit who gives Fotheringay his powers); Torin Thatcher (*Observer*, semi-divine spirit).

SYNOPSIS

Many people are unaware that the legendary H. G. Wells wrote screenplays. His memorable *Things to Come* (1936) has a few apocalyptical elements, but *The Man Who Could Work Miracles* actually depicts the complete destruction of the world. While both films are highly regarded, *Things to Come* soon became dated, while *The Man Who Could Work Miracles* still seems fresh and charming, one of the greatest fantasy films ever made.

The story opens in the heavens, where three semi-divine spirits share their thoughts. One of them has been granted the ability to bestow power by "the Master." Player is fascinated by Earth, and he tells the others that he plans to give all its inhabitants special powers. His companions try to dissuade him, and Player agrees to give only one of them power, as an experiment to see what is in the human heart. They settle back and watch as Player haphazardly selects a meek British clerk, George Fotheringay, as the recipient of all the power he is able to bestow.

In the small town of Essex, England, Fotheringay is about to enter his regular pub, the Long Dragon, where a discussion is taking place about the nature of miracles. Fotheringay proposes a definition of what constitutes a miracle, but the others quibble over his terminology. The clerk then proposes a demonstration, saying that he will try to turn a lamp upside down by using only his force of will. If he could do it, that would be a miracle. To everyone's surprise, the lamp spins over in midair. Startled, Fotheringay mutters, "It's got to drop," and at that instant the lamp falls and shatters on the floor. The owner, alerted by the noise, kicks Fotheringay out of the pub for practicing silly magic tricks. The confused man goes to his bedroom, where he tries the same trick again with his candlestick. When it works, he exclaims, "It is a blooming miracle!" He tries a series of other stunts, levitating his bed and making a series of animals appear and disappear. Becoming sleepy, he orders all his conjurations to disappear. When he awakens the next morning, the clerk assumes it was only a dream, but when he tries to summon up a rabbit, a small white bunny appears on his bed. He somberly thinks to himself that he has to seriously consider the implications of his new power.

Fotheringay is late reaching his job at Grigsby and Blott, a drapery (better known as a dry goods store in America). The other employees are busy at their tasks. Bill Stoker talks to lovely Ada Price, teasing her about their dithery co-worker, George Fotheringay. Maggie Hooper, her arm in a sling due to a sprain, chats with Effie, who is self-conscious about her freckles. Fotheringay tells his secret to Maggie and cures her arm as proof. Believing he is a healer, she asks him to clear up Effie's complexion and he obliges. The other employees discuss this development over lunch. Stoker urges him to accumulate all the money he possibly can, but Maggie insists that he reserve his power for doing good deeds and healing the sick. Stoker adds that Fotheringay could do that as well, perhaps by visiting the hospital once a week and cleaning it out. Fotheringay admits that his power frightens him. Maggie suggests he visit the local minister for advice. The gentle clerk daydreams for the rest of the day, and at closing time, his department is in shambles. When Major Grigsby, his boss, demands that he tidy up, the clerk waves his hands and says, "Apple pie order!" All the clothes and boxes put themselves away, and a flying whisk broom dusts off the counter-top. Grigsby is astonished by this fantastic spectacle.

On his way home, Fotheringay makes a rose tree grow in the middle of the road. Constable Winch comes by and starts to argue with him, threatening his arrest. Upset, Fotheringay mutters, "Go to blazes," and the policeman instantly disappears. In hell, Winch looks around for an escape as flames roar around him. Fotheringay is startled when his casual comment is carried out, and he decides to send Winch to San Francisco instead. Befuddled, the constable appears in the middle of a traffic jam, and he runs as two San Francisco cops who try to arrest him. He later tells his remarkable story to two reporters, but their editor refuses to believe Winch's preposterous yarn.

Stoker and Ada Price are out on a date. On her way home she runs into Fotheringay, who has a crush on her. When he tries to cast a spell that would make her return his feelings, his power fails. She stomps off indignantly, and the clerk determines that there is a limit to his powers: he is unable to affect either the human heart or soul. The next day, Grigsby tries to convince Fotheringay to sign an exclusive contract to limit his miracle working to his firm exclusively. He brings him to see Bamfylde the banker to talk about the prospects of a worldwide chain of stores run by Fotheringay's powers. The clerk resists the idea, demonstrating that if he wanted money, he could just pluck it out of thin air. The elderly banker almost has a fit after this demonstration, saying that the clerk could destroy the banking system by simply making money. It would lead to chaos and destroy the social system. Fotheringay listens but makes no commitment.

When Stoker hears of Grigsby's proposal, he advises the clerk not to become a tool for others but instead to run the entire world himself and do it right. Fotheringay takes the idea under advisement and quietly goes back to work in the store. After Ada teases him that he is stingy with his miracles, he conjures up for her a diamond tiara and a pearl necklace, finally dressing her an elegant costume worn by Cleopatra, but when a customer enters the room, he transforms her back into her original clothes.

That night, Fotheringay visits Simon Maydig, the local Baptist minister, for advice. He makes a tiger appear to convince the skeptical cleric. The startled minister advises Fotheringay not to bother with piecemeal healing, but instead to banish all disease in one fell swoop. But the miracle worker now envisions a catch to any of his possible actions. Maydig promises to stay up all night to plan a logical series of good deeds. As Fotheringay goes, the minister asks him for a small token favor, a miraculous deed involving Colonel Winstanley, Maydig's pompous neighbor.

Next door, the colonel coughs loudly after taking a drink from his decanter. He summons his butler and blames him for causing his whiskey to go flat. A crash is then heard in the next room, and after checking, the butler reports that each piece in the colonel's priceless sword collection has been changed into a plowshare. The police are summoned, and when Inspector Smithells arrives, he claims the transformation is another of a series of unexpected miracles that have occurred in the district during the past two days. As an example, Smithells shows Winstanley a cable from San Francisco from one of his officers who was transported there as if by magic. The inspector believes a local resident named Fotheringay is somehow behind the pattern of events. The colonel demands that Fotheringay be brought to his garden the following morning.

At first, the pompous colonel tries to bully Fotheringay, demanding an explanation. The clerk replies that it was only a symbolic act suggested by Reverend Maydig, his neighbor. The clerk discloses his intent of bringing about a new era of peace and plenty. He will begin the golden age that very afternoon, and Fotheringay restores the colonel's liquor and weapon collection as a sign of good faith. Winstanley still has doubts, so the clerk transports them both to Bombay and back as further proof. The colonel is now overwhelmed and tries to dissuade Fotheringay from Maydig's vision of a world where people will lack any competitive drive and instead spend their time promoting brotherly love. He bellows that this new millennium will result in bedlam, but the meek clerk responds that he wants to give the new way a try.

Colonel Winstanley summons Grigsby, Bamfylde and other members of the old order to discuss ways of stopping the lunatic schemes of Maydig and Fotheringay. He proposes that they take drastic action. Meanwhile, the clerk talks with Maydig about his doubts. Since he cannot change people's hearts, will they be happy in the proposed new world? After the Colonel tires to shoot him, Fotheringay declares himself invulnerable to any harm. This assassination attempt has finally roused Fotheringay, who declares that only he himself will decide his future course of action.

Fotheringay calls forth the creation of a great palace, and costumes himself as the Prince of the World. He changes Maydig and Bamfylde into counselors, and Winstanley into his captain of guards. He then orders up various groups of people to populate his new order. Ada Price appears as Cleopatra, and Maggie Hooper materializes as his queen. He next summons the most beautiful women, the greatest bankers, businessmen, teachers and politicians of the world all to appear. Prince Fotheringay begins a speech and orders all those who rule the world "to run it better!" He then demands an end to war. If these people of influence fail to organize a better world—a good, happy, sensible world—the clerk vows to wipe them all out. When their reactions seems resentful, Maydig urges Fotheringay to give them more time. The sun is setting, and he proposes to give everyone the night to think it over. Fotheringay replies instead that he will order the sun not to set until all his plans are instituted. When Maydig continues to protest, Fotheringay orders the earth to stop rotating.

Every building and person on the entire planet hurtles off into space as the world is destroyed when its rotation is abruptly halted. The three heavenly beings watch this event in complete amazement. "Well, that's the end of your nasty little pets upon their silly little planet," Indifference says mockingly. But Fotheringay, who is invulnerable, is still alive as his body spins wildly in outer space. The clerk wishes for time to return to the point three days earlier when he went to the pub. He then wishes away his incredible power. Player is impressed by this choice and decides to nurture the planet, to give all its inhabitants power gradually, bit by bit over time and throw added wisdom into the mix. His two companions are still in doubt, but Player is confident that Earth will have a bright future.

Back at the Long Dragon pub, Fotheringay again attempts to turn the lamp over by force of will, and he seems both relieved and forlorn that he no longer has the power to perform miracles.

CRITIQUE

This is one of those rare films that improves with repeated viewings. Many British films from the 1930s do not play well for American audiences, but this is a true exception. Neither are there any dull stretches in the entire film, which moves forward at a brisk pace. There are so many clever lines and asides that it is hard to keep track of them. Unlike numerous fantasies, the film wastes little time getting started, but jumps right into the story. The film's humor is both whimsical and infectious. The most incredible element, however, is the film's apocalypse, which is simply incredible. The climatic event sneaks up unexpectedly, as Fotheringay abandons his previous caution and lets rip with a poorly worded command that halts the earth's rotation. The consequences are instantaneous and terrible, certainly amounting to one of the most unexpected end-of-the-world moments ever portrayed on film. Apocalyptic films usually fuel their drama with suspense over the fate of the planet. This film, on the other hand, unveils its destruction as an utter surprise, a conjuror's trick by H. G. Wells to make his startling point: no individual is capable of wielding absolute power. The subtle, dangerous repercussions of the gift bestowed on Fotheringay serves as the pivotable point of the film. It is just that the audience never expects the catastrophe and is completely unprepared for it when it happens.

Hungarian-born producer Alexander Korda was the brightest light of the British film industry, and this picture clearly illustrates the reason, since its quality is of the highest order. It is hard to envision a more scintillating or innovative script than the one developed by H. G. Wells, although he did have some uncredited assistance. There is some hilarious social satire in the script as well, particularly in the stereotypical depictions of Grigsby as the businessman, Bamfylde as the banker, Winstanley as the military man, Smithells as the policeman and Maydig as the clergyman. It is very amusing trying to follow the ramifications and the logical arguments of each of these characters, and how they represent the various elements of society. One of the wittiest comments is that disease should not be eliminated because it would put doctors out of work. The throwaway lines contained in some of the scenes when they try to make their case to Fotheringay are priceless. For example, when Colonel Winstanley picks up a scythe that replaced one of his valuable swords, he mutters under his breath, "Bolshevik contraption!" The cinematography, editing and special effects are all of the first order. The miracles portrayed in the film were state-of-the-art for the time, and the screen magic they provide is still enjoyable today.

The cast is also ideal. Roland Young is superb as the unpretentious and modest hero, and his last-minute transformation after being the target of a gunshot is ingenious. Young is largely remembered as the original Cosmo Topper in a series of "Topper" films, as well as being a memorable Uriah Heep in *David Copperfield* (1934). Nevertheless, this film is probably the crowning moment of his career. Ralph Richardson, who made his screen debut in *The Ghoul* (1933) with Boris Karloff and Ernest Thesiger, here appears in remarkable makeup as an elderly, stuffed-shirt British Colonel. One would never discern that the actor playing this role was only thirty-four years old. It is an incredible performance. Ernest Thesiger also has a meaty part as the Baptist minister who has a mad gleam in his eye as he dreams of a perfect world. It is a quintessential role for the eccentric actor, rivaling his memorable Dr. Pretorius in *The Bride of Frankenstein* (1935). The film is filled with brilliant moments that offer the cast an opportunity to shine. George Zucco, perhaps, has the best line, which he delivers perfectly: when accused of diluting his employer's stock of whiskey, he replies in utter sincerity that he would just as soon poison a baby. The picture also includes early career gigs for future stars George Sanders and Michael Rennie.

It has been reported that Eddie Murphy and other actors have been considering a remake of the film. As wonderful a talent as Murphy is, the role is really not suited for him. Someone such as Steve Buscemi or Jeffrey Combs, on the other hand, might be excellent as a modern-day Fotheringay if given the opportunity.

REPRESENTATIVE QUOTES

"These men, they are such silly little creatures, swarming and crawling. Why has 'The Master' permitted them?" (Observer, speaking about the earthlings)

"They are pitifully small, but I like them. . . . If they were not weak, they might not be so pitiful, but their lives are so short, their efforts are so feeble." (Player, commenting to his colleagues)

"A miracle, I say, is something contrariwise to the usual course of nature done by an act of will, something that couldn't happen, not being specially willed." (Fotheringay's definition of a miracle at the pub debate)

"I can assure you, I have studied these questions, very profound questions, before you were born. Human society is based on want. Wild-eyed visionaries, I name no names, may dream of a world without need. Cloud Cuckoo Land! It couldn't be done!" (Bamfylde to Fotheringay)   "It hasn't been tried." (Fotheringay's reply)

"Oh sir, I've got my weaknesses, but I would as soon poison a baby as tamper with whiskey." (Moody the butler to his employer)

"They were apes only yesterday. . . . There is something in every one of those creatures like a little grain of gold glittering in sand, a flash of indignation when they think things are false. That's godlike . . . that is why they interest me." (Player to his fellow spirits at the conclusion of his experiment)

Mars Attacks! (1996)

Rating: ✴✴✴✴✴   Threat: Alien invaders

Warner Brothers. Written by Jonathan Gems based on a storyline developed by the Topps Company; Photographed by Peter Suschitzky; Special effects by James Mitchell, Michael L. Fink & David Andrews (supervisors); Edited by Chris Lebenzon; Music by Danny Elfman; Produced by Tim Burton & Larry Franco; Directed by Tim Burton. 106 minutes.

ANNOTATED CAST LIST

Jack Nicholson (*James Dale*, U.S. president; *Art Land*, Las Vegas casino developer); Glenn Close (*Marsha Dale*, first lady); Natalie Portman (*Taffy Dale*, their daughter); Annette Bening (*Barbara Land*, Art's wife); Pierce Brosnan (*Dr. Donald Kessler*, President Dale's science advisor); Martin Short (President Dale's press secretary); Rod Steiger (*Gen. Decker*, President Dale's military advisor); Paul Winfield (*Gen. Casey*, head of U.S. armed forces); Michael J. Fox (*Jason Stone*, GNN News anchor); Sarah Jessica Parker (*Nathalie Lake*, Jason's wife and talk show hostess); Lisa Marie (Martian disguised as pretty woman); Tom Jones (*Tom Jones*, casino headliner); Jim Brown (*Byron Williams*, former heavyweight champ and Luxor casino host); Pam Grier (*Louise Williams*, Byron's estranged wife and bus driver); Ray J (*Cedric Williams*, their son); Brandon Hammond (*Neville Williams*, their second son); Janice Rivera (*Cindy*, Casino hostess); Danny DeVito (pushy gambler); Lukas Haas (*Richie Norris*, Donut World employee); Joe Don Baker (*Glenn Norris*, Richie's father); O-Lan Jones (*Sue Ann Norris*, Richie's mother); Sylvia Sidney (*Florence Norris*, Richie's grandmother); Jack Black (*Billy Glenn Norris*, Richie's brother); Christina Applegate (*Sharona*, Billy Glenn's girlfriend); Barbet Schroeder (*Maurice*, president of France); Jerzy Skolimowski (*Dr. Ziegler*, inventor of universal translator); Brian Haley (*Mitch*, Secret Service agent); Timi Prulhiere (White House tour guide); Joseph Maher (White House decorator): Julian Barnes (White House waiter); Ken Thomas (White House photographer); John Finnegan (*Chet Brickmore*, Speaker of the House); Coco Leigh (press conference journalist); Josh Weinstein (hippie with dove); Steve Valentine (*Ian*, Nathalie's TV director); Vinny Argiro (casino manager); Rebeca Silva (Donut World employee); Chi Hoang Cai (*Mr. Lee*, Kentucky rancher); Tommy Bush (farmer on tractor); Jeffrey King (NASA technician); Rance Howard (Texan investor); Richard Assad (*Sheik Ramullah*, Saudi investor); Valetta Carlson (elderly slots player); Kevin Mangin (trailer lover); Jonathan Emerson (newscaster); Willie Garson (corporate man); Gregg Daniel (lab technician); J. Kenneth Campbell, Jeanne Mori (alien autopsy doctors); Ed Lambert, John Gray (old men in nursing home); C. Wayne Owens, Joseph Patrick Moynihan (strangers); Enrique Castillo, Don Lamoth, Roger Peterson (the colonels in

Pahrump); Gloria Hoffman, Betty Bunch, Gloria Malgarini (Vegas nuns); John Roselius (GNN boss); Michael Reilly Burke, Valerie Wildman, Richard Irving (GNN reporters); Tamara Curry, Rebecca Brousard (prostitutes); Darelle Porter Holden, Christi Black, Sharon Hendrix (backup singers for Tom Jones); Sylvia Nightingale (woman in crowd); Slim Whitman (favorite singer of Grandma Norris); Frank Welker (Martian vocal effects); Poppy (*Poppy*, Nathalie's dog).

SYNOPSIS

There is apparently no middle ground of opinion regarding *Mars Attacks!* You either "get it" and find it to be one of the most hilarious spoofs ever made or you "don't get it" and find it a bewildering series of vignettes. In truth, the film is not aimed at today's teenage audience but at baby boomers, film enthusiasts who grew up in the 1950s loving the science fiction films typical of the era from *War of the Worlds* (1953) and *Earth vs. the Flying Saucers* (1956) to *Target Earth* (1954) and *Invasion of the Saucer Men* (1957). Many of the incidents, situations and characters refer, either directly or obliquely, to many of these pictures, and the sarcastic slant is usually right on target.

Mars Attacks! is extraordinarily episodic, which is not surprising because it is based on a legendary series of bubble gum cards developed by the Topps Company in the early 1960s. Some of the events in the film correspond to striking visual episodes from the series. Because of the rapid-fire way the story is presented, the usual in-depth summary is not suited to this film, so the synopsis will be in more general terms.

Behind the main credits we see an invasion force of hundreds of flying saucers heading toward Earth. This army consists of three-foot-tall Martians with enormous heads and pulsating brains. Their language consists solely of the sounds "Ack, ack," and these pesky fiends aim to totally eradicate the human race. At first, they feign friendship. A landing is set up in the desert outside of Las Vegas, where the Martian ambassador speaks through a translation machine saying, "We come in peace." A hippie in the crowd releases a dove, which the ambassador kills with a ray gun, then firing on the crowd and reception committee. President Dale broadcasts a secret message to the Martians, saying the incident was a cultural misunderstanding. Laughing at his gullibility, the ambassador asks to address the U.S. Legislature. The head Martian whips out a ray gun during his speech and wipes out Congress. The president finally realizes it is a full-scale invasion, and the world's governments fight back but are ineffectual against the invaders, until a surprising defense is discovered in Kansas. These events are related through various groups of people: President Dale and his entourage in Washington, D.C.; entrepreneur Art Land and the casinos of Las Vegas; and the Norris family, inhabitants of a trailer park in rural Kansas.

President Dale is a shallow man, driven by polls and concerned principally with his popularity rating. His wife, Marsha, concentrates on White House decor. She is eventually crushed by a chandelier during an alien attack on the White House. His teenage daughter, Taffy, is normal and well-meaning but finds Washington a superficial and insincere place. Presidential press secretary Jerry Ross is sex obsessed. He is slain by a Martian posing as a hooker, whom he brings to the "Kennedy room," a secret tryst in the White House. Dr. Kessler is Dale's muddled-headed science advisor who is convinced the Martians are really benevolent. He is captured during the sneak attack at the Capital, and his head is removed from his body and kept alive as a Martian experiment. He passes his last moments flirting with Nathalie Lake, a TV fashion show hostess whose head has been attached to the body of her Chihuahua, Poppy. Nathalie's husband, Jason Stone, a conceited anchorman for GNN, is killed at the time of Nathalie's capture. General Casey, head of America's armed forces, is an empty-headed yes man who believes the best way to get ahead is never to express an opinion. The Martian ambassador kills him with a ray gun at their photo-op meeting in the desert. General Decker is suspicious of the aliens, and he is continually ignored by Dale when he urges military resistance to the Martians. He is eventually shrunk to the size of a mouse and stomped down by a Martian. Other Washington residents are bus driver Louise Williams and her sons, Cedric and Neville. She is the estranged wife of former heavyweight champ Byron Williams, now a host at the Luxor Hotel and Casino in Las Vegas.

Art Land is a sleazy, scheming conniver determined to develop the most impressive casino in Nevada. His wife, Barbara, is a former alcoholic who initially believes the Martians have arrived to create a New Age haven for man. After witnessing the attack in the desert, she tries to convince her husband of the threat. He ignores her and is killed while promoting his plans to investors when the aliens invade Vegas. Barbara flees Vegas with the help of Byron Williams, showgirl Cindy and pop superstar Tom Jones. Byron gives them an opportunity to escape at the airport, holding off a gang of aliens, challenging them to a boxing match. Jones pilots Land's private jet and flies the others off to Lake Tahoe, where they hide out in a remote cave.

In Kansas, the pride of the Norris family is Billy Glenn, a redneck soldier. His parents idolize him and ignore his brother, Richie, who works in a local donut shop. Richie also cares for Grandma Norris and visits her in the nursing home whenever possible. Billy Glenn disgraces himself on national television during the Martian attack in the desert when his rifle falls apart and he tries to surrender. When the Martians attack the trailer park, Richie heads to the nursing home to try to save his grandmother.

Worldwide, the planet is almost powerless in the face of the Martian attack. A montage shows worldwide chaos, as the Martians bowl down the statues on Easter Island, recarve Mount Rushmore with Martian faces and blow up famous sites such as the Taj Mahal and Big Ben. The Martians break into the war room at the White House, where Dale makes a desperate plea, beseeching, "Why can't we just get along?" At first the Martian ambassador seems moved, and he starts to cry. He shakes Dale's hand, but this is revealed as a trick as his hand breaks off and pokes through Dale's heart.

At her nursing home, Grandma Norris is blissfully unaware of the attack while listening on a headset to her record player. The invaders sneak up upon her, but her headphone plug is pulled out of the phonograph, and the falsetto pitch of her favorite singer, Slim Whitman, causes the Martians' heads to explode. Richie and Grandma Norris head to the powerful nearby radio station to broadcast Slim Whitman songs. Soon, all of Earth's defenders learn about this weapon, start to play Slim Whitman records and save the earth as all the invaders perish and their flying saucers crash.

Richie Norris and his grandmother are decorated in Washington by Taffy Dale, the only surviving individual with any connection to the government. Byron Williams has survived his fist fight with the aliens and arrives in Washington to reunite with his wife and children. Barbara, Cindy and Tom Jones emerge from their cave to see Lake Tahoe filled with the wreckage of alien spacecraft. In celebration, Tom Jones starts to sing his trademark song "It's not Unusual," as the end credits roll.

CRITIQUE

When released, the film seemed to draw numerous critical attacks from both the cultural left and right wings, no doubt since the targets of the script's satirical jabs cut across the political spectrum. Many critics seemed to resent the equal broadsides and gave the film a cold shoulder. Burton throws down the gauntlet in the pre-credit sequence when he opens the film with a stampeding herd of cattle, all in flames: it is a Hollywood rule of thumb not to show animals mistreated in the course of a story. In *Mars Attacks!*, Dale's dog and numerous birds are zapped, and Natalie's Chihuahua is the subject of a mad experiment. Political correctness is cleverly lampooned, as well as numerous other targets, from New Age culture to *Playboy* magazine.

While much of the humor is broad, some of it is quite subtle. Even the titles establishing time and location are capricious at times. When President Dale has a news conference on Thursday, May 12 at 4:03 P.M., he opens it by saying, "Good morning," indicating how completely out of touch he actually is. Interestingly enough, *Mars Attacks!* is one of the few films that maintains proper depictions of day and night when showing montage scenes from around the world. Multiple viewings are necessary to catch many of the references, including numerous film tributes, from the Orson Welles classic *Citizen Kane* (1941), when Jason and Nathalie have their own version of the famous breakfast scene, to the notorious *Alien Autopsy* documentary. These allusions are not forced or highlighted. When a viewer detects one, it is an added bonus, but it is not essential to identify them all to enjoy the film. The script does an amazing job balancing and incorporating all these elements. Tim Burton worked uncredited with Jonathan Gems in fine-tuning the screenplay, which is also remarkable for its breakneck pacing and many dazzling vignettes. As for the idea of using Slim Whitman as Earth's salvation, it ranks as the most ingenious touch ever employed in a satirical film. Besides "The Indian Love Call," they should also have used Whitman's version of "Una Paloma Blanca," which would have complimented the Martian's bird phobia.

Another brilliant aspect of the film is the phenomenal score by Danny Elfman, the most innovative and exceptional film composer of the last fifteen years of the twentieth century. His infectious, jaunty main theme is an ingenious reworking of the "Dies Irae," which you will find yourself humming long after the film's conclusion. Elfman also cleverly uses occasional electronic effects that recall Bernard Herrmann's score to *The Day the Earth Stood Still* (1951). Seldom does music add so much to the overall film as in this case, especially when you add Slim Whitman and Tom Jones to the mix.

The other technical work and special effects are stunning, but the film went seriously over budget with the soaring cost of computer-generated images. Burton initially wanted to use stop action animation, as Ray Harryhausen employed in many classic films of the 1950s and 1960s. The flying saucers in the film are based principally on Harryhausen's effects for *Earth vs. the Flying Saucers*. The giant walkers used by the Martians are a cross between *War of the Worlds* as envisioned by H. G. Wells in his original novel and devices used in *Return of the Jedi* (1983). The Martians themselves, based on the bubble gum cards, are craftily designed with big pop eyes, skull-like faces and oversized domes that seem to bulge with brain tissue. Their "Ack-ack" speech is a fascinating touch. When their brains explode, it is reminiscent of the deaths of the bizarre brain creatures in Richard Gordon's *Fiend wthout a Face* (1958). The picture also references the many "living head" films of the 1950s with the experiments done on Dr. Kessler, Nathalie and Poppy, whose doghead was attached to Nathalie's body. When the camera pans by the alien lab, you can also spot Jason's severed hand, reanimated and walking about, a tribute to *The Crawling Hand* (1963).

The talented cast is outstanding, and most of them manage to make the most of their brief screen time. Nicholson is excellent, but the gimmick of his dual role should have been expanded to the Kansas scenario, as with the troika performance by Peter Sellers in *Dr. Strangelove* (1964). Rod Steiger practically steals the show as General Decker. He plays him like an over-the-top General Patton, ranting and calling for action. The hilarious thing is, although he seems like a nut, he actually is right on target with his advice compared to the rest of the president's muddled brain trust. Pierce Brosnan plays Dr. Kessler like a head-in-the-clouds Fred MacMurray from *The Absent-Minded Professor* (1961). His overconfident perception of the invaders as benevolent is a marvelous touch (for which he eventually pays with his head). Brosnan's performance is an interesting spin, far different from his niche in the James Bond series. Sylvia Sidney's career dates back to the 1920s, and she plays Florence Norris with a wacky zest that is unforgettable. Almost all the other performers shine as well, especially Jim Brown, Pam Grier, Paul Winfield, Martin Short, Michael J. Fox, Annette Bening, Glenn Close and Danny DeVito. There are a few let-downs, such as Jerzy Skolimowski, who is totally flat as Dr. Ziegler, inventor of the universal translator. A better actor, such as Vincent Schiavelli, would have been magnificent in the part. Two other members of the cast deserve special attention. Lisa Marie is completely bewitching as the disguised Martian who attempts to assassinate President Dale. Adding Tom Jones to the cast is another wonderful touch, and he comes across so well that it is surprising that he has not been tapped for other film roles.

Mars Attacks! will gain status in the future as a unique cult film, an affectionate memento of a bygone film era grafted with caricatures of more recent sociological trends. Human gullibility can be seen as a serious undercurrent to the satire. Humanity is unable to cope with the threat largely because they refuse to believe in it. When Glenn Norris sees his son dissolved by the alien ray gun, he states, "It didn't happen." When President Dale is called by the French president, who just signed a deal with the Martians, Dale immediately knew that it was a phony ploy, yet moments later he naively seems to believe that he and the ambassador can "just get along." Another example of gullibility is the Martian's use of the translator, with which they broadcast the message, "Do not run. We are your friends," while murdering people left and right. The shadows of the Soviet Gulag and the German concentration camps are clearly present here. The apocalyptic threat of total human genocide remains powerful, even when cloaked as comedy. In many instances, *Mars Attacks!* takes chances and does not play it safe. It is undeniably a unique masterpiece and one of the most significant satires in the genre.

REPRESENTATIVE QUOTES

"A powerful memory is in the making, not just for me, but for all mankind." (President Dale, announcing the sighting of the fleet of Martian flying saucers)

"I'm feeling so optimistic because of the Martians, and it is so perfect that it is happening at the beginning of the new millennium. Our planet was suffering with the ozone and the rainforest and so many people unhappy in their lives, and the Martians heard our global cosmic cry for help. People say they're ugly, but I think they came to show us the way. I think they've come to save us." (Barbara Land at her AA meeting)

"They blew up Congress!" (Florence Norris with total delight while watching television in the nursing home)

Meteor (1979)

Rating: ****   Threat: Meteor collision

American International. Written by Stanley Mann & Edmund North; Photographed by Paul Lohmann; Special effects by Margo Anderson, Glen Robinson & William Cruse; Edited by Carl Kress; Music by Laurence Rosenthal; Produced by Arnold Orgolini & Theodore Parvin; Directed by Ronald Neame. 107 minutes.

ANNOTATED CAST LIST

Sean Connery (*Dr. Paul Bradley*, astrophysicist); Brian Keith (*Dr. Alexei Dubov*, top Soviet scientist); Natalie Wood (*Tatiana Nikolaevna Donskaya*, Dubov's assistant); Karl Malden (*Harry Sherwood*, head of NASA); Carole Hemingway (*Gladys*, his secretary); Martin Landau (*Gen. Adlon*, head of Project Hercules); Trevor Howard (*Sir Michael Hughes*, British astronomer); Henry Fonda (U.S. president); Richard Dysart (secretary of state); Joseph Campanella (*Gen. John Easton*, military liaison officer to NASA); Bo Brundin (*Rolf Manheim*, chief technician of *Hercules*); Katherine De Hetre (*Jan Watkins*, trajectory analysis officer); James G. Richardson (*Alan Marshall*, Jan's assistant and boyfriend); Roger Robinson (*Bill Hunter*, tracking technician); Michael Zaslow (*Sam Mason*, NASA commander); John McKinney (*Peter Watson*, NASA flight director); John Finlater (*Tom Easton*, astronaut on *Challenger II* and son of Gen. Easton); Paul Tulley (*Bill Frager*, astronaut on *Challenger II*); Allen Williams (*Michael McKendrick*, astronaut on *Challenger II*); Gregory Gaye (Soviet Premier); Bibi Besch (*Helen Bradley*, Paul's estranged wife); Clyde Kusatsu (*Yamashiro*, astro-tracker in Hong Kong); Burke Byrnes, (coast guard officer who tracks down Bradley); Henry Olek (Adlon's translator); Peter Bourne (Security Council president); Stanley Mann (Canadian representative); Ronald Neame (British representative); Philip Sterling (Soviet Representative); Arthur Adams (Ghana representative); Fred Carney (American representative); Sybil Danning (skier at Swiss resort); Meschino Paterlini (her skiing companion); Osman Ragheb (Zurich television reporter); Jon Yune (Siberian man); Eileen Saki (Siberian woman); Yu Wing (Hong Kong fisherman); Yan Tsui Ling (his wife); Joe Medalis (bartender); Selma Archerd (woman in subway); Domingo Ambriz (boy with radio in subway); Clete Roberts (American television announcer); Stu Nathan (British television announcer); James Bacon, Yani Begakis (reporters); Chris Baur, Paul Camen, Dorothy Catching, Bill Couch, William Darr, Joan Foley, Paul Laurence, Johnny Moio, Reed Morgan, Conrad Palmisano, Tony Rocco, Jesse Wayne (communication center technicians); Peter Donat (narrator).

SYNOPSIS

When initially released, *Meteor* was critically panned as a total disaster with no redeeming features, but years later the reputation of the film has recovered, and for many it has achieved cult status as one of the most entertaining entries in the cycle of disaster films initiated by *The Poseidon Adventure* (1972). Although featuring an impressive cast of major stars, it actually was made on a relatively modest budget compared to other disaster films such as *The Towering Inferno* (1974). In fact, one-third of its budget was spent on an awkward publicity campaign that failed to bring viewers to the theaters. In any case, the film plays better on a small screen, where the special effects seem less shoddy, and viewers can concentrate on the remarkable series of performances (some over-the-top), the eccentric editing and the exhilarating musical score.

Dr. Paul Bradley is sailing in a boat race when the coast guard overtakes his ship to transport him to an emergency meeting at NASA. The scientist had resigned from NASA five years earlier and is upset by his recruitment. Harry Sherwood, head of NASA, and General Easton explain the unprecedented crisis. A new comet was observed entering the solar system, and Sherwood diverted the flight of *Challenger II*, en route to Mars, to monitor its passage through the asteroid belt. Unexpectedly, the comet struck Orpheus, a major asteroid, shattering it. *Challenger II*, commanded by General Easton's son, was destroyed by the debris, and the largest chunk of Orpheus, five-miles-wide, is headed directly toward Earth. Years earlier, Bradley had devised *Hercules*, a satellite with nuclear weapons that was intended to be used to destroy any dangerous meteors that approached Earth. However, the military took over the satellite to use as a weapon to threaten Russia, which was why Bradley resigned. Now NASA needs his help to destroy the meteor that is threatening the planet.

In the Soviet Union, Dr. Alexei Dubov, their leading scientist, is advised of the approach of the meteor. Meanwhile, Bradley and Sherwood meet with the secretary of state to brief him on the threat. Since the existence of *Hercules* is secret, there is some controversy about its use by General Adlon, who is in charge of the project. The president decides to place Bradley back in charge of *Hercules* with his mission to eliminate the threat from the meteor. The communications center for the project was built in an abandoned subway station situated beneath the AT&T Building in lower Manhattan. Bradley determines that the nuclear rockets on *Hercules* are insufficient to divert the meteor. To save the planet, they will need help from the Soviets who are believed to have a space-based weapon similar to *Hercules*.

The president addresses a news conference to describe the global danger. He says that both Russia and the United States have prepared for this possibility with foresight by placing satellites with atomic missiles in space. The Soviet premier watches this speech, amazed at how these illegal weapons are being transformed into devices of humanitarian concern by the American leader. The premier decides to send Dubov to America as a gesture, but the scientist demands full authority if the planet is to be saved.

Sir Michael Hughes, a British astronomer from Jodrell Observatory, calls and informs Bradley and his team that additional smaller meteors, fragments of Orpheus, will begin to strike the Earth within twenty-four hours. The largest chunk will hit on Sunday, December 7. That evening, Dr. Dubov arrives with his assistant and translator, Tatiana Donskaya, a lovely young woman. Bradley brings them into the secret communications center over the objections of General Adlon. At first, communication is hampered between the Russians and Americans because of old suspicions, but Bradley makes a special effort to work out details on a theoretical basis. Dubov uses this opening to share all the information he can, so they can start the technical work to synchronize their missiles. The Russian weapon is named *Peter the Great*, and together both satellites have enough fire power to divert the meteor. Both weapons first need to be realigned from their current positions facing Earth. While Dubov catches a catnap on the cot in Adlon's office, Bradley and Tatiana chat and become friends. She learns that Bradley is separated from his wife and explains that her own husband was a cosmonaut who was killed while on a mission.

At the United Nations, the Security Council debates the issue of Soviet-American teamwork. In Siberia, an Eskimo family is killed when a meteor falls near their tent, and they are the first victims of the catastrophe. Later a meteor shower occurs over Pisa, Italy, but they burn up, causing no damage. General Adlon assumes the emergency is over. He becomes hysterical when Bradley disagrees, and he stomps off, saying he will convince the president to put him back in charge of *Hercules*. Dubov also has an outburst, and he calls the Russian Ambassador. Shortly afterward, the log jam at the Security Council is broken and Russia pledges full cooperation.

Hercules and *Peter the Great* are repositioned in space. To prevent the meteor from striking, *Peter the Great* must launch its missiles first. Forty minutes later, *Hercules* must launch its weapons. Both sets of rockets will impact the meteor in coordinated waves, forever diverting it from Earth. The Soviet missiles look like giant pencils with red erasers, while the American ones look like huge, plastic-capped crayons. Meanwhile, at a Swiss resort, a small meteor hits, causing a massive avalanche that swallows the town, killing thousands. The president meets with the NASA chief for a briefing. Sherwood explains that once launched, NASA will be unable to control the rockets. If five or more missiles fail, then Earth will face an immense cataclysm.

Another meteor strikes the Pacific Ocean, and Hong Kong is engulfed by a hundred-foot tidal wave. General Adlon returns to the communications center to apologize to Bradley and Dubov, offering to help in any way. The Soviet missiles launch successfully. Sir Michael calls with a warning that another destructive meteor is due to hit New York City momentarily. Bradley refuses to launch the *Hercules* weapons early, since the timing needs to be exact. Fortunately, the meteor does not strike until fifteen seconds after the missiles take off, but New York City is totally devastated. The communications center suffers major damage, as equipment topples and a partial cave-in occurs. Many personnel are killed, including General Adlon. The survivors, including Bradley, Sherwood,

Dubov and Tatiana, struggle out through an escape route that leads to the regular subway system. This passage becomes flooded with mud as the group tries to make its way to safety.

General Easton, at NASA headquarters in Houston, takes over monitoring the missiles when contact with the communications center is lost. He informs the president when three rockets fail, but the remaining missiles are successful and the earth is saved. The evacuees from the communications center emerge in a subway station where, they mix with other disaster refugees. A boy with a radio picks up a news bulletin that the danger is over, and Bradley, Sherwood, Dubov and Tatiana, all covered in mud, embrace in celebration.

Later, a departure ceremony at the airport is held in honor of Alexei Dubov. Bradley kisses Tatiana goodbye, and she is hopeful that Bradley will visit her soon in Moscow.

CRITIQUE

This wacky production has a wonderful sense of humor, which comes close, but never crosses the line into parody. Much of this involves the editing and sound effects, and in fact the sound team was nominated for an Academy Award. The special effects for the most part are derivative and cheap. The avalanche sequence, for example, was almost totally lifted from an earlier effort called *Avalanche* (1978), which starred Rock Hudson and Mia Farrow. Some other effects were cribbed from various sources, such as the collapsing building shot from three or four different angles, which was feebly employed to represent the total destruction of New York City. The matte paintings, however, are quite good, the most outstanding one showing a gash-like crater in Central Park and the rest of the city in shambles. Most visual effects concentrated on the meteor twirling in space, a potato-shaped fragment of iron ore. There are numerous sound effects in space, where in reality there is nothing but complete silence. The comet roars, and whenever the meteor chunk appears, the sound track would huff and swish with strange sounds as if the meteor had an outlandish case of asthma. These meteor shots were also placed in the film in deliberately odd places. For example, the Soviet premier answers his telephone, and then the meteor appears as if it were on the other end of the line; or Sean Connery looks up an elevator shaft, and again we cut directly to the meteor, as if it were in the shaft. This loony editing is intentional, set up by an early shot in the film where Connery is reading a report about *Hercules* and, as he lowers the paper, the satellite in the sky appears directly behind the report. Even after seeing the film many times, these innovative and peculiar jump cuts are fascinating and provoke a smile.

Another interesting factor is the hell-bent-for-leather musical score, filled with extravagant fanfares and pulsating rhythms. Classical music buffs might detect that some of the music was inspired by an oddball composition by Russian composer Alexander Glazunov (1865-1936) entitled *Suite from the Middle Ages*. Laurence Rosenthal is a very prolific film composer, and many of his scores, from *Becket* (1964) to the television series *Young Indiana Jones* and the mini-series *Peter the Great*, have a unique vitality.

The storyline has numerous twists and turns, but it manages to keep things moving at a brisk pace. At each of the disaster sites, the story focuses on one particular individual, whether an attractive skier in the Alps or a humble fisherman in Hong Kong, and sticks with them until they become victims of the onslaught from the sky. The script is loaded with many colorful asides, particularly for Sean Connery, and these clever and occasionally vulgar quips are quite memorable. The weakest point, dramatically, of the film is near the conclusion, when the technicians from the *Hercules* control center have to stagger through the subway tunnel as it fills with mud and water. This sequence is dull and distracts from the main event, which is whether the missiles will successfully deflect the meteor. The plot is uncertain at times as to whether they intend to destroy the meteor or merely alter its course. When the president addresses the nation, he says the intention is is the latter. Another unusual element is the name of the American spacecraft destroyed early in the film, *Challenger II*. Seven years after the release of this film, the original *Challenger* exploded in a tragic accident. The newspaper headline seen in the film, "*Challenger*: What went wrong?" seems eerily prophetic. Incidentally, the year when the story is set is nebulous. A deep-space mission to Mars seems to push these events well into the 21st century. Of course, referencing the calender date of December 7, Pearl Harbor day, as the appointed time of the apocalypse is another bizarre facet of the story, as is the canteen where the *Hercules* technicians eat, since it is furnished with a number of old-fashioned "shoot 'em up" pinball machines. The threat portrayed in the film is a credible one, although the comet-asteroid collision segment seems contrived as most of the debris seemed to head straight for Earth. The size of the anticipated meteor strike in the film is roughlt equivalent to the one which destroyed the dinosaurs, so the threat is a genuine and feasible one. The onscreen scrawl at the end of the film describes a real-life study which scientists are undertaking to head off such a threat when it materializes. Statisticians predict that such an event will probably not happen for another 50 million years, but the possibility still exists it could happen anytime.

The stellar cast is the most interesting aspect of *Meteor*. Sean Connery, veteran of many exciting James Bond features, is sharp and on edge for most of the picture. Natalie Wood is effectively cast as Dubov's assistant and possible romantic interest for Connery. She is charming and manages to strike the right tone throughout. Karl Malden plays his role straight, and his bluster seems a handy commodity left over from his performances in *The Streets of San Francisco* TV series. The film is actually stolen by Brian Keith, who speaks only one line in English in the entire film. His reading as Dr. Dubov is masterful, colorful and beguiling. He smiles, gestures and enlivens every scene in which he appears. When you consider his role as the local lawman in *The Russians Are Coming, the Russians Are Coming* (1966), his casting as the Soviet astrophysicist is ironic and a stroke of genius. In his scenes set in Russia, his character seems like a Soviet version of Charlie Chan, with an appropriate aphorism for every situation. The Soviet premier, incidentally, is veteran actor Gregory Gaye, who was a murder victim in *Charlie Chan at the Opera* (1937) and the title character of the Republic serial *Flying Disk Man from Mars* (1947). Another exceptional performance is that of Martin Landau as the paranoid and zany General Adlon. He brings much color and enthusiasm to a role that seems thankless on the surface. His well-controlled hysteria is among the highlights of the film. On the other hand, Henry Fonda plays the role of the President as an understated satire of his performance in *Fail Safe* (1964). His trademark "My Gawd" exclamation as he watches the television news is another unforgettable moment in the picture. The other players also are excellent in their parts, particularly Joseph Campanella as the general who watches the destruction of his son's spacecraft, and Sybil Danning as the attractive lady skier at the Swiss resort. There are also cameos in the Security Council scene by screenwriter Stanley Mann as the Canadian Ambassador and director Ronald Neame as the British ambassadors.

If you are among those who dismissed *Meteor* at the time of its release, the film is definitely worth another look. It is a very diverting and colorful picture, a film whose special effects may lack magic but that makes up for its numerous deficiencies in most unusual ways. On the whole, the picture is extraordinarily entertaining.

REPRESENTATIVE QUOTES

"The asteroid belt, a vast junkyard of metal and rock orbiting between Jupiter and Mars, thousands of fragments, some as small as a fist, some as large as a city and amongst these, Orpheus, twenty miles in diameter and undisturbed for countless generations . . . until now." (Final portion of opening narration)

"A mass of rock one mile wide, traveling at 30,000 miles per hour, would cause a crater fifty miles across and five miles deep. Orpheus is five miles wide. Its striking force is equal to 2,500,000 megatons of TNT. That is ten orders of magnitude above the largest earthquake ever recorded." (Bradley at the meeting with the secretary of state)

"The Volga is about to overflow its banks, and we are discussing swimming lessons." (Translation of Dubov's comment to the Soviet premier)

"Fook the Dodgers!" (Dr. Dubov's only attempt at English, quoting what a cab driver told him)

"In 1968, at the Massachusetts Institute of Technology, a plan was designed to deal with the possibility of a giant meteor on a collision course with Earth. This plan is named *Project Icarus.*" (True-life fact reported in end title card)

Moonraker (1979)

Rating: ∗∗∗   **Threat:** Lethal nerve gas

United Artists. Written by Christopher Wood based on the novel *Moonraker* by Ian Fleming; Photographed by Jean Tournier; Special effects by Derek Meddings (supervisor); Edited by John Glen; Music by John Barry; Produced by Albert R. Broccoli, William P. Cartlidge (associate) and Michael G. Wilson (executive); Directed by Lewis Gilbert. 126 minutes.

ANNOTATED CAST LIST

Roger Moore (*James Bond*, British Secret Agent 007); Lois Chiles (*Dr. Holly Goodhead*, scientist and CIA agent); Michel Lonsdale (*Hugo Drax*, industrialist who plans to exterminate and repopulate the world); Richard Kiel (*Jaws*, hired assassin); Corinne Clery (*Corinne Dufour*, assistant working for Drax); Bernard Lee (*M*, head of British Secret Service); Geoffrey Keen (*Frederick Gray*, British defense secretary); Desmond Llewelyn (*Q*, head of weapons research); Lois Maxwell (*Moneypenny*, M's executive secretary); Toshio Suga (*Chang*, Drax's henchman); Emily Bolton (*Manuela*, Brazilian agent assigned to assist Bond); Blanche Ravalec (*Dolly*, girlfriend of Jaws); Mike Marshall (*Col. Scott*, NASA assault force leader); Michael G. Wilson (Scott's assistant); Leila Shenna (hostess in private jet); Jean Pierre Castaldi (pilot of private jet); Anne Lonberg (glass museum guide); Walter Gotell (*Gen. Gogol*, head of KGB); Lizzie Warville (Gogol's mistress); Douglas Lambert (Mission Control director); Arthur Howard (*Cavendish*); George Birt (747 pilot); Denis Seurat (747 officer); Kim Fortune (RAF officer on shuttle transport); Claude Carliez (gondolier in Venice); Guy di Rigo (ambulance guard); Chris Dillinger, George Beller (Drax technicians); Albert R. Broccoli, Lewis Gilbert (two observers in St. Mark's Square); Chichinov Kaepper, Christina Hui, Francoise Gayat, Nicaise Jean Louis, Irka Bochenko, Catherine Serre, Beatrice Lipert (Drax's harem of followers); Johnny Trabers Troupe (circus performers).

SYNOPSIS

The most popular motion picture series of the last half of the twentieth century, the James Bond films, periodically has apocalyptic elements. In *You Only Live Twice* (1967), archvillain Ernst Stavro Blofeld tried to provoke a nuclear war between the United States and the Soviet Union, with the evil organization SPECTER on the sidelines, hoping to pick up the pieces after the conflict. In *The Spy Who Loved Me* (1977), madman Carl Stromberg had a similar scheme to make land masses unlivable and force humankind to set up communities under the sea. *Moonraker*, however, is the purest example of a total apocalyptic scenario, as the messianic Hugo Drax plans to wipe out all the human race while he and his followers take refuge in a space station. This entry is also the Bond film with the greatest reliance on science fiction in its presentation, no doubt inspired by the success of *Star Wars* (1977).

In the pre-title sequence, a British 747 aircraft is transporting *Moonraker*, a new space shuttle, when it is hijacked in mid-air by two men who were concealed in the shuttle. They launch *Moonraker*, which destroys the transport plane as it blasts off. The British defense minister alerts M, head of the Secret Service who plans to assign 007—their best agent, James Bond—to investigate. Bond is returning from his latest assignment by private jet. The pilot and hostess of the jet, however, are in the employ of Jaws, a menacing giant with gleaming metallic teeth. Jaws is an assassin who was an adversary of Bond in *The Spy Who Loved Me*. Bond is thrown out of the jet without a parachute. He glides through the air and manages to snatch the parachute away from the pilot, who also fell out of the plane. Jaws jumps and tries to attack Bond in the air, but is unsuccessful when 007 opens his chute. When his own parachute fails, Jaws manages to crash land onto a circus tent. This leads directly to the main title sequence, featuring images of Bond with his parachute and silhouettes of shapely female acrobats tumbling across the screen.

Bond meets with Defense Minister Frederick Gray and M to be briefed on his mission. Gadgetry specialist Q gives Bond a wristwatch that can fire darts by wrist muscle control. Agent 007 begins his inquiry by visiting industrialist Hugo Drax, whose California-based company built the shuttle. Bond flies to Los Angeles, where he is met by a beautiful helicopter pilot, Corinne Dufour, who flies him to Drax's headquarters (a large factory complex on an estate featuring an ornate baroque palace brought stone by stone from France), which Drax uses as his personal residence. From the air, Bond watches a large number of attractive women who are training in Drax's astronaut program. Bond meets with Drax, who behaves as if he were a great French aristocrat from the past. When Drax discovers that Bond knows the *Moonraker* was stolen, he orders Chang, his bodyguard, to kill him. Bond is given a tour of the facilities by Dr. Holly Goodhead, a NASA scientist on loan to the Drax Corporation to oversee space shuttle construction. She shows him the centrifuge trainer, a huge machine that rotates a passenger compartment at high speeds to simulate the pressure experienced by an astronaut when launched in a rocket ship. Holly is called away as Bond tests the equipment. Chang relieves the technician in control, and he sets the apparatus to spin at 20 Gs, a level considered to be fatal. Bond saves himself by shorting out the control panel with a dart from his wristwatch. That evening, with Kerns help, 007 locates a safe hidden within an antique clock. He photographs a set of plans for an elaborate space station that he finds in the safe. Drax is furious when he discovers his plans have been violated. He organizes a hunting party, setting a trap for Bond, but the secret agent spots Drax's sniper and shhots him out of a tree while pretending to aim at a pheasant flying by. After Bond leaves, Drax takes out his frustration by setting his dogs on Corinne and they tear her to pieces.

Next, 007 investigates one of Drax's subsidiaries, a glass factory in Venice,

Italy. He tours the museum of rare glass objects and the adjacent facility. He bumps into Holly Goodhead, who is in Venice to deliver a lecture at a symposium. When Bond later takes a gondola ride, several attempts are made on his life, but he easily escapes due to the special design of his boat. When a speedboat chases him, he converts his gondola into a hovercraft, and he glides through St. Mark's Square. That night, Bond breaks into the factory and follows a man into a highly advanced special laboratory that can only be accessed by a musical code, the five-note motif of the alien spacecraft used in *Close Encounters of the Third Kind* (1977). Two scientists are working on a highly dangerous chemical formula. Bond manages to obtain a sample vial when the men leave the room; however, he misplaces a sealed beaker when the men return. Observing from a airtight chamber, Bond watches as one of the scientists accidentally knocks over this beaker, and the two men fall dead almost instantly. Agent 007 escapes from the lab with his sample, but Chang attacks him as he attempts a getaway. They have an epic fight in which all the exhibits in the glass museum are destroyed. Chang is defeated and killed. Bond then sneaks into Holly's hotel room and questions her. He identifies her as an American agent after discovering several unusual CIA weapons among her personal effects. Bond also spots airline tickets to Rio di Janero in a drawer. He suggests that they cooperate, and they pass the night together. When 007 leaves at daybreak, however, Holly checks out immediately. M and the British defense minister are escorted to the hidden lab by Bond, but they find that the room has been converted into a huge study, where Hugo Drax reacts with mild disdain at their intrusion. Grey mutters an apology to Drax and asks M to remove Agent 007 from the case. Bond gives M the vial with the lethal sample and says he will visit Rio pretending to be on holiday.

Jaws is hired by Drax to replace Chang, and he is also dispatched to Rio. Manuela, a Brazilian agent, is assigned to help Bond. Bond uses the carnival to mask his break-in to Drax's warehouse in Rio, but he finds it deserted. One of the street revelers is Jaws in disguise, but he is swept away by the festive crowd. The next day Bond heads to Pão de Açúlar, the scenic mountain in Rio's harbor, which is reached by cable car. Holly is also there, observing Drax's cargo planes as they leave the airport. The two agents finally agree to cooperate, but their cable car stalls as they descend Pão de Açúlar. Jaws arrives alongside in a second car and jumps across. Bond and Holly sling a chain over the cable and slide down to the mainland. Jaws follows in the cable car, but it travels too fast and crashes into the terminal. Dolly, a small blonde woman with pigtails, helps Jaws out of the wreckage. They look at each other, and it is love at first sight, as the soundtrack plays *Romeo and Juliet* by Tchaikovsky. Meanwhile, Bond and Holly are captured by some thugs, who drive off with them in an ambulance. Bond manages to escape but is unable to rescue Holly. He encounters a band of gauchos who brings him to a monastery, which is a front for a commando training school operated by the British Secret Service. He meets M and Q, who explain that the sample in the vial contained a highly toxic nerve gas fatal to humans but causing no harm to animals. The formula is based on a rare orchid found only on a remote river in the Brazilian jungle. Q equips Bond with a special boat for his journey into the interior. As he nears the area, his speedboat is shelled and he is chased by other boats, one of them led by Jaws. Bond gets trapped in rapids heading toward a waterfall. He converts the top of his vehicle into a hang-glider, soaring over the falls while Jaws goes crashing over the edge.

After landing, Bond observes a small community in the jungle, and he follows some of the women, whom he recognizes as members of Drax's entourage. When he draws nearer, the rock he is standing on tilts over and he is tossed into a pool with a giant python, but he vanquishes the snake with a pen knife. Jaws returns and captures him as he emerges from the pool. Drax shows him that his base is actually a sophisticated launch complex for numerous space shuttles. The industrialist explains that he and all his followers will soon be transported to his space station, which is already in orbit. The planet will be cleansed of human life using his special nerve gas, which will not affect plants or animals. Then he and his followers will return to a world of his design with a race of perfect physical specimens. Bond asks why he hijacked *Moonraker* from the British. Drax explains that one of his own shuttles developed a flaw, and he did not have enough time to construct another. Drax orders 007 to be taken to a chamber underneath the launch pad, where Holly Goodhead is also a prisoner. They will be incinerated during the next take-off. As the countdown commences, Bond blows a hole through a hatch, and they make their way down a shaft moments before the rocket's vapor can reach them. They overpower two shuttle pilots and take their places for the next flight.

Holly notes that their flight course is prearranged, and they rendezvous with an elaborate space station. Bond comments that it is Drax's version of Noah's ark. He also deduces that the huge complex has some device that cloaks it from detection. Bond disables the jamming equipment. On Earth, Colonel Scott at NASA telephones General Gogol in the Soviet Union about the space station, explaining that they intend to attack the complex at once.

Drax delivers a speech to his followers, saying they will all be like gods and that he will form the ultimate dynasty. He orders Operation Orchid, the eradication of all human life on Earth, to commence. Jaws captures Bond and Holly and takes them to Drax, who is alerted that the United States has launched a spacecraft against him. He plans to destroy the ship with a laser beam. When Bond questions Drax about his standards of physical perfection, Jaws realizes that Drax eventually intends to eliminate both him and his girlfriend. Jaws decides to join forces with Bond, and they overpower Drax's guards. Bond pushes a button on the guidance control panel that disrupts the rotation of the station, causing a loss of gravity. This gives the NASA spacecraft a chance to dock and commence its attack. A formidable battle begins, as American forces with laser guns invade the complex. Bond kills Drax, ejecting him into space through an airlock. The space station starts to break apart. Agent 007 makes his way with Holly to an armed shuttle in order to destroy the three globes of nerve gas that were previously launched. Jaws helps them launch when the docking release clamp becomes jammed. Jaws and Dolly are thrown clear from the station in an escape pod. Holly pilots *Moonraker* in a desperate attempt to overtake the globes, and Bond destroys them with a laser cannon. They barely reach the last globe in time, as it starts to enter the atmosphere. NASA makes visual contact with *Moonraker* after they complete their mission, and Bond and Holly are shown in a weightless embrace. "My God, what's Bond doing?" Frederick Gray grumbles, and Q replies, "I think he's attempting reentry." Bond shuts off the video camera as Holly asks him to take her around the world one more time, and the end credits appear.

CRITIQUE

Although this film presents the deadliest threat in the entire Bond series, in tone it is perhaps the lightest and most humorous of the adventures. This is largely due to the cartoon-like nature of the rivalry between Bond and Jaws which resembles that of Road Runner and Wile E. Coyote. Time and again Bond engineers a daredevil escape, while Jaws faces the consequences and crashes into a circus tent or tumbles over a waterfall. Yet he always emerges unscathed, just like any toon character in *Who Framed Roger Rabbit?* (1988). These set pieces are brilliantly conceived and executed but repetitive of similar chases and scenes in earlier Bond movies. The opening sky-dive sequence is most original, and a very challenging sequence to top. *Moonraker* finally does top it with the dynamic battle in space, a remarkable action masterpiece. There are countless loopholes throughout the story, but the action is so swift that the viewer has little time to consider them. One that particularly stands out is the seasonal factor. Since it is carnival time in Rio, it must be late February or early March. But Bond has just left Venice where it appeared to be summer. The subliminal ads throughout the film are another major annoyance. When Bond opens the drawer of Holly's bureau in her Venetian hotel room, a box of Marlboro cigarettes is seen lying conveniently adjacent to her airplane tickets. Prominent billboards for Marlboro and Seven-Up soda dot the roadway when Bond and Holly are being driven away as prisoners in the ambulance in Rio. Similar ads are above the entrance to the cable car to Pão de Açúlar. Then, when Bond is riding with the Gauchos, the soundtrack plays Elmer Bernstein's theme from *The Magnificent Seven* (1960), the same theme that was used in Marlboro television ads. In later films, "product placement" became more subtle, but in *Moonraker*, its use is clumsy and distracting.

The apocalyptic threat in *Moonraker* is intriguing and unique: a nerve gas based on a botanical model that proves fatal only to humans but leaves animals and plants unharmed. It receives slightly more screen time than the usual Bond threat, and we are even presented with a chemical breakdown of the formula onscreen. The anthropological story attached to the plant—that it wiped out the civilization that bred it because the pollen of the plant produced sterility—is a fascinating detail in the story. The "necklace of death" with which Drax intends to envelope the earth is a chilling metaphor, but additional details would have been useful. How long would the deadly gas have remained potent? Could gas masks prove an effective defense against it?

As usual, the technical aspects of *Moonraker*, like any Bond film, are superb. John Barry's music score is excellent, with a beguiling title theme (sung by Shirley Bassey) and then the traditional Bond motifs, with which filmgoers are quite familiar. The cinematography is outstanding, particularly in the scenes in Venice, Rio and the spectacular Iguacu waterfalls. Like all Bond films, it is far preferable viewed in the letterbox format which preserves the integrity of each shot. The editing is crisp and fast paced, and editor John Glen later directed a number of Bond pictures of his own, such as *Octopussy* (1983). The only glitch is that the pigeon who does a double take watching Bond's hovercraft in St. Mark's Square looks just like what it is, a stilted and artificial editing trick.

The cast leads are very well played. Roger Moore's Bond is more whimsical and tongue-in-cheek. Incidentally, the very first Bond was Barry Nelson, who played him as an American agent in a television version on *Climax* in the 1950s opposite Peter Lorre as Le Chiffre, the first Bond villain. Like Sean Connery, Moore played Bond seven times, and although his conception of the part was more formula driven, he managed to keep his performances charming, flippant and entertaining. Lois Chiles, a fine actress, was originally considered to play the heroine in *The Spy Who Loved Me*. She makes an atypical "Bond girl," since she is fully trained as a CIA operative as well as a scientist. She is one of the few heroines who surpasses Bond intellectually as well. Chiles appears natural and at ease throughout the film, and she gives the appearance that she is the one, rather than Bond, who chooses to keep their romance casual. French actor Michel Lonsdale is very interesting as Hugo Drax, a role originally intended for James Mason. He is cool, detached and utterly regal. He underplays his role magnificently and is one of the most believable of all Bond villains. In his speech after landing on the space station, his "god complex" is utterly convincing. Lonsdale is best remembered as the abbot in the exceptional *Name of the Rose* (1986), which Sean Connery as a medieval monk who resembles Sherlock Holmes. Lonsdale also stood out in *Day of the Jackal* (1973) and *Jefferson in Paris* (1995) where he played King Louis XVI. Richard Kiel, the 7 foot giant who plays Jaws, is colorful and handles his role with genuine comic panache. His remarkable facial expressions are among the highlights of the film, especially as he is about to crash into a wall or tumble over a waterfall. His character is pure burlesque, and he is as indestructible as Bond himself. He is given one line in the film, "Well, here's to us," as he shares a glass of champagne with his girlfriend while the space station starts to disintegrate. It is a great moment, except that the station no longer has gravity, so it would have been impossible to pour the beverage. There is a slight parallel between Jaws and Darth Vader, and one can see similarities between the revolt of Jaws against Drax to Vader's turn against the emperor in *Return of the Jedi* (1983). Kiel has appeared in a considerable number of films over the years, including the strange, huge alien creature who resembled Farfel (the dog puppet from Nestle's Quik commercials) in *Phantom Planet* (1961). Kiel also played. the prehistoric man in *Eegah!* (1962), the large but gentle mental patient in *Brainstorm* (1965) and appeared in the recent

Disney effort, *Inspector Gadget* (1999). Jaws will deservedly remain his best re-membered part. *Moonraker* was the last screen appearance of Bernard Lee as M, a role he had essayed since *Dr. No* (1961). His film career dated back to the 1930s and included such memorable films as *The Third Man* (1949) and *Father Brown* (1954). There are also cameo appearances in the film by producers Michael G. Wilson and Albert R. Broccoli, as well as director Lewis Gilbert.

Despite its many strengths, *Moonraker* is not a particular favorite among Bond film enthusiasts, who find the boat chases repetitive and the humorous encount-ers with Jaws too silly. The crown jewel of the film, the battle in outer space, is without doubt one of the best sequences in the entire series, but to some 007 purists, it is too far a leap into science fiction. *Moonraker* also has a cadre of loyalists as well, but for the general public, it is simply a great popcorn movie.

REPRESENTATIVE QUOTES

"Even in death, my munificence is boundless. When this rocket lifts off, I shall be leaving you in your own private crematorium. Mr. Bond, Dr. Goodhead, I bid you farewell." (Drax as he places Bond and Goodhead in the chamber beneath the launching pad)

"No doubt you have realized the splendor of my conception. First, a necklace of death above the Earth, fifty globes each releasing its nerve gas over a designated area, capable of killing 100 million people. The human race, as you know it, will cease to exist. Then, a rebirth." (Drax to Bond while launching his second globe of nerve gas)

"Take a giant step for mankind." (Bond to Drax as he staggers backwards into the air lock)

The Night the World Exploded (1957)

Rating: ***   **Threat: Worldwide earthquakes**

Columbia. Written by Jack Natteford & Luci Ward; Photographed by Benjamin H. Cline; Special effects by Willard Sheldon; Edited by Paul Borofsky; Musical direction by Ross DiMaggio; Produced by Sam Katzman; Directed by Fred F. Sears. B & W, 64 minutes.

ANNOTATED CAST LIST

Kathryn Grant (*Laura Hutchinson*, assistant research scientist); William Leslie (*Dr. David Conway*, inventor of the earthquake predictor); Tristram Coffin (*Dr. Ellis Morton*, head of seismology lab); Raymond Greenleaf (*Cheney*, governor of California); Charles Evans (*Gen. Bartes*, military head of Civil Defense); Marshall Reed (general's aide); John Zaremba (*Daniel Winters*, assistant secretary of state); Frank Scannell (*Quinn*, sheriff from Los Cerritos, Nevada); Paul Savage (*Kirk*, Carlsbad park ranger killed by E-112); Fred Colby (*Brown*, Carlsbad park ranger); Natividad Vacio (doctor at Carlsbad Hospital); Otto Waldis (*Professor Hangstrom*, Stanford University mineralogist); Terry Frost (foreman of Carlsbad rescue team); Dennis Moore (military short-wave operator).

SYNOPSIS

This modestly budgeted film brings a fresh and unusual approach to an end-of-the-world story. which has considerable potential that is largely wasted due to the use of scientific gibberish for explanations. Instead of engaging the audience, the script confounds them whenever it attempts to describe what is happening, missing a chance to create a minor gem of a film.

The story begins as Dr. Morton arrives at his seismology laboratory. He learns that his associate, Dr. Conway, has worked all night to complete his invention, the pressure photometer, which can forecast earthquakes. In fact, the machine has already predicted that a major tremor will occur within twenty-four hours. Morton and Conway immediately go to see the governor, who is hesitant about following through on the prediction because their machine has not yet been tested. He does alert the Disaster Council to prepare for the possibility of a disaster. When the scientists return to their lab, their assistant, Laura "Hutch" Hutchinson, offers to spend the night to help monitor the new machine. Hutch mentions to Dr. Morton that she may leave the project soon if she decides to accept the marriage proposal from her boyfriend, Brad. Actually, Hutch has a crush on Dave Conway, but he is so absorbed in his work that he never notices her. Morton implores her to stay on.

The next morning at 5:45 A.M., the earthquake strikes with devastating results. A montage of disaster footage flashes by while a narrator describes the damage. The narrator concludes by saying that "what escaped their notice was that the axis of the Earth had shifted three degrees." Dave asks Hutch to accompanying him on a return trip to see Governor Cheney. The seismologist tells a board of officials that another earthquake of twice the intensity will occur in several days. There will also be a series of earthquakes worldwide, each of increasing intensity. Some new force is exerting pressure beneath the earth, and unless it is relieved, the planet will be destroyed. Morton goes to Washington, D.C., to brief the secretary of state with the same news.

Dave plans to set up his new machine at the deepest point of the Carlsbad Caverns to get the most precise readings. While descending by rope ladder to their staging area, Hutch gets a panic attack and is unable to move. Dave taunts her, calling her a baby, and she becomes so angry that she continues down the rope without incident. At the bottom of the drop, Dave apologizes for the insult, saying he was just trying to get her mind off the depths below her. They set up the pressure photometer and start to record the readings.

Morton receives a report that Southern California has been struck by the second earthquake and the ground has tilted another four degrees. This is followed by a fresh series of quakes around the world, and a montage reveals the destruction. General Bartes is sent to California to confer with the governor and help coordinate the Department of Civil Defense. In the cavern, Kirk, a park ranger helping the scientists, discovers an unusual rock in the depths of the cave. Neither Dave nor Hutch can identify it. Kirk takes the rock back to his quarters to analyze it. He places it on a table, and while his back is turned, the rock grows in size and gives off steam. Finally a huge explosion kills Kirk and destroys the building. Dave and Hutch help sift through the wreckage, wondering if the newly discovered rock was to blame.

In the cavern, Dave locates other, similar rocks. He places it on a bench, and moments later it starts to grow and produce steam. It burns through the wooden bench and falls into a pool of water, which seems to render it harmless. Dave calls his discovery Element 112. He believes this new element is the cause of the worldwide quakes. Buried deep in the earth, rocks composed of this element are being pushed up to the surface, where they dry off, and then expand and explode, causing tremendous earthquakes.

Back in Washington, Dave meets with Daniel Winters, assistant secretary of state, and warns him of this new development. Winters arranges an emergency meeting at the Smokeridge Proving Grounds, a military base, and promises to cut through any red tape so the meeting can be held as soon as possible. The world's top scientists are briefed about the new element, now called E-112. Dr. Hangstrom, the leading mineralogist, participates in experiments demonstrating the growth rate and explosive qualities of E-112 when completely dry. "It has an explosive power of tilting anything, even the Earth," Dave explains. But when water is added, E-112 shrinks and becomes harmless. Each scientist is given a sample of E-112 and asked to brief their appropriate government agencies, such as the Committee of Public Safety, about the threat.

Hutch is trapped by a cave-in at Carlsbad Caverns. Information from the pressure photometer reveals that Carlsbad will be ground zero for the next earth-quake, and a rescue team rushes to dig Hutch out in time. Racing against the clock, Dave and the rescue team break through, moments before the expected quake. Hutch recovers at the Carlsbad Hospital, and as Dave visits her, he real-izes he is in love with her.

The Datatron, a master computer, predicts the earth will be destroyed in twen-ty-eight days unless E-112 is controlled. The only way to achieve this is to flood any area with signs of E-112 activity. Large-scale engineering feats and massive cloud-seeding with dry ice are the two main methods in this scheme. Many "tilted" zones are drenched with water, but it is more difficult to find a remedy for arid areas. Hutch returns to work, and when Dave asks why she does not spend time with Brad, Hutch says she is already with the man she loves. "What do you want from me with the world collapsing, maidenly reticence?" Dave replies that he hopes it is not too late for them.

Reports worldwide show that the water projects appear to be working and the earthquakes are decreasing. A TV broadcast from Athens is interrupted by a quake, and the Greek newsman dives beneath his desk as debris starts to fall in the studio. Dave is called by Sheriff Quinn from Los Cerritos, Nevada, who re-ports that a volcano has developed overnight in his town. Dave calculates that the only way to pacify the area is by releasing the water from the Horseshoe Dam. He calls the facility but is told that the workers at the site are dying of poison gas released from the volcano. Dave plans to blow up the dam himself using his research supply of E-112.

Dave and Hutch fly by helicopter to the dam to plant a supply of E-112 that should produce a large enough explosion. Sheriff Quinn joins them in the dan-gerous assignment. Dave also brings along nitric acid, which accelerates the ex-plosive cycle of E-112. While running through the huge dam complex, the group faces more danger when the nitric acid is overturned by one of the dying workers, who upsets a table as he falls. They return to the helicopter just in time as the E-112 starts to explode. The ensuing flood ends the danger to the last area threatened by the new element.

Finally, with the threat over, the series of earthquakes cease. Dave calculates that the problem may reappear in another hundred years. He and Hutch survey the countryside from a hilltop, and they begin to plan their own future together. After they kiss, Hutch jokingly wonders if the danger is really over since she felt the earth starting to move again when they embraced.

CRITIQUE

This Columbia feature from the enterprising poverty-row studio mogul Sam Katzman (one of the most successful producers who specialized in cheaply-made quickies) could have been a low budget classic if the screenwriters had proposed a relatively sound scientific basis for their story. Instead, they used mumbo-jum-bo while trying to explain their plot. Their descriptions are so nonsensical that they undermine the entire concept, which is unfortunate because a rational explanation could easily have been devised. Instead the story spouts doubletalk about "the tilting of the Earth's axis" and other phrases that are incoherent and make no sense. For example, if they described a fifty-mile area as "bulging from the center" instead of "tilting," then the concept would seem more conceivable. To say an area is tilting, however, means one end of the area is up and one end is down. Then there would be a fall-off where the land returns to normalcy. The way it is described, however, comes across as absolutely meaningless.

Outside of this major irritation, *The Night the World Exploded* does almost everything else right, and the result is a very entertaining screen yarn produced on a shoestring. The story proceeds at a relatively quick pace, and the romantic subplot of the workaholic scientist with an admiring assistant is whimsical and well handled. The use of stock footage is very heavy, but well integrated into the film. The true-life newsreel footage is very powerful since the reality is so very apparent. There are also a number of special effects shots lifted from Republic serials, such as *Manhunt of Mystery Island* (1945) and *Daredevils of the Red Circle* (1939). The impressive action sequence at the dam is also reminiscent of some of the Republic serials, which frequently used a large industrial complex as a backdrop. The sequence is well staged and serves as a credible climax to the film. The Carlsbad Cavern scenes are also effective, well staged and reasonably convincing. The picture is competently directed by Fred F. Sears, who died of a heart attack at the age of forty-four, shortly after completing the film.

The cast is pleasant, if somewhat low key. Kathryn Grant as Hutch is both perky and appealing. She plays her character as very professional and non-stereotypical for the 1950s. Grant even manages to handle the awkward line about rioting in the churches without making it seem ridiculous. She also shows some range in the part, such as few wistful scenes as well as her panic attack while climbing down into the cave. Grant's real name was Kathryn Grandstaff, and her close friend, actress Marla English, had jokingly nicknamed her "Kathryn Grandstuff." Grant shortly retired from acting when she married Bing Crosby. William Leslie was a journeyman actor who handled this rare lead role as Dave Conway moderately well. The same year as this film, he costarred with Ronald and Nancy Davis Reagan in *Hellcats of the Navy* (1957). Tristram Coffin was a veteran of over a hundred films, mostly Westerns and serials. He was often cast as the villain, but he also served as an action hero in *King of the Rocketmen* (1949). He is dependable as Dr. Morton, and if you observe him closely, he brings some interesting nuances to this supporting role. Note the scene where he brings his family to the lab out of concern for their welfare. The other bit players are also credible, including veteran performers such as John Zaremba, who appeared in scores of films such as *Frankenstein's Daughter* (1959) and *20 Million Miles to Earth* (1957). His real forte was television where he appeared in hundreds of shows such as *Perry Mason* and *I Led Three Lives,* where he was Richard Carlson's FBI contact, Jerry Dressler.

Producer Sam Katzman was a legendary Hollywood showman noted for the "Jungle Jim" series, developing the concept of the East Side Kids and the remarkable and colorful series of Bela Lugosi Monogram horror films during the 1940s. Katzman continued to turn out cheaply-made exploitation films up until his death in 1973.

REPRESENTATIVE QUOTES

"Those who lived to tell the tale remember the day began with fragile, breathtaking beauty. The temperature was cool, in the low fifties. The air mountain pure, even downtown. It was a day unreal enough to serve as a setting for the birth of a world or the death of it." (Opening narration)

"It looks like something in the Earth is expanding, creating enough force to literally tilt the surface. . . . If that pressure keeps increasing, there will be explosions powerful enough to reduce this planet to dust." (Dave Conway to the governor and his council)

"I wanted to pray and be with other people, not by myself. There was nothing but rioting in every church. People fighting to get in. I couldn't make it, so I prayed by myself." (Hutch to Dave, relating how she spent her time off)

Noah's Ark (1929)

Rating: ✳✳✳   **Threat: Global Flood**

Warner Brothers. Written by Anthony Coldeway & De Leon Anthony based on a story by Darryl F. Zanuck & on the *Bible*; Photographed by Barney McGill & Hal Mohr; Special effects by Fred Jackman; Edited by Harald McCord; Music arranged by Louis Silvers; Produced by Darryl F. Zanuck; Directed by Michael Curtiz. B & W, Original version, 135 minutes; Restored version, 100 minutes; Youngston version, 75 minutes.

ANNOTATED CAST LIST (Biblical story characters are listed first.)

Dolores Costello (*Miriam*, Japheth's betrothed; *Marie*, German wife of Travis); George O'Brien (*Japheth*, Noah's youngest son; *Travis*, American tourist); Paul McAllistar (*Noah*, the arkbuilder; the army chaplain); Guinn Williams (*Ham*, Noah's second son; *Al*, friend of Travis who dies in combat); Noah Beery (*King Nephilim*, wicked ruler of Akkad; *Nikoloff*, Russian schemer); Malcolm Waite (*Shem*, Noah's eldest son; *Bulkah*); Louise Fazenda (ceremonial maiden in temple; *Hilda*, Al's friend at the inn); Myrna Loy (slave girl; theater troupe dancer); Anders Randolf (leader of Nephilim's troops; German man on train); Armand Kaliz (leader of Nephilim's personal guards; Frenchman on train); William V. Mung (Nephilim's guard; innkeeper); Nigel de Brulier (Nephilim's high priest; soldier); Noble Johnson (broker); Otto Hoffman (trader); John Wayne (extra).

SYNOPSIS

This picture was one of the most expensive productions of the late 1920s, and it went seriously over budget. It was the brainchild of the young Darryl F. Zanuck, who planned to outdo Cecil B. DeMille, taking *The Ten Commandments* (1923) as his model. Like the earlier film, the main story takes place in modern times, with an extended flashback to the *Bible*, telling the story of the flood. All of the major players undertook dual roles in the modern and biblical plots. The scenes with Noah were depicted on a large scale, with broad brush strokes and impressive effects. The film included a synchronized soundtrack and musical score, as well as several short talking sequences. These, however, were all in the modern story. An alternate silent version was also released.

The film begins at the end of the flood story, with God making a covenant with Noah, promising never again to destroy the Earth with a massive deluge. The film continues, portraying both the story of the tower of Babel and the worship of the golden calf. The picture then links the golden calf to the activities of the stock market on Wall Street. (Interestingly, the stock market crash of 1929 happened four months after the original release of the film.) The setting finally focuses on the Orient Express as it starts its journey to Constantinople in July 1914. The train derails after a bridge collapses, and the survivors recuperate at a nearby inn. The central figures of the story are present at the inn. These include two Americans, Travis and Al; Marie, a German girl they rescue from the train; Nikoloff, a Russian secret agent who has designs on Marie; and an evangelist who is mocked for reading the *Bible*. Nikoloff and Travis fight over the girl. French police arrive with the news that war has been declared, and Marie flees with Travis and Al before Nikoloff is able to turn her in as a German national. In Paris three years later, Travis marries Marie. Al joins the army when the United States enters the war. Travis later decides to join, in a burst of patriotic enthusiasm after seeing Al marching in a parade of American troops, leaving Marie feeling totally abandoned. At the front, Al is killed in combat and Travis becomes a hardened soldier. Marie joins a traveling dance troupe to survive. Nikoloff notices her at a show and tries to blackmail her into submitting to him. When she refuses, he plants false papers on her and she is arrested as a spy. Marie is sentenced to death by firing squad, and by a remarkable coincidence, all the main characters are reunited. The army chaplain who consoles her is the same evangelist from the train wreck. Travis is a member of the firing squad, and he is astonished to find his wife in the crosshairs of his rifle. He demands that the execution be halted. Shells from a long-range German canon explode nearby, and everyone topples into an ancient underground catacomb. They are trapped, and the minister tries to keep the survivors calm by relating the story of Noah's ark.

The script expands the biblical story, focusing on the city of Akkad in the land of Ur of the Chaldees. King Nephilim is their ruler, and his reign symbolizes the wickedness of humanity. He worships the idol Jagbuth with human sacrifice and plans to find the fairest virgin for this ritual. In the entire world, only Noah and his family remain faithful to Jehovah. Noah's sons, Ham, Shem and Japheth, are admirable men. Japheth is betrothed to Miriam, a servant of their household. Soldiers of Nephilim seize Miriam as the intended victim of the sacrifice. Japheth follows her into Akkad to rescue her, but he is seized by Nephilim, blinded, and put to work as a slave in the king's stone mill, where he is forced to crush rocks into powder by pushing a massive grindstone. God summons Noah to the heights of Tersgah, where He informs the patriarch of the coming worldwide deluge and tells him to construct a great ark.

Noah and his family undertake God's instructions. Soldiers of Nephilim mock and stone them as they work, but God sends a ring of fire to protect them. The day of the sacrifice arrives, and Noah interrupts the ceremony with a warning of God's wrath. A fierce storm suddenly arises. Nephilim orders an archer to kill Miriam, but a bolt of lightning electrocutes the man when he stretches his bow, and a blast of wind knocks over the other archers. Nephilim appeals to the massive statue of Jagbuth to vanquish the storm, but the figure crumbles after another lightning hit. The stone mill is also destroyed, setting Japheth free. He stumbles his way to the Temple and rescues Miriam.

At the ark, the animals start to arrive in pairs and board the huge ship. Below in Akkad, a massive wall of water sweeps through the city. People scramble wildly trying to escape the raging tide, and soon everything is engulfed. A number of refugees make their way to the ark, seeking rescue. In a miracle, God restores sight to Japheth and the doors of the ark open automatically to receive him and Miriam, but the doors close to other stragglers and Nephilim himself has his fingers crushed by a wooden shutter while attempting to get aboard. The rising waters lift the ark while the rest of humankind perishes.

The chaplain finishes his story of Noah, comparing the flood to the deluge of blood spilled in the war. Nikoloff dies from his injuries. A rescue team breaks into the underground vault, and as they are rescued, the survivors learn that an armistice has been signed and the war is over. The picture ends in jubilation as all the troops celebrate the end of the conflict.

CRITIQUE

The highlight of this film, the flood, is very impressive and memorable, but the rest of the plot seems painfully contrived and quite corny. The script is downright absurd at times, particularly the plot twist that Travis is a member of a firing squad about to kill his wife. Story loopholes abound, in both the war and biblical stories. Nikoloff denounces Marie because she is German, a problem she could easily solve by revealing that she is the wife of an American soldier. At this juncture of the story, Russia had pulled out of the war, so what standing would a former Russian agent have in giving orders to American troops? The biblical story spends time documenting how the poor suffer under King Nephilim, yet God shows no mercy or concern for these suffering souls. The plot leaves the impression that the flood was summoned merely to save Miriam and Japheth. After Noah appears at the Temple to warn of the deluge, he then simply vanishes leaving Miriam to fend for herself until blind Japheth stumbles in long after to finally rescue her. The flood arrives so quickly, that the whole event occurs within one or two hours instead of the biblical forty days. The scenes in Akkad, nevertheless, are the most remarkable in the film, and the large scale of the sets, the elaborate costumes (based on ancient Babylonian garb) and the use of crowds are vivid and striking.

The acting is generally good, although over the top at times. Dolores Costello makes a very appealing heroine. She was married to John Barrymore, and her granddaughter, actress Drew Barrymore, bears a distinct resemblance to her. George O'Brien carries the brunt of the film's action, and his reading is rather hokey. The scene in which he deserts his wife in a crowd to chase after his buddy Al, whom he spots in a parade of American troops, is exaggerated, but nowhere as overwrought as the depiction blind Japheth, who endlessly grimaces while imploring God to send down his wrath. O'Brien was more successful in his career when he specialized in cowboy roles. Guinn Williams, often known by his nickname, "Big Boy," is the most natural performer, and the only one to be completely successful in the brief sound sequences. His death scene is also well handled. Unfortunately, he is given little to do as Ham. Noah Beery is su-

perb in his dual role, and both his villains are decidedly different. Paul McAllistar is magnificent as Noah, but his twentieth-century counterpart is stuffy and a
bit clichéd. John Wayne worked in the film as an extra, appearing as a soldier in
the war sequences.

The musical score is trite, using snatches of classical and popular music pretty
much at random to convey the intended mood of each scene. The cinematography is exceptional, and the special effects portraying the great flood still pack a
tremendous power. These scenes proved to be exceedingly dangerous to film,
and some blame director Michael Curtiz for having little concern for the safety of
his extras. Fifteen thousand tons of water were stored in reservoirs, which
poured onto the set through special causeways concealed behind the temple set.
When this water was released, many extras were startled by the force, and their
struggle to escape was genuine. Reportedly, there were three deaths and numerous injuries. Unlike the death of actor Vic Morrow on the set of *The Twilight Zone—The Movie* (1982), there was little publicity surrounding this tragic
occurrence.

The film was originally debuted in June 1929 with a running time of 135
minutes, which was later trimmed by a half hour prior to general release. The
film recovered only a mere portion of its production cost, partially due to poor
reviews and the effect of the downturn in the economy after the stock market
crash. In the 1950s, producer Robert Youngston totally recut a version of
Noah's Ark for rerelease. Youngston had been very successful in issuing feature-
length compilations of silent shorts by the great comedians, including Buster
Keaton, Harry Langdon and Laurel and Hardy. This version eliminated all title
cards as well as the brief sound sequences and employed a non-stop narrator, who
not only told the story but commented on the performers, their careers and their-
acting style. The sequence of events was also reshuffled, with the World War I
story reduced considerably and placed later in the film. Interestingly, the scenes
of the flood still conveyed great power on the big screen, and this release proved
to be successful.

With the total destruction of the existing world, *Noah's Ark* qualifies as an
apocalyptic film. The story of the flood has been retold many times in films,
cartoons and television. *The Bible* (1966) included a forty-minute segment that
was one of the more succesful versions, in which John Huston directed himself
as both Noah and the voice of God. The destruction of the earth by the flood
was hardly covered in the film, which concentrated instead on Noah's interaction
with the animals during their long voyage. Most critics hailed Huston's folksy
and charming performance as the highlight of the three-hour epic. In 1976, a
Robert Ripley-style documentary, *In Search of Noah's Ark*, also restaged the
biblical tale. A mini-series called *Noah's Ark* appeared in 1999, with John
Voight as Noah. This version took much wider latitude with the biblical story,
adding a pre-flood variation of the story of Sodom and Gomorrah as a teaser to
the great flood and adding large doses of comic relief into the mix. Mary Steen-
burgen played Noah's flighty wife. The silliest segment had a peddlar, played by
James Coburn, who floats by the ark in a ramshckle craft and trades goods with

Noah and his family. The computer-generated effects were subpar and the miniseries is not in the same league with the 1929 film.

REPRESENTATIVE QUOTES

"And the Lord said . . . I will not again curse the ground any more for man's sake . . . neither will I again smite anymore everything living, as I have done." (Opening title card)

"The Flood . . . it was a Deluge of Water drowning a World of Lust." (The title card of the minister addressing the survivors trapped in the underground catacomb)

No Blade of Grass (1970)

Rating: **   Threat: Global famine**

MGM. Written by Sean Forestal & Jefferson Pascal based on the novel *The Death of Grass* by John Christopher;   Photographed by H.A.R. Thomson; Special effects by Terry Witherington;   Edited by Eric Boyd-Perkins & Frank Clarke;   Music arranged by Burnell Whibley;   Produced & directed by Cornel Wilde.   97 minutes.

ANNOTATED CAST LIST

Nigel Davenport (*John Custance*, architect fleeing London with his family); Jean Wallace (*Ann Custance*, John's wife);   Nigel Rathbone (*Davy Custance*, their son); Lynne Frederick (*Mary Custance*, their teenage daughter); John Hamill (*Roger Burnham*, scientist and Mary's boyfriend); Patrick Holt (*David Custance*, John's brother and owner of a large farm); Anthony May (*Andrew Pirrie*, gun shop clerk); Wendy Richard (*Clara Pirrie*, his wife);   Christopher Lofthouse (*Spooks*, Davy's schoolmate);   George Coulouris (*Mr. Sturdevant*, gun shop owner);   Ruth Kettlewell (fat lady in pub); M. J. Matthews (*George*, her companion);   Michael Percival (police constable);   Tex Fuller (*Mr. Beasley*, John's lunch companion in flashback);   Simon Merrick (TV announcer);   Anthony Sharp (*Sir Charles Brenner*, government ecologist);   Norman Atkyns (*Dr, Cassup*, head of Davy's boarding school);   John Avison (Yorkshire sergeant); Jimmy Winston (rapist killed by Ann);   Richard Penny, R. C. Driscoll (gang members);   Geoffrey Hooper (roadblock spokesman);   Christopher Wilson (roadblock gunman);   William Duffy (farmer slain by Pirrie);   Mervyn Patrick (*Joe Ashton*, group leader killed by Pirrie);   Joanna Annin (*Emily*, Slain leader's wife);   Ross Allan (*Alf Parsons*, recruit who joins Custance);   Joan Ward (Alf's wife);   Karen Terry (Alf's daughter);   Bruce Miners (*Bill Riggs*, recruit);   Margaret Chapman (*Prudence Riggs*, Bill's wife);   Michael Landy (*Jess Arkwright*, recruit);   Louise Kay (*Susan Arkwright*, his wife);   Brian Crabtree (*Joe Harris*, recruit);   Susan Sydney (*Liz Harris*, Joe's wife);   Bridget Brice (*Jill Locke*, pregnant woman);   Christopher Neame (*Locke*, Jill's husband);   Derek Keller (*Scott*, recruit);   Suzanne Pinkstone (Scott's wife);   Surgit Soon (*Surgit*, Indian recruit) John Buckley (captain);   Malcolm Toes (sergeant-major);   Cornel Wilde (Narrator; short-wave radio broadcaster).

SYNOPSIS

This is a bleak and unsettling film that escorts the viewer into an unvarnished tour through the darkest regions of human nature. The downward spiral is inexorable, and the audience is offered no ray of hope or comfort in the entire plot. The quality of the film is remarkable, employing a full repertoire of cinematic techniques. It also manages to avoid a preachy tone except for the awkward opening that is reminiscent of the clichéd public service announcements of the 1960s with a teary-eyed Indian. After this stumbling start, the film is near perfect in its portrayal of a world gone mad as all society breaks down and even decent people have their moral standards stripped away as they fight for survival.

The picture opens with a montage of global pollution while Cornel Wilde, as narrator, describes how the ecosystem of the planet was abused during the decade of the 1970s until a worldwide famine began. Because of the pollution, a lethal virus has appeared, which destroys all plant life, leading to the collapse of all agriculture. The title song, resembling a folk tune, describes this green blight where no blade of grass can survive. The proper story begins in 1979 as Roger Burnham calls his friend John Custance with a warning that martial law is about to be declared and the city of London will be closed. John, a distingiuished-looking man who wears a patch over one eye, alerts his wife, Ann, and teenage daughter, Mary, to prepare to escape to his brother's sizable farm in the remote hill country. Roger joins them, and as they set off in two cars, they hear increasingly ominous news over the radio. The Chinese are bombing their own cities, killing 300 million people, in an attempt to stretch their meager food supplies. Other organized governments are collapsing, and there are reports of cannibalism. Each of the characters has a flashback of events leading up to the current crisis. The travelers find their way blocked by a street riot as looters pillage the remaining stores. After the police quell the riot with firearms, John decides that they will need to obtain guns if they are going to survive.

They stop at the home of Sturdevant, who runs a firearms store for hunters. HIs shop is closed, but he opens up for his old customers. He refuses to sell them guns when they do not have the proper permits. They try to explain that their need is desperate and that they are going to a safe refuge in the country. Custance invites the shopkeeper to join them, but he refuses. Sturdevant is then shot and killed by his own clerk, Pirrie, who asks the Custances to allow him and his wife to join them. Now with three cars, the caravan encounters a military blockade, and they get into a gunfight provoked by a belligerant officer who threatems to shoot Roger, a a few soldiers are killed in the battle. The Custances pick up their young son Davy at his boarding school. When Ann learns that Davy's friend Spooks is now an orphan, she invites him along. While on their way, the boys are warned by Ann never to speak with Pirrie or his wife.

Bulletins on the radio report that the country is falling into anarchy and martial law has been proclaimed by the prime minister. Pirrie and his wife had originally planned to rob and abandon the others but now think it is wiser to stay with them, finding safety in numbers. One car gets separated from the others by the barricades at a railroad crossing, which turns out to be an ambush. After overpowering John, a gang of bikers kidnaps Ann and Mary, dragging them off and raping them. Burnham and Pirrie revive Custance and rescue the women. One of the thugs is wounded in the scuffle and begs for his life. Ann Custance grabs the rifle out of Pirrie's hands and kills the rapist with one shot.

Continuing on their way, the group monitors the latest developments on the radio. A citizens' committee topples the British government when it learns of plans to use nerve gas on the populace of London. The prime minister flees the country and the revolutionary committee attempts to restore order. At another roadblock, a citizens' militia commandeers their vehicles and rations, leaving them only their clothes, but Pirrie manages to conceal a pistol. They set off on foot and decide to raid a local farmhouse, killing the owners. Custance has difficulty explaining the violence to his son, but after Spooks compares the situation to a Western, the boys seem to take it in stride. They tune in America on a short-wave radio in the house and learn that almost all governments have ceased to exist except in North America. The U.S. president starts to speak, but the signal fades away. After resting, the group sets out again, walking through a rainstorm. They pass the night in an abandoned barn. While there, Pirrie catches his wife trying to seduce Custance, and he shoots her. Custance asks him not to let the boys know of this episode.

The landscape gets more rugged as they continue on their way. Mary begins spending more time talking with Pirrie, and her father tries to stop her. A confrontation is avoided between Custance and Pirrie only when Mary says she feels safer being with Pirrie, and that it is her own choice. In her eyes, he has become a more preferable than Roger. Near a picturesque aquaduct, they chance upon an armed band of stragglers. Custance approaches them, saying that if they band together, they will have a better chance of survival. He says his brother's farm can serve as a sanctuary which they can share and help defend as civilization disintegrates. Joe Ashton, their leader, is hostile and tries to start an argument; he is finally shot by Pirrie. Custance tries to make peace with the others, stating his that proposal is still open. First one family and then another decides to join with Custance until the group swells to a sizable band. The large group pushes forward relentlessly until the women are too exhausted to continue. John is concerned when he sees that the green blight has already progressed so far north, and the countryside is covered with dead animals who have eaten the diseased grass. A women goes into labor, and Pirrie sets up an armed perimeter with a handful of men to protect their makeshift camp. Custance helps the mother deliver the new infant, but the baby dies moments after its birth.

The next day, as their outfit probes deeper into the hill country, they encounter an army unit that is in rebellion. They avoid contact and circle around this war zone, but another group, a gang of bikers with horned Norse helmets detects them and lauches an assault. They encircle them, and the battle is a bloody one, and the bikers break off their raid after their leader is killed.

Weary, the survivors finally reach the outskirts of the farm of David Custance. The boundry of the farm is very well fortified, and several sniper shots are fired as they approach. A voice shouts out for them to move on. John Custance proceeds with a white handkerchief on a stick, proclaiming his identity. David appears out of the scrub, and the brothers embrace. David is shocked that his brother has so many people with him. He will make room for John's family and Roger, but no others. David himself has a large assembly billeted on his land and fears they may already exceed the capacity of the farm to support them.

John pleads for his associates, but his brother remains adament. Returning to his followers, John notifies them that they will either have to move on or fight their way in. That night, they try to sneak onto the land through the woods. David's men are on the alert, and another onslaught occurs. Pirrie and David Custance kill each other in the fracas. After a number of deaths, a truce is declared and John is recognized by all survivors as the new leader. The victims of this last fight are buried, and John leads a forlorn prayer at their graves, asking God's forgiveness for everyone. Ann tries to comfort John over the death of his brother, but he repliess coldly, "If Pirrie hadn't killed him, what would I have done?" As the survivors return to their compound, the scene is inverted as in a photographic negative, suggesting their that days are numbered. The film ends with a reprise of the folk tune reinterating that no blade of grass will survive. At one point, Cornell Wilde considered adding an another scene set one year later, in which a member of the compound takes a walk and finds a sole blade of grass growing in a barren field, but Wilde discarded the idea.

CRITIQUE

No Blade of Grass is a genuine masterpiece of apocalyptic cinema. Cornel Wilde's direction is exceptionally hard-edged and brilliant, but the film is so unrelentingly dark that it is difficult to watch. Many viewers are unable to handle such a pessimistic vision. One must commend Wilde for the picture's unflinching integrity. There is no compromise, and Wilde allows no sentimentality to intrude on his black depiction. At one point, in the childbirth sequence, there seems to be a hint of redemption—of a future—but this comes crashing down when the baby perishes. Not surprisingly, the film was a commercial disaster, and MGM wound up dumping it as the second half of a double feature. The picture's only rallying point was its ecological message, but this turns out to be the plot's weakest link. The conjecture that the plant virus was caused by the residue of soil pollutants could simply be a wrong assumption by bungling scientists. Britain's top ecologist in the film, Sir Charles Brenner, is an unreliable fool. Theoretically, the green blight in the film could have appeared unrelated to the terrible state of pollution. Except for the awkward opening, the ecological message remains a side issue and is not the dominant focus of the plot.

The style of the picture is very sophisticated, and to a certain extent *No Blade of Grass* is really an art film. The editing is phenomenal and innovative. The techniques include, not only flashbacks, but flashforwards as well. Early in the film, Mary suggests to David that they begin a sexual relationship, that she wishes to lose her virginity and become a woman. At this point, a quick cut reveals her being raped in the future. These flashforwards to future events occur regularly throughout the film. The cinematography is memorable. The scene in which Custance persuades a rival group to join his band is actually quite beautiful, with an impressive background of a giant aquaduct and a rolling hillside. The script of the film is compelling. The radio bulletins are particularly colorful and interesting as humankind slips further and further down the vortex. The last message on short wave from the United States describes how all European royalty and heads of government have sought asylum in North America. The president then begins a cliché-filled speech about the lofty ideals of civilization, and he is soon drowned out by static. When his voice resumes, no one remains to listen to his empty words. This is a subtle and effective moment. The only poor technical aspect of the film is the weak and irritating musical score. The ballad that opens and closes the picture is particularly trite and empty.

Some critics have described this picture as merely a reworking of *Panic in Year Zero* (1962), which is unfair since the approach of both films is vastly different. *Panic in Year Zero* depicts a temporary loss of the veneer of civilization, with hope always present. But in *No Blade of Grass*, the decline of civilization is permanent, with no real hope possible. *Panic in Year Zero* also stresses aspects of the American character, where *No Blade of Grass* seems to subtly deride the British character. For instance, in the pub flashback, the television shows scenes of famine in China and Africa, which most of the patrons ignore as they gorge themselves while making disparaging remarks about the Chinese. Time and again, there are lines of dialogue suggesting a sense of arrogance—that Britain is above the problems of the rest of Europe and the world. At other points, the stoic British character seems to be mocked.

The characters in the film are unconventional and richly portrayed. John Custance reminds one at times of Wotan, the weary head of the Germanic gods in Richard Wagner's opera cycle, *Der Ring des Nibelungen*. Like Wotan, he is silver-haired, wears an eye patch and is forced into making devastating choices. Nigel Davenport plays Custance with flawless precision, as his character violates his moral code again and again in the name of survival. He has one remaining dream, an idyllic fantasy of his brother's farm, where the green virus will never spread and where people may live in harmony and dignity as human beings. Of course, he then winds up inviting so many people to come with him that his proposal becomes only another cruel illusion. By the end of the film, John is only an empty shell of a man, and his prayer at the graveside of the victims is hollow and lifeless.

Cornel Wilde's wife, Jean Wallace, delivers a powerful performance as Ann. Previously married to Franchot Tone, Jean Wallace appeared in many films with Wilde, notably the film noir classics *The Big Combo* (1955) and *Storm Fear* (1955). In this film, her character ranges from minor petulance in flashbacks, when she is troubled that her petunias may catch the blight, to earth-shattering rage, when she grabs the rifle to personally dispatch the thug who raped her and her daughter. In another film, her performance might have garnered an Academy Award nomination. Lynne Frederick, who was later married to both David Frost and Peter Sellers, is splendidly convincing as the daughter. She is coquettish and playful at first, but after she is attacked she becomes morose and hardened. Like her father, she is forced to make painful choices, such as when she betrays David and selects Pirrie as her future mate because she feels he can protect her. Pirrie is probably the most remarkable character of all. In any other movie, he would be seen as a psychopath and a monster, but in this film, the gun crazy rake is practically the hero. With the downfall of civilization, he has become the most valuable individual traveling with Custance due to his cunning and ruthlessness. He saves the situation time and again, and he and Custance develop a grudging respect for each other. When they openly quarrel over Ann, Pirrie restrains his natural "shoot-first" instinct for the only time in the picture. He always refers to John as "Mr. Custance" with a sense of esteem, even when he is shot and dying in the guerrilla attack on the farm. Pirrie is the only one who seems to fit into the savage world, and at times he seems like a modern version of Doc Holiday, brutal and calculating but with a certain code of honor. Anthony May is brilliant as Pirrie, and he pushes the envelope in a marvelous reading. Again, if this were a more popular film, May would have been a contender for an Academy Award for best supporting actor. Another worthwhile cameo is turned in by verteran George Coulouris, whose long line of credits include such varied films as *Citizen Kane* (1941), *The Master Race* (1944) and *Man without a Head* (1958). He is perfectly cast as the crusty gun shop owner, a stickler for details and a traditionalist with total confidence in Her Majesty's government.

Despite the high quality of the production on many levels, this remains an uncomfortable film to watch. The brutal procession of events is too unrelenting and the battle scenes too repetitious. There is no nobility or unselfishness to be found in anyone. Neither is religion invoked to provide any consolation, until the vapid prayer at the film's conclusion. Some might appreciate the work more if they consider it as a poker-faced black comedy, a portrait of Murphy's law gone mad. Otherwise, the film is simply too desolate. In this sense, it almost resembles Alexander Solzhenitsyn's towering work, *The Gulag Archipeligo*, the three-volume chronicle of the Soviet slave labor camps. Both works challenge their audience to chart out unblinkingly the lowest depths of humanity.

REPRESENTATIVE QUOTES

"It will be worse here than it is in Africa or Asia where they are used to famine." (David Custance to his brother and Roger Brunham as they are dinning in a pub)

"The guilty don't deserve to die as quickly as the innocent." (Pirrie, while threatening the rapist with his rifle)

"Everything is different now, boys. We have to fight to live. Do you understand?" (John Custance to Davy and Spooks, after the killing of the farmer and his wife)

"This motion picture is not a documentary, but it could be." (Cornel Wilde's closing narration)

No Survivors Please (1964)
AKA *Der Chef Wünscht Keine Zeugen*
(*The Chief Wants No Survivors*)

Rating: ***   **Threat:** **Nuclear war caused by aliens**

Shorcht. Written by Peter Berneis; Photographed by Henry Hubert; Edited by Claus Von Boro; Music by Herman Thieme; Produced & directed by John Albin & Peter Berneis. B & W, 88 minutes.

ANNOTATED CAST LIST

Robert Cunningham (*Fawnsworth*, renowned American ambassador); Maria Persehy (Ginny Desmond, his secretary); Uwe Friedrichsen (*Howard Moore*, Parisian newspaper reporter); Wolfgang Zilzer (alien chief); Gustavo Rojo (*Armand*, agent for the chief); Karen Blanguernon (*Vera*, alien impostor); Stefan Schnabel (General Ruskovski, Soviet official); Rolf Wanka (*Dr. Hans Walter*, rocket scientist); Armin Dahlen, John Elwenspoek, Ralph von Nauckhoff, Ralph Illig, Ted Turner.

SYNOPSIS

In the late 1950s and early 1960s, the German film industry produced a number of oddball features in both German-language and English-language versions. Many of these were based on mysteries by Edgar Wallace, and others were either horror or science fiction. *No Survivors Please* is an excellent example of the latter. Most of the principals speak English, and those with noticeable accents are dubbed, sometimes with inappropriate voices for their characters. These films have a unique style combining elaborate camera angles and imaginative settings but with storylines that are sometimes ponderous.

The picture opens in New York City where an airline pilot is ordered by a mysterious chief to crash his plane over the Yucatan peninsula while transporting Ambassador Fawnsworth on his mission to Costa Rico. The chief insists, "No survivors please!" Ginny Desmond, Fawnsworth's secretary, sees her boss off on his chartered flight. During the flight, the pilot goes back to talk with the ambassador, calmly reassuring him as a fire breaks out and the plane spirals down to crash in the jungle. Fawnsworth's body is revived shortly after by an alien posing as the wife of an explorer. She welcomes the new alien who now inhabits Fawnsworth's body and briefs him on how to pass as a human being.

In Washington, D.C., the chief meets with the alien posing as Senator Taylor, and they select rocket scientist Hans Walter as the next candidate for replacement. The scientist decides to take an ocean cruise, but he disappears while walking the deck at night. Later the news circulates that Dr. Walter has been miraculously rescued from the ocean by another ship. In the Soviet Union, General Ruskovski, a leading Soviet official, appears to die during an operation, but then mysteriously revives. His doctor, Suchinkoff, another alien impostor, reports his success to the chief, who announces an upcoming meeting in New York City.

Howard Moore, a reporter for a Paris newspaper, has become intrigued that so many famous people had recent brushes with death, which he finds a startling coincidence, including such people as Fawnsworth and Dr. Walter. He convinces his editor to publish a series of articles about the phenomenon. Moore attempts to court Ginny Desmond, hoping she will persuade Fawnsworth to agree to an interview. He obtains handwriting samples of some of the alien substitutes indicating a complete alteration of their personalities. Meanwhile, at his New York meeting, the chief discusses plans for the destruction of humankind by provoking their goverments to start a nuclear war.

Ginny asks Fawnsworth if he would agree to an interview, and she is startled when he concents. The chief orders Fawnsworth to dispose of Moore and assigns Vera and Armand, other substitutes, to work with him. Moore interviews Fawnsworth while in flight to South America. He tells a fanciful story that he survived after the crash by charming birds down from the trees, killing them and drinking their blood. Fawnsworth observes a growing bond between Ginny and Moore that he finds fascinating. Planning to kill the reporter during a street festival in Rio, a masked Vera lures him into a side street, where Armand appears with a knife. Ginny, directed by Fawnsworth, shows up and deflects the sneak attack. Fawnsworth confesses to Suchinkoff, the doctor who revived Ruskovski, that he permitted this rescue due to an emotional impulse. Suchinkoff says that he himself has became contaminated after reading a love poem and has requested to be returned to his home world. Ginny begin a romance with Moore and they rendezvous at a Rio beach. They see Suchinkoff drive his car over a cliff, and his body is totally incinerated. Fawnsworth asks the chief if he could go home as well, but his request is denied. The chief sends him to Paris on another mission, insisting again that Moore be killed. At a Kremlin meeting, Ruskovski lays the groundwork for a nuclear attack.

Moore meets with his editor at a Paris bistro, but when Armand tries to shoot him with a rifle, Fawnsworth again interferes, using his own body to block the assassin's target. Vera and Armand plan their next move. Vera attempts to seduce Moore, but the experience changes her and she is unable to kill him. Armand visits Moore's editor, and when he refuses to cancel the series of articles, he arranges for the editor to be poisoned. A substitute takes over as editor and assigns Moore to cover the Grand Prix at Le Mans. Armand arranges a traffic accident when the reporter drives home. The next time Moore and Ginny meet, he has been replaced, and she finds the substitute to be cold and distant.

Armand implores the chief to send him home. When Moore reports to the chief, he is told that the war will start very soon. Fawnsworth travels by aircraft to meet with Dr. Walter at a secret base from which an atomic missile will be launched at Moscow, provoking the nuclear holocaust. He brings Ginny with him. In flight, the ambassador confesses the entire alien plot to her and explains how the concept of human love has made his task of destroying life on Earth very difficult. She makes one final appeal on behalf of humanity. Ginny moves him, and he orders their plane to crash, allowing another chance for the human race to survive.

A short time later, the chief is formulating new plans to destroy humankind, and the resurrected body of Ginny is his new assistant. Moore visits Ginny as she recovers in the hospital. Even though they are now alien, they still can recollect the experience of love. To inspire their resolve, the chief and Senator Taylor take a walk to observe humans. The film ends with a montage of faces, old, young, beautiful and ugly as the Rio carnival music is reprised on the soundtrack. An underground nuclear test is then shown as the film ends.

CRITIQUE

Very few people have seen this film, and even fewer expended the energy to seriously consider it. It has enough depth to make a serious study worthwhile. This eccentric picture begins as if it is going to be hilariously bad, but by the time the character of the reporter enters the scene, it becomes compelling instead. The plot is labyrinthian and complex, but with far more substance than expected. It is the naive personalities of the aliens that make the film seem so rich. Except for the chief, they all develop an immediate sympathy for the human race and the concept of love. Some. like Armand and Ruskovski, resist the impulse. Others, like Fawnsworth and Vera, find they are unable to continue their mission. It is this quiet, internal conflict that makes the film fascinating. The technical work is excellent. The cinematography resembles an art film, always playing with light and shadows. There is a concentration on unusual faces throughout the film, culminating in the final, impressive montage. The luminous close-ups of Karen Blanguernon are gorgeous. The worldwide locales are also very impressive, particularly scene between Moore and his editor on the balcony with the Cathedral of Notre Dame framed in the distance. The music is unusual and catchy throughout, ranging from a Latin American samba to a melodramatic dirge.

One major flaw is the inadequate dubbing. For example, the drawling voice with a Southern accent provided to the co-pilot while he jokes about smoking is so absurd that it provokes gales of laughter, from which it takes time to recover. The editing is uneven, and a few sequences are poorly cut, such as the scenes with Dr. Walter on the luxury liner. The Le Mans scenes are also a bit of a stretch, and seem thrown in simply because they had available stock footage of a crash at the Grand Prix. For the most part, the other stock material is well integrated and does not stand out.

The international cast does a fine job. Many of them were regulars in the German film industry, but Robert Cunningham is American born and raised in Kansas, although most of his film work consists of bit parts filmed in Europe. He played Henry Fonda's second in the famous duel scene in *War and Peace* (1956). He is fascinating in the key role of Fawnsworth. He has a few curious lines that echo memorable statements prior to World War II. In the pre-credit scene, as the genuine Fawnsworth, he says he is seeking "peace in our time," recalling Neville Chamberlain. Then at the conclusion of the film, when explaining the alien's designs on Earth, he says they are doing it because they need more "living space," bringing to mind Hitler's use of the same phrase. Wolfgang Zilzer made a number of American films, including a lead role (under the name Paul Andor) in Monogram's *Enemy of Women* (1944) as Dr. Josef Goebbels. Stefan Schnabel, son of the legendary classical pianist Arthur Schnabel, also appeared in a number of American films including *The 27th Day*. Maria Persehy and Karen Blanguernon both had decent screen careers. Gustavo Rojo was a fixture in Spanish films, but also appeared in efforts such as *The Valley of Gwangi* (1969).

The final insertion of the underground atomic test is intriguing. It suggests that the chief will eventually complete his task, yet the previous poignant scene with the meeting of the alien Howard Moore and alien Ginny Desmond implies the opposite, that the distant memory of love will continually thwart the chief. The German version of the title, *The Chief Wants No Survivors*, makes one wonder if he will ever get his wish.

REPRESENTATIVE QUOTES

"Have you ever seen two pieces of meat tied to a string and thrown to the gulls? There are always two who will grab and swallow the pieces at the same time, and neither one can let go so in the end they'll choke to death. I'm going to throw them the world, and they will swallow from both ends until they choke on it too." (The Chief to Senator Taylor describing how he will provoke a nuclear war)

"Don't forget that there are few of us and many of them. We are an expeditionary force sent to Earth to eliminate mankind. The human bodies of great and important men we temporarily occupy are now nothing but empty shells, ruled by our superior intelligence instead of primitive human emotions. Do not try to remember or understand human emotions." (The chief at the meeting with alien impostors)

"Here we are only human." (Armand to Vera)

One Night Stand (1984)

Rating: ****   **Threat: Nuclear war and fallout**

Astra Film Production. Written by John Duigan; Photographed by Tom Cowan; Edited by John Scott; Music by William Motzing; Produced by Richard Mason; Directed by John Duigan. 97 minutes.

ANNOTATED CAST LIST

Cassandra Delaney (*Sharon Smith*, usherette at the Sydney Opera House); Saskia Post (*Eva*, Czech émigré and Sharon's friend); Tyler Coppin (*Sam*, AWOL American sailor); Jay Hackett (*Brendan Pizzy*, janitor at Sydney Opera House); David Pledger (*Tony*, Brendan's friend); Ian Gilmour (Sharon's boyfriend in flashbacks); Jennifer Miller (Sharon's teacher in flashbacks); Monica McDonald (Sam's old girlfriend in flashbacks); Peggy Thompson (Sam's mother in flashbacks); Michael Conway (security guard at Sydney Opera House); Lois Ramsey (Salvation Army worker); Alec Morgan (Scottish piper); Tsukasa Furuya (large nutcracker robot); John Krummel (TV news commentator); Richard Morecroft, Helen Pankhurst (TV reporters); Frankie Raymond (*Frankie*); Todd Boyce, Michael Cloyd, Justin Monjo (American sailors).

SYNOPSIS

This Australian production is a bizarre compound that seems like a cross between *Waiting for Godot* and the "Porky's" series. At times it seems like a rambling and silly frolic, but then it switches tone and becomes vivid, intense and emotionally wrenching. The unexpectedness of some segments could even compare to the initial impact that Alfred Hitchcock's *Psycho* (1960) had on viewers. When the film sustains this mood it is magnificent, but it occasionally squanders its advantage with an awkward gesture. This quirky film has yet to be discovered by many movie aficionados, who may someday grant it cult status.

The picture opens with an anti-American protest march greeting the arrival of a U.S. warship in Sydney harbor. Most people ignore the protestors, however, since it is the Christmas season. The camera follows two pretty girls, Sharon and Eva, who are observed by two young men dressed as Santa Claus. They strike up a conversation and persuade the girls to go out with them that evening. Tony and Brendan decide to take their dates to a rock program in the concert hall at the Sydney Opera House. The story spends considerable time with typical teenage banter as the girls size up their dates. The two couples return to the girls' apartment, where a television report describes a serious world crisis due to an incident in Central America. Sharon and Eva finally decide to dump the guys, and they give them a quick brush off.

Christmas passes, and Sharon is at work as an usherette at the Sydney Opera House on New Year's Eve. After the show ends, Eva arrives and the girls plan to go to a party. Sharon notices that one of the patrons, a young man, is hiding in the bathroom. She recognizes him as an American sailor who has jumped ship and was reported missing in the newspaper. He admits that he has been hiding out in the complex for the past three days. His name is Sam, and he shows the girls his hideout in a control booth. While they are talking, a janitor cleaning the stage begins to sing, pretending he is giving a concert. Sharon recognizes him as Brendan, and she activates the control panel, causing the lights to flash and a giant nutcracker robot to advance on the bewildered janitor. The girls go down to the stage following their prank, roaring with laughter. They start to tease Brendan when Sam shouts in alarm that the radio has just announced that nuclear war has started in Europe. All citizens of Sydney are advised to stay indoors, since a nuclear bomb has been dropped on a military base near the city.

The four young people decide to remain at the art complex. The girls search for a phone to try to make a call. Performers still in costume are using the telephones trying to reach their families. When Eva finally locates a phone, it is inoperative. She starts to panic, but Sharon calms her by commenting that they will have to set an example for the two guys. They decide to dress up in exotic costumes from the wardrobe department. Sam and Brendan likewise agree to put up a brave front for the sake of the girls.

Each of the characters has numerous flashbacks as the film continues. Eva is a Czech émigré in Australia who was the object of ridicule by schoolmates until Sharon befriended her. Sharon herself recalls her heartbreak when she broke up with her first boyfriend. Sam remembers his girlfriend in New York, an ice skater, and how his mother got drunk when he brought the young lady home for supper. He also thinks about his visit to Paris on shore leave from the navy. Brendan is haunted by images of ballroom dancers performing *The Blue Danube Waltz* by Johann Strauss, Jr.

After some chatter about what creatures might survive a nuclear blast, Eva reads the daily horoscope forecasts for each of them. They listen again to the radio, which reports the belief that there will be no further nuclear strikes against Australia. Brendan has a key to the bar room at the complex, and they go there to down a few drinks. They loosen up as they gab about sex. At midnight, they peek out to watch the city from a balcony. At first they expect to hear some sounds of celebration for the new year, but the hour passes with only a lonely church bell tolling in the distance.

They go to the movie theater in the complex and run the projector. A long segment of Fritz Lang's classic *Metropolis* is shown. A security guard interrupts them, and they pass by the concert hall, where an organist is playing to the empty seats. The four decide to play a game of strip poker, and the girls dress up with more elaborate clothes from the wardrobe department. They joke about how the British royal family is coping in their fallout shelter. The poker game continues until Brendan loses and completely strips for the girls, who chortle uncontrollably and then wander off. Sam goes to a grand piano and starts playing *Gymnopedie No. 3* by Eric Satie. The melancholy theme makes Brendan feel sad, and after dressing, he seeks out Sharon in the wardrobe department. She tries to cheer him up, saying that if this is their last night, they should make the most of it. She starts to remove her clothes and they embrace.

Eva passes through the Opera House business office and turns on the television. Barely able to speak, a newswoman reports that most of Europe has virtually ceased to exist. A transmission from the United States shows graphic footage of the victims of an atomic attack in upstate New York. Eva is devastated by the scene and switches off the set when Sam enters the room. She tells him the set in inoperative when he asks about it. At the same time, Sharon and Brendan look outside from the lobby. The sky is strangely illuminated by continuous flashes of light. They agree not to inform their companions, but they find Eva in tears when they return. Sam tries to comfort her, and Sharon wonders if prayer might help.

A voice over a loudspeaker warns that everyone in the Opera House must relocate immediately to the subway station. The four take off at once, mingling with other people pouring out of the complex toward the underground entrance. Clips from *Metropolis* are intercut into this sequence. The subway platform is filled with people on the verge of panic. An old lady and a guitarist are performing a blues ballad. When they finish, a Salvation Army worker asks if anyone else is able to sing. Sharon and Eva volunteer and start to sing "It Might As Well Rain until September." In the middle of their number, a massive explosion is heard and the lights go out. People start to scream, but the girls continue their song until their voices and the fading rumble of the nuclear blast are the only sounds remaining. Sam lights a match, and everyone looks up anxiously as the end credits appear onscreen.

CRITIQUE

One Night Stand takes an unusually long time to launch its main story, which serves to lure the audience into a false sense of security. It gives the impression that we are watching a Down Under version of *Happy Days*. The date sequence of the girls with Brendan and Tony has a very frivolous air as they wisecrack and gossip. The background news reports about a world crisis would be almost overlooked except for the camera taking note of the somber reflections of one rather ominous commentator. The tone continues to remain light as the scene shifts to the Sydney Opera House. Showcasing the various facilities at the complex also seems part of the film. Then the war starts, but as in Joe Dante's superb film *Matinee* (1993), the war scare does not seem to be the main thrust of the film. Subtly and gradually this changes. The characters pick up more depth with the brief flashbacks. Their fun-loving facades slowly begin to crack, and each one tries to maintain the illusion that nothing is really happening. Their self-delusion and escape into alcohol and sex last only so long. The genuine crux of the film is concentrated in the short, horrifying television footage that Eva sees about the aftermath of an atomic blast. This crucial sequence is among the most powerful moments to appear in any film. The scene lasts only ninety seconds, but its impact is cataclysmic and overwhelming, both to Eva and the viewing audience.

Another element that enriches the picture is its imaginative use of scenes from *Metropolis* (1926). The film is first viewed by the two couples on the big screen of one of the theaters, and they seem mesmerized by it. Images of the stars of the silent German classic, Brigitte Helm, Rudolf Klein-Rogge and Gustav Fröhlich, are used very deftly. The clips from *Metropolis* are carefully arranged, but not in the proper chronological sequence from the original Fritz Lang film. Even more potent is the later use of these images, which counterpoints the scenes of people fleeing to the subway station, in a sequence of tragic sweep and intensity.

The picture also benefits from moments of pure surrealism. In some scenes, we see performers in Shakespearean garb reacting to the nuclear nightmare. Sharon and Eva also try to turn their backs on modern times by dressing in fanciful costumes. Placing the strip poker contest on a fanciful stage set is also surreal, as is the nutcracker robot with whom the characters often interact. When the robot finally topples over, it vainly continues its mechanical movements on the floor, a fine visual metaphor for the activities of the main characters. In addition, the mid-summer Christmas season seems somewhat unreal to residents of the Northern hemisphere.

Unfortunately, the power of the film is undercut at times by some heavy-handed and clumsy choices. A good example is the close of the film, which ends with genuine cinematic poetry. A reprise of the Satie piece on solo piano would have been perfect for the end credits over the freeze frame of the four actors looking upward in disbelief. Instead, this poignant conclusion is ruined by a corny medley of 1960s protest songs. Similar missteps occur at several points throughout the film, such as the awkward and unnecessary demonstration march.

The young cast members are good, but none of them appeared in anything more than a mere handful of additional films. Cassandra Delaney and Saskia Post are outstanding, and Delaney in particular seems to have the makings of a star. She is fresh and appealing, and she effectively portrays a wide and subtle range of emotions. Her singing voice is also fairly good. Post is wonderfully compelling as Delaney's alter ego, who anticipates her every mood change. When she emotionally collapses after the shattering TV broadcast, her anguish is most expressive and convincing. Their male counterparts, Tyler Coppin and Jay Hackett, are not as strong or interesting. Coppin struggles throughout at trying to approximate an American accent. At best, he sounds as if he were doing a weak impersonation of Jack Nicholson. Hackett is both more credible and vulnerable in his role. Some of the other performers are excellent in their short roles, particularly Helen Pankhurst who stands out dramatically as the distraught news commentator.

The cinematography is exceptional throughout, and the use of bright colors throughout the film contrast masterfully with the storyline as the plot grows ever more somber. The editing is equally superb, and the Sydney Opera House itself makes a fascinating locale, which the film exploits expertly. The music heard is quite a melange, from snatches of Richard Wagner to pop and rock melodies. If only writer/director John Duigan could have avoided his sporadic heavy-handedness, this picture might have created a major sensation. But by 1984, it was almost too late for a tenable antinuke parable.

REPRESENTATIVE QUOTES

"There is one unthinkable conclusion . . . Armageddon. For surely, it is in just this climate of almost hysterical recrimination that a fatal misunderstanding would occur, and the button be pushed. This, of course, would be beyond comprehension." (TV news commentator whose report is ignored by Sharon and Eva)

"Even the corgis have their own underground kennel." (Brendan to the others, while discussing how the British royal family is coping with the crisis)

"It was horrible on the television in the office. The people, you couldn't even tell they were people anymore. They've been burned alive. They were screaming, and their skin was hanging from their faces. . . I didn't want to tell you." (Eva to the others after viewing the television broadcast)

"Nothing's happened yet. Maybe it's a false alarm." (Sam's observation a moment before the final nuclear explosion)

On the Beach (1959)

Rating: *****   Threat: Radiation sickness

United Artists. Written by John Paxton based on the novel *On the Beach* by Nevil Shute; Photographed by Guiseppe Rotunno; Special effects by Lee Zavitz & Linwood G. Dunn; Edited by Frederic Knudtson; Music by Ernest Gold; Produced & directed by Stanley Kramer. B & W, 134 minutes.

ANNOTATED CAST LIST

Gregory Peck (*Dwight Lionel Towers*, American submarine captain); Ava Gardner (*Moira Davidson*, Australian socialite); Anthony Perkins (*Lt. Peter Holmes*, Australian liaison officer to Towers); Donna Anderson (*Mary*, his wife); Katherine Hills (*Jennifer*, their baby); Fred Astaire (*Julian Osborne*, nuclear scientist); John Tate (*Adm. Bridie*, head of Australian Navy); Lola Brooks (*Lt. Osgood*, his assistant); Guy Doleman (*Bob Farrel*, first officer of the *Sawfish*); Peter Williams (*Jorgenson*, professor with theory of fallout dissipation); Peter O'Shaughnessy (his associate); John Meillon (*Ralph Swain*, yeoman who jumps ship in San Francisco); Joe McCormick (*Ackerman*, first sailor to get radiation sickness); Kevin Brennan (*Dr. King*, physician who treats Ackerman); Lou Vernon (*Davidson*, Moira's father); Harp McGuire (*Sundstrom*, sailor who explores the San Diego refinery); Ken Wayne (*Benson*, requisitions officer on the *Sawfish*); Richard Meikle (*Davis*); Keith Eden (*Dr. Fletcher*, government physician who informs Holmes about the suicide pills); Basil Buller-Murphy (*Sir Douglas Froude*, Mary's uncle); Jim Barrett (*Chrysler*, Australian officer on the carrier *Melborne*); Frank Gatcliff (radio officer); John Royle (his supervisor); Ken Baumgartner (chief petty officer on the *Sawfish*); Stuart Finch (*Jones*, communications operator on the *Sawfish*); Lucian Endicott (planesman on the *Sawfish*); Jack Boyer (medic on the *Sawfish*); Jerry Ian Seals (*Fogarty*, crewman on the *Sawfish*); Harvey Adams (*Sykes*); Grant Taylor (*Morgan*, Holmes party guest); Rita Paunceford (Holmes party guest); Audine Leith (*Betty*, Holmes party guest); Paddy Moran (Pastoral Club member concerned about the wine supply); C. Harding Brown (*Dykers*, Billiards player at Pastoral Club); John Casson (Salvation Army preacher); Cary Paul Peck (boy); Dale Van Sickel (stunt driver for Fred Astaire).

SYNOPSIS

This film is perhaps the first and foremost example of mainstream apocalyptic cinema. It is a film made even more intense by the low-key delivery of most of the cast. There are few histrionics in this cerebral approach. The story portrays no mass rioting, no reverting to the law of the jungle as civilization fades away. There is little genuine action in the picture as most of the drama is internal, and it proceeds towards doom with a leisurely but inevitable rhythm that is mesmerizing. Compared to most other apocalyptic films, *On the Beach* has an emphasis on human dignity which is truly unique and timeless.

On the Beach projects a storyline five years in the future. It is January 1964, and the entire population of the world except Australia has succumbed to the deadly fallout from a brief, but lethal, nuclear exchange between the major world powers. In a small apartment, Lieutenant Peter Holmes prepares tea for his sleepy wife, Mary, and a bottle of milk for his infant daughter. The young couple talks as if the world were still normal, but Peter has been summoned to meet with Admiral Bridie, head of the navy. He is assigned as liaison officer to the American submarine *Sawfish,* which recently docked in Melbourne. Bridie explains that he will review the appointment in four months. The deadly residue of fallout is due to reach Melborne in five months, according to the top government scientists.

Dwight Towers, the captain of the *Sawfish*, is a quiet, friendly man, and Peter takes an instant liking to him. They go to the exclusive Pastoral Club for lunch. Peter later meets his wife on the beach, explaining that he invited Captain Towers as their weekend guest. Mary agrees, as long as Peter promises to keep the conversation away from morbid topics. They plan to hold a party with Towers as guest of honor, and they also plan to invite Moira Davidson as female companionship for Towers. In fact, Moira meets the captain at the train station when he arrives. Peter's friend Julian Osborne, a nuclear scientist, attends the party. He explains the recent war as a colossal blunder probably caused by faulty vacuum tubes and transistors. Another party guest blames the scientists, however, which upsets Julian, who finally speaks the unspeakable: that everyone is doomed. Mary shouts for him to stop, saying that some hope has to exist. Moira, like Julian, is a heavy drinker who uses alcohol to keep from focusing on the truth. She and Towers later sit on the porch at night and watch the stars. He speaks calmly and rationally about the approaching doom, but when he refers to his wife and children, he speaks as if they are well and happy back in Connecticut. Moira does not comment on this idiosyncrasy, as she and Towers form a warm attachment.

At a scientific conference, Professor Jorgenson proposes a theory that the radioactive elements may be dispersing more quickly than previously anticipated. He proposes to Admiral Bridie that a reconnaissance mission be sent as far north as Alaska to measure the radiation levels and attempt to verify his theory. Towers agrees to undertake the mission by submarine, and Julian Osborne is assigned to go with them to perform the necessary tests. The admiral also informs Towers about an intermittent message that has been picked up from San Diego. It seems the sender of the message does not know Morse code, but there is a definite pattern to the signal. On their journey, the *Sawfish* will try to track down the source. Later, Moira visits the *Sawfish* and asks Towers for a tour of his vessel. When she sees Julian coming aboard, she teases him that drinking is not allowed on submarines. Later Moira and Towers relax by sailing and walking by the ocean. When asked by Moira what would be his favorite last activity, Towers replies that he would wish to go trout fishing in a clear stream. Their bantering suddenly stops when Towers accidentally calls her Sharon, his wife's name. Down the beach, Peter talks with Dr. Fletcher about the suicide pills that the government is preparing to dispense at the appropriate time. He later visits Mary's uncle, Sir Douglas Froude, who helps Peter obtain a supply of the pills.

Before leaving on his mission with the *Sawfish*, Peter leaves Mary two of the pills for herself and the baby in case she contracts radiation sickness before he returns. She bitterly rejects the idea. Meanwhile, Towers and Moira go to a nightclub and spend a night out on the town. She tells him she felt honored when he called her by his wife's name. Towers backs away from their relationship, and he explains the only way he can continue to function is to maintain the illusion that his family is still living and is safe at home. He fears a romance between them would undermine this safety mechanism. Moira breaks off their date and leaves. She gets drunk and visits Julian, who is working on a racing car, a Ferrari, which he recently purchased. He wants to race it before he dies. She tells him that previously no man has ever meant anything to her. Now she has fallen in love with Dwight Towers, but he is still married to his memories. Julian reveals that the *Sawfish* is leaving on its mission in the morning.

The journey of the *Sawfish* is uneventful. Off Point Barrow, Alaska, Julian finds the radiation level still to be extremely high, disproving Professor Jorgenson's optimistic theory. Peter has a long talk with Julian, sharing his concerns about facing the end with Mary. Julian merely tells him to be grateful his wife loves him so deeply. The boat proceeds down the West Coast to San Francisco. Towers surveys the city through the periscope, observing the desolate streets, which are free from any nuclear damage. No sign of life is visible, not even a bird. One member of the crew, Swain, whose home town is San Francisco, jumps ship through the escape hatch. When the sailor later fishes from a pier in San Francisco Bay, Captain Towers speaks to him by loudspeaker from the submerged sub and wishes him well. Swain discloses that he prefers to die at home.

The *Sawfish* next tracks down the mysterious radio signal to a coastal refinery in San Diego. Julian becomes depressed after discussing the cause of the war with the crew, and Towers arranges for him to have a drink. A crewman volunteers to explore the refinery, and he is dressed in a special protective outfit to carry out this task. He discovers the message was caused by a window shade cord attached to a half-filled coke bottle resting on the transmitting key, a set-up apparently devised by the last user of the refinery's radio room. The sailor then taps out an explanation in Morse code, describing his findings. Towers chuckles in amazement as he listens to this message, and he realizes his mission was simply a wild goose chase. They set course immediately for Melborne.

As the scene shifts back to Australia, all the characters makes a decision about how they choose to spend their last days. Moira is staying at her father's ranch, hoping that she will hear from Towers when he returns. He shows up unexpectedly, embraces her without reserve, and they agree to spend their last days together. Julian drops by to invite them to an upcoming Australian Grand Prix, where he plans to compete in his Ferrari. Admiral Bridie calls with news that Towers is appointed commander of all remaining U.S. naval forces. The message came from the American base at Brisbane in northern Australia just before they went off the air permanently.

All of Julian's friends gather to watch the Grand Prix. It is a wild, freewheeling race, with the drivers going all out to win, and many of them crash in the event. Moira cannot bear to watch, but Peter and Mary cheer Julian on to victory. Towers and Moira go on a trout-fishing trip. The resort they choose becomes quite crowded. At night the revelers sing "Waltzing Matilda," but Moira and Towers notice no one but each other.

When Towers returns to the shipyard, he learns about the first case of radiation sickness among his crew. Dr. King informs the captain that time is drawing very short. The Salvation Army sets up a round-the-clock crusade in downtown Melbourne. The hospitals start to distribute suicide pills, and long lines form to receive this "medication." Towers asks his crew to take a vote about their wishes, and they decide to return to sea and head back to America. He calls to tell Moira about their choice, and she rushes to his side for a final rendezvous. Everywhere things are winding down. Admiral Bridie shares a drink with his female aide and realizes that she loves him. At the Pastoral Club, only an elderly waiter is still alive, and he passes his time shooting billiards. Julian locks himself in his garage and races the motor of his Ferrari until the fumes overcome him. Peter and Mary have a final intimate conversation as they remember when they first met on the beach. She asks him to prepare a final cup of tea for the pills and to see that their daughter receives the correct portion. The *Sawfish* disembarks in the harbor as Moira alone watches the boat leave. A final montage shows that Melbourne is now deserted. The banner from the Salvation Army crusade, reading "There is still time . . . brother," sways gently in the breeze as the picture fades to darkness. There are no end titles.

CRITIQUE

When released, *On the Beach* was either praised or criticized largely on the basis of the political interpretation of the reviewer rather than the film itself. It was seen through the prism of the contradictory "Better Dead Than Red" and "Better Red Than Dead" philosophies. Even years later, the political leaning of the commentators seemed to influence their perceptions. For the most part, the film evades the soapbox approach. Fred Astaire mouths a few platitudes while discussing the war with crew members of the *Sawfish*. In the novel, the atomic war was actually a conflict between China and Russia, with the United States drawn in later after Washington was nuked by Egyptian fanatics. If the disaster portrayed had been an act of God (such as a zone of intense radiation coming from space), most of the dialogue would have required very little change. To fully appreciate this film, it should be regarded in purely apocalyptical terms as a series of character studies of individuals who confront their own end as well as the end of humankind. In this light, the film gains formidable stature even after all these years. This is not to say there are not many shortcomings in the story. It seems odd that Australia is the only oasis of survival. What about the countless other islands in the South Pacific and South Atlantic, not to mention New Zealand? Moreover, the prevailing sense of universal resignation seems to be defeatist. No one wants to try very hard to save the human race. For example, supplies could be stockpiled for a select group who might possibly survive in a refuge or shelter, perhaps in Antarctica. Instead, nobody seems to care, or even to try. This lack of any effort weakens the palette of the picture to a degree, and the palette would have been enriched if at least one character had a sense of determination not to "go gentle into that good night," in the words of Dylan Thomas. The concept of the British stiff upper lip is simply too pervasive. The scene of people calmly lining up for their suicide pills provokes a shudder and calls to mind the events at Jonestown. Criticism from the late 1950s claimed that total destruction with the weapons of the day was not credible. These comments overlook the fact that the story was set five years in the future, and the development of deadlier weapons producing greater radiation is certainly credible. Other objections mentioned the film's length, ponderousness and lack of action. Some critics tried to regard it as a standard adventure film instead of what it is, a character study of a small group of people.

In essence, *On the Beach* resembles a mosaic, each section highly polished with the highest technical standards. The cinematography is breathtaking, a masterful use of black-and-white photography. The editing is excellent and received an Academy Award nomination. Ernest Gold's music score is quite good, but his reliance upon "Waltzing Matilda" becomes somewhat overdone by the end of the film. It would have been far more effective if he just used it for the opening credits, the trout-fishing sequence and the finale. Instead, it is repeated almost nonstop and becomes somewhat wearing. Stanley Kramer's direction is sensitive, thoughtful and totally lacking in the self-indulgence of which he is sometimes accused. Since Australia lacked extensive filmmaking facilities, Kramer found himself deeply engrossed with many day-to-day details of the project, including camerawork, initial cut editing and even wardrobe management. One of Kramer's major problems occurred when the U.S. Navy decided to halt cooperation with the film maker after he prematurely announced their agreement at a press conference, and Kramer was forced to use a British diesel sub for the exterior shots of the nuclear-powered *Sawfish*. On the other hand, the interiors of the boat were accurate in every detail, and they were shot at a mockup at the Melborne Fairgrounds.

There are numerous special touches that deserve mention. There is the cyclical balance of the picture, which opens with the surfacing sub and Holmes preparing tea for his wife and closes with Holmes and his wife drinking the poisoned tea followed by the scene of the *Sawfish* diving beneath the water. The conversation of two old codgers discussing the supply of port at the Pastoral Club is a priceless vignette. The relationship of Admiral Bridie and his loyal assistant is another quiet, well handled episode. According to some sources, the name of the aide is Lieutenant Hosgood, but instead, the admiral clearly calls her

Osgood throughout. Indeed, at one point this suggests a subtle tribute to the real-life father of Anthony Perkins, actor Osgood Perkins (1892-1937). When the admiral exclaims, "Osgood," Anthony Perkins appears in the doorway behind him, center screen, and the timing of this seems quite deliberate. Then there is the remarkable Grand Prix sequence, where each of the participants courts death openly while indulging in their passion. The author of the novel, Nevil Shute, was himself a sports car enthusiast who raced under the name N. S. Norway (his actual last name). In fact, Shute drove a red Ferrari at the time *On the Beach* was filmed. At first he was heavily involved with the production, but then he and Stanley Kramer had a falling out over the project and his input became minimal. On the whole, the script follows Shute's story in a fairly close manner. Many minor details are changed, such as the sub's name, which is *Scorpion* in the novel, and Swain leaves the boat in San Francisco, certainly a more dramatic locale than the small town depicted in the novel. The main thrust of the story remained pretty much intact. Shute died of a stroke while working at his typewriter on a new book a year after the release of *On the Beach*.

A final major strong point of the film is its cast. Gregory Peck is ideal as Captain Towers, well balanced and functioning, with his pain tightly locked away, yet always present whenever he makes a comment about his family. Incidentally, Peck's ten-year-old son Cary has a cameo in the film as well. Ava Gardner has never been more radiant or compelling on the screen as Moira, and she tosses off some of the best lines in the film magnificently. (Gardner and Peck were good friends, and upon her death in 1990, Peck adopted her dog into his own home.) Anthony Perkins is excellent as Peter, but his Australian accent is erratic and unconvincing. There is also an expression in his face that reminds one of Norman Bates as he prepares the poison tea. Of course, his next film project was *Psycho* (1960) for Alfred Hitchcock. Donna Anderson is adequate as Mary, but one wishes that Mia Farrow would have been old enough to tackle the role since she was ideally suited for it. Fred Astaire is brilliant as Julian, and this dramatic part launched a new phase of his career. Astaire's son accompanied him to Australia and served on the film crew as best boy. The rest of the cast are uniformly good, although the accents of some of the American sailors seem to have an Australian twang, despite the fact that Kramer endeavored to cast these parts with American-born actors.

A new film adaptation of the novel called *On the Beach 2000* was in production in late 1999 with Armand Assante in the lead role as Dwight Towers. Rachel Ward assumed the role of Moira, and her real-life husband, Bryan Brown, plays the part of scientist Julian Osborne. The new project faces a difficult challenge when it comes to matching the eloquence and style of its predecessor.

REPRESENTATIVE QUOTES

"Our scientists disagree as to when radiation will reach Australia. The atomic war has ended, but the prime minister reports no proof of survival of human life anywhere except here." (Radio broadcast after the opening credits)

"The background level of radiation in this very room is nine times what it was a year ago. Don't you know that? Nine times! We're all doomed you know, the whole silly, drunken, pathetic lot of us. Doomed by the air we are about to breathe. We haven't got a chance." (Julian Osborne's drunken tirade at the party)

"He is married to a girl named Sharon, and they have two children. But if things were different, if she were alive, I'd do anything, any mean trick I know, to get him. Even if I could make him forget, there isn't time. No time to love, and nothing to remember, nothing worth remembering." (Moira to Julian, discussing Dwight Towers)

"It's all over, and I want you to know that I could never have been happier with anyone in the world but you." (Peter to his wife as they decide to take the pills)

Quiet Earth (1985)

Rating: ****   **Threat:** Alteration of the electron

Mr. Yellowbeard Productions. Written by Bill Baer, Bruno Lawrence & Sam Pillsbury based on the novel *Quiet Earth* by Craig Harrison; Photographed by James Bartle; Special effects by Addenbrook; Edited by D. Michael Horton; Music by John Charles; Produced by Sam Pillsbury & Don Reynolds; Directed by Geoff Murphy. 100 minutes.

ANNOTATED CAST LIST

Bruno Lawrence (*Zac Hobson*, New Zealand scientist); Alison Routledge (*Joanna*, woman who befriends Zac); Peter Smith (*Api*, truck driver who joins Zac & Joanne); Anzac Wallace (man who tries to drown Api); Norman Fletcher (*Perrin*, scientist who oversees Project Flashlight); Tom Hyde (scientist who lectures on videotape).

SYNOPSIS

This is a thoughtful, intelligent film made in New Zealand. The narrative unfolds in a very subtle manner, with important bits of information scattered throughout the picture. For example, a quick close-up of an object in one scene has no relevance until much later in the film. The same is also true of certain lines of dialogue. It requires multiple viewings to understand many elements of the story. The script plays a clever guessing game with the viewers, only revealing certain points after dropping a number of hints. For the synopsis, I am abandoning this sophisticated technique to relay the plot in a more linear fashion.

Zac Hobson is a scientist in New Zealand who is working on a complicated process to create a world power grid called Project Flashlight. This experiment would allow energy to be transmitted instantly to any location. Airplanes in flight would no longer need fuel, for example, because their engines would be fed directly through the power grid. This same concept, in a different form, was actually used in the serial *Manhunt of Mystery Island* (1945). Hobson detects much danger in this undertaking, and he comes to believe the American developers of the process may be withholding important information about the possible side effects. Hobson is so upset by his fears that he decides to take his own life with an overdose of sleeping pills.

The film proper opens with the audience unaware of any of this background, as Zac is lying motionless in his bed at home. At precisely 6:12 A.M., the fabric of the entire planet undergoes a change on the molecular level. Zac opens his eyes and begins to get dressed. He makes a phone call, but there is no response. He drives down the road and stops at a gas station, which no one is attending. He looks around the back of the station, and shuts off a pot of coffee, which is boiling away. He continues down the road, honking his horn, but no one appears. He stops at a house at random, trying to locate anyone. There are signs of recent activity: the shower is running and the breakfast is half eaten. Continuing on his way to the city, Zac becomes more and more perplexed by the total desolation, with cars and trucks abandoned everywhere. He investigates a fire, which appears to be the wreckage of a large airplane that has crashed, but no victims are at the scene.

Zac eventually goes to his worksite, a laboratory beneath a colossal satellite dish. He locates a teletype message that mentions Project Flashlight. As he goes enters the underground lab, he sees the figure of Dr. Perrin, head of the facility, seated in front of a control panel, and a computer screen before him states the message, "Operation Flashlight complete." The world power grid has been established. When Zac touches Perrin, his body topples over and hits an emergency alarm and the laboratory automatically seals. Zac rigs an explosive with a gas tank and retreats to his office. He activates his mini tape recorder and dictates a new message: "One: There has been a malfunction at Project Flashlight with devastating results. Two: It seems I am the only person left on earth. Three: Perrin has been incinerated at the grid control. Four: I am sealed . . ." The explosion rips through the facility before Zac can complete his memo. Water sprinklers are set off, and Zac escapes through an opening caused by the explosion.

Zac broadcasts an appeal at the radio station that he arranges to play in an endless loop, asking any survivors to contact him. He scrawls a message on a large billboard, asking, "Am I the only person left on earth?" Time passes in an erratic jumble. Zac dons a policeman's hat and drives around broadcasting in a patrol car. After moving to a large mansion, Zac visits the mall, exploring all the stores and taking any items he wants. Bit by bit, he seems to be going mad. He dresses in a nylon slip and shoots out his television screen while playing a videotape of a scientist discussing Project Flashlight. Indulging in a fantasy, Zac creates an audience on the mansion's lawn using giant cutout figures of Adolf Hitler, Queen Elizabeth II, Pope John Paul II, Richard Nixon, Nikita Khrushchev and other well known figures. He sets up a dozen tape recorders with sounds of cheering and stages a political rally. Suddenly, the electricity fails, and Zac finishes his harangue in total darkness.

The next day, he wanders into a church and blasts the figure of Jesus Christ on the cross with a shotgun, demanding, "Where are you?" He then hacks at some electrical wiring, muttering to himself, "And now I am God?" His madness continues as he smashes through another building in a giant tractor, and he finally places the barrel of a shotgun in his mouth but is unable to pull the trigger. He goes for a swim in the ocean and seems to regain his grip on sanity after emerging from the water.

After returning to his mansion, Zac installs a large electric generator. He resumes wearing normal clothes, and starts to work on a computer to track and monitor any changes in the environment. A young woman suddenly emerges from his terrace while he is concentrating on the computer. She holds a gun on him, but lowers it a moment later and the two embrace, overjoyed that they are no longer alone.

The woman, Joanna, and Zac get to know one another, discussing their experiences since the rest of humanity vanished three weeks earlier. Zac mentions that he has observed many subtle changes, such as that the water now spirals down the drain in the opposite direction. Joanna mentions that she saw the body of a baby in a hospital. While driving down the road, they come across the scene of an old accident, with several bodies present. They wonder why these corpses did not vanish with everyone else. Deciding to search for other survivors, they split up to explore different areas of the city, using walkie-talkies to keep in contact. Both notice a strange shift in the fabric of existence, as if the entire world trembled momentarily. Zac confides his fears about Project Flashlight to Joanna. All reserve between them falls away, and they begin a physical relationship.

Continuing his research, Zac makes a startling new discovery. The unit charge of the electron has changed. Since this factor has always been a constant, and it is now unstable, he suspects this is the catalyst that caused all human and animal life to vanish. He presumes the power grid is responsible, and since the grid is still operational, it continues to influence the atomic structure. Zac calls this apocalyptic reaction "the effect," and he starts to calculate if and when the effect might reoccur.

A third individual, Api, captures Zac in an ambush. Api is a black trucker, and at first his manner is threatening to Zac and Joanna. His hostility soon passes, and he joins with them wholeheartedly. Api shows the others that some fish also survived the effect, and they have a cookout. Api explains that a man was trying to drown him in the river when the effect took place and his attacker simply dematerialized. Joanne reveals that she was almost electrocuted while the effect happened due to a short in her hair dryer. The audience also learns that Zac had taken an overdose of pills when the effect struck. All three were at the point of death, and the effect revived them at the same time it erased the living. This also explains the presence of the other bodies. They, too, were dead when the effect struck, but their lives ebbed away again due to their massive injuries or to neglect, as in the case of the baby in the hospital.

Joanne finds herself drawn to both men, and as Zac concentrates on his research, she starts to spend more time with Api. Zac makes a new discovery: the sun itself is in danger of collapsing due to the effect. Zac and Api have a misunderstanding over Joanna, who makes it quite plain that she will tolerate no fighting over her. Another serious fluctuation in the grid occurs. Zac then tries to explain the danger posed by the grid, and they decide to blow up the laboratory in the hope that the entire grid will collapse if one key station stops functioning. They load up a truck with explosives and head toward the lab, where they discover that the level of radiation has risen to a fatal level. Zac leaves the others outside the lab, saying he will fetch a device he invented that could operate the truck by remote control. Left alone, Joanna and Api share an intimate moment, after which Api reveals that he will drive the truck into the lab compound if Zac's device fails. Suddenly, they hear the noise of the truck starting and discover that Zac was bluffing about the device, instead intending to sacrifice himself for them. Zac smashes the vehicle against the wall of the laboratory, crashing through to the lower level, where he detonates the explosives. But the effect reoccurs at that precise moment.

Zac mysteriously awakens on a beach. He looks around and realizes he is no longer on Earth since a giant ringed moon now appears in the sky. His face reflects his amazement and wonder as the picture concludes.

The ending of the film could be interpreted in different ways. The new effect could have propelled Zac into an alternate dimension, where he is completely alone. Alternately, the effect could have completely transformed reality before the grid was destroyed, and Joanne and Api are still present in another location. The variations and possibilities are many, but the sense of wonder on Zac's face suggests that whatever happened, he will be able to adapt and survive.

CRITIQUE

Numerous critics praised *Quiet Earth* upon its release, but many felt the picture went downhill after the appearance of the other two survivors. They believed the scenes with Zac alone were fascinating. Of particular appeal was the scene where Zac is able to rummage and play through an empty shopping mall. This must be a popular fantasy for filmgoers. The explanation behind the effect was regarded as confusing, and many failed to pick up on the clues sprinkled about the film. *Quiet Earth* requires close concentration, and the events of climax of the story are properly foreshadowed in the script. The open ending also led to some negative reactions. The alternate dimension interpretation seems to be the proper one, given some of the earlier clues. Zac was thrown clear into this new dimension by the effect, which struck at the moment he set off the explosives. The real mystery of the ending is the fate of Api and Joanne. One option no one has considered is that the original world might have been fully restored after the collapse of the grid, with Api and Joanne back among a revived human race.

In any case, the movie is a fascinating one that grips and intrigues the viewer in the first half, and adequately explains the backstory in the second half. The picture is completely successful because it is fresh, thought-provoking and entertaining. There is a superficial resemblance to *The World, the Flesh and the Devil* (1959) since the last three survivors include a woman and two men, one black and one white. But *Quiet Earth* does not appear to have any racial overtones because the race question never actually becomes an issue. When Zac insults Api, his remark is aimed at his intelligence, not his racial background. Joanne likewise seems color-blind. The relationship of the three individuals never seems contrived.

The performances of the three leads are exceptional. Bruno Lawrence seems like a modern-day everyman, a bedraggled, balding man who happens to have a flair for science. Lawrence successfully carries the opening half of the film all by himself, a genuine accomplishment, and his portrayal during Zac's breakdown is most vivid. It reminds one at times of *Sofi* (1968), the extraordinary one-man film with Tom Troupe that chronicles a nineteenth century clerk and his descent into total madness. Zac is also a poor communicator, and he is forced to rely on his tape recorder in order to get the others to understand the results of his experiments and observations. There is also an anti-American bias in Zac. When he sets up his audience of giant cardboard figures, he places Nixon next to Hitler. His character seems to believe that there is a sinister motive behind the American plan for the power grid. His suspicions seem grounded in an active dislike of anything American. The only drawback to Lawrence's performance as Zac is his accent, which seems rather thick when compared to the other leads in the film. Alison Routledge is marvelous as the free-spirited Joanne, who delights in dressing like a pixie. Her charm and playful spirit make her every scene a true delight. Peter Smith is fully convincing as Api. His performance has range, and he gives the impression that, while in his previous life Api was not an admirable individual, his experiences after the effect have transformed him and helped him grow into a finer human being. The music and cinematography are good, and the editing is truly exceptional. The cinematic techniques used by director Geoff Murphy are polished and never awkward or self-conscious. This is a demanding film for the viewer, but anyone who tries to study the picture will find their efforts well rewarded.

REPRESENTATIVE QUOTES

"I get the feeling that we are either dead or in a different universe. Are you from a different universe? Are you a woman or a child?" (Zac to Joanna after she has fallen asleep during their first night together)

"We were just one small unit in a whole network of stations around the world acting simultaneously. Besides, we might not have been responsible. God may have just blinked." (Zac describing Project Flashlight to Joanna)

"I reckon 'the effect' was a cosmic event like the creation, and nobody has ever explained that one. On the other hand, perhaps nobody disappeared, only me. I am 'the effect' . . . and you are not real. You are only in my mind." (Zac to Api and Joanna as they load the truck with explosives)

Robot Monster (1953)

Rating: ✳✳   **Threat: Alien death ray**

Astor. Written by Wyott Ordung; Photographed by Jack Greenhalgh; Special effects by Jack Rabin & David Commons; Edited by Bruce Schoengarth; Music by Elmer Bernstein; Produced by Phil Tucker & Al Zimbalist; Directed by Phil Tucker. B & W, 63 minutes.

ANNOTATED CAST LIST

George Nader (*Roy*, scientist and astronaut); Claudia Barrett (*Alice*, his girlfriend); John Mylong (*George*, professor and Alice's father); Selena Royle (*Martha*, her mother); Gregory Moffett (*Johnny*, Alice's younger brother); Pamela Paulson (*Carla*, Alice's younger sister): George Barrows (*Ro-Man*, alien Invader; *Great Guidance Ro-Man*, alien leader); John Brown (voice of Ro-Man).

SYNOPSIS

Robot Monster is frequently cited, along with Edward D. Wood Jr.'s *Plan Nine from Outer Space* (1959) as the worst film ever made. While cheap, goofy and amateurish may be accurate terms to describe them, no one can deny that they are also fascinating films, mesmerizing in their camp value and tremendously entertaining. Movies that provide so much pleasure to audiences confirm the adage, "They're so bad they're good!" In fact, these films seem to have a surreal logic at times. In actuality, the worst films ever made are dull, boring, ponderous and impossible to sit through. None of these terms applies to *Robot Monster*. So the solid two star rating for *Robot Monster* is earned through its sheer entertainment value, not quality of the production.

The credits of *Robot Monster* display a background of science fiction comic books. Each actor appears in an iris as his or her name is displayed, but Selena Royle's name is misspelled as "Royale." Some prints also integrate footage of dinosaurs in a pre-credit sequence that may have been added later to lengthen the film for television broadcast. Children Johnny and Carla are playing a game of spaceman in Bronson Canyon. They come across two archeologists, Roy and George, digging in the cavern. (Perhaps they do not know Bronson is actually a man-made test boring.) Johnny's mother and big sister call for him, having laid out a comfortable blanket in a field of rocks. Johnny asks his mother if they are ever going to have a new father, and if so, will he be a scientist? After eating heartily, everyone falls asleep but Johnny, who sneaks back to the cave so he can explore. At this point, everything changes.

A strange ray from the sky hits the cave, and Johnny stumbles and hits his head. Dinosaurs appear and indulge in a terrific fight. Johnny gets up and sees strange equipment in the cave and a large gorilla wearing a diving helmet. This bizarre figure is Ro-Man XJ2, who has just conquered Earth. He activates a tele-screen to report to Great Guidance, another gorilla wearing an identical diving helmet. Ro-Man informs him that all human life has been annihilated, but Great Guidance contradicts him, saying eight humans still survive, and he orders that them to be destroyed. Ro-Man turns to another machine that is producing a cloud of bubbles. Johnny comes out of his hiding place and runs off. George, the older of the two archeologists, is pacing in an open cellar surrounded by sparking wires. When Johnny appears, he now calls George "Pop," and Martha, his mother, scolds him for leaving the compound. The professor explains that the wire barrier hides their presence from Ro-Man, the terrible invader. Johnny reveals that Ro-Man's headquarters is in a nearby cave.

Ro-Man calls them on their view screen. He asks them to surrender and he will provide a painless death. Roy is observing Ro-Man as he finishes his broadcast, and he heads to the compound. where he tells the family that two oth-ers, Jason and McCloud, have survived. Roy theorizes that the professor's anti-biotic serum, which they all received, has also made them immune to Ro-Man's death ray. Jason and McCloud are planning to blast off in a rocketship to reach the space platform. They plan to share the serum with the garrison of men sta-tioned there. Alice, also a scientist, has two days to get a message that Ro-Man is unable to monitor through to the space platform.

Alice and Roy work day and night but fail to complete the task. Ro-Man calls them, and boasts that the rocket which has launched and the space platform will both be destroyed. Great Guidance sends out a cosmic blast and both targets are obliterated. Ro-Man tells them: "Calculate your chances! Negative, negative. Is there a choice between a painless surrender death and the horror of resistance death?" Ro-Man gives them one hour to capitulate. Martha urges George to call Ro-Man and try to reason with him.

Minutes later, Ro-Man is startled to get a call from George on his view screen. "What do you have to fear from us?" He shows each of his family members on the screen, and Ro-Man is annoyed when Johnny sticks his tongue out at him, bellowing, "The boy is impertinent!" Then Ro-Man makes a re-quest. He wants to see a close-up of Alice. He suggests they send her to him as negotiator. Roy insists that she not go and ties her up. Johnny slips out of the compound to meet Ro-Man.

The alien is furious to find Johnny at the meeting place. He tries to kill him with his calcinator death ray, but Johnny is unharmed. Johnny lets slip that his father's serum protects him, and Ro-Man plans to recalculate the death ray to overcome the serum. While searching for Johnny, Roy and Alice stumble across Ro-Man so they hide in the brush. They talk to each other in silence, as if play-ing charades, pledging love and deciding to marry. It almost seems that when Roy tied her up in the earlier scene, he unleashed her heart at the same time. Ro-Man returns to his cave and calls Great Guidance. He explains the source of their immunity to the death ray, and Great Guidance suggests he use physical force to eliminate the people.

When Roy and Alice return to the compound, they ask George to marry them. Roy removes his shirt for the occasion. George delivers a maudlin ceremony. Roy and Alice leave on a honeymoon. Carla tries to follow them and runs directly into Ro-Man, who is waddling down a dirt path at his usual lumbering pace. He kills her, and wanders back to his telescreen to boast to Great Guidance about his great achievement. He also tries to talk his superior into altering the plan to include one living human "for reference," but Great Guidance insists they all must die. Ro-Man continues his search, comes across the kissing couple, and pushes Roy over a cliff. He then carries Alice back to his lair. She asks him why he is so strong, and he replies, "We Ro-Mans obtain our strength from the Planet Ro-Man, relayed for individual energizers." He says his energizer is in the cave. Ro-Man, as if taking a page from Roy's book, ties Alice up.

George calls Ro-Man on the viewer screen, but the alien tries to put him off. He is presently too busy conversing with Alice, asking if she would like him better if he was "Hu-Man." Great Guidance monitored the last message and now calls to berate XJ2 for his delaying tactics. Becoming confused, Ro-Man asks, "To be like the Hu-Man, to laugh, feel, want! Why are these things not in the plan?" Great Guidance tells him to follow his orders at once or be destroyed. Becoming more incoherent, Ro-Man apologizes to Alice and then chases after Johnny who appears at the mouth of the cave, taunting him. As he lumbers off in pursuit of the boy, George and Martha enter the cave and untie Alice. George tries to smash Ro-Man's energizer. As Ro-Man closes in on Johnny, who does not even try to elude him, Great Guidance decides to pull the plug on XJ2 and sends out a calcinator death ray to him. Ro-Man collapses besides Johnny.

Speaking to no one in particular, Great Guidance starts to rant and says he will release cosmic Q rays which will revive prehistoric reptiles to finish off George, Martha and Alice. Apparently this plan is too slow, and Great Guidance instead decides to send powerful vibrations to smash the planet Earth out of the universe. Earthquakes erupt, and large fissures start to swallow the dinosaurs. The planet begins to disintegrate.

The scene shifts back to the opening picnic. Roy carries Johnny and calls to his mother. Johnny looks around and asks if everyone is still alive. Roy comments on the bump on the boy's head. Martha invites George and Roy to dinner, and the group heads off. Suddenly, the sound of the calcinator death ray is heard, and the image of Ro-Man emerges from the cave three times, reaching out to the audience, before the end title appears.

CRITIQUE

Robot Monster was intended to be a 3-D release, but the process never worked correctly. In an interview with the author, Claudia Barrett provided many details about the making of the film. Originally, the storyline presented was intended to be reality, not a dream. After the main section was completed, director Phil Tucker had a change of heart and framed it as Johnny's nightmare, but he also wanted to leave open the possibility that it might come true. The concept was that perhaps George and Martha would fall in love and marry, and then the entire sequence of events would come to pass. That is why the calcinator death ray initially strikes before Johnny hits his head and why, at the conclusion, the image of Ro-Man keeps reappearing in the cavern. Such an interpretation is ruined, however, by George's line of dialogue to Ro-Man where he states Martha is his wife of twenty-three years.

The entire production was shot very rapidly and with much chaos, largely due to Tucker. Barrett recalls that two different cameras were used, and the two cameramen often confused the cast with conflicting instructions. She reports that in the sequence in which she is carried away by Ro-Man, she was first instructed to be frightened and kicking, but then Tucker decided to have her flirt with him instead. The scenes where Claudia appears to be laughing with Ro-Man were not intended to be in the film either. She and George Barrows were merely horsing around while the camera was test shooting, and somehow these playful shots wound up in the final film.

Claudia finally describes Phil Tucker and executive producer Al Zimbalist as lacking in humor and failing to detect any of the underlying sense of burlesque throughout the entire picture. Claudia now finds the film "tremendously funny" and is happy to be remembered as the gleam in Ro-Man's eye.

One major talent, that of screen composer Elmer Bernstein, had his career launched by *Robot Monster*. Bernstein's colorful score is among the best things in the picture, with one miscue, the juvenile "nyah-nyah" kid's chant tune that accompanies the first appearance of the children. The quality of the cinematography is quite good in itself. The images seen in negative, used to signify the death ray, are decent effects. The bubbles from the bubble machine in the cave even have a macabre appearance when seen in negative. On the whole, the picture is clumsily stitched together, and the endless stock footage clips from serials, the silent *Lost World* (1925) and *One Million B.C.* (1940) are overused and make little sense. The bubble machine is one of the most preposterous props seen in any film. We never get a chance to inspect Ro-Man's energizer. Many commentators have mentioned that the dubbing for George Barrows failed to match his gestures at all time. However, there also is a scene in *Star Wars* (1977) where Dave Prowse as Darth Vader gesticulates with his arm to Peter Cushing with no accompanying dialogue. If we can overlook the flaw from George Lucas, perhaps we should also tolerate it from Phil Tucker. Come to think of it, is there not some similarity between Darth Vader and Ro-Man? Both start as totally cold-hearted, but then their emotions are stirred. Vader, however, is far more successful in implanting his ideas on the emperor than Ro-Man is with Great Guidance.

The cast of *Robot Monster* is actually quite distinguished for such a bargain-basement film. George Nader had just made his screen debut in *Monsoon* (1952) and was regarded as an up-and-coming star. Selena Royle and John Mylong were both esteemed veteran performers with an enormous list of credits. Claudia Barrett had already acted onscreen with Humphrey Bogart and Peter Graves. George Barrows was a well known stunt man who earned quite a few extra dollars with his gorilla costume in numerous pictures and TV shows. He did *Robot Monster* as a favor to Tucker. The concept was ludicrous, since Ro-Man was originally intended to be a mechanical man. Yet it is quite impossible to think of him as a robot as he appears in the film. Great Guidance is even more bizarre, batting bubbles around with a pointer as he monitors the hapless XJ2 Ro-Man. Great Guidance's sense of timing in the story is wonderful, as is his superb idea to re-create the dinosaurs for the sole purpose of killing George, Martha and Alice. One feels he really has it in for Alice, who ruined a perfectly good Ro-Man with her charms. *Robot Monster* is a film that merits multiple viewings, since there are always fresh insights to be drawn from it. One critic found in it a powerful allegory about the Holocaust and the facelessness of evil when people obey orders blindly. Even if the writer's tongue was planted firmly in cheek, the fact that the picture could be regarded in such a light is a tribute to this crazy but appealing film, the most absurd extreme of apocalyptic cinema.

REPRESENTATIVE QUOTES

"The Hu-Man knew about atomic energy, but had not mastered the cosmic ray. Wherever I directed the calcinator beam, they groveled. At first the fools thought it came from one among their many nations. They began destroying each other with hydrogen bombs. I announced myself to keep them from wiping out cities, which will give our people much amusement. Too late they banded against me. Their resistance pattern showed some intelligence, but all are gone now." (Ro-Man to Great Guidance)

"Dear Lord, you know I am not trained for this job, but I have tried to live by your laws, the Ten Commandments, the Beatitudes, the golden rule. I would like you to look down on Alice and Roy and give your blessing. Even in this darkest hour, we have kept the faith. In your grand design there may be no room for man's triumph over this particular evil that has beset us. But if, by any chance, victory should be on our side, I want you to give a long life to Alice and Roy, and a fruitful one." (Wedding ceremony performed by George)

"I cannot, yet I must. How do you calculate that? At what point on the graph do must and cannot meet? Yet I must, but I cannot." (Ro-Man's soliloquy about following his orders)

Runestone (1991)

Rating: **   **Threat:** Ragnarök

Hyperion. Written by Willard Carroll based on a novella by Mark E. Rogers; Photographed by Mischa Suslov; Special effects by Max W. Anderson & John Eggett; Edited by Lynne Southerland; Music by David Newman; Produced by Harold E. Gould Jr. & Thomas Wilhoute; Directed by Willard Carroll. 105 minutes.

ANNOTATED CAST LIST

Peter Riegert (*Capt. Gregory Fanducci*, New York City homicide detective); Joan Severance (*Marla Stewart*, an artist); Tim Ryan (*Dr. Sam Stewart*, her husband and an archaeologist); Mitchell Laurence (*Martin Almquist*, museum director possessed by Fenrir); Dawan Scott (*Fenrir*, wolf creature from Norse mythology); Alexander Godunov (*Sigvaldson the clockmaker*, actually Tyr, a Norse god); William Hickey (*Lars Hagström*, eccentric scholar of mythology); Donald Hotton (*Ask Franaq*, Norse scholar); Chris Young (*Jacob*, his grandson); Lawrence Tierney (*Richardson*, New York City police chief); Erika Schickel (*Angela*, Martin's assistant); Bill Kalmenson (*Lester*, art critic); Arthur Malet (*Stoddard*, medieval art expert and curator); John Hobson (*Marotta*, museum guard); Anthony Cistaro (detective); Merilyn Carney (*Tawny*, museum patron); Greg Wrangler (*Bob*, museum patron); Ed Corbett (janitor); William Utay (Truck driver who delivers the runestone); Sam Menning (wino killed by Fenrir); Gil Perez (*Alberto*, mugger killed by Fenrir); Gary Lahti (*Sanders*); Ralph Monaco (cabbie); Peter Bigler (*Harris*, policeman); Richard Moliware (*Pulaski*, policeman); Rick Marzan (*Strange*, policeman); Kim Delgado (*Reynolds*, policeman); Joshua Cox (*Crossley*, policeman); Vanessa Easton (nurse who tends Stewart); Carl Parker (elevator operator); Matthew Boyett (Tyr's apprentice); David Newman (*Graves*); Josef Rainer, Christopher Holder, Susan Lentini, Kelly Miller (Magnussen board members and their wives); Carol Hickey, Lisa Dinkins (bespectacled guests at fundraiser); Eben Ham, Layne Beamer (policemen summoned to the museum).

SYNOPSIS

A basic knowledge of Norse mythology helps to raise this artful, but confusing, horror film from the level of an offbeat werewolf film to a modern-day setting of Ragnarök, the Norse doomsday. A brief mythological primer is helpful to decifer the plot. Odin, the foremost of the gods, is alarmed when his sometime adversary, Loki the trickster, sires three monstrous offspring. The worst is Fenrir, a monstrous wolf who grows more dangerous each day. Only one god, Tyr, is brave enough to confront Fenrir, and he imprisons him with magic, losing his hand to the monster in the process. For various misdeeds, the gods are cursed, and when Odin consults the oracle, he learns about Ragnarök, the doom of the gods, when all life on Earth will be destroyed by fire and water. A sequence of events will trigger Ragnarök, including the freeing of Fenrir from his captivity. If Fenrir is recaptured, Ragnarök will be postponed indefinitely. If he is not, universal destruction is imminent. The basic outline of this myth is used as the framework for *Runestone*, making it one of the most atypical of apocalyptic films. Unfortunately, the film gets sidetracked at several points along the way, and only minimal clarification is provided for filmgoers unfamiliar with Norse mythology.

As the film begins, a mysterious clockmaker is observed at his work in a room filled with clocks. He has a young apprentice as a companion. He becomes concerned when his large grandfather clock stops a few seconds before midnight. The scene switches to a coal mine in Pennsylvania where a strange artifact, a huge stone with runic markings, is discovered in a lower shaft that is being excavated. The unusual object, undoubtedly of Norse origin, is shipped to a New York museum run by the Magnussen foundation, but when it is unloaded from the truck to the museum's freight elevator, an accident happens and a building employee is crushed to death.

Two elderly men, devotees of Norse legends, are upset when they learn about the new discovery. Lars Hagström insists that his ill friend inform him where he has hidden a legendary weapon, but the other scholar, film theater owner Ask Franaq, remains silent. Jacob, his grandson, is upset by their beliefs, which he claims gives him nightmares. Lars visits Martin Almquist, the head of the museum, to warn him about the terrible danger locked away in the stone. Archaeologist Sam Stewart and his wife, Marla (Martin's former fiancée), are summoned by the museum to translate the runic carvings on the stone. Sam is unable to decode the message and suggests only Lars Hagström would be able to translate it. After they leave, Martin examines the runestone himself, and a strange force is released, transforming him into a giant wolf-demon. The beast commences a killing spree, and the museum janitor and security guard are torn to pieces. Later, homicide detective Fanducci and chief Richardson inspect the carnage with the Stewarts. They report that Martin was also on the premises and is now missing.

The next morning, Franaq falls into a coma and is brought to the hospital. Martin, acting strangely but restored to his normal form, visits Marla and frightens her with his advances. When Sam enters the room, Martin struggles with him and stabs him. Later at the hospital, Sam reports Martin's strange behavior to Fanducci. The detective says that lab tests on the museum victims reveal they were killed by a monstrous canine or wolf. Marla visits Lars while her husband is recovering, and the eccentric scholar tells her that he and Franaq are the last of a group of watchmen on guard for signs of Ragnarök, the apocalypse foretold in Norse mythology. The release of the beast Fenrir is the most important sign. Lars claims he will soon die, but someone else will appear to assist in the struggle against Fenrir. Moments later, Fenrir breaks into the apartment and kills Lars. Marla flees to the street below, but Fenrir follows, chasing her through Central Park. Two muggers try to hold her but are killed by Fenrir, and Marla jumps into a cab and escapes.

Fanducci assigns six men to guard the Stewarts day and night. They go to the hospital to see Franaq, but he is still in a coma. Jacob is shocked when told about the death of Lars. He never believed in Fenrir and does not know the location of the secret weapon. They visit the Cloisters, the medieval branch of the Metropolitan Museum of Art, where Stoddard, an elderly curator, shows them a cycle of art about the imprisonment of Fenrir in a rock by the god Tyr. Fanducci sends the Stewarts to the mine in Pennsylvania where the runestone was found. His examination of photos of the site suggests that the rock was originally positioned in another chamber much higher up, and he thinks there could be additional ruins there that might be helpful. At the mine, Sam locates the right shaft and squeezes up to an alcove where he photographs the runes, from which he learns that Tyr will resurface and battle Fenrir with the aid of a mortal named Jacob. Back at the museum, an exhibit of living tableaux draws a large crowd. The clockmaker, actually the god Tyr, attends the show drawn by the presence of Fenrir, who smashes into one of the exhibits and rampages through the crowd. Fanducci and a team of men are summoned, and they sweep through the museum. The detective encounters the beast, who chases him across the roof. Fenrir pushes him over the side, but Fanducci grabs a large banner proclaiming the exhibit and shimmies down to the street unharmed.

When the Stewarts return from Pennsylvania, Fenrir attacks them at their apartment. Fanducci's guards are killed, and the monster appears impervious to bullets. A backup team arrives and the beast runs away under machine gun fire. As the remaining cops take a body count, Tyr enters the apartment and offers his assistance. Fanducci takes him to Captain Richardson, who is transfixed by his hypnotic stare. The chief puts a hundred men at his disposal. He takes Fenrir's hair samples, which the police had collected, and sets a trap for the beast at the runestone in the museum. Tyr tells Marla that Fenrir's cunning was limited in the remote past because his host was illiterate. He is now more dangerous with Martin, an educated man, as his host. Marla must also serve as bait, since Martin is still obsessed with her. Sam and Fanducci remain on watch with them.

Franaq awakes from his coma and tells Jacob the location of the weapon, an ancient battle axe, hidden behind a mural in his theater. Fenrir appears at the museum, bursting through the police who shoot their weapons in a vain attempt to slow him down. The wolf-demon and Tyr face off in the main chamber and their ancient battle resumes. Tyr is unable to fend off the beast usung a fireman's ax, and at one point, when Marla is knocked over, Fenrir speaks to her in Martin's voice, saying, "Forgive me. I'm not myself today." Jacob arrives with the weapon and tosses it to Tyr. The Norse warrior wields it, and with Jacob's help, eventually drives Fenrir back to the runestone where he is again imprisoned, asthe body of Martin collapses on the floor. Tyr withdraws and vanishes into a cloud of smoke. Fanducci, recovering from his wounds, chips off a fragment of the runestone as a souvenir. He suggests to Jacob and the Stewarts that they keep silent about the details of the battle, and find someplace new to hide the runestone. Tyr reappears in his room of many clocks where his young apprentice is napping, waiting for him. The large grandfather clock has resumed ticking, and it chimes the hour as the end credits roll.

CRITIQUE

The main problem with *Runestone* is that it seems unwilling to commit itself to a single style. At times it resembles a standard horror movie or a distant cousin to Clive Barker's *Rawhead Rex* (1986) with a Manhattan setting. At other times, it seems like a lampoon of the trendy art world, with a lot of clever dialogue satirizing the fashionable art crowd in two major sequences, first the fundraiser where patrons get to smash specially designed walls with sledge hammers to the music of "The Teddy Bears' Picnic," and the second with the living tableaux, showing a family watching television and a woman in curlers doing the ironing. When Fenrir attacks and kills the model, the observers think it is part of the show with the subliminal message, "Housework kills." Then there is the parody of the police, and it becomes a game to figure out how many will be torn apart before the picture ends. Finally there are the sequences that relate to the Norse myths, the foundation of the story. This dichotomy is interesting, but it never really works. The second major weakness is the muddled way in which the plot unfolds. We are never really shown, for example, how Martin is seduced by Fenrir. We learn that the possession is voluntary and assume Martin's motivation is his longing for Marla, who married his rival, Sam Stewart. It is also left unclear how the freeing of Fenrir leads to Ragnarök. In the Norse myths, we know that Fenrir's release triggers the liberation of the other imprisoned monsters and evil forces, including his father, Loki; the serpent, Jormungand; the Fire Giants; and the other adversaries of Odin and his host of gods and heroes. In their great battle, Earth is destroyed by fire and almost all the gods are slain. This outcome is hinted at in the film, but never fully described. The audience is just informed it will be doomsday, and it is left as that. The film would have been improved if more dialogue had been devoted to these events. At the end of the picture, many filmgoers no doubt assume Fenrir was killed instead of being merely rebound in the runestone, and with Ragnarök merely deferred. On the other hand, these myths have seldom been utilized onscreen and the film legitimately tries to explore new ground. Of course, some films such as the *Star Wars* saga have adapted the myths, with Darth Vader assuming the role of Odin. The story of Tyr is also among the oldest mythological figures, even predating Odin. In Germanic myths, he was called Tiwaz, and the third day of the week, Tuesday, was named in his honor. *Runestone* embellishes his myth as the clockmaker, and it is uncertain exactly who his young apprentice represents—perhaps Thor's son Magni, since the film equates Tyr as the companion of Thor. The film errs by showing Tyr with a black glove on his left hand, since it was his right hand that Tyr lost when originally binding Fenrir.

The technical work in the film is adequate except for the lapses in script focus, as well as some clumsy editing. The music by David Newman is first rate, and Newman himself has a cameo in the film. He comes from a musical family, since his father was Alfred Newman, the distinguished composer of *Wuthering Heights* (1939) and *The Robe* (1953), and his brothers are Thomas Newman and Randy Newman, also noted composers.

The cast provides some decent performances. William Hickey is most impressive as Lars, and it is unfortunate he is disposed of so early in the picture. Screen veteran Lawrence Tierney, one of the icons of film noir, also has an excellent turn as the chief of detectives. Peter Riegert is not immediately appealing as Fanducci, but both the interest in his character as well as his performance improve as the film develops. Joan Severance is strong throughout in her reading as Marla. Stuntman Dawan Scott (Bigfoot Harry from the television series *Harry and the Hendersons*) is outstanding as the ferocious Fenrir. Alexander Godunov is the major problem in the cast. He looks wonderful as Tyr, but his delivery is so often mumbled that it is impossible to follow what he is saying. Born Boris Godunov, the performer used his middle name instead for billing when he became a headline ballet dancer for the Bolshoi. No doubt the notoriety of the historic usurping Tsar and the fame of the opera by Modeste Mussorgsky influenced that decision. He made a name for himself as an actor with powerful performances in *Witness* (1985) and *Die Hard* (1988). Godunov died unexpectedly at the age of forty-six in 1995. Writer/director Willard Carroll is largely to blame for not calling for retakes or overdubbing when the actor's lines are unclear. Perhaps he felt that Tyr would be unused to conversation and his speaking style would be stilted, but it still leaves the audience in the lurch. The pronunciation of "Fenrir" by different characters also varies widely throughout the picture, no doubt further bewildering the audience. Despite its uneven and faulty execution, *Runestone* still should be admired as a fresh and worthy effort, a most unusual variation of *Götterdämmerung*.

REPRESENTATIVE QUOTES

"You are a non-believer. There are no atheists in foxholes, and you are in one now. The runestone is the major player in the Norse doomsday scenario, and we are the supporting cast. I warned Martin, but I suspect it was already too late. . . Every dogma must have its day. Fenrir. It is good to be on a first name basis with evil." (Lars ramblings to Marla, moments before he is killed)

"Fenrir took off Tyr's hand when he realized he'd been tricked. He wasn't pleased." (Stoddard to Jacob and the Stewarts)

"I think you can kiss your security deposit goodbye." (Fanducci to the Stewarts after Fenrir's attack at their apartment)

"You've done an excellent job so far. You have forced the beast back tonight, but Fenrir becomes stronger every day. He will adapt to everything." (Tyr to Fanducci)

The Satan Bug (1965)

Rating: **   Threat: Killer virus

Mirisch Corporation. Written by Edward Anhaut & James Clavell based on the novel *The Satan Bug* by Alistair MacLean; Photographed by Robert Surtees; Special effects by A. Paul Pollard; Edited by Ferris Webster; Music by Jerry Goldsmith; Produced & directed by John Sturges. 114 minutes.

ANNOTATED CAST LIST

George Maharis (*Lee Barrett*, intelligence officer and security expert); Richard Basehart (*Charles Reynolds Ainsley*, wealthy madman who poses as Dr. Gregor Hoffman); Dana Andrews (*Gen. Williams*, head of military intelligence); Anne Francis (*Ann Williams*, the general's daughter and Barrett's girlfriend); Henry Beckman (*Dr. Baxter*, director of Station Three); John Larkin (*Dr. Leonard Michelson*, scientist who replaces Baxter); Richard Bull (*Eric Cavanaugh*, Head of intelligence squad); Frank Sutton (*Donald*, Ainsley's top henchman); Ed Asner (*Veretti*, henchman); Simon Oakland (*Tasserly*, deputy administrator of Station Three); John Anderson (*Regan*, slain head of Station Three security); John Clarke (*Raskin*, Station Three security officer); Hari Rhodes (*Johnson*, Station Three security officer); Martin Blaine (federal agent posing as Henry Martin); Harry Lauter (phony intelligence agent); James Hong (*Dr. Yang*, research scientist at Station Three); Harold Gould (*Dr. Oster*, research scientist at Station Three); James Doohan (security agent who dies of botulism).

SYNOPSIS

This is a curious, edgy film that does not fit comfortably into any traditional category. It has a mercurial nature that frequently shifts gears so that the viewer is never sure exactly where the plot is going. This uncertainty actually works in the film's favor while the story unfolds, but it makes it seem weaker in retrospect. There is a feeling of disappointment when the film concludes, a sense that the picture just did not live up to its potential. The opening two-thirds are indeed excellent, but the last third is confusing, with an abrupt finish. The overall atmosphere is good and sense of tension is well maintained. The threat of global extinction is credible, but the thrust of the story gets bogged down as the picture nears its denouement.

The story begins as a truck makes a delivery of two large crates to Station Three, a remote chemical weapons research facility in the desert Southwest. Moments later, a helicopter with Security Chief Regan arrives at the same facility. He checks over the elaborate security of the underground lab. Since it is late Friday afternoon, most of the scientists are leaving, except for Dr. Baxter, the director of the project, who is deeply involved in his work at E Lab. Regan urges him to take some time off, but Baxter insists his work is at a crucial stage. After Regan leaves, two intruders suddenly appear. One of them emerges from E Lab, locking its vault-like door. He then walks past the main security post with his face obscured as he puts on Baxter's hat and coat. Outside the facility, Regan notices something strange about Baxter's car as it passes through the front gate, and he returns to the underground lab. Later the security detail becomes alarmed when Regan fails to answer their calls on the intercom.

The scene shifts to a marina later the same night, where Lee Barrett, a former military intelligence officer, is approached by a shady individual who offers him a huge sum to deliver a vaccine stolen from Station Three. Thinking he is a spy, Barrett pulls a gun on the man, who is actually a federal agent assigned to test Barrett's loyalty. Cavanaugh, head of an elite Pentagon security team, then appears to recruit Barrett's help. Regan, Barrett's successor at Station Three, has just been found murdered at the site, and Barrett is needed to assist in the investigation. Dr. Baxter, the head of the project, has also been reported missing.

Cavanaugh, Barrett and germ warfare expert Dr. Leonard Michelson arrive at Station Three by helicopter at daybreak. They interview Dr. Gregor Hoffman, the last scientist to leave the laboratory the previous night, and he recommends that the vault door to E lab be sealed in concrete. He warns them about the newly developed Satan bug, an indestructible artificial virus that is lethal enough to kill all life on earth if it is released. This virus is stored in E Lab, along with additional vials containing a deadly botulinus. If someone has tampered with the Satan bug, opening E lab will cause the end of the world. Barrett volunteers to enter the lab to learn what happened. Dressed in a hermetically sealed suit, Barrett explores the lab and discovers the murdered body of Dr. Baxter. The flasks with the Satan bug and deadly botulinus are all missing.

Barrett reports to General Williams, head of military intelligence, who is staying incognito at a nearby estate with his daughter Ann, Barrett's old girlfriend. The general had recently learned of the existence of the Satan bug, and had an appointment scheduled with Dr. Baxter. Barrett learns how the intruders penetrated E lab concealed in two large wooden crates. They murdered Baxter and stole the vials. One of them impersonated Baxter to leave the premises. The other killed Regan when he came to investigate, and later escaped by cutting through the wire fence that surrounds the compound. Barrett believes that someone on the inside must have aided the break-in. General Williams receives a threatening telegram demanding that Station Three be shut down immediately. Barrett speculates that a madman with a messianic complex is behind the theft. The Satan bug could serve as the ultimate blackmail weapon. Dr. Hoffman reveals that Baxter had been working day and night on an antidote to the virus. The authorities plan to keep secret all developments on the case.

The next scenes are rather elliptical and perplexing. Two men meet on the porch of a house overlooking the desert. They were the intruders, and they discuss the completion of their recent assignments in Florida and Los Angeles. They are puzzled that their boss, a man known as Ainsley, is not at their hideout. The first man, Donald, calls the home of Dr. Oster, looking for Ainsley.

Just at that moment, Barrett arrives at Oster's house to check on his whereabouts. He answers the ringing phone, and Donald hangs up after asking for Ainsley. Ann Williams then arrives with a message for Barrett and discovers Dr. Oster's body floating in his swimming pool. They wonder if Oster had helped the thieves.

General Williams is informed that the deadly botulinus has been released in Florida. Washington has authorized the General to manage the crisis. Hundreds were killed in this attack, but since this form of the virus totally dissipates after eight hours contact with the open air, there is no residual danger. A film taken by helicopter over the affected area is reviewed. Bodies are strewn everywhere: on boats, in the street, on a golf course, wherever the victims were at the time the botulinus was released. Williams assigns Barrett to investigate Dr. Hoffman, the only lab employee who has not yet been cleared. The general also suggests following up on the lead provided by the mysterious phone call at the Oster home looking for Ainsley.

Barrett interrogates Dr. Hoffman, who has been working at Station Three for the past five months after being hired out of Vienna, Austria. Cavanaugh interrupts the interview, exclaiming that they have identified a suspect named Charles Reynolds Ainsley, a reclusive millionaire and crackpot, who is probably behind the theft. Ainsley had disappeared about eight months earlier, and no existing photograph of him can be located. Meanwhile, Donald receives a phone call from Ainsley telling him where the Satan bug is hidden. Finally, General Williams is called by Ainsley, who threatens to release the botulinus in Los Angeles unless all his demands are met. This threat forces the authorities to reveal the danger to the public, and a total evacuation is ordered for the city.

Following a lead, Barrett discovers that Dr. Hoffman's car was disabled in a canyon outside of Station Three early that morning and that he had to hitch back to the laboratory. On a hunch, Barrett and Ann Williams go to the remote spot near a stream. Barrett suspects that Hoffman himself had possession of all the deadly flasks except for the two that he passed to the intruders. These were the flasks that were placed in Florida and Los Angeles. He then killed Oster, but on his way back to Station Three, his car developed a flat that he could not repair because his jack broke. So he must have hidden the Satan bug and the other vials near this spot. Ann discovers a metal box submerged in the stream. Ainsley's two henchmen show up, abduct Barrett and Ann, and take control of the deadly flasks. They bring their hostages back to their hideout. After Hoffman arrives, they all leave in a van. The intelligence agents spot the vehicle and follow it by helicopter. The van stops at a secluded location where Hoffman switches cars and takes the Satan bug with him.

A rather bewildering game of cat and mouse ensues between Cavanaugh's security team and Ainsley's clique. At one point, two federal agents and Barrett are locked in a garage by the intruders. Donald tosses a flask with botulinus through a window, and the men desperately try to smother the released virus with dirt and kerosene. The two officers die, but Barrett escapes and sets the garage on fire to destroy the deadly virus. This entire encounter is well staged and one of the highlights of the movie. Barrett winds up being captured again when Hoffman arrives on the scene to investigate the fire. This time Hoffman admits that he is actually Charles Reynolds Ainsley, who killed and impersonated the real Gregor Hoffman. Dropping his thick foreign accent, Ainsley admits he is also a chemist and could easily pose as the obscure Austrian scientist. Ainsley's car is finally overtaken by security agents, but moments later they turn out to be members of Ainsley's gang posing as federal agents. They rendezvous with a small helicopter. Ainsley reveals to Barrett that he himself is immune to the Satan bug, since Dr. Baxter had been successful in developing a vaccine that would resist the fatal virus. It was Baxter's discovery that prompted Ainsley to stage the theft. Oster was killed, not because he aided the thieves, but because he knew about the antidote.

Meanwhile, Cavanaugh lays a clever trap to capture the van with Ann Williams and the henchmen. They stage a phony road accident, and agents posing as motorists surround the van while complaining about the delay. Then they storm the vehicle, rescuing Ann. The two intruders are killed in a gun duel, and all of the remaining botulinus flasks are recovered. The Satan bug, in Ainsley's possession, is still missing.

General Williams and his daughter return to the henchman's original hideout, hoping to find a clue to the whereabouts of the vial hidden in Los Angeles. A doodle left by one of the thugs resembles a baseball diamond, so the general orders an intensive search of Dodger Stadium. The police frantically look for the flask, and it is finally located, attached to a small explosive, hidden in a beverage cooler at a stadium concession stand.

Flying over Los Angeles, Ainsley mocks the people stuck in the giant traffic jam that is clogging all the roadways leading out of the city. Barrett presses him to reveal the location of the flask, but Ainsley refuses. Barrett finally attacks him, and as they struggle, the helicopter goes out of control. The pilot falls out the open door, and Barrett grabs the vial with the Satan bug as it rolls off the seat. Ainsley still refuses to reveal the location of the flask, declaring, "Los Angeles will be my epitaph," as he unexpectedly jumps. Barrett regains control of the helicopter and activates the radio. He tells General Williams that he has retrieved the Satan bug but was unable to learn where the other flask is hidden. He is told that the unit had been discovered and already disarmed. "For God's sake, make a good landing," Williams advises. The picture then ends abruptly with the helicopter still in midair.

CRITIQUE

This film is an unconventional one that has characteristics of being both a major studio thriller and a conventional TV movie. This dichotomy is apparent on many levels. For example, the sets switch from an ultramodern, sophisticated underground lab to long sequences in the desert scrublands of Southern California, the same landscape that serves as backdrop to countless television programs. The impact of the small screen is also apparent in the cast, which is stocked with many performers who are best known for their work on television. They include George Maharis from *Route 66*; Richard Basehart and Richard Bull, the admiral and doctor from *Voyage to the Bottom of the Sea*; Anne Francis from *Honey West*; Ed Asner from *The Mary Tyler Moore Show* and *Lou Grant*; Frank Sutton, who played Sergeant Carter on *Gomer Pyle*; Simon Oakland from *The Night Stalker*; and even James Doohan, Scotty from *Star Trek*. In some cases their television fame came after this movie, but still, the presence of so many television stars seasons the flavor of the film. The few special effects are unimpressive. When Donald tosses the deadly flask into the garage, it wobbles unnaturally through the air, obviously on wires.

The plot line begins to plummet downhill after Ainsley and his thugs drive off with his hostages. The meanderings that follow seem rather pointless. Ainsley and his henchmen split up for no apparent reason, and then, after Barrett escapes death from the virus at the garage, the coincidence of Ainsley arriving at the same location to recapture him is too much to swallow. There is simply no reason why two additional members of Ainsley's gang pose as intelligence officers (except, of course, to mislead the viewers). The end structure of the film is very inept. The audience watches as the hidden flask with the virus is discovered at Dodger Stadium. This knowledge completely undercuts the impact of the next scene, where Barrett desperately attempts to learn the flask's location from Ainsley. Finally, the picture literally ends up in the air, since if Barrett crashes while landing, Los Angeles will be destroyed. The film could have ended more effectively if Barrett had a problem landing the helicopter, perhaps engine trouble or a sputtering motor caused by a stray bullet. Then the picture could have finished on a high dramatic note, with the triumphant reunion of Anne and Barrett at the airfield. Instead, Barrett and General Williams relay some obsolete plot points dryly over the radio, and the end credits roll as Barrett flies to the airport, hoping his landing skills are not too rusty. With the excellent buildup and development through most of the picture, this fizzling end is a total misstep on the part of writers Edward Anhaut and James Clavell and director John Sturgis. Barrett's cryptic final line, "We are back where we started," seems like a total cop-out.

A dynamic ending would have saved the picture, since many of the earlier scenes are top-notch. The fervent score by Jerry Goldsmith and the sharp and compelling cinematography seem squandered after the half-hearted conclusion. The cast also performs well, although both Dana Andrews and Anne Francis are more or less wasted in the script. Andrews seems present merely to clarify what plot developments have taken place. Richard Basehart, on the other hand, gives an exceptional performance. He is totally convincing as the Austrian scientist who is concerned and overwrought by the events at Station Three. The effect is chilling when he drops his characterization as Dr. Hoffman and becomes the calm, but totally psychotic, Ainsley. His final line as he leaps from the helicopter is delivered brilliantly. His suicide is totally unexpected and catches the audience by complete surprise. George Maharis also turns in a strong performance, and he is at his best playing against Basehart in their many scenes. Better editing and a sharper finale would have made this picture a genuinely memorable thriller. Oddly enough, Basehart later starred in another picture with a similar theme called *And Millions Will Die* (1973). World destruction was not an element in this film, but Basehart was compelling in his role as an expert who had to track down a cache of nerve gas hidden in the sewers of Hong Kong.

REPRESENTATIVE QUOTES

"If I took the flask which contains it and exposed it to the air, everyone here would be dead in a few seconds. California would be a tomb in a few hours. In a week, all life, and I mean all life, would cease in the United States. In two months at the most, the trapper in Alaska, the peasant on the Yangtze, the aborigine in Australia, dead, all dead because I crushed the flash and exposed a green-colored liquid to the air. Nothing, nothing can stop the Satan bug. Who will be the last to go? Perhaps a great albatross winging its way across the bottom of the world. Perhaps an Eskimo deep in the Arctic . . . one day soon they too would die." (Ainsley, as Dr. Hoffman, describing the power of the Satan bug)

"Some scientists thought the H-bomb would start a chain reaction that would blow up the world. Nobody really knows about this. Theoretically, yes, but it hasn't yet been put to the real test. Perhaps it will destroy all life. Perhaps. Certainly, it will destroy millions. Do you want to test it?" (Ainsley to Barrett while forcing him to lower his gun)

"What are your plans for the world, Ainsley? War? Peace? Back to the Middle Ages or forward to the future? It is not going to make any difference what you choose because it all means one thing to you. . . . Power! Power for its own sake!" (Barrett taunting Ainsley in the helicopter before attacking him)

The Seventh Sign (1988)

Rating: ****   **Threat:** **Biblical apocalypse**

Tri Star. Written by George Kaplan & W. W. Wicket; Photographed by Juan Ruiz Anchia; Special effects by Michael L. Fink & Ray Svedin (supervisors); Edited by Caroline Biggerstaff; Music by Jack Nitzsche; Produced by Robert W. Cort, Ted Field & Paul R. Gurian (executive); Directed by Carl Schultz. 97 minutes.

ANNOTATED CAST LIST

Demi Moore (*Abby Quinn*, artist expecting a baby); Michael Biehn (*Russell Quinn*, her husband, a lawyer); Jürgen Prochnow (*David*, actually Jesus Christ in disguise); Peter Friedman (*Father Lucci*, actually Kartaphilos, Pilate's doorkeeper who struck Christ and was cursed); Manny Jacobs (*Avi*, Jewish scholar who assists Abby); John Taylor (*Jimmy Szaragosa*, Russell's death row client); Lee Garlington (*Dr. Inness*, Abby's doctor); Akosua Busia (*Penny*, lawyer); Harry Basil (Kids Korner salesman); Arnold Johnson (synagogue janitor); Rabbi Baruch Cohan (synagogue cantor); John Walcutt (novitiate); Hugo Stranger (*Harold Berne*, priest murdered by Lucci); Patricia Allen (nursery school administrator); Michael Laskin (Israeli colonel); Ian Buchanan (*Huberty*, meteorologist); Manko Tse (Abby's practical nurse); Leonard Cimino (cardinal heading committee); Richard Devon (second cardinal); Rabbi William Kramer (*Rabbi Ornstein*, linguistic scholar); Blanche Rubin (*Mrs. Ornstein*, his wife); John Heard (minister consulted by Avi); Joe Mays (motel clerk); Jane Frances (TV game show contestant); Glynn Edwards, Robin Groth, Dick Spangler (newscasters); Darwyn Carlson, Harry Bartron, Dale Butcher, Dorothy Sinclair, Larry Eisenberg (reporters); Sonny Santiago (medical technician); Frederic Arnold (surgeon); Adam Nelson, David King (paramedics); Kathryn Miller, Karen Shaver, Lisa Hestrin, Christiane Carman, Irene Fernicola, Yukiko Ogawa (nurses); Robert Herron, Hank Calia, Gary Epper, John Sherrod (prison guards).

SYNOPSIS

Any apocalyptic film that utilizes religious themes is treading on delicate ground since many people are averse to mixing their religious convictions with entertainment. A film about the historic life of Jesus Christ is one thing, but the Second Coming is another. In the light of this challenge, *The Seventh Sign* manages fairly well, sidestepping any tone of offensiveness. The resulting film is heartfelt yet still entertaining.

The film opens on Christmas Day in Haiti where an other-worldly stranger named David walks through a busy town to the edge of the ocean carrying an envelope with an elaborate wax seal bearing the image of an angel. After breaking the seal open, the beach starts to fill with dead fish being washed ashore. The scene shifts to the Negev Desert in Israel three days later. A meteorologist is transported by the Israeli army to a small village, which is inexplicably suffering a storm of snow and ice. A priest, Father Lucci, shows up at the same site. He reveals that in ancient times this locale was the site of the cursed city of Sodom. In a pile of snow, Lucci notices the fragments of a broken seal.

In Los Angeles, Abby Quinn is concerned about her pregnancy since she miscarried her last child. She and her husband, Russell, a struggling lawyer, plan to rent out an apartment over their garage to help meet expenses. Russell is handling an appeal case for a murderer condemned to death, Jimmy Szaragosa, a retarded youth who killed his parents when he discovered they were brother and sister. Jimmy, who is deeply religious, felt compelled to this act by the biblical law of Moses as described in *Leviticus*. Russell becomes consumed by the case, believing that Jimmy's original lawyer was incompetent, and that Jimmy's mental uncapacity should help mitigate his sentence.

The stranger, giving his name as David Bannon, visits Abby and asks to rent the apartment. He tells her he is a teacher of ancient languages. When David moves in, Abby notices an unusual sealed envelope among his belongings. He joins the Quinns for dinner, and a sparrow flies into their living room through an open door. David protects the bird when Abby advances on it, telling her the story of the Guf, where unborn souls are kept in heaven, and how sparrows are reputed to see souls when they descend from the Guf.

While shopping the next day, Abby thinks she sees David enter a building and follows him. It turns out to be a synagogue, where the *Kaddish*, the prayer for the dead, is being chanted by a cantor. David breaks open another seal inside the synagogue. As Abby leaves, she suffers a seizure and is taken to the hospital. Her unborn baby is saved, but her doctor informs Russell that her condition is delicate. When David visits Abby, they watch television, and David is upset by the many examples of human misery on the news. He remarks, "I used to think the world would change, but it hasn't." He speaks darkly that the course of humanity appears to remain focused on death. In Rome, Father Lucci submits a report to a panel of cardinals in which he strongly debunks reports of signs of the approaching apocalypse.

Abby sneaks into David's room and tries to peek into the sealed envelope. She steals a paper filled with ancient writing with the heading 2/29, which is the date for which her Caesarian is scheduled. When she is distracted, the envelope with the seal drops to the floor. She steps on it, breaking the seal as she leaves. An earth tremor strikes as she descends the stairs, and she sees a dead sparrow on the ground. Abby goes to Russell's office and reveals her fears that David means some harm to her unborn child. Russell, preoccupied with Jimmy's approaching execution, dismisses her worries as foolish. Abby then brings the paper to Rabbi Ornstein, a linguistic specialist, but offends the Hasidic scholar when she touches him. The rabbi's wife chases her out of the apartment, and Avi, a Jewish student who lives across the hall, tells her that she violated a taboo. He offers to translate the paper, which is written in an obscure, secret form of Hebrew that ancient scholars used to protect their writings. Avi explains that 2/29 is not a date but a biblical reference, and the paper opens with a passage from *Joel*, chapter 2, verse 29, which refers to the apocalypse. Avi promises to translate the entire document. Abby goes to the library to research the Guf and learns that the seventh and last sign of the apocalypse occurs when the Guf is empty and the first soulless child emerges into the world, stillborn.

When Abby returns home, she encounters David. She is frightened by him, fearing he is a fanatic who thinks he will end the world by killing her baby. She grabs a knife and stabs him in the abdomen, but he is unharmed. His wound glows and is healed. David reveals he is Jesus Christ. "I can't die again, Abby, I wish I could." Abby has a revelation in which she witnesses a Roman soldier who strikes Christ on the way to the cross. She protests, and the soldier barks at her, "Will you die for him?" Abby shrinks back, and her vision ends.

Upon learning Abby has collapsed, Russell rushes to the hospital. The doctor tells him that she has suffered a delusional episode, but that her fetus is still doing well, and with rest she will be fine. Having translated the entire paper, Avi becomes convinced that the last seven signs are indeed happening. He meets with a minister and asks about the Christian interpretation of the apocalypse.

Father Lucci arrives in Los Angeles and is given a room in a Novitiate House. An elderly priest, Father Berne, is amazed when he sees Lucci, thinking he resembles Father Morell, a priest he knew in his youth. He locates a photo of Morell and is shocked to discover that Lucci is indeed Morell, and he has not aged a day in fifty years. Later Berne confronts Lucci, who kills him after revealing he is actually Kartaphilos, the doorkeeper of Pilate's Hall of Justice who struck Christ on his way to judgment. He has been cursed to roam the world to await the Second Coming. Kartaphilos wishes to facilitate the end of the world and fears that Abby has the power to prevent it. Meanwhile, Abby returns home and is visited by David. She asks him if her baby will be born if one of the seven signs does not come about. He replies that it would break the cycle, but that it would require someone who is willing to sacrifice everything. Then God would grant the world another chance. Abby promises David that she will try.

The next morning a massive hailstorm strikes Los Angeles. Lucci rescues Abby from the street, pulling her into a doorway. He says he wants to help her and then questions her about David. The priest tells her it is impossible to stop a sign. Only three signs remain, the death of the last martyr, an eclipse and earthquake and the stillbirth of the soulless child. When he tells her to abandon all hope, Abby recognizes Lucci as the soldier who struck Christ in her vision. Kartaphilos tells her that it was no vision, that she indeed was there as a Jewish maiden who refused when asked, "Will you die for him?" Abby has been reincarnated to be given a second chance to reply to the original question by Kartaphilos. She flees from the man and meets up with Avi. They consider how they may stop one of the signs. It is now late at night, and they stop at a motel in order to pick up a Gideon *Bible*. Avi reads *Revelations* 6, which describes the opening of the seals. They conclude that Jimmy Szaragosa must be the last martyr who represents this sign, and in the morning, a solar eclipse is scheduled.

Russell has failed in all his attempts to gain a postponement for Jimmy. The young man is still confident in his belief that he was carrying out the word of God. Russell accompanies the young man to the gas chamber. As the new day breaks, Abby and Avi rush to the prison in a desperate attempt to prevent the execution. But Kartaphilos is there as well, and he draws a gun when Abby and her friend burst into the execution chamber. The police guards shoot the priest, but he is unharmed. Abby throws herself in front of his gun when he fires at Jimmy, but the bullet passes through her and kills him. An ambulance races the wounded Abby to the hospital, and she goes into labor. An earthquake occurs at the point when the solar eclipse reaches total blackout. Abby is rushed to the delivery room, where her son is born. She sees that her baby is alive and well before she herself dies. Russell holds the newborn infant as David enters the operating room and says that the Hall of Souls is full again due to Abby's sacrifice. As he leaves, David asks Avi to write a new gospel and tell the world what he saw. David then walks off, vanishing into the light.

CRITIQUE

The script by George Kaplan and W. W. Wicket is remarkable, displaying extraordinary skill. The film is filled with a number of biblical passages, quoted with accuracy. They expertly blend in the concept of the Guf found in the *Talmud*, where it is described as the place in heaven where souls are kept until brought to Earth. The *Talmud* also says "the son of David" will not appear on Earth until each soul in the Guf descends to Earth. Jewish scholars interpret this as a sign of the worth of each individual in the divine plan. Another element of the plot is the story of Kartaphilos, which first appeared in *The Chronicle of St. Albin* in 1228. This was one of the earliest variants of the tale of the Wandering Jew, the human cursed to live eternally until the Final Judgment. As portrayed in this film, this figure was originally not a Jew but a Roman soldier. The screenplay raises a number of difficult issues in an intelligent manner, such as the case of Jimmy Szaragosa, a retarded, self-confessed murderer who felt his crime was justified, indeed compelled, by his faith. Morally, this is one of the most complex controversies portrayed in modern film. Also thoughtful is Avi's discussion with the Protestant minister, when he comments that devout followers of each faith think that their group alone will be the one recognized by God.

Most of the production aspects of the film are also first rate. The music, cinematography and editing are consistently good. The acting is somewhat uneven, but understated and refined. The German actor Jürgen Prochnow, who gained international fame in *Das Boot* (1981) and became active in American films shortly after, has the key role, and if he had not been convincing as the returned Christ, the entire picture would have collapsed. His performance is well-crafted and credible. He has numerous powerful but quiet moments that could have been easily ruined if they were overstated or bland. Prochnow manages always to hit the right note. Demi Moore, on the other hand, is not really convincing as Abby, and her approach to the part is all over the map. Perhaps this is intentional, a symptom of her character's pregnancy. She does not actually harm the film, but she fails to give it an extra lift as she does in *The Juror* (1996) and other films. Peter Friedman is also inconsistent as Lucci, particularly in his early scenes. At first, he wants to impress others around him that these signs are wondrous and supernatural. Then he debunks them in front of the cardinals. One would imagine that he would have worn the mask of the doubter all the time, and not just assumed it for the cardinals. Oddly enough, the cardinal who questions him most closely, Richard Devon, played Satan in a fascinating Roger Corman film called *The Undead* (1957). Others in the cast, such as John Taylor, Michael Biehn and particularly Manny Jacobs, are exceptional in their roles. Director Carl Schultz also adds verisimilitude to the cast by having an actual rabbi play the Hasidic rabbi in the film.

Not surprisingly, *The Seventh Sign* was only modestly successful at the box office, and some filmgoers might consider it blasphemous despite the care of the screenwriters. Others might find it pretentious or even comic, but credit must be given for the earnestness and poise of the entire production. It is certainly one of the best apocalyptic films of the religious category. It takes numerous chances, and although several ideas fail, a majority succeed, and succeed well.

REPRESENTATIVE QUOTES

"There is a story about the newborn child and the sparrow's song. It's ancient Hebrew. They believe that in Heaven, God's mansion has many halls, and that one of these halls is the Hall of Souls. It's called the Guf. They say, whenever a baby is born, this is where its soul comes from. As the soul descends from heaven, only the sparrows can see it, and so they sing." (David to Abby after rescuing the sparrow)

"There are only a finite number of souls in the Guf, and that it is when the last soul is used and the Guf is empty that the world will end. The first infant born without a soul, born dead as such a soulless child must be, heralds the death of the world, and so it is called the final sign." (Abby, reading aloud from a library research book)

"I came as the Lamb, and I return as the Lion. Now I am His Wrath." (David to Abby, revealing his true identity as Jesus Christ)

"Who will be saved, Reverend? I mean, the Jew doesn't think it will be the Moslem, and the Moslem doesn't think it will be the Christian. The Christian doesn't think it will be the Buddhist. So, what if nobody is saved? What if we are all wrong?" (Avi discussing the apocalypse with a minister)

"Remember it all. Write it down. Tell it so people will use the chance she has given them." (David to Avi at the end of the picture)

Solar Crisis (1990)
AKA *Starfire*

Rating: **   **Threat: Giant solar flare**

Vidmark. Written by Joe Gannon & Crispin Bolt based on the novel *Explosion of the Sun* by Takeski Kawata; Photographed by Russ Carpenter; Special effects by Neil Krepela (producer); Edited by Richard Trevor; Music by Maurice Jarre & Michael Boddicker; Produced by Richard Edlund, James Nelson, Morris Morishima, Takehito Sadamura & Takeshi Kawata (executive); Directed by Richard C. Sarafian under the name Alan Smithee. 112 minutes.

ANNOTATED CAST LIST

Tim Matheson (*Steve Kelso*, commander of the mission to save the planet); Charlton Heston (*Adm. Skeet Kelso*, his father); Corin Nemec (*Mike Kelso*, Steve's son); Peter Boyle (*Arnold Teague*, Head of IXL); Jack Palance (*Travis Richards*, eccentric desert dweller); Annabel Schofeld (*Alex Noffe*, genetically enhanced human); Tetsuya Bessho (*Dr. Ken Minami*, designer of *Ra* probe); Dorian Harewood (*Borg*, executive officer of *Helios*); Paul Koslo (*Dr. Gunter Haas*, scientist who learns Teague's plans); Sandy McPeak (*Gurney*, officer in charge of search for Mike); Silvanna Gilardo (*T. C.*, communications officer on *Helios*); Scott Allan Campbell (*McBride*, navigator of *Helios*); Dan Shor (*Harvard*, crewman); Frantz Turner (*Lamare*, Crewman); Richard S. Scott (*Lt. Meeks*, engineer of *Helios*); David Ursin (*Kovac*, Teague's security chief); Brenda Bakke (*Dr. Claire Beeson*, IXL scientist who debunks the Starfire theory); Rhonda Dotson (Little Al's waitress); Roy Jenson (bartender); Roy T. Fukagawa (cook); Michael Berryman (*Matthew*, wanderer who rescues Dr. Haas); Jimmie F. Skaggs (Biker); Chris Nash (Corvette driver); John Blyth Barrymore (*Avery*, communications officer in *Skytown*); Carole Hemingway (*Rhonda*, TV reporter); Don Craig (TV anchorman); Jerry Hauck (*Corp. Flynn*, Guerney's assistant); John Hugh (*Dr. Dufait*, Medical officer on *Helios*); Bob Maroff (camel rider); Steve Welles (*Prophet,* thug at Little Al's); Eric James (*Louisiana*); William A. Wallace (*Pohl*); Tammy Maples (Steve's wife, viewed in photographs); Ted Montue (bridge officer on *Helios*); Richard Terrile (hologram operator); Michael Stanhope (astronomer); Kathryn Spitz (IXL receptionist); Ann C. Fink (vidphone operator); Jimmy Austin, Richard Eden (technicians); Robert Hawkins, John Tabler (security officers); Mindy Rickles, Nick Gambella, Lehua Reed (astronauts); H. M. Wynant, Paul Carr (IXL executives); Milt Kogan, Arnold Quinn, Louie Elias (IXL search squad); Rick Dorio, Mario Roberts, Larry Duran, Stacy Elias, Eurlyne Epper, Bill Hart (bandits); Paul Williams (voice of Freddie); Stephen R. Kujala (robotruck voice); Tracy Jones Stateman (voice of *Helios* computer); Terrence Beasor (narrator).

SYNOPSIS

This film, completely financed by Japanese sources, encountered a number of problems while developing a final cut, and director Richard Sarafian used the pseudonym "Alan Smithee," which numerous directors have used since 1967 when they want to drop their own name in the credits of a film (usually due to artistic differences regarding the final cut). Among the directors who have used the moniker are Don Siegel, Jackie Cooper, Dennis Hopper and David Lynch. Distribution for the picture was almost nonexistent, although it had a respectable run in Japan under the title *Kuraisisu 2050* (*Crisis 2050*). With spectacular special effects, a talented cast and a relatively fresh plot, most of the film's troubles seem due to a muddled storyline, unfocused character development and poor editing, which is often incoherent. Since the plot itself is complex, this is a serious handicap. Nevertheless, the outlines of a decent film are discernible.

The picture opens with narration that pointlessly duplicates the onscreen scrawl. In the year 2050, scientists, concerned by the dramatic increase in solar activity, have developed the Starfire theory, which postulates that the sun is on the verge of producing an immense solar flare that could extend to the orbit of Venus or beyond. Since their calculations conclude that this flare will occur in the direction of Earth, they believe all life will be destroyed. The only plan to save the planet would be to explode a unique anti-matter device on the opposite side of the sun, which would generate the flare on its far side of the sun in a direction 180 degrees away from Earth, which would produce only a minor effect on our world. The spaceship *Helios* will undertake this crucial assignment of transporting and launching this bomb, nicknamed Freddie, into the interior of the sun in a special space probe, called *Ra* , which was designed to withstand intense heat. Many scientists, led by the distinguished Dr. Haas, are skeptical of the Starfire theory. Magnate Arnold Teague, head of the IXL Corporation, openly mocks the theory and schemes to hamper the mission of the *Helios*. He plans to use the panic that would follow this failure to cheaply buy up most of the Earth's resources and make IXL the most powerful force in the world. At an IXL board meeting, Dr. Haas reveals that his initial calculations were wrong and the monstrous solar flare will indeed destroy the Earth within forty eight hours. Dr. Beeson, an IXL board member, still refuses to believe it. Teague instructs Kovac, his security chief, to implement the sabotage of *Helios*.

The man placed in charge of the *Helios* mission is Captain Steve Kelso, son of the famous Admiral Skeet Kelso, who believes that it is a suicide mission. The admiral learns that his grandson, Mike, has disappeared from his boarding school on Earth. He tells Steve that he will track down Mike himself and make sure that he is safe. Meanwhile, Mike is trying to travel to *Skytown*, the space station where *Helios* is docked to see his father before he leaves on his mission. His space rover crashes in the wastelands, and he meets an old squatter named Travis who lives in a hut in the desert. He agrees to drive Mike to the nearest spaceport. After his motorcycle breaks down, they stop a robotruck, a large, computer-operated vehicle, and hitch a ride until a gang of bandits hijack the vehicle. The bandits take Travis and Mike to Little Al's, a desert truck stop.

While briefing the crew of *Helios*, Captain Kelso reveals that the *Ra* probe will require a human pilot to guide it through the electromagnetic interference into the sun. Alex Noffe, a genetically enhanced woman and key member of *Helios*, is seized by Kovac, who programs her to sabotage the mission. *Helios* sets off with a crew of sixteen. When Dr. Haas learns about the sabotage plans, Teague flies him out to the desert and abandons him. Nearing the point of death, the scientist is found much later by Matthew, a desert wanderer, who brings Haas to Little Al's. Mike helps tend to Haas who tells him about Teague's attempt to sabotage *Helios*. After Haas dies, Travis arranges to have Mike driven into town. The waitress at Little Al's, however, calls IXL and they send a security team that uncovers that Haas spoke with Mike. Kovac proceeds to capture both Mike and Travis, torturing the old man to death. Admiral Kelso follows Mike's trail to Little Al's and learns he was abducted by IXL. He then raids IXL headquarters with a squad of soldiers.

Mike is brought before Teague in his flying transport, who continues to mock the concept of the solar flare because it was not predicted by Nostradamus. He flies Mike to a rocky gorge and orders Kovac to kill him. Mike runs off, and when the security chief pursues, Mike ambushes him, gaining control of his gun. Kovac refuses to back off, and Mike is forced to shoot him as they both topple over a cliff. Injured, Mike sets off a distress call with Kovac's portable phone, and the admiral and his men rescue him. Mike explains about Teague's sabotage plot, and the admiral tries to send a warning message to *Helios*. He then shoots Teague's flying transport out of the sky, killing the mad industrialist as he tries to escape. An oxygen tank blows up on *Helios*, almost crippling the mission and reducing their air supply in half. Captain Kelso suspects that a saboteur is behind the explosion. Freddie begins to malfunction, threatening to explore prematurely. After the crisis is averted, Freddie reveals that Alex was responsible for his miscalibration. Alex collapses, and when she recovers, she explains that she was programed by an intruder to cripple the mission. Now back to normal, Alex volunteers to pilot the probe carrying Freddie into the sun. Kelso refuses, planning to helm *Ra* himself. Alex knocks him out and sets off in the probe. She travels deep into the sun, and when Freddie explodes, the monster flare discharges away from Earth as planned. The crippled *Helios* turns back to *Skytown*, arranging for a rendezvous with a transport ship before their air supply is depleted. The planet is saved and the end credits roll.

CRITIQUE

Solar Crisis is an ambitious, big-budget science fiction thriller, but multiple viewings are required to sort out the many plot threads, which never really fit together. The plot is set well into the future, but in the earth scenes, technology seems to have stood still. The subplot of Mike's adventures and the pursuit by his grandfather are basically a dead end, since by the time the admiral sends off his warning message, the damage on *Helios* has been done and since Captain Kelso figures out what is going on without any outside alert. The earth scenes, therefore, seem extraneous. The film also references *2001: A Space Odyssey* (1968), particularly when Alex plunges into the sun in the *Ra* probe, which recalls Keir Dullea's journey inside the monolith during the finale of the Kubrick film. Both sequences feature a colorful light show with alternating cuts of the awestruck astronaut. Freddie is reminiscent of HAL the computer in *2001*, in both manner of speech and attitude. The threat of increased solar activity is well portrayed. Scientists used to estimate that an increase in the sun's temperature would occur in about five billion years. New computer models have cut this projection down to a half billion. Considering that Earth has been capable of supporting life for four and a half billion years, our planet is, from a galactic point of view, now entering its last phase. *Solar Crisis*, of course, accelerates this process wildly, but we are told state that releasing the megaflare will insure Earth an additional ten million years of solar tranquility.

The special effects are the strongest element of *Solar Crisis*, and they are excellent and impressive throughout. The weakest aspects are the script, the editing and the music. Maurice Jarre, the distinguished French composer of such scores as *Dr. Zhivago* (1965) and *Witness* (1986), seemed to be asleep at the switch during this film. The most impressive music sequence featuring the *Ra* probe is a paraphrase of the opening of *Carmina Burana* by Carl Orff. The cast delivers wildly varied performances. Tim Matheson, Charlton Heston, Peter Boyle and Annabel Schofeld are superb, particularly Boyle, who manages to bring considerable charm to the villainous Teague. When he smiles at Mike and tells him his father sounds like a good man, it really goes against the stereotype of corporate screen megalomaniacs. Schofeld manages to steal most of the scenes aboard *Helios*, and she has considerable charisma. On the other hand, Jack Palance overacts shamelessly as the old desert rat, and his performance borders on satire. Corin "Corky" Nemec fails to ignite interest as Mike, and David Ursin appears to be doing a pale imitation of Robert Shaw in *From Russia with Love* (1963). Director Richard Sarafian, best known for his extensive television work dating back to *The Twilight Zone*, provides very little personality to the picture, but since he disowned the final print, it is unfair to pass judgment on his intended vision.

REPRESENTATIVE QUOTES

"The sun, the mother of all life, begins the final event by threatening to cast a colossal megaflare that will destroy all of the earth's creatures. The cremation of the planet is at hand." (Opening narration)

"IXL invests in the future, an optimistic future, and I refuse to believe that a megaflare or even God Himself is going to end it. That's not the way I see it." (Teague to his board of directors)

"Scientists! The world is full of experts and scientists who say God has spoken through them. One thing I have learned. No one knows anything. All their theories change like the tide." (Teague to Mike)

Star Trek—The Motion Picture (1978)

Rating: ****   **Threat:** Alien device

Paramount. Written by Harold Livingston based on a story by Alan Dean Foster & Gene Roddenberry with Isaac Asimov (advisor); Photographed by Richard H. Kline; Special effects by Douglas Trumbull, Richard Yuroch & John Dykstra (supervisors); Edited by Todd Ramsay; Music by Jerry Goldsmith; Produced by Gene Roddenberry; Directed by Robert Wise. Original version, 132 minutes; Expanded version, 143 minutes.

ANNOTATED CAST LIST

William Shatner (*James T. Kirk*, Starfleet admiral); Leonard Nimoy (*Spock*, Vulcan Starfleet officer); DeForest Kelley (*Dr. Leonard McCoy*, chief medical officer of the Enterprise); James Doohan (*Montgomery Scott*, engineer of the *Enterprise*); George Takei (*Hikaru Sulu*, helmsman of the *Enterprise*); Walter Koenig (*Pavel Chekov*, chief weapons officer); Nichelle Nichols (*Nyota Uhura*, communications officer); Majel Barrett (*Dr. Christine Chapel*, medical officer); Stephen Collins (*Willard Decker*, captain of the *Enterprise*, later reduced to executive officer); Persis Khambatta (*Ilia*, navigator); Grace Lee Whitney (*Janice Rand*, transporter chief); John D. Gowans (Rand's assistant); Mark Lenard (Klingon captain); John Rashad Kamal (*Sonak*, Vulcan science officer killed in transporter accident); Susan Sullivan (woman killed in transporter accident); Billy Van Zandt (alien ensign); Roger Aaron Brown (*Epsilon* technician); Michele Ameen Billy (*Epsilon* lieutenant); Gary Faga (airlock technician); Howard Itzkowitz (ensign who gives Kirk permission to board); Marcy Lafferty (*DeFalco*, officer who replaces Ilia); Terrence O'Connor (*Chief Ross*, Chekov's backup); Michael Rougas (*Lt. Cleary*); Joshua Gallegos (*Perez*, security officer who escorts Ilia); Leslie C. Howard (yeoman who gives Kirk directions); Doug Hale (voice of *Enterprise* computer); David Gautreaux (*Com. Branch*); Sayra Hummel, Junero Jennings (technical assistants); Edna Glover, Norman Stuart, Paul Weber (Vulcan masters); Ralph Brannen, Ralph Byers, Paula Crist, Iva Lane, Frank L. Seales, Bjo Tremble, Momo Yashima (crew members); Jimmie Booth, Joel Kramer, Bill McIntosh, Dave Moordigian, Tom Morga, Tony Rucco, Joel Schultz, Craig Thomas (Klingon crew).

SYNOPSIS

Nine years after the original *Star Trek* television series was canceled, a revised version of the series was planned for production. But with the enormous success of *Star Wars* (1977), this project was suspended and replaced by a major feature-length film with a large budget. While wholeheartedly welcomed by fans, many felt the picture short-changed the regular cast in favor of elaborate special effects and an ethereal storyline. It was not until after its original theatrical run that eleven minutes of edited footage was reinstated to the film, and this material, centering on cast regulars, helped restore the overall balance of the film and was a genuine improvement, and the extended version is the basis for the synopsis and critique.

The film opens with an extended musical prologue with a blank screen, a throwback to the film overture that major pictures such as *Ben-Hur* (1959) and *Lawrence of Arabia* (1962) used to employ. The story proper opens with three Klingon starships encountering and being destroyed by an enormous space anomaly, a cloud containing a mysterious alien vessel. Space Station *Epsilon* tracks the course of this cloud and finds that it is headed directly toward Earth. The only Starship capable of intercepting the cloud is the *Enterprise*, which is undergoing the last stages of a major refit. Admiral James T. Kirk, who commanded the *Enterprise* during a previous five-year mission, persuades Admiral Nogura, head of Starfleet, to return to him command of his old ship in this hour of crisis. Kirk informs Scotty, engineer of the *Enterprise*, of his restored position, and the engineer treats Kirk to a leisurely shuttle ride around the *Enterprise* before he assumes command. The transporters on the *Enterprise* are untested, and as Sonak, the Vulcan science officer assigned to the *Enterprise*, attempts to beam aboard, he and a female crew member are killed when the unit malfunctions. Kirk confronts Will Decker and relieves him as captain of the *Enterprise*. Decker is stunned and somewhat bitter as he is temporarily reduced in rank to serve as Kirk's executive officer. The crew members who previously served under Kirk—Pavel Chekov, Nyota Uhura, Hikaru Sulu, Christine Chapel and Janice Rand—are thrilled to be serving under him again. A new officer aboard is Lieutenant Ilia, a Deltan, a species noted for their overpowering sexuality. In order to serve with humans in Starfleet, Deltans are required to take an oath of celibacy. Years earlier, when he served on Delta, Will Decker had formed an attachment with Ilia, a relationship both of them find difficult to forget. Dr. Leonard McCoy is beamed aboard after the transporters are repaired. He complains that Admiral Nogura drafted him, but Kirk reveals that it was his doing because he needs McCoy's support in dealing with the threat facing Earth. Kirk holds out his hand to his friend, whom he affectionately calls "Bones," and McCoy responds in kind. Kirk holds a general meeting for the entire crew, and an emergency transmission from *Epsilon* shows the destruction of the space station by a plasma energy attack from the mysterious cloud.

Enterprise leaves the space dock, and Kirk urges Scotty to implement warp speed. An engine imbalance creates a wormhole. Decker countermands an order by Kirk when an asteroid obstructs their path in the wormhole. In private, Kirk demands an explanation and discovers that Decker saved the ship because the phaser weapon that Kirk wanted to employ was made inoperative by the engine imbalance. McCoy warns Kirk that he is pushing the crew too hard and is competing with Decker.

A shuttle brings Commander Spock aboard, and he requests activation as science officer. He had interrupted the ritual of Kolinar, by which all emotion is purged, because he sensed the approach of a new, powerful entity, undoubtedly the intelligence contained within the cloud. The other members of the crew are excited by the return of their old comrade, but they find him distant, uncommunicative, even glacial. Spock works with Scotty to adjust the engines, and the *Enterprise* manages to achieve warp speed, providing enough leeway to intercept the cloud well before it reaches Earth.

The crew is awed by the magnitude of the cloud. Spock reveals that the energy required to generate the cloud exceeds the energy output of the sun. They broadcast messages of friendship but receive no response. The ship is attacked with an outburst of plasma energy, but *Enterprise's* defense shields protect the ship. Spock, who has developed a psychological link with the intelligence inside the cloud, senses it is puzzled that *Enterprise* has not responded to its hail. He discovers that their signals are incredibly complex and of extremely short duration. He broadcasts a response to the alien entity, and the attacks cease.

The crew becomes mesmerized by the beautiful patterns formed by the clouds. An alien probe in the form of a shaft of glowing light invades the bridge of the *Enterprise*, and it downloads information from the ship's computer until Spock smashes the control panel. The shaft then stuns Spock, and finally vanishes after seizing Ilia. Decker is outraged, since he had previously told Kirk that allowing the ship to be drawn into the cloud was an "unwarranted" risk. He snaps at Kirk, "This is how I define unwarranted!" A tractor beam from the entity draws the *Enterprise* into the interior of the cloud.

An intruder in the image of the missing Ilia appears on the ship. She claims to be a representative of "V'ger" sent to observe and study the carbon-based units infesting the *Enterprise* (by which she means the crew). She tells Kirk that V'ger is traveling to Earth "to find the creator," with whom V'ger wishes to become one. McCoy examines the intruder and finds she is a mechanical reproduction of Ilia, down to the smallest detail. When Decker enters the room, Ilia reacts differently to him, as if he were an equal rather than a carbon-based unit to be studied. Kirk decides to assign Decker to guide Ilia, since Spock believes Ilia's empathy with Decker may still be intact. Communication with V'ger's proxy is essential to avoid any danger to Earth.

The cloud containing Enterprise is only a few hours from Earth when Spock decides on a bold course. He plans to link minds directly with V'ger (a Vulcan technique), and he dons a spacesuit to travel outside the ship to physically touch V'ger itself. His mind meld proves overwhelmingly traumatic, and Kirk himself heads out in a thruster suit to rescue his friend. After recovering, Spock relates that V'ger is a living machine, lonely and without hope, that is trying to discover its real purpose, which it can only do by joining with its creator. Spock returns to his post, but he seems changed, more appreciative of his emotions and his friendship with the people around him.

V'ger's cloud dissipates as it approaches Earth, and it broadcasts a simple radio signal. Ilia is upset, saying that the creator has failed to respond. V'ger plans to destroy all the carbon-based life forms on Earth since V'ger believes they somehow prevent the creator from responding. Spock advises Kirk to treat V'ger as if it were a child. Kirk then bluffs, claiming he knows why the creator has not responded but will only reveal the reason directly to V'ger. An air envelope forms outside the ship and the *Enterprise* is pulled by a tractor beam alongside V'ger itself. Kirk, Spock, McCoy, Decker and Ilia disembark from the ship on foot and walk across a field of large, hexagon-shaped tiles to a recessed platform where V'ger is housed. Kirk steps up to the object, which is actually a large, metallic ball. He notices writing on it with the lettering "V GER." Wiping off some rust obscuring some letters, he reveals the full name, "VOYAGER 6." The entity is an old probe launched by NASA in the twentieth century which fell into a black hole and was found and repaired by a planet totally populated by machines. They repaired and enhanced the unit which they named V'ger from its incomplete lettering. They endowed it with tremendous technology so it could fulfill its original mission: to learn all possible data and transmit it back to Earth. Kirk asks Uhura to obtain the response code for *Voyager* from the computer files and broadcast it. When she transmits the sequence, V'ger deliberately burns out her reception wires. Ilia reports that V'ger wants the creator personally to transmit the code. Kirk reveals that the carbon-based units are the creator, and that V'ger was wrong in assuming the creator was a living machine. Ilia starts to look longingly at Decker, and he volunteers to manually enter the last numbers of the binary code that V'ger is expecting. Kirk warns that there may be unforeseen results for the individual who attempts this. Staring at Ilia, Decker says he wants to do it. Decker is bathed in an other-worldly glow, and he starts to evolve into pure energy. Ilia reaches forward and embraces him, and she also starts to glow. Spock signals to the others that they must return quickly to the *Enterprise* as the entire area is being transformed into pure energy. They run back to the ship as all remaining sections of V'ger undergo a metamorphosis and it spreads out and seems to disappear into another dimension. Kirk is amazed as he and the others return to the bridge, and McCoy likens it to the birth of a new life form that has evolved into another plane of existence. Kirk contacts Starfleet to report that Earth is now out of danger and lists Decker and Ilia as missing. He decides to take the *Enterprise* off on a shakedown cruise. When asked for a heading, Kirk waves his hand toward the view screen and says, "Out there, thataway!" The *Enterprise* breaks into warp speed, and a closing title card reads, "The human adventure is just beginning."

CRITIQUE

The cost of this film was in excess of $42 million, and because of this expense, it was only modestly successful. It did launch the franchise as a viable film series, and several of the later films are also apocalyptic in nature. *Star Trek IV: The Voyage Home* (1986), the best of the series, had a similar theme to the first film. An alien device from deep space arrives at Earth and broadcasts a signal to which no one can respond. The machine begins to devastate the planet, and Spock determines that the signal is, in fact, a whale call. Since whales are extinct in this future era, the main characters travel back in time to the twentieth century to procure a pair of whales. Earth is saved when the whales reply to the call and the device leaves Earth in peace. In *Star Trek (VIII): First Contact* (1996), the villainous mechanized race known as the Borg are defeated by Federation forces. They send a scout ship back in time to undermine human history so they would instead emerge victorious. The *Enterprise* under Captain Jean-Luc Picard then travels back in time to undo their interference and again save the world.

Although the picture is far more successful in the longer version, there is still some trepidation about the metaphysical plot. Stars William Shatner and Leonard Nimoy themselves felt the plot left them staring at the viewscreen in silence. The film actually avoids action and concentrates instead on creating a cerebral mood of wonder and awe. It is very successful in this endeavor, but a large number of filmgoers were expecting a fast-paced escapade (and indeed, this is what they got in the excellent 1982 entry, *Star Trek II: The Wrath of Khan*.) Instead, this film unfolds at a leisurely pace, which almost undercuts the urgency of the mission of the *Enterprise*. Near the beginning of the film, Scotty ferries Kirk over to the *Enterprise* in an extended, almost dream-like passage. This permits a detailed study of the refurbished *Enterprise*, as well as an opportunity for composer Jerry Goldsmith to develop his lyrical and expressive main theme. To the non-fan, the sequence is static and almost intolerable, but to a *Star Trek* devotee, this rare moment is a solemn celebration: after years of waiting, *Star Trek* has returned and fans can simply pause, sit back and indulge in their affection for the show.

The subplot of Decker and Ilia is perhaps given too much weight in the storyline, crowding out the regulars. Kirk, Spock and the others are merely background spectators. It is only the expanded version that allows a few special moments for them to be the center of attention. In truth, it is the special effects that are showcased in the film, and they are breathtaking and quite beautiful at times, representing a rare instance where abstract art and motion pictures become intertwined. A few technical aspects of the film are not as successful. The new uniforms for the crew are awful, particularly Kirk's short-sleeved shirt. The skin-tight spandex look is very unflattering, and each cast member wears an oversize packet on his stomach, which also looks foolish. There are also a number of gaffes and missteps, both in plot and execution. The "let's-wrap-it-up" banter on the bridge at the conclusion is painful in its awkwardness, especially McCoy's comparison to the delivery of a baby. The passionate looks of longing that Decker and Ilia constantly exchange, particularly at the climax, also seem silly. The expanded version has a priceless goof when Kirk leaves the ship in his thruster suit. If you observe closely, you'll see the rafters and studio ceiling above him. Apparently the special effects crew never completed their work for this shot, assuming it would not be used. Critics can also nitpick the film in plot terms. For instance, why didn't the machine planet repair crew working on V'ger take a moment to clear its name plate and uncover the entire name VOYAGER at the time of their renovation?

The positive aspects far outnumber the weaknesses. The set design of the new ship is not bad, and visually the exterior of the *Enterprise* is stunning. Jerry Goldsmith's musical score is exceptional, and his main theme was later adopted by the second television series, *Star Trek: The Next Generation*. The cast performs very well, given the material with which they had to work. William Shatner deserves genuine credit for his performance. His Kirk is complex, with many nuances, and his dark side is also on display until tempered by McCoy. Leonard Nimoy is more distant and impassive as Spock than at any other point in his history of the role. The encounter with V'ger is a turning point, and a more relaxed, balanced Spock emerges. It is a seminal moment in *Star Trek*, in which Spock finally integrates his human and Vulcan halves, and Nimoy follows through with this precise character development in *Star Trek II*. DeForest Kelley is reliable as ever as Dr. McCoy, even sporting a southern accent in his opening scene. Stephen Collins felt like an outsider on the set, but this no doubt contributed to the fine edge that he brings to his role as Decker. Persis Khambatta is magnificently alluring and exotic as the bald alien, Ilia. One must note the appearance of Mark Lenard as the Klingon captain. Lenard also played the father of Spock, Sarek, on the television show and in later films. He was the only actor to play all three major alien races in the *Star Trek* saga. Many longtime fans of the show, including Bjo Tremble who was a leader in the "save the series" movement when cancellation was threatened after the second season, appear as crew members and aliens in the Recreation Deck scene, the largest number of people ever to appear in a single shot in the history of *Star Trek*.

This film is an extraordinary effort, but in terms of plot and the balance of characters, as well as dramatic thrust, the picture did not synthesize the right formula to please both Trekkers and the public at large. The three following *Star Trek* films, however, did zero in on the right combination, and on a more modest budget. Despite its flaws, there is something uniquely noble and magnificent that the later, superior films lacked. There is a certain boldness to the plot, portraying a sentient machine search for God, a role that man inadvertently fulfills in the guise of Decker. In awarding the four-star rating, I again stress that this is a very subjective impression, but the film seems to strike a special chord with a minority of film lovers who treasure its unusual tempo and emphasis. Much of this seems due to the direction of Robert Wise, who stressed the ethereal qualities of the film throughout and brought to it a rather spiritual tone.

One final interesting note is that *Star Trek—The Motion Picture* was actually not the first *Star Trek* film. A 70 minute Turkish film called *Turist Ömer Uzay* (1970) was actually the first *Star Trek* feature. It was unauthorized by Paramount, and the film was distributed principally in Turkey. Kirk was played by Sadri Alisaçk, Spock by Erol Amaç and McCoy by Feibrei Mertay. The story of the film recycled plots from two television episodes, "The Man Trap" and "Amok Time," grafted to a third original story about a current-day Turkish bridegroom who is beamed aboard the *Enterprise* during his wedding feast. The costumes and various details of the show were captured to a remarkable detail, including even the character's hair styles. The McCoy counterpart is younger, but the Spock equivalent does a particularly fine job. A video of this Turkish language film is available in the collector's video market. This bizarre curiosity item is "fascinating" (as Mr. Spock would undoubtedly observe), and it would be a hilarious treat for any unabashed Trek enthusiast.

REPRESENTATIVE QUOTES

"An alien object of unbelievable destructive power is less than three days away from this planet. The only Starship in interception range is the *Enterprise*. Ready or not, she launches in twelve hours." (Kirk to Scotty)

"I remember when you recommended me for this command. You told me how envious you were and how much you hoped you would find a way to get a Starship command again. Well, sir, it looks like you found a way." (Decker to Kirk after learning of the admiral's assumption of command)

"I saw V'ger's planet, a planet populated by living machines, unbelievable technology. V'ger has knowledge that spans this universe, and yet, with all its pure logic, V'ger is barren, cold, no mystery, no creativity . . . (At this moment, Spock grasps Kirk's hand) This simple feeling is beyond V'ger's comprehension. It has no meaning, no hope. Jim, it has no answers. It's asking questions: 'Is this all that I am? Is there nothing more?' " (Spock after his mind meld with V'ger)

"I weep for V'ger as I would for a brother. As I was when I came aboard, so is V'ger now, empty, incomplete and searching. Logic and knowledge are not enough." (Spock to the others when they notice his tears)

Target Earth (1953)

Rating: ✳✳✳   **Threat:** **Army of alien robots**

Allied Artists. Written by William Raynor based on a treatment by James Nicholson & Wyott Ordung of the novella *Deadly City* by Paul W. Fairman; Photographed by Guy Roe; Special effects by Dave Koehler; Edited by Sherman A. Rose; Music by Paul Dunlap; Produced by Herman Cohen; Directed by Sherman A. Rose. B & W, 75 minutes.

ANNOTATED CAST LIST

Richard Denning (*Frank Brooks*, traveling salesman); Kathleen Crowley (*Nora King*, widow who attempted suicide); Richard Reeves (*Jim Wilson*, gambler who won the daily double); Virginia Grey (*Vicki Harris*, his girlfriend); Robert Roark (*Davis*, escaped killer); Mort Marshall (*Charles Otis*, man killed while fleeing hotel); Arthur Space (*Gen. Wood*, officer in charge of defense); Steve Pendelton (colonel); Jim Drake (lieutenant); Whit Bissell (*Tom*, top government scientist); House Peters Jr. (*Barton*, electronics lab technician).

SYNOPSIS

Conceived as a low-budget variation of the famous *War of the Worlds* (1953), *Target Earth* actually surpasses its rival with an impressive and eloquent opening half hour before faltering due to inferior and laughable special effects and a subplot padded with stock footage.

The film opens at a rooming house in a major Midwestern city. The panning camera notes a ticking clock displaying the time as 1:30 PM. A sleeping woman is slowly coming to her senses, and there is an open bottle of sleeping pills next to her hand on the bed. She gets up sluggishly and starts to get dressed. When she notices that her electricity is off, she knocks at the doors of her neighbors, but there is no response. The whole building is deserted, so she heads to the streets, which are totally empty. Every store is closed, and she becomes frantic, randomly pushing buttons of different apartments as she seeks an explanation. She finally comes across the corpse of a woman in a doorway and, backing away, she bumps into a man. Assuming the stranger has murdered the woman, she runs off in panic until the man catches her in an alley. He tries to calm her down, introducing himself as Frank Brooks. He had arrived in town the previous evening from Detroit and was passing time waiting for another train when he was hit over the head and robbed. He awoke at midday and has been searching for other people in the deserted city. The woman, Nora King, says she overslept and missed learning what had happened. They trade theories as to why the city is deserted. Since both the telephones and electric power are disconnected, Frank assumes it was a mass evacuation. They decide to head to the center of town where they might learn the facts. Frank decides to break into a store to locate a transistor radio, but he is unable to find any batteries. They hear music coming from a bar, where they find Jim Wilson and his girlfriend Vicki Harris helping themselves to free drinks. They were aware of the evacuation but never learned the reason. Jim used the opportunity to visit the high-class nightspots he never could afford. Frank tries to sober them up by suggesting they eat a solid meal. When he suggests it is ti,e to move on, Wilson declines, saying he never had it so good. More subtle, Nora suggests that the best area nightclub is Club Royale, five miles south of town. Wilson agrees with this idea, and everyone heads outside to locate a car. When they locate a convertable, they open the door and the body of the driver tumbles out. The sight of the corpse sobers Wilson up, and he tries to start the car. However another man, Charles Otis, appears, and explains that a necessary part, the distributor arms, is missing from every vehicle he has tried. Otis has been fleeing from the northern suburbs, which is in shambles, with bodies scattered everywhere.

On a wall across the street, Vicki suddenly spots an ominous shadow, apparanetly caused by a mysterious entity patrolling on the roof of one of the buildings. Frank leads the others into the lobby of a hotel where Otis finds a newspaper with the startling headline, "INVASION BY MYSTERY ARMY." It reports that an enemy force of extraterrestrial origin had landed north of the city during the evening, and Civil Defense had ordered the immediate evacuation of the entire populace of the city. Otis panics after reading the news and he flees the hotel. A clunky-looking robot notices him and kills him with a ray projected from its helmet. Frank suggests they hide in a suite on one of the upper floors of the hotel and try to sneak out of town after dark. They also hope that the National Guard or the army might rescue them.

The scene switches to military headquarters, where the top brass are baffled about how to confront the alien invasion. All units sent against them have been entirely wiped out. An air strike is launched over the city against the invaders, but the aliens destroy the planes with ease. Watching from the hotel, Frank and his companions are shocked by how quickly and effortlessly the aircraft are destroyed. They also realize that it is no longer possible to escape from the city. When Frank says that their prospects are bleak, Nora leaves the room shaking with fear. Frank follows her, and Nora confesses that she missed the evacuation because she tried to overdose on sleeping pills. Her husband was killed in a car crash a few months earlier, and she felt she no longer had any reason to live. Meeting Frank has changed her outlook and made her believe she has a future, but now it is too late.

The military considers firing an atomic missile to destroy the city and the alien army. A dormant robot is found by an advance guard and brought to military headquarters and Tom, a top scientist, is placed in charge of studying it. He determines that the alien machine was rendered inactive when its cathode ray tube, the glass-like faceplate in its helmet, was somehow cracked. Tom tries a series of experiments to cause a crack, but all attempts fail.

Frank and Wilson slip down to the hotel kitchen to retrieve some food, after which Nora and Vicki try to sleep. During the night, an armed intruder breaks into their hotel suite and holds the four survivors at gunpoint. Vicki recognizes the man as Davis, a killer who was arrested a month ago. He killed a guard and escaped while the prisoners awaiting trial were being evacuated. Davis corners Nora and propositions her, saying he has a plan to use the others as decoys while they escape through the sewer and double back behind the lines of the robot army. When she rebuffs him, Davis figures she is also expendable. Meanwhile, at the army electronics lab, Tom concludes that the best way to crack the cathode ray tube is by sound oscillations and he sets out to determine which frequency might work.

Davis brings his hostages to the hotel lobby. He orders them to head out the door, but Vicki confronts him instead. The desperate criminal shoots both her and Frank. Wilson knocks his gun away and they struggle until Wilson chokes him to death. Only winged by a bullet, Frank tries to help Vicki, but she dies. An alien robot breaks into the lobby, and Frank, Nora and Wilson run up the stairs to the roof. The robot follows, and Wilson deliberately distracts it, hoping to give Frank and Nora a chance to escape. The automaton kills Wilson and starts to corner Frank and Nora when an army jeep in the street below passes, blaring a high-pitched sound through loudspeakers. The robot collapses, and Frank and Nora rush down to the army vehicle. The soldiers explain that the alien machines can be destroyed by sound, and they transport them to a medical unit to treat Frank's gunshot wound.

CRITIQUE

When I first saw this film on television as a child, I was utterly spellbound for the first forty minutes, considering it to be the finest science fiction film I had ever seen. However, this was only until the robot shows up as Otis leaves the hotel. Its appearance was so incredibly awkward and idiotic that I crumpled up my bag of chips and tossed it at the set. Thirty-eight years later, my opinion has changed little. The first half hour is surreal and elegant, with evocative camera angles, moody photography and superb visuals. The opening shot in Nora's room is worthy of Alfred Hitchcock, as the camera pans from the clock to the bottle of pills and finally to Nora herself. What other B film would have the audacity to launch its apocalyptic story with the failed suicide attempt of the heroine? The film intrigues the viewer as it slowly unfolds. When Wilson and Vicki appear in their drunken fling, the picture becomes reminiscent of the play *Waiting for Godot*. The dialogue throughout the film is rich and literate, even when the action becomes ludicrous. The acting has an intensity quitee atypical of a low-budget quickie.

The quality level crashes when the scene switches to military headquarters, where the performances are hackneyed and run-of-the-mill. The stock footage seldom seems to match up. The story is supposed to be set in the Midwest, but the terrain in these shots is the desert Southwest. The action sporadically returns to the survivors hiding out in the hotel, but it cuts away every few minutes to the military lab, where another experiment fails. Interest revives again at the hotel when the armed killer enters the scene, but it sinks to the ridiculous when the robot breaks into the hotel. The scene of the bulky, clumsy automaton trying to climb the staircase is totally inept and hilarious. Seldom has one weak effect ruined so much in a basically worthwhile film. I generously rated the film with three stars, but in actuality the first half rates five stars and the second half rates one, so three stars is a compromise.

Note that only one robot is ever seen, although there is supposed to be an army of automatons. The metal man on patrol near the hotel and the prone figure in the lab are obviously the same. Couldn't a little money have been invested to make the figure more believable? On *Tales of Tomorrow*, there is an episode entitled "Read to Me, Herr Doktor," in which they use a similar robot made out of cardboard, and even that robot is marginally more effective. It would be a highly entertaining experiment if a first-rate computer-generated robot were superimposed over the original in this film, similar to the additions made by George Lucas to his special edition of *Star Wars* in 1997. Film promoter Wade Williams also did some doctoring, adding new special effects, for his video release of *Rocketship XM* (1950). Would *Target Earth* suddenly emerge as a classic? Perhaps, but then the faltering military scenes would still stand out like a sore thumb. It is also worth noting that the first few minutes of *Target Earth* directly inspired the pilot episode of *The Twilight Zone* written by Rod Serling and entitled "Where is Everybody?" The defeat of the alien army is parodied by *Mars Attacks!* where the singing of Slim Whitman produces the necessary pitch to overcome the alien invaders.

The six actors who play the parts of the stragglers missed by the evacuation are uniformly excellent. Robert Roark, oddly enough, bears a marked similarity to Rod Serling, both in appearance and manner of speech. His calculating and odious Davis makes an excellent contrast to the killer robots. Virginia Grey is one of the most underrated actresses in history. She had a long film career, dating back to Little Eva in *Uncle Tom's Cabin* (1927), and including a remarkable number of roles in such varied films as *The Great Ziegfeld* (1936), *House of Horrors* (1946), *Crime of Passion* (1956), *Portrait in Black* (1960) and *Airport* (1969). Grey was always convincing in her performances, and she shines here as the blustery but dependable Vicki. Dick Reeves is another first-rate character actor who was usually cast in roles less meaty or complex than the hard-luck gambler Jim Wilson. His part was originally written with Lon Chaney in mind for the role. Kathleen Crowley appeared in about twenty films, but none of her other parts has the depth or variety of Nora King, one of the most unusual heroines in B films. Even when her character is subjected to traditional traumas, such as the amorous advances by Davis, Kathleen brings more substance to her part than usual. Richard Denning is good, although a trifle blunt and foursquare. His opening confrontation with Kathleen is his weakest moment. He says he is not going to hurt her, but then gives her a solid slap across the face. Whit Bissell and Arthur Space are adequate as the research scientist and General Wood. They merely seem to walk through these parts and probably each worked only one afternoon on the film.

A telefilm titled *Target Earth* played in the late 1990s, but it was unrelated to the original film.

REPRESENTATIVE QUOTES

"Ever try to empty a sack of sugar? Some of the grains always stick to the sack like the two of us. Something tells me we better get out of here fast. . . . The only reason they would clear out an entire city like this would mean to get away from certain death. And that would mean anyone still here is a dead pigeon." (Frank Brooks to Nora)

"You don't need a reason to die, Frank, just one to live. Somehow I thought I didn't have one anymore." (Nora to Frank, discussing her suicide attempt)

"You mean the city and the whole world is safe again?" (Nora to the soldier) "Maybe 'til the next time. . . . From what I was told, if they had used a certain metal instead of glass in that tube, all the oscillators in the world couldn't have stopped them." (The soldier in reply)

Them! (1954)

Rating: ***** **Threat: Giant ants**

Warner Brothers. Written by Ted Sherdeman & George Worthing Yates; Photographed by Sid Hickox; Special effects by Dick Smith & Ralph Ayers; Edited by Thomas Reilly; Music by Bronislau Kaper; Produced by David Weisbart; Directed by Gordon Douglas. B & W, 93 minutes.

ANNOTATED CAST LIST

Edmund Gwenn (*Dr. Harold Medford*, renowned entomologist); Joan Weldon (*Dr. Pat Medford*, his daughter and associate entomologist); James Arness (*Bob Graham*, FBI agent); James Whitmore (*Sgt. Ben Peterson*, New Mexico police officer); Christian Drake (*Ed Blackburn*, his partner); Onslow Stevens (*Gen. Robert O'Brien*, Air Force Intelligence commander); Sean McClory (*Maj. Kibbee*, Air Force Intelligence officer assigned to the case); Sandy Descher (young girl who encounters the ants); Luz Potter (girl as seen from airplane); John Close (*Johnny*, pilot who spots the girl); Mary Alan Hokanson (*Mrs. Lodge*, mother of lost boys); Scott Corell (*Jerry*, her son, trapped in an LA storm drain with the ants); Richard Bellis (*Mike*, her second son); Olin Howlin (*Jenson*, alcoholic who sees ants from hospital window); Joel Smith (*Smith*, Ben's jeep driver in storm drain); William Schallert (Medic who rides with girl in an ambulance); Cliff Ferre (police lab man); Don Shelton (*Fred Edwards*, police captain); Matthew McCue (*Gramps Johnson,* desert store owner killed by Them); Fess Parker (*Crotty*, pilot detained in Texas); Joe Forte (*Putnam*, coroner in New Mexico); Russell Gage (coroner in LA); Ann Doran (psychiatrist treating the girl); Fred Shellac (attendant); Norman Field (*Gen. James*, Army Intelligence officer); Otis Clarke (admiral who orders the sinking of the *Viking*); Leonard Nimoy (sergeant who receives UFO report); Janet Stewart (WAVE); Wally Duffy (airman); Warren Mace (*Viking* radio operator killed by ants); Dub Taylor (railroad yard watchman); Robert Berger (*Sutton*, LA cop who finds Lodge's body); John Bernardino (*Ryan*, Sutton's partner); Lawrence Dobkin (L.A. city engineer); Victor Sutherland (senator); Dorothy Green (matron); Frederick J. Foote (*Dixon*); John Maxwell, Marshall Bradford, Waldron Boyle (doctors); Willis Bouchey, Alexander Campbell (government officials); Booth Coleman, Walter Coy (reporters); Harry Tyler, Oscar Blanke, (winos interviewed by Bob); Harry Wilson, Ken Smith, Kenner Kemp, Richard Boyer, Eddie Dew, Dick Wessell, Dean Cromer, James Cardwell, Gayle Kellogg, Charles Perry, Jack Perrin, Hubert Kerns, Royden Clark (soldiers and policemen).

SYNOPSIS

The dawning of the nuclear era provided great impetus to films with an apocalyptic theme, not limited to the concept of nuclear warfare alone. *Them!* is a pivotal film, one of the first to link nuclear radiation with giant mutants, an idea that became a major theme in the realm of science fiction. Many of these giant mutants threaten the human race as the dominant species on Earth, but none more convincingly than *Them!*

Although the film is in black and white, the letters of the title *Them!* are tinted in red and blue, making it stand out in a unique fashion. The picture opens in the desert wastes of New Mexico. The state police are following a report by a passing motorist of seeing a little girl wandering about in a daze. A plane spots the child and radios her location to two officers, Ben Peterson and Ed Blackburn. The young girl, dressed in pajamas and a robe, is in a state of total shock, and the police conclude she came from a trailer they spotted parked off the road. When they investigate, they find that the entire side of the trailer has been torn apart. Ed spots an unusual print in the ground near the trailer. He summons an ambulance and a crime scene technical team. When the crew arrives, Ben hears a strange, high-pitched sound in the distance. The policemen check out a general store, which is in shambles, with one entire wall smashed down. After they find the dead body of the proprietor, Ben returns to headquarters, leaving Ed on guard at the scene. After a few minutes, Ed hears the strange sound again and, while searching for it, screams and is killed offscreen.

The next day, Ben is shaken by the loss of his partner, and the police learn that the trailer belonged to an FBI agent on vacation with his family. The FBI assigns Agent Bob Graham to the case, and he forwards a photo of the print found near the trailer to the FBI lab in Washington, D.C. The FBI responds by sending two scientists from the Department of Agriculture to New Mexico, a father and daughter team of entomologists named Harold and Pat Medford. They ask to be taken to visit the young girl who is still at the hospital. She has not spoken since being discovered, but when the elder Dr. Medford gives her formic acid to smell, the odor snaps the girl out of her catatonic state and she starts to scream out, "Them! Them!"

Ben and Bob take Pat and her father to the scene of the wrecked trailer. Dr. Medford becomes more alarmed when he finds additional, fresh prints. A dust storm arises, and the strange sound reoccurs. Pat wanders near a mound when a giant ant almost twelve feet length comes after her. Dr. Medford instructs Bob and Ben to shoot at its antennae, and the creature collapses in a hail of gunfire. Dr. Medford proclaims it to be a fantastic mutation caused by the residue radiation from the first atomic bomb test at nearby White Sands.

General O'Brien and Major Kibbee from the military join the operation under Dr. Medford's authority. They search the desert in two helicopters, and Pat spots the ant colony. Her father outlines a plan of action using cyanide to wipe out the nest at noon the following day, when the entire ant population should be present in the colony. since ants dislike the heat of the sun. An exploratory team searches through the nest after the cyanide release to ascertain if all the ants were destroyed. Unfortunately, Pat discovers evidence in the queen's chamber that two hatchlings and their mates had already fled the nest to form additional colonies.

In Washington, D.C., Dr. Medford makes a presentation to an executive committee about the danger posed by the ants. If the two colonies are not quickly located and destroyed before further queens are born, he predicts that the giant ants will overwhelm and wipe out the human race within two years. He shows the skeptical group a film that documents the destructive power of the ants. (The use of a technical film to explain the threat later became a cliché in this type of film.) In addition, Dr. Medford recommends that secrecy be maintained about the existence of the ants to avoid panic among the general populace.

Without revealing the nature of the threat, a nationwide effort is launched to monitor any unusual phenomena that might signify the presence of the giant ants. After several weeks pass, the team hears about a pilot who reported seeing unconventional UFOs over Texas. Bob and Pat travel to interview him, and he tells them that the UFOs resembled giant, winged ants and were flying eastward. Bob informs the doctors who are treating the pilot that he must be kept isolated for the sake of national security. A colony appears in a cargo ship, the *S.S. Viking* in the Gulf of Mexico. The navy investigates and sinks the ship after determining there were no survivors to the ant attack. The winged queen flying over Texas had entered the ship to nest while it was docked in the harbor. With this colony eliminated, only one more nest remains, but Dr. Medford warns that as time passes, the likelihood increases that additional queen ants will be hatched.

Ben and Bob fly to Los Angeles to inquire into a large sugar theft at a rail yard. The side of a boxcar was torn apart, indicating that giant ants were to blame. They also investigate the death of a man named Lodge who was discovered mangled after disappearing on a Sunday morning outing with his two sons. Bob and Ben interview the widow to learn where her husband had been planning to go with the children, but they had gone to a different spot each week. They question the cops who discovered Lodge's body, which leads them to interview an alcoholic in the drunk tank who claims to have seen giant ants at the entrance of the Los Angeles storm drain system. They find a model airplane belonging to the Lodge boys in the same area. Dr. Medford and Pat are summoned to Los Angeles, and they order a massive search of the storm drain system by the army. They authorize breaking the news of the giant ants to the public, and Los Angeles is placed under martial law. On television, a city official proclaims a public curfew and describes in detail the danger posed by the mutant ants.

Ben, Major Kibbee and Bob take the lead in the search as military jeeps probe through the storm drains. Ben locates the two boys, alive and well, in an unfinished side tunnel. He undertakes a rescue, sending the boys through a small passage to safety, but is himself killed before he can join them. Soldiers using flamethrowers advance on the ants. They locate the egg chamber and discover three newly hatched queens. Dr. Medford and Pat conclude that no additional queens have escaped, and the nest and the remaining ants are torched. Bob wonders if other monsters have been created by other nuclear tests, a question Dr. Medford is unable to answer as the film concludes.

CRITIQUE

Them! was an extraordinarily popular and influential film which was often imitated in later films featuring giant locusts, crabs, shrews, scorpions, spiders and even rabbits. One later film, *Empire of the Ants* (1977), based on a story by H. G. Wells, was somewhat ridiculous and only emphasized the effectiveness of the original *Them!* Along with *The Thing* (1951), *The Day the Earth Stood Still* (1951) and *Destination Moon* (1950), this film became one of the undisputed classics of 1950s science fiction.

Gordon Douglas mounted the film with exceptional care, and it is probably his finest achievement. Even when viewed today, the film has an intensity and a degree of craftsmanship that is remarkable. Almost all the technical elements excel, particularly the cinematography and editing. According to cast members I interviewed, Christian Drake, Sandy Descher and Luz Potter, the ants were transported around mounted on trucks and hydraulics were used to produce movement. All the giant ants were full scale, not models, and considerable resourcefulness was required to maintain the illusion of a large number of these enormous nine to twelve foot long monsters. Douglas also used clever camera placements to augment the effect. Today, the audience would be overwhelmed with computer graphics such as those used in *Starship Troopers* (1997), but given the range of possible effects in the early 1950s, Douglas did exceedingly well.

The original script intended the final colony of ants to be located in the New York City subway system, but that would have been prohibitively expensive. The substitution of the Los Angeles storm drain system works quite well. The pacing of the script is quite good, slowly building to the appearance of the monsters. Christian Drake filmed a scene where he was attacked on screen, but the later revelation during a desert windstorm is far more effective. It is also salutary that the ants behave as authentic ants and do not display enhanced intelligence, as they do in *Empire of the Ants*. The script also breaks a few rules, such as killing James Whitmore in the climax of the film. A romantic subplot, usually a distraction in similar films, is only hinted at between James Arness and Joan Weldon, and their relationship seems more realistic. Edmund Gwenn is superb as the crusty old scientist, and he has the best lines of dialogue in the picture. His character is partially based on a similar role played by Cecil Kellaway in *The Beast from 20,000 Fathoms* (1953), but he added unique touches that made his role distinct. It is fun to compare how both Gwenn's and Kellaway's scientists approach using communications equipment. Gwenn's sotto voce asides about repeating the phrase "Over" are delightful, and they endow small, inconsequential moments of the film with interest and pleasure. Similar small moments, such as the interview with the winos and the heartfelt concern shown to Mrs. Lodge help this film stand out from later similar efforts. Gwenn was a screen veteran whose career dated back to 1916, and he had many memorable roles, including Kris Kringle in *Miracle on 34th Street* (1947). Gwenn was in his late seventies when he appeared in *Them!* James Whitmore and James Arness handled their roles with grace and ease. Sandy Descher, who was first sighted by Gordon

Douglas while she and her family were vacationing at Jackson Hole, Wyoming, recalled how deeply committed the director was to all aspects of the production. She also recalled an amusing incident. When Douglas was directing Descher on location in the Mojave Desert, he kept urging her, "Don't blink, don't blink" while he backed into a cactus, and had to have the spines removed with tweezers from his backside. In my interview with Luz Potter, the midget who served as Sandy Descher's double, she recalled that the greatest difficulty shooting in the desert was the blowing sand which really stung the eyes of the performers. Joan Weldon also commented on the difficulty of shooting the windstorm sequence. Her performance as Dr. Pat Medford is understated and appealing. Her character is protective of, and affectionate to, her famous father, and he, in turn, treats her with professional respect, calling her "Doctor" as often as he calls her "Pat." Two minor players in the film also went on to fame, Fess Parker as the pilot who sights the flying ants, and Leonard Nimoy, as the sergeant who brings the UFO report to the attention of his superiors. Sean McClory, the charming star of later films such as *Valley of the Dragons* (1961), is excellent in the role as Major Kibbee, although his screen time is limited.

Mutation is frequently overstated as a threat in films, and it was the success of *Them!* that helped to popularize the concept as a standard motif. The picture does stress that the development of the giant ants is an accident of nature, an unforeseeable byproduct of the nuclear age. In that sense, the ants can be seen in symbolic terms. Other unusual interpretations have been made regarding the film. Some have seen the picture as an anticommunist allegory with mutant ants representing the Communist movement. This interpretation is far-fetched and certainly never intended by the filmmakers. *Them!* can stand on its own as an exercise in terror which captured the public's imagination and created an unforgettable image of an apocalyptic possibility.

REPRESENTATIVE QUOTES

"We may be witnesses to a biblical prophecy come true. And there will be destruction and darkness come upon creation, and the beasts shall reign over the earth." (Dr. Medford to the others after the destruction of the first giant ant)

"No, we haven't seen the end of them. We only had a close view of the beginning of what may be the end of us." (Dr. Medford to Bob after the nest is eliminated)

"If these monsters got started as a result of the first atomic bomb in 1945, what about all the others that have been exploded since then?" (Bob's question at the end of the film) "Nobody knows, Robert. When man entered the atomic age, he opened a door into a new world. What we eventually find in that new world, nobody can predict." (Dr. Medford's reply)

Virus (1980)
AKA *Fukkatsu No Hi* (*Day of Rebirth*)

Rating: **   **Threat:** Virus and nuclear weapons

Toho. Written by Koji Takaga, Gregory Knapp & Kinji Fukasaku based on the novel *Fukkatsu No Hi* by Sakyo Komatsu; Photographed by Daisaku Kimura; Special effects by Ichiro Higa; Edited by Akira Suzuki; Music by Teo Macero; Produced by Haruki Kadokawa; Directed by Kinji Fukasaku. Original version, 155 minutes; International version, 106 minutes.

ANNOTATED CAST LIST

Chuck Connors (*McCloud*, British submarine captain); Glenn Ford (*Richardson*, U.S. president), Olivia Hussey (*Marit*, sole survivor from Norway Station): George Kennedy (*Adm. Richard Conway*, commander of Palmer Station) Masao Kusakari (*Dr. Yoshizumi*, seismologist from Showa Station); Edward J. Olmos (*Capt. Lopez*, head of Frey Station); Henry Silva (*Gen. Garland*, head of Joint Chiefs of Staff); Bo Svenson (*Maj. Carter*, Conway's assistant) Robert Vaughan (*Senator Barkley*, head of Defense Oversight Committee); Stephanie Faulkner (*Sarah Baker*, member of Palmer Station) Stuart Gillard (*Dr. Edward Meyer*, inventor of MM88); Cec Linder (*Dr. Latour*, French doctor in Antarctica); Isao Natsuki (*Dr. Nakanishi*, head of Showa Station); Sonny Chiba (*Dr. Yamauchi*, member of Showa Station); Chris Wiggins (*Dr. Borodinov*, Soviet head of Mirny Station); John Evans (*Capt. Nevsky*, military expert, Mirny Station); Eve Crawford (*Dr. Irma Ollich*, Palmer Station member); John Granik (*Dr. Turowicz*, Soviet scientist); John Bayliss (*Major King*, Palmer Station officer); Ara Hovanessian (*Major Giron*, Palmer Station officer); Ted Follows (*Major Barnes*, Palmer Station officer); George Touliatos (*Colonel Rankin*, Military head of Operation Phoenix); Larry Reynolds (*Morrison*, cabinet member); David Gardner (*Watt*, cabinet member); Dan Kippy (*Reed*, cabinet member); William Binney (*Simmons*, cabinet member); Ron Hartman (*Dr. Rogers*, scientific head of Operation Phoenix); Ken Pogue (*Dr. Krauss*, bacteriologist in Leipzig); Ken Camroux (*Jones*, second-in-command of *Nereid*); Gordon Thompson (radio operator of *Nereid*); Matt Hawthorne (navigator of *Nereid*); Yumi Takigawa (*Noriko*, Tokyo physician); Jan Muszynski (*Ensign Smirnov*, acting commander of Soviet submarine); Charles L. Campbell (TV reporter).

SYNOPSIS

Although impressive and eloquent on many levels, the reach of this ambitious epic seems to extend its grasp. The film seems hampered by a labyrinthian plot, which causes it to ramble. The story awkwardly includes a double apocalypse, since the world is first destroyed by a virus and then the survivors in Antarctica learn they are the target of nuclear missiles from a computer defense program that is about to be triggered. Therefore, it gives the impression of two different plotlines stitched together. Moreover, the international version was edited down considerably from the two-and-a-half-hour Japanese original, which makes it seem even more of a disjointed patchwork.

The film begins with a bedraggled figure stumbling along a desolate landscape. After the title card, the action flashes back years earlier to a bacteriological lab in Leipzig, East Germany, where Dr. Krauss is trying to smuggle a sample of a deadly virus to a colleague in Switzerland who could possibly develop a vaccine. The virus, MM88, was stolen from a lab in the United States, and Krauss considers it an unstoppable doomsday germ that would destroy the world if it were ever released. The transaction is interrupted by armed men, shooting breaks out, and Krauss is killed. The men carrying the virus escape in a private plane, which crashes while flying over the Alps. The vial containing MM88 is shown smashing against some rocks outside the wreckage.

One month later, a terrible plague known as the "Italian flu" is ravaging Europe. In the United States, Dr. Meyer is visited by Colonel Rankin, who reports that government agents were unable to recover MM88, which they had traced to Dr. Krauss in East Germany. Krauss is now dead and the espionage team has disappeared. Meyer is frantic that the virus be found, since it is invulnerable to everything except extremely low temperatures. Rankin is worried that Meyer might reveal what he knows to Senator Barkley, head of the Defense Oversight Committee. Since MM88 was an unauthorized project (known as Operation Phoenix), Rankin and Dr. Rogers, head of the project, decide to detain Meyers in a mental institution.

Worldwide, the virus is having a devastating impact. In Washington, D.C., President Richardson and his cabinet are given a detailed report about the plague and the civil discord sweeping the world. Crowds in Washington are demanding government action and distribution of the vaccine, which might stop the disease. Richardson is informed, however, that the vaccine is ineffective, a mere placebo. General Garland demands that the president activate the automatic Defense System (AS), in case the deadly flu outbreak is actually a case of germ warfare by the Soviet Union. At that moment, the hot line from the Kremlin rings and Richardson is informed that the Soviet leader has just died from the Italian flu. Garland does not believe the report.

A montage chronicles the collapse of civilization around the globe. In Tokyo, doctors and nurses desperately struggle in an attempt to treat the overflow of patients. An overworked doctor collapses, unable to continue, and panic sets in. Back in Washington, Senator Barkley breaks into to see Richardson with important news. He has learned the Italian flu is caused by MM88, a virus developed by a top-secret military project called Operation Phoenix. The president has never heard of it and questions Garland. The general claims it was only a theoretical study when the senator brings Dr. Meyer into the Oval Office. When the president learns that MM88 was stolen from the government lab and Meyer was illegally detained, he dismisses Garland. Meanwhile, the devastation continues, and massive bonfires of dead bodies are lit in every city.

A few days later, Richardson and Barkley meet in private. Both men are hacking uncontrollably. They lament that Meyer died before finding a cure. As Richardson rambles on forlornly about his inability to do anything, Barkley mentions the effect of the cold in stopping MM88 and reminds the president of the outposts in Antarctica. He places a call to Palmer Station in Antarctica. Admiral Conway, in charge of the scientific station, replies and informs the president that no trace of the disease is present in the entire continent. Richardson says the rest of the world is doomed, and he urges them and the other scientific missions to set up a total quarantine. He wishes them well, and urges them to work together to survive, and carry on human life on Earth. Richardson and Barkley die moments later. General Garland, becoming unhinged, takes an elevator that leads to a chamber far beneath the White House and programs the computer that activates the AS. A final montage surveys the major cities of the world, and in each of them, not a single survivor remains.

At Palmer Station, Conway organizes a group to represent each of the scientific communities and plan for their general survival. The major active stations are operated by major countries, including Russia (Mirny Station), Japan (Showa Station), France (D'Urville Station), Chile (Frey Station) and Norway Station. A case of mass suicide occurs at Norway Station, and the one survivor, a pregnant woman named Marit, is rescued by two members from the Japanese team. She is in shock because her husband had tried to kill her. Dr. Yoshizumi agrees to stay with her until she gives birth.

The Federal Council of Antarctica meets and determines there are 855 men and 8 women present in the scientific stations, the last survivors on Earth. A message is received from a Soviet sub, T232, requesting permission to land. The ship is carrying the Italian flu, and Dr. Borodinov, head of the Soviet Station, has to refuse their request. Smirnov, acting commander of the sub, says they will land nevertheless. He is interrupted by another voice coming from the *Nereid*, a British submarine. Dr. Borodinov gives McCloud, captain of the British sub, permission to destroy the Soviet vessel. Following this action, McCloud and his crewmates are given permission to land after it is learned they are free of the deadly virus. When the Council is notified by Yoshizumi that Marit has given birth to a girl, they issue their first official proclamation, a message of greeting to the newborn child.

One of the women in Palmer Station is raped. The Council is at a loss how to proceed when another woman suggests that a new set of ground rules has to be developed for human sexuality, given the difference in numbers between men and women. Unless this problem is confronted, there will be no future, since many children need to be conceived as quickly as possible to support the continuation of the human race.

The *Nereid* goes on a mission to determine if there is any other pockets of survivors but find none. A air sample reveals that the virus is still prevalent in the atmosphere. Dr. Latour requests they retain a sample so he can work on a vaccine. Time passes, and additional children are born at Palmer Station.

Yoshizumi has fallen in love with Marit. He continues working in his special field, seismology, and makes the interesting discovery that there will be a major earthquake in the ocean off the coast of Washington, D.C., within a month. This news upsets Major Carter, who fears that the AS, a retaliatory missile network, was engaged during the last days of the plague. If an earthquake hits Washington, this system would interpret it as an attack and nuclear missiles would be launched against Russia. Captain McCloud confirms that they received an activation signal at that time. Captain Nevsky then reveals that the Soviet Union had its own automated missile system and that one of the targets is Palmer Station. If any nuclear weapons strike Russia, Palmer Station is doomed. The only way to prevent this chain of events is to send someone to Washington to shut down the AS before the earthquake. Conway sets up a lottery, but Carter volunteers as the only one with knowledge of the computer complex beneath the White House. Yoshizumi wants to go with him, and they have a pointless battle in the snow until Carter agrees to bring him along. The women and children plus a crew will be sent out of harm's way in an icebreaker. Conway lends his quarters to Yoshizumi and Marit so they can spend their last night together.

Before the *Nereid* leaves for Washington, Dr. Latour gives Carter and Yoshizumi a vaccine he developed that might protect them against the virus. After a ten-day voyage, they reach Washington, which is already beginning to experience tremors. Carter and Yoshizumi make their way through the nightmare landscape of the deserted US capitol. After they enter the underground complex beneath the White House, the main shock hits and the computer launches its missiles. Carter is pinned by heavy debris, and Yoshizumi tells his dying friend that they were too late. He broadcasts a message to McCloud that Dr. Latour's vaccine appears to have been successful.

Four years pass, and Yoshizumi is walking through the barren landscape, repeating the opening scene of the film. His clothes are threadbare, and his beard is long and tangled. He has been hiking from Washington down to the tip of South America, hoping to meet up with the survivors from the icebreaker. They are living in a small group of hovels. Dr. Latour is urging them to move north now, where a sustainable community could flourish. He knows his vaccine has overcome the virus. Marit is despondent and no longer believes in a future. But then she goes outside to the beach and sees the figure of Yoshizumi approaching in the distance. She runs to him and they embrace. He utters, "Life is wonderful," as the rest of the community rushes to greet him. It is the day of rebirth.

CRITIQUE

This was the most expensive film undertaken by a Japanese studio, but box office worldwide was very poor and the picture recouped less than 10 percent of its total cost. Some of the expense went to recruit the well-known international cast, but more went to obtain impressive location footage in Japan, Canada, Alaska and Antarctica itself. Second-unit footage also covered many of the major cities of the world such as New York, Washington, Moscow and Rome.

The novel on which the film is based is highly regarded, but it strongly reflects the atmosphere of the 1960s in its concepts and axioms. The names of many characters have interesting connotations. President Richardson seems a cross between Richard Nixon and Lyndon Johnson. Admiral Conway in his sanctuary in Antarctica calls to mind the explorer Conway who was brought to Shangri-La in the snowbound wilds of Tibet in the novel *Lost Horizon*. Captain Nevsky reflects the legendary Russian hero Alexander Nevsky. Even the secret military Operation Phoenix has a great irony, both because the project uncovers the virus that eventually destroys the world, and because it reflects the eventual rebirth suggested in the Japanese title of the book and film.

The care that went into the entire production is evident, especially with its cinematography, but much of the effort is not well utilized. For instance, the scene where Masao Kusakari keeps attacking Bo Svenson has one of the most spectacular ice and mountain backdrops ever filmed, but the scene itself is so clumsy and pointless that the wonderful scenery is simply wasted. These missteps occur again and again, but most of the problems stem from the basic story which is filled with clichés and loophole in the plot. Consider the crisis which Palmer Station faces, with the possibility of a nuclear strike in several weeks. Why is not the entire station evacuated on the icebreaker instead of just the handful of women and children and a skeleton crew? This makes no sense. If the ship could not accommodate them all, it could have made two trips and others could have left on the *Nereid* or journeyed to some of the other stations that were still manned and in operation. As George Kennedy shouts at one point after he conceives of his lottery, "This is stupid!" Similarly, having the bulk of the survivors wait around as sitting ducks when they have ample time to escape is also stupid. Palmer Station's handling of their rape case is dim-witted as well. Instead of offering the women protection, they decide to line them up instead to service all the men. These are supposed to be scientists and military officers, yet this demeaning solution is the best they can propose? Worse yet, the idea originates with the women themselves. Instead of gaining in power, which is what would likely happen with such a ratio, the women are turned into a commodity that should be equally shared by all the men.

The heroic and monumental trek of Kusakari from Washington to South America is also without logic and poorly thought out. Although he is immune to the virus, he obviously would have faced fatal doses of radiation from the nuclear weapons that struck the United States. Even if Central and South America were undamaged by the bombs, the walk through the southern United States surely would have proven fatal. Why is he in such pitiful state with disintegrating shoes and rags for clothes? Couldn't he have gotten new clothes along the way in South America? Couldn't he have located and fixed up a jeep or a fast motor boat? The picture tried to conclude on an "up" note with the rebirth of hope by the survivors who are amazed by the return of Kusakari, but his leaves other aspects unresolved. What was the fate of the *Nereid*? Did the crew perish when the Russian missile hit Washington? It seems they should have been safe since they had ample advance warning and could have dived deep enough to avoid destruction. The fate of the people from the other stations is not addressed either. Perhaps some of this is explained in the original novel, but none of it is clarified for the filmgoer.

There are many ludicrous scenes in the first half of the film as well. The staging of the airplane crash at the beginning of the film is poorly staged and unconvincing. The small plane explodes as it crashes into a mountain. Then the vial containing the virus is seen spinning through the air until it smashes against some rocks. This is illogical. Did someone from the plane throw it up in the air moments before the crash? Either the wreck should not have included an explosion or the aircraft should have broken apart above the ground. The filmmakers must have concluded that the virus would have perished in the explosion and later added the insert shot showing the vial breaking against the rocks. The Oval Office scene with the ill Glenn Ford and Robert Vaughan dressed in granny shawls while hacking away madly is one of the most unintentionally funny sequences ever recorded. Here they are coughing violently, yet they try to butter each other up with lavish praise until their dying sniffle. Henry Silva, however, seems totally immune to this flu, and one expects that he would still be patrolling the computer complex when Bo Svenson and Masao Kusakari show up at the film's sputtering non-climax.

The cast struggles well as best it can with the faulty script. Chuck Connors is miscast as a British naval officer, and he underplays his character in a deadpan style instead of faking a British accent. Glenn Ford, Robert Vaughan, Bo Svenson and George Kennedy try their best to appear as earnest and troubled leaders, but the script does not allow them much opportunity to be convincing in these roles. Olivia Hussey, whose career never fulfilled the promise of her early success in *Romeo and Juliet* (1968), is the most sympathetic character in the film, but she seems to struggles through a amazing set of difficulties pokerfaced, displaying hardly any emotion. Edward J. Olmos is pathetic as the Chilean leader, and the sentimental Spanish song he sings when Hussey and Kusakari share their last night together is completely maudlin and corny. For the most part, Masao Kusakari is wonderful, although his English is sometimes difficult to understand. His performance is undercut by his ridiculous scene with Swenson that was already described. Cec Linder as Dr. Latour provides the best acting in the entire film. Of Canadian background, Linder was an exceptional actor who paradoxically never drew much notice. He was Felix Leiter in *Goldfinger* (1964) and was also effective in *Crack in the Mirror* (1959) opposite Orson Welles. Stuart Gillard was excellent in the key role as Dr. Meyer. Gillard later became more successful as a television director, helming the pilot episode of the revamped *Outer Limits* and *Beast*, a TV mini-series based on a novel by Peter Benchley. Ken Pogue and Chris Wiggins brought uncommon intelligence to their roles. The weakest reading in the film was delivered by Henry Silva as the sneaky head of the Joint Chiefs of Staff. Of course the part is a thankless one, but note how brilliantly Martin Landau handled a similar role in *Meteor*, filmed a year before *Virus*. Silva plays the role like a robot, and his reading more or less ruins his scenes with Glenn Ford and Robert Vaughan.

In conclusion, one must note the sincere effort of director Kinji Fukasaku, who attempts to infuse the film with special moments of pure screen poetry. He indeed makes a noble effort, and the epitaph of this film may well be represented by Chuck Connor's words to Kusakari by radio, "We all tried, Yoshizumi, we all tried." The filmmakers worked very hard to create a poetic epic, but the 1960s message of the need for world governments to work together was just plain hackneyed by the 1980s, and the double-apocalypse plot was just too awkward and contrived to be successful.

REPRESENTATIVE QUOTES

"MM88 is an accident, a Frankenstein monster masquerading as a virus. Soon after it was found we could take DNA apart and reassemble it in different ways, an American geneticist developed this MM88. When we heard of its characteristics, we decided to borrow some of it. . . . Essentially it is a mimic. A mimic attaches itself to an existing virus such as polio, influenza, etc., increasing both the toxicity level and the reproductive level of the host disease. In other words, it hits so hard and multiplies so fast, it simply overwhelms any vaccine known. . . . Unless we neutralize this monster, we are left with a doomsday weapon." (Dr. Krauss, describing the virus)

"This may be the last sunset we will ever see. 'If we only had a little more time.' Those were Dr. Meyer's last words." (Richardson to Barkley) "The entire civilization just sputtered out with those words. As the speechwriters were so fond of having to say about history, those who can't remember the past, are condemned to repeat it." (Barkley's reply)

"Women have become our most valuable natural resource. And, has just been pointed out, one to one relationships are no longer possible. This means that each woman, however reluctantly, will have to accommodate more than one man. Of course we will have to go against deep personal feelings, but this is an extremely serious matter. Somehow we must find the will to suppress our instincts. . . . Can we control our instincts with reason?" (Dr. Irma Ullich proposing a new sexual order)

"Submarine *Nereid*, this is Yoshizumi speaking. We were too late. Save yourselves if you can. Warn Palmer Station to evacuate. We tried! We tried!" (Yoshizumi's message to McCloud) "We all tried, Yoshizumi, we all tried." (McCloud's reply)

Voyage to the Bottom of the Sea (1961)

Rating: **   **Threat: Ring of fire in the sky**

20th Century Fox. Written by Irwin Allen & Charles Bennett; Photographed by Winton Hoch & John Lamb; Special effects by L. B. Abbott & Davis S. Horsley; Edited by George Boemler; Music by Paul Sawtell & Bert Shefter; Produced & directed by Irwin Allen. 105 minutes.

ANNOTATED CAST LIST

Walter Pidgeon (*Adm. Harriman Nelson*, scientist who designed the *Seaview*); Peter Lorre (*Com. Lucius Emery*, Nelson's advisor and friend); Robert Sterling (*Lee Crane*, captain of the *Seaview*); Joan Fontaine (*Dr. Susan Hiller*, psychiatrist studying men under stress); Frankie Avalon (*Lt. Chip Romano*, *Seaview* officer); Michael Ansara (*Miguel Alvarez*, survivor picked up by *Seaview*); Barbara Eden (*Lt. Cathy Connors*, Nelson's secretary and Crane's fiancée); Regis Toomey (*Dr. Jamieson*, medical officer aboard *Seaview*); Henry Daniell (*Dr. Emillo Zucco*, Viennese physicist critical of Nelson's work); Howard McNear (*Llewellyn Parker*, congressman visiting the *Seaview*); John Litel (*Vice Admiral B. J. Crawford*, Naval Bureau of Marine Exploration officer); Mark Slade (*Jimmy Smith*, seaman who operates mini-sub); Charles Tannen (*Gleason*, chief petty officer aboard *Seaview*); Del Monroe (*Kowski*, volatile crew member); Anthony Monaco (*Seaview* cook); Robert Easton (*Sparks*, radio operator); Jonathan Gilmore (*George Young*, crewman anxious to see his newborn son); George Diestel (*Lt. Hodges*, engineer on *Seaview* who sabotages the generator); Kendrick Huxham (UN chairman); John Giovanni (Italian UN delegate); Art Baker (UN commentator); Skip Ward, William Herrin, Richard Adams, Michael Ford, Robert Buckingham, James Murphy (*Seaview* crew members).

SYNOPSIS

Filmmaker Irwin Allen broke into films with an Academy award-nominated documentary, *The Sea around Us*, in 1950. He later concentrated on fantasy, adventure and disaster films, including a remake of *The Lost World* in 1960. *Voyage to the Bottom of the Sea* was inspired in part by the publicity generated by the exploits of the nuclear submarine *Nautilus* and its historic voyage beneath the polar ice cap. Allen was intrigued by the discovery of the Van Allen radiation belt in the late 1950s, and setting his story twenty years in the future, he based his submarine plot on an apocalyptic crisis resulting when this belt inexplicably catches fire.

The picture opens with Frankie Avalon crooning the pop title tune as the credits roll. The *Seaview*, undergoing a test run in Arctic waters, is an elaborate research submarine developed by Admiral Harriman Nelson, one of America's top scientists. The most interesting feature of the *Seaview* is the observation windows positioned in the nose of the vessel. Three observers are aboard to verify the tests: Vice Admiral B. J. Crawford, Congressman Llewellyn Parker and psychologist Dr. Susan Hiller. The shakedown cruise is interrupted by the unusual phenomenon of the polar ice caps melting. The submarine surfaces, and the sky appears to be ablaze. Contacting Washington, D.C., the crew learns that the Van Allen radiation belt which, rings the planet, has caught fire. Nelson is ordered by the president to head to a science conference at the United Nations in New York City. A man, Miguel Alvarez, is discovered stranded on an ice flow and is rescued. He and his dog are the sole survivors of a scientific expedition.

Commodore Lucius Emery is aboard the sub, researching sharks and other marine life. A top scientist himself, he joins Nelson in a brainstorming session to solve the crisis. Nelson develops a plan to seed the Van Allen belt with additional radiation and explode it outward, away from the earth. His solution requires a missile to be fired from an area of the Pacific near the Mariana Islands sixteen days later. Nelson and Emery present their plan to the International Scientific Committee. Dr. Zucco, an eminent physicist, believes the belt will burn itself out when its temperature reaches 173 degrees, and he denounces Nelson's plan. The majority of the committee agrees with Zucco, but Nelson, undeterred, leaves in his sub and orders Crane to plot a course at full speed to the Marianas. Alvarez and Dr. Hiller are trapped aboard as the *Seaview* heads off. Many members of the crew resent Nelson's actions.

Nelson attempts to contact the president and obtain his approval. Radio communications are no longer possible due to the effects of the Van Allen fire. The admiral orders that the underwater telephone cable between Brazil and Europe be tapped when the *Seaview* passes near it. Crane leads a team of underwater divers to patch into the cable, but when Nelson talks to London, he learns that they have already lost all contact with the United States. Nelson address the crew by intercom, saying he intends to implement his plan since he believes it is the only chance to save the planet. Most of the crew turns hostile, and Crane himself starts to lock horns with Nelson, questioning his every move. The *Seaview*'s race to the designated launch site is delayed when the sonar generator is sabotaged. Nelson orders that full speed be maintained, even though the ship will be running blind without sonar, and the boat gets trapped in an old mine field. The mini-sub is launched and destroyed as it frees *Seaview* from entanglement with a large mine.

The admiral starts to receive threatening notes. The crewman who sabotaged the generator commits suicide, and Crane warns Nelson that he is driving the men too hard and that rebellion is in the air. Someone sets a fire in the admiral's quarters while he is sleeping, but he is rescued when his secretary, Lieutenant Connors, sounds the alarm. The *Seaview* surfaces to air the smoke out of the vessel. They encounter a derelict ship, four days out of Honolulu. Everyone aboard is dead of exposure, and a newspaper on the ship relates that the *Seaview* is now a hunted ship by all the navies of the world. Kowski, a member of the crew, approaches Crane, demanding that they set course back to America. Nelson offers the crew full supplies to leave on the derelict ship. A number of men take this opportunity to desert. Crane files an official protest of Nelson's actions. Dr. Hiller tells Crane that the Admiral has become delusional. After Nelson strikes Lieutenant Romano, whom he finds resting in sickbay, Crane decides to arrest the admiral, but Emery and Connors try to talk him out of it. At this moment, the *Seaview* comes under sudden attack from another submarine. Nelson advises a crash dive, and the hostile sub follows, firing its torpedoes. At a depth of 3,200 feet, the attacking boat explodes and the *Seaview* is slightly damaged. A giant squid attaches itself to the front of the vessel, and Crane sends a charge of electricity through the hull to free the *Seaview*. Dr. Hiller tries to sabotage the atomic pile, but she falls into the shark tank maintained by Emery when the submarine unexpectedly lurches to one side. Nelson orders the launching of the missile, but Alvarez grabs an explosive, which he threatens to detonate unless Nelson cancels his plans. He holds the submarine hostage, but Emery and Crane arrange to launch the missile with a remote detonator. Streaking across the sky, the missile performs exactly as Nelson planned and the Van Allen belt is hurled away from the earth.

CRITIQUE

This film irritated many traditional science fiction buffs with its many loopholes, but it was a large commercial success. To be enjoyed, the story has to be regarded as a comic book adventure, and indeed, the pastel color scheme of the production calls comic strips to mind. On this level, the picture can be regarded as pure escapist fun. The *Seaview* itself is rather elegant to watch as it glides underwater. The interior of the ship is less impressive, beyond the glass nose and the control room. The decor of Admiral Nelson's office, the recreation room, the sickbay, and other rooms are implausible because objects are positioned on tables and in cabinets and no account is taken of the pitch and yaw movement that a submarine continually encounters. One wonders how Commodore Emery's shark tank reacts when *Seaview* breaks the surface at a 45 degree angle as it does in the opening shot. The story never resolves how the *Seaview* is a government ship but not actually part of the navy.

The major difficulty with the plot is that it all seems very contrived and very little of it flows smoothly. The main scientific problem is the credibility of the threat, since the Van Allen belt is three hundred miles above the earth in a vacuum, and there is no oxygen present that would permit a fire. The behavior of the crew is also unbelievable. They seem a collection of misfits ready to fall apart at any adversity. If Crane hand-picked each of his crew members, he did a miserable job. The rest of the sub's complement are equally treacherous, as both Hiller and Alvarez do their best to prevent the world from being saved. The only individuals who consistently support Nelson are Commodore Emery and Lieutenant Cathy Connors.

The special effects of the film are wonderful. The burning sky effect is quite impressive, even though the satellite view from space shows that the flames exist only over the central portion of the earth, far from the North Pole where the *Seaview* firsts observes the phenomenon. There are two squids in the picture. One grabs Crane while he is scuba diving in search of the underground cable. This life-size model is phony-looking. On the other hand, the giant squid that attacks the *Seaview* after it dives to avoid the enemy sub is excellent. The underwater photography by John Lamb is top notch. The music is also good, apart from the schmaltzy opening number sung by Avalon.

Overall the cast is a mixed bag. Walter Pidgeon never seems to settle into the role of Nelson. Named after Admiral Horatio Nelson, the character has too much arrogance and bluster, more like the stereotype of an admiral than a genuine one. Also, Nelson's scientific and teaching background is stressed, which makes one wonder when he ever had time to rise through the ranks to admiral. Peter Lorre and Joan Fontaine play their parts well. When Frankie Avalon was added to the cast, the role of Chip Morton was changed to Chip Romano to accommodate him, and he does an adequate job. Sterling and Eden are earnest, but their parts are rather shallow. Michael Ansara casts a dark pall over the proceedings in his role as the scientist who becomes a religious fatalist. He always carries his pet dog, an unusual touch that never figures into the plot. Character actors John Litel and Regis Toomey flesh out their parts nicely, as does Howard McNear, later known for his performance as Floyd the barber on *The Andy Griffith Show*. Henry Daniell is colorful when he goes over the top as Dr. Zucco. His character's name seems to be a tribute to George Zucco, who died in 1960 while the script was being written. Oddly enough, both Zucco and Daniell played Professor Moriarty in the Sherlock Holmes film series with Basil Rathbone.

A number of years later, Allen used the sets and stock footage from the film to create a television version of the film, which lasted for four seasons. Richard Basehart assumed the role as Admiral Nelson with far greater assurance than Pidgeon, and David Hedison took the role of Captain Crane. Ironically, Hedison had declined the part for the motion picture when it was offered to him. 110 one-hour episodes were filmed, and the second season episode entitled "The Sky's on Fire" is a remake of the plot of the film. The role of Chip Romano reverted back to Chip Morton for the series, but attention was seldom focused on this role. Unfortunately, the character of Commodore Emery was eliminated, so Nelson no longer had a scientific equal with whom he could share his thoughts, a limitation that undercut the range and variety of the plot lines. Only one cast member of the original film cast reprised his role in the television series, Del Monroe, although his character's name was altered from the awkward Kowski to Kowalski. Coincidentially, both actors who played the role of Admiral Nelson, Richard Basehart and Walter Pidgeon, died within days of each other in 1984.

REPRESENTATIVE QUOTES

"Not even Jules Verne dreamed of anything like this." (Nelson while conducting a tour of the *Seaview*)

"This planet is impaled on a roasting spit, slowly but inexorably being seared and blistered by the fire in the sky.   If the Van Allen belt continues to burn, the world will burn with it, and no one can doubt that civilization as we know it will disintegrate if the temperature should rise to 175 degrees. . . . Our planet has a life expectancy of about three weeks." (Nelson's UN speech)

"You offer defeatism. May I remind you this is a federal ship and these are federal seamen. By what right do you dare preach of imminent death, of meek resignation to the inevitable? Nothing is inevitable except defeat for those who give up without a fight." (Crane to Alvarez as he orders him not to talk with the crew)

"God's will is written across the heaven." (Alvarez to Nelson as he holds the *Seaview* hostage)

The War of the Worlds (1953)

Rating: ***   **Threat:** Alien Invasion

Paramount. Written by Barré Lyndon based on the novel by H. G. Wells; Photographed by George Barnes; Special effects by Gordon Jennings, Wallace Kelley, Chester Pate, Bob Springfield, Eddie Sutherland, Paul Lerpae, Aubrey Law & Jack Caldwell; Edited by Edward Douglas; Music by Leith Stevens; Produced by George Pal & Frank Freeman Jr.; Directed by Byron Haskin. 85 minutes.

ANNOTATED CAST LIST

Gene Barry (*Dr. Clayton Forrester*, astronuclear physicists); Lewis Martin (*Matthew Collins*, pastor of the Linda Rosa Community Church); Ann Robinson (*Sylvia Van Buren*, his niece, a library science teacher); Les Tremayne (*Gen. Mann*, Army Intelligence chief); Houseley Stevenson Jr. (his aide); Robert Cornthwaite (*Dr. Pryor*, Pacific Tech scientist); Sandro Giglio (*Dr. Bilderbeck*, Pacific Tech scientist); William Phipps (*Perry*, guard at landing site); Paul Birch (*Alonzo Hogue*, guard); Jack Krushchen (*Salvatore*, guard); Henry Brandon (cop at landing site); Carolyn Jones (giddy blonde radio listener); Pierre Cressoy (her companion); Walter Sande (*Bognany*, Linda Rosa sheriff); Alex Frazer (*Dr. James Hettinger*, Pacific Tech scientist); Ann Codee (*Dr. DuPrey*, blood specialist); Charles Gemora (Martian at farmhouse); Ivan Lebedeff (*Dr. Gratzman*, Pacific Tech scientist); Alvy Moore (*Zippy*); Frank Kreig (*Fiddler Hawkins*, square dance caller); David McMahon (minister of first church); Jameson Shade (deacon); Cliff Clark (Spanish priest hearing confessions in LA); Russell Conway (*Rev. Bethany*, minister of third church); Gertrude Hoffman (elderly news vendor); Freeman Lusk (secretary of defense); Herbert Lytton (chief of staff); Sydney Mason (Linda Rosa fire chief); Peter Adams (forest ranger station lookout); Robert Rockwell (companion forest ranger); Ted Hecht (radio reporter); Edgar Barrier (*Prof. McPherson*, Canadian scientist interviewed by reporter); Vernon Rich (*Col. Ralph Heffner*, officer in charge of troops surrounding the cylinder); Ralph Dumke (*Buck Monahan*, first man to approach the alien cylinder); Ralph Montgomery (Red Cross leader); Jimmie Dundee (Civil Defense official); Bob Morgan (injured Civil Defense worker); Hugh Allen (brigadier general); Don Kohler (colonel); Russ Bender (*Dr. Carmichael*); Al Fergusen (police chief); Edward Wahrman (cameraman); George Pal, Frank Freeman Jr. (bums listening to radio); Anthony Warde, Joel Marston (military police); Ned Glass, David Sharpe, Dale Van Sickel, Fred Graham (looters); Douglas Henderson, Stanley Orr, Charles J. Stewart, Fred Zender, Jim Davies, Dick Fortune, Martin Coulter (marines); Paul Frees (First narrator and announcer at bomb site); Cedric Hardwicke (second narrator); Eric Alden, Ruth Barnwell, Hazel Boyne, Nancy Hale, Patricia Iannone, Rudy Lee,

John Mansfield, Mike Mahoney, John Maxwell, Bill Meader, Cora Shannon, Gus Taillon, Dorothy Vernon, Waldon Williams.

SYNOPSIS

The most dramatic and gripping of the novels of H. G. Wells, *The War of the Worlds* was etched into the American consciousness by a radio version performed by Orson Welles and his Mercury Theater Troupe in October 1938. With some justification, this show is regarded as one of the greatest radio programs, and certainly the most influential. Many famous individuals considered tackling a film version, including Alfred Hitchcock, Cecil B. DeMille, Sergei Eisenstein, Alexander Korda and Orson Welles himself. Producer George Pal inherited the project after the success of *Destination Moon* (1950) and *When Worlds Collide* (1951), and he pared the concept down until he came up with a script that fell within his budgetary range. The resulting picture is regarded as a full-fledged classic by some and a missed opportunity by others.

The picture begins in awkward fashion, with multiple prologues. A pre-credit sequence reviews battle tactics during World War I and II and hypes the terrible weapons to be used in *The War of the Worlds*. The second prologue, with a different narrator, discusses the plans of alien intelligences on Mars. This narration then veers off into what seems to be a third prologue, a travelogue of each planet in the solar system, featuring impressive astronomical drawings by artist Chesley Bonestill. After this diversion, the narrator returns to the story of the Martian invasion, which starts one summer evening when a mysterious objects crashes into the hills of California near the town of Linda Rosa. The fire department rushes to the crash site to extinguish the brush fire caused by the fallen object. A number of villagers come to watch, and the local officials ask one of three scientists on a fishing holiday to look it over. Dr. Clayton Forrester becomes suspicious when he discovers the object is radioactive, and he believes that it might be hollow. He plans to wait until the object cools to undertake a complete investigation. Matthew Collins, pastor of the local church, and his niece Sylvia invite Forrester to stay at their home for the night. The scientist accompanies Sylvia to the local square dance. Three guards left at the crash site hear strange noises from the object. A round hatch starts to unscrew like a lid on a cylinder and the three men realize that it is a spacecraft, but they are killed by a mysterious ray when they try to approach the ship. A power blackout occurs in Linda Rosa, and Forrester returns with the sheriff to the landing site. He ascertains that the earth has been invaded by aliens and tells the sheriff to summon the military at once.

Additional alien cylinders are reported falling worldwide with increasing frequency. The military units surround the crater with the alien spacecraft, and a host of observers gathers outside their perimeter. A radio reporter interviews Forrester about his speculations. Reinforcements are brought in after the aliens start to shoot their heat ray at the crowd. General Mann, head of U.S. Army Intelligence, comes to Linda Rosa to confer with Forrester about the situation.

Mann gives the scientist an ominous report: whenever the aliens move from their original landing site, total destruction seems to follow. The landings occur in clusters of three. Linda Rosa is the only location where the military had time to set up an organized defense around an alien ship.

An alien machine, a strange flying tank, rises out of the crater. Reverend Collins makes a final attempt to approach them in peace. Reading the Twenty-third Psalm, the minister approaches the machine, which fires its ray and blasts the man out of existence. Two additional flying machines emerge and attack the army, routing it. The heat ray disintegrates everything in its path. The machines themselves are protected by an invisible shield and are unharmed by any return fire. Forrester urges Mann to report that traditional military tactics are useless against the invaders. He and Sylvia make their escape from the scene of the massacre in a small plane, but they crash and are forced to take refuge in a farmhouse. The air force launches an attack against the alien machines, but all their jets are destroyed.

General Mann sets up headquarters in Los Angeles and organizes Civil Defense and the local authorities to prepare for an immediate evacuation of the city. He is concerned when he learns that Forrester is missing. Meanwhile, at the farmhouse, Sylvia discusses her fears with Forrester and he tries to comfort her. Their respite is broken when an alien machine, in trouble, crashes into the building. A Martian emerges from a companion machine, and the couple hides amid the rubble. The alien's tentacle, with three fingers, brushes against Sylvia, and Forrester shines a flashlight at its face, which has three eyes grouped in a circle. The light is painful to the creature, and it dashes off when Forrester throws a brick at it. The Martians attempt to trap them in the ruins of the farmhouse by barricading the doors. Forrester finds a viewer used by the alien and a cloth soaked with Martian blood. They bolt from the building seconds before it is destroyed by the alien heat ray.

The narrator comments on the perfection of the Martian invasion, and a montage shows glimpses of the world in chaos, with masses fleeing the relentless alien attack. There seems to be no possible defense to the onslaught. The capitals of all major nations have fallen and are destroyed except for Washington, D.C. General Mann briefs the secretary of defense and military leaders from around the world about the tactics used by the Martians in their campaign of total destruction. The secretary agrees to ask president to authorize the use of nuclear weapons against the invaders. Forrester and Sylvia make their way to Pacific Tech, where scientists have gathered to study the aliens and find their weaknesses. The alien viewer, used by them like a periscope, reveals that their optics and the rest of their technology is based on the number three. They also learn that Martian blood is extraordinarily anemic. One of the scientists, Bilderbeck, calculates that, at the present rate, all human life on the planet will be destroyed in six days.

An atomic bomb is detonated over a nest of alien machines, but their shields remain intact and their machines are completely unharmed by the nuclear explosion. Undeterred, General Mann urges the scientists to work nonstop until they develop a practical weapon to repel the invaders. Considering the composition of their blood, Forrester believes a biological weapon may be their only hope against the Martians.

Los Angeles comes under direct attack. While leaving the city, the convoy of trucks from Pacific Tech is assaulted by a mob of looters. Forrester is knocked unconscious, and when he recovers, he sets out to find Sylvia who was driving the bus that led the caravan. He searches in vain as the alien machines advance. Recalling her religious faith, Forrester searches for her at various churches, finally locating her. A Martian machine crashes outside the church. After a brief period of silence, Forrester investigates. The Martian tries to leave its vehicle and dies. Down the street, another Martian machine crashes. "We were all praying for a miracle," Forrester concludes quietly. The narrator explains that the Martians fell victim to earthly germs, from which they had no resistance.

CRITIQUE

The excellent Los Angeles sequence, with the desperate citizens trying to escape, ends the picture on a high note that compensates for earlier shortcomings. The original turn-of-the-century setting would have been preferable, but Orson Welles illustrated the effectiveness of updating the story. This production, however, fails to follow through with many of the concepts brilliantly pioneered by Welles in his radio drama. Unfortunately, the California locale works against the film for the most part, turning it into an artificial, back-lot production that fails to open up to the broader canvas that the story demands. The montage sequences that try to suggest broader dimensions are weak and second rate, and some of the plot meanderings, such as the square dance sequence, are downright annoying. The script does attempt some worthwhile subtleties. Like the technology of the Martian invaders, much of the film is organized in groups of three. The three-part opening narration is an example. The main body of the story also falls into three parts: the Linda Rosa landing; Forrester's encounter with the Martians and his Pacific Tech research; and the destruction of Los Angeles.

Many of the special effects are very commendable, particularly the sound effects of the Martian heat ray. The flying machines, actually standing on invisible magnetic legs according to Forrester, are impressive, even though the wires that hold them up are occasionally visible. The visual consequences of the heat ray, where vehicles glow and disappear, are adequate but derivative of similar shots in *The Day the Earth Stood Still* (1951). The shots of the solitary Martian in the farmhouse are very well handled, deriving maximum effect while showing the creature only minimally. The major disappointment is at the end of the picture when the Martians start to die, since only one tentacle is shown and not the entire dead creature. Most audiences feels cheated that the special effects were cut back here and that this critical shot was done on the cheap. On the whole the film is really too short and gives the impression of being padded, such as in the multiple introductions. A number of critics also questioned the religious tone injected at the end of the picture, but this seems entirely vindicated by the events at this point of the story. It certainly foreshadows the ending of both the film and the original text of the novel, where divine intervention is credited with human salvation. The cinematography and editing are particularly good in the last third of the film but very static and prosaic at the cylinder landing site. The only shot that is outstanding in the sequence is when Pastor Collins makes his desperate attempt to communicate with the invaders. At one point, Pal considered filming the last third of the film in 3-D, starting with the sequence in which the nuclear bomb was detonated. It was originally intended as a sign for the audience to don their 3-D glasses when the characters in the film don special glasses to observe the nuclear explosion. This clever idea was abandoned, however, perhaps due to the prohibitive additional expense. As for the music, the score by Leith Stevens never seems to click. In fact, the main title theme sounds as if a jungle epic were unfolding.

The cast is adequate, but never outstanding. Gene Barry, capable of excellent work in such films as *Naked Alibi* (1954) and *Thunder Road* (1958), only manages to catch fire toward the end of the film, after the Pacific Tech truck convoy is hijacked. Ann Robinson starts off quite well as Sylvia, but after her opening appearance her performance falls somewhat flat. She is given some excellent dialogue in the farmhouse sequence, but she merely says the lines without expression and fails to bring her part to life. Les Tremayne, as General Mann, is very earnest and provides the most consistent performance. The scientific colleagues of Forrester at Pacific Tech are well played, but the script provides none of them with a moment to shine with the exception of Sandro Giglio as Dr. Bilderbeck. Producer George Pal himself is briefly glimpsed as one of two bums listening to Forrester being interviewed on the radio. His sidekick in the scene is associate producer Frank Freeman Jr. Cedric Hardwicke does an exceptional job as the second narrator, a role originally offered to Cecil B. DeMille himself by George Pal.

Much of this film was brilliantly satirized in *Mars Attacks!* (1996). Watching both films back-to-back actually makes them both seem better. Another interesting footnote is that the 1989 television series *War of the Worlds* references both the Orson Welles radio show and the George Pal film. Footage from the film was actually used on the show, which presumes that the invaders did not die but merely went into hibernation due to the bacterial infection. Their bodies were preserved instead of destroyed, and now these bodies have revived to continue their war on mankind. There also were a number of differences in the series. The invaders are now revealed to have come from a distant solar system forty light years from Earth, called Mortax. They now have special powers to assume human shape as well. This show was quickly canceled when the second season was revised to involve an additional set of invaders.

One of the main handicaps of the film is that it suffers by comparison to the original H. G. Wells novel, as well as the Orson Welles radio version. If this film were titled *The Conflagration from Outer Space* or something similar, it would have had far more impact. If a little more time and money had been spent on refining the plot and improving the ineffective montages and on increasing and improving the effects with additional detail, then this picture could have been the major classic that many envision it to be. As it stands, however, only the last third is worthy of that status.

REPRESENTATIVE QUOTES

"No one would have believed in the middle of the twentieth century that human affairs were being watched keenly and closely by intelligences greater than man's. Yet, across the gulf of space on the planet Mars, intellects vast and cool and unsympathetic regarded our Earth with envious eyes, slowly and surely drawing their plans against us." (Opening by the second narrator)

"If they are more advanced than us, they should be nearer the Creator for that reason." (Pastor Collins to his niece)

"The Martians had no resistance to the bacteria in our atmosphere to which we have long since become immune. Once they had breathed our air, germs which no longer affect us began to kill them. The end came swiftly. All over the world their machines began to stop and fall. After all that men could do had failed, the Martians were destroyed and humanity was saved by the littlest things which God in his wisdom had put upon this Earth." (Closing narration)

When Worlds Collide (1951)

Rating: ****   Threat: Interplanetary collision

Paramount. Written by Sydney Boehm based on the novels *When Worlds Collide* & *After Worlds Collide* by Philip Wylie & Edwin Balmer; Photographed by John F. Seitz, W. Howard Greene & Farciot Eduoart (process photography); Special effects by Gordon Jennings & Harry Barndollar; Edited by Arthur Schmidt; Music by Leith Stevens; Produced by George Pal; Directed by Rudolph Maté. B & W, 83 minutes.

ANNOTATED CAST LIST

Richard Derr (*Dave Randall*, pilot); Larry Keating (*Dr. Cole Hendron*, American astronomer); Barbara Rush (*Joyce Hendron*, his daughter); Peter Hanson (*Dr. Anthony Drake*, physician and fiancé of Joyce); John Hoyt (*Sidney Stanton*, crippled millionaire); Frank Cady (*Harold Ferris*, Stanton's attendant); Hayden Rorke (*Dr. Emery Bronson*, South African astronomer who discovered the threat); Stephen Chase (*Dr. Dean Frye*, technology expert); Jim Congdon (*Eddie Garson*, technician); Judith Ames (*Julie Cummings*, Eddie's girlfriend); Sandro Giglio (*Dr. Ottinger*, scientist who mocks the collision theory); Frances Sanford (*Alice*, Hendron's secretary); Freeman Lusk (*Rudolf Marston*, philanthropist); Joseph Mell (*Glen Spiro*, philanthropist); Art Gilmore (*Paul*, Bronson's assistant); Keith Richards (*Stanley*, Bronson's assistant); Rudy Lee (*Mike*, youngster rescued by Dave); John Ridgely (customs inspector); Hassan Khayyam (UN committee president); Ramsay Hill (French UN delegate); James Seay (*Donovan*, newspaper publisher); Gene Collins (newspaper hawker); Mary Murphy, Kirk Alyn, Robert Chapman, Charmine Harker (spaceship passengers); Paul Frees (narrator).

SYNOPSIS

When Worlds Collide was one of the first apocalyptic films produced by a prominent studio, and although the budget was economical, it was sufficient with George Pal's creative expertise to appear as a major production. Pal had just completed the highly successful *Destination: Moon* (1950), and *When Worlds Collide* was intended as a blockbuster successor. While not achieving the same level of success, the film was significant nevertheless and quite influential, becoming the standard against which future celestial disaster films would be measured.

The picture begins with a reference to the *Bible* about Noah and the flood. At a remote observatory in South Africa, astronomer Emery Bronson makes a frightening discovery. Two heavenly bodies, which he names Bellus and Zyra, will enter our solar system, and their paths will intersect the orbit of Earth, de-

stroying the planet. Dr. Bronson hires Dave Randall, a freelance pilot, to serve
as courier to bring all his calculations and data to Dr. Cole Hendron, the world's
foremost astronomer, at the Cosmos Observatory in the United States. Dave is
unaware of the nature of the material he is conveying, and he is met in New
York City by Joyce Hendron, daughter of the illustrious scientist, who assumes
Dave knows the contents of the briefcase that is chained to his wrist and is impressed by his cool demeanor. When Dr. Hendron briefs his staff about the coming disaster, Dave is included in the conference. Hendron confirms Bronson's
findings. In less than a year, Earth will collide with Bellus, which is three times
larger, and there will be no escaping the destruction. Another planet, Zyra, almost a twin of Earth, will pass by nineteen days before Bellus.

Joyce and her fiancé, Dr. Tony Drake, take Dave to dinner at a nightclub.
Now knowing the short time until doomsday, the pilot reacts with carefree nonchalance. A day earlier he proclaimed that nothing was more valuable than cash,
but now he lights up his cigarette using money, and Joyce is amused by his attitude. She finds herself attracted to the pilot and puts off Tony when he suggests
they marry at once.

Several days later at a UN meeting, Hendron and Bronson announce their findings about the end of the world, but they are ridiculed. They propose that a portion of humanity might be saved by escaping to Zyra, which they believe has
vegetation and may be inhabitable. The French ambassador mocks the idea as a
space age Noah's ark. Another famous scientist, Dr. Ottinger, claims Bronson's
calculations are wrong and denounces Hendron for needless panic and headline
hunting. This strong statement makes it impossible for Hendron to convince
any governments to fund an emergency rocket program. Two wealthy philan-
thropists advance Hendron enough funds to launch a private program. Joyce
confides to her father that she has suspended her engagement with Tony because
she has fallen in love with Dave Randall. Hendron promises to keep Dave on
the project.

A dour, wheelchair-bound millionaire, Sidney Stanton, offers to pay for the
entire project himself if he can choose the survivors. Hendron declines, saying
there will be room for only forty people and livestock and so the selection must
be made scientifically. If Stanton funds the projects. Hendron will offer Stanton
himself passage on the spacecraft. The miserly businessman grumbles but accepts the offer, and Hendron prepares a breakneck schedule.

Top scientists gather under the direction of Dr. Dean Frye to design the spacecraft. The ship will be mounted on a mile-long slide that will help slingshot the
vessel into space instead of a traditional launch technique. The best engineers,
mechanics, technicians and agricultural specialists are gathered for the project.
Every detail ensuring survival for the flight is prepared. The final selection for
the available seats will be done by lottery, with every participant having an equal
chance. A number of individuals, including Frye, Stanton, Joyce, Dave and
Tony Drake, have been preselected by Hendron for the flight. An equal number
of men and women are to be chosen. Dave believes that he does not deserve special treatment. He tells Dr. Hendron that he will not board the ship at the ap-

pointed hour, but asks him to keep his decision secret.

As the threat continues to approach Earth, international scientists finally accept Bronson's theory. When the governments of the world announce the certainty of doom, panic breaks out. A montage shows crowds filling the St. Peter's Square in Vatican City and other places of worship around the world. Newspapers in every language proclaim the coming of doomsday. Martial law is declared, and coastal areas are evacuated to avoid the massive tidal waves when Zyra passes close by Earth. Nothing can be done, however, to prepare for the collision with Bellus.

The streets of New York City are displayed as the hour of Zyra's passing is at hand. The city is deserted. Massive tidal waves approach and sweep through the corridors of the city, filling Times Square like a raging whirlpool. Earthquakes are triggered worldwide, and engineers rush to protect the spacecraft from damage. After the carnage, Dave and Tony fly a helicopter to drop needed medical supplies to a nearby group of survivors. Tony is upset that he has lost Joyce, and the two men start to argue. When Dave rescues a young boy clinging to the roof of a house in a flood zone, he leaves the helicopter and fears his companion might abandon him. At first Tony flies off but returns to get Dave, and their differences are reconciled. The young boy, Mike, becomes a symbol of hope for the members of the project, and his name is added to the list of passengers along with that of his pet dog, the mission's unofficial mascot.

Repairs to the spaceship cause the mission to fall behind schedule, and all are urged by a persistent voice over the loudspeaker to redouble their efforts. Tony tells Dave that Dr. Frye has a heart problem and may not survive the blackout phase during the launch and that Dave's presence on the flight is essential as the only other individual who can operate the ship, so the reluctant pilot agrees to rejoin the crew.

With only a few hours left until take-off, the names of the lottery winners are posted. One of the technicians, Eddie Garson, has a winning number, but after he learns that his girlfriend, Julie Cummings, failed to win a slot, he goes to Hendron and declines his selection. Ferris, Stanton's servant, draws a gun and demands that he be allowed to assume the slot, but Stanton shoots him with a hidden weapon. The millionaire warns the others to expect an uprising from others not selected in the lottery. Dave suggests accelerating the boarding of the passengers and animals onto the ship and locking the ramp gate. Hendron decides to add Julie Cummings and Eddie Garson to the selected list.

Stanton's prediction proves correct, and the losers of the lottery try to storm the ship. At the last moment, Dr. Hendron refuses to board the vessel, and he wheels Stanton away from the ship, saying, "The new world isn't for us, it is for the young." The doors close, and Stanton rises from his wheelchair and tries to walk to the ship, but it is too late. The ship's engines ignite and the voyage begins. The force of the launch causes everyone to lose consciousness. Moments later, Bellus is observed crashing into the Earth, destroying it.

Dave is among the first to revive and is startled to see that Dr. Frye had recovered before him. He looks back at Tony and realizes that there was no problem with Frye's heart: the doctor invented the problem to ensure that Dave would join the flight. As the spacecraft approaches Zyra, Dave assumes the controls and crash-lands the ship in a snow-filled valley. He quickly opens the doors of the craft and discovers the air is breathable. The passengers survey their new domain and see mountains, strange plants and a lake in the distance. On the horizon, surrounded by fog, are two pyramids. Mike rushes to check if his pet has survived the trip and discovers the dog has given birth to a litter of puppies. The animals and people start to disembark, and a wordless chorus is heard on the soundtrack as the survivors watch dawn break in their new home. Dave and Joyce walk down the gangplank hand-in-hand. The message, "The first day on the new world had begun . . ." appears on the screen (instead of "The End") as the music swells to a climax.

CRITIQUE

This ambitious film came very close to being a total success except for the scientific gaffes that dilute the storyline and the failure to provide consistent first class special effects. Pal's previous film, *Destination: Moon*, was noted for the accuracy of its technical and scientific details. *When Worlds Collide*, on the other hand, makes no attempt to do this, and these lapses pile up. The script itself seems confused about the nature of Bellus. At times, it is described as a world but at other times it is called a star. A star three times the size of Earth would be a very small sun indeed. If it is a star, Earth would broil long before it could be harmed by a collision. If it is a world, how could the vegetation and moderate climate of Zyra be explained if that planet traveled though the interstellar void with Bellus. Of course, the planet Jupiter is a gas giant, which is known to give off heat, but it is also a hundred times larger than Earth, while Bellus is described as only three times larger than Earth. A greater weakness than the nature of Bellus is the future orbit of Zyra. If this planet is captured by our sun and assumes a similar orbit to Earth, then the future habitation of Zyra is possible. If it slingshots beyond our solar system, then relocating to Zyra is pointless. Yet this key question is never raised in the course of the story. If Zyra assumes the orbit, won't it also be under continual threat year after year from colliding with the leftover fragments of Earth and Bellus? Many critics, including Arthur C. Clarke, took this picture to task for these technical mistakes. Without a convincing scientific basis, any apocalyptic film suffers, but there are additional problems beyond the scientific lapses. What happened to the character of Dr. Bronson, who disappears during the second half of the film? What happened to the sister spacecrafts that were being built in other countries. Dr. Hendron mentions them several times in the first half of the film, but then they also are never mentioned again. Wouldn't the constant haranguing on loudspeakers, telling people to "Hurry, hurry" be distracting and slow down work rather than speed it up? Why is the effect of the passing of Zyra given so much screen time, while the big show, the greater disaster caused by Bellus, is largely ignored? Finally, what is the meaning of the two pyramids seen at the end of the film? Does this imply that Zyra has, or had, intelligent life? Or is it merely a bizarre natural phenomenon? The large number of plot defects are annoying and prevent this admirable effort from achieving top-drawer status.

Noting these weaknesses, *When Worlds Collide* is still an impressive effort. Interestingly, Cecil B. DeMille had considered making a film based on the novels after their initial appearance in the early 1930s. It is fascinating to speculate how impressive a DeMille version might have been. George Pal had also initially considered a far more costly version of the film before scaling back to a more frugal production. The thesis of an interplanetary collision is realistic, given the cataclysmic history of our solar system. The asteroid belt, it has been theorized, is either a destroyed planet or a planet that never took form. The axis of Uranus, tilted almost 90 degrees, shows evidence of a near-collision in the remote past. One of Neptune's satellites travels in orbit completely different from that planet's other moons, signaling that it was a rogue asteroid that almost hit the planet but was captured instead. The thesis of planetary encounters is scientifically sound. *When Worlds Collide* works effectively within this premise, mixing the activities of a number of interesting characters within the framework of a desperate race for salvation. The characters seem human, and the audience cares about them.

Rudolph Maté's direction is crisp and even eloquent at times. The cast is excellent, and Richard Derr makes a very appealing hero as Dave Randall. (Douglas Fairbanks Jr. had been originally considered for the part.) Derr had only a modest film career, and his physical resemblance to Danny Kaye might have limited the number of roles he was offered, however, his similarity compliments his part in this film. Derr is simply delightful in the nightclub sequence. Having just learned of Earth's doom, he displays a unique exuberance that sets him free from his earlier conventions, and his sheer relish displayed by lighting his cigarettes using flaming money is one of the most memorable images in the film. Barbara Rush is also captivating as Joyce, and although her selection of a mate seems incongruous against the backdrop of a world facing destruction, this plot device works due to her earnestness and believability. This film was one of her earliest efforts, and the picture helped propel her into a very successful career, ranging from *It Came from Outer Space* (1953) to *The Bramble Bush* (1960) and *Come Blow Your Horn* (1963). She even managed to shine in the otherwise dismal film *Can't Stop the Music* (1980). Peter Hanson is successful in the thankless role of Dr. Tony Drake. Hanson had a modest film career, usually in pictures directed by Maté. John Hoyt is memorable as the calculating skinflint Stanton, a role he plays to perfection. His final rise from the wheelchair was later satirized by Joe Flarherty on the *SCTV* series as obnoxious station owner Guy Caballero. The other cast members do splendid jobs, including Hayden Rorke, best remembered as Dr. Bellows on the *I Dream of Jeannie* series; Frank Cady, later notable as grocer Sam Drucker on *Green Acres;* and Larry Keating, who later played a straight man and neighbor of Gracie Allen on the *Burns and Allen Show*. The music is adequate for the most part, but the passages with a pseudo-religious chorus are a bit hokey. The editing and cinematography are exceptional. There is one moment often overlooked in the film that deserves special praise: the rescue of young Mike from the rooftop of his flooded home. Note the handling of the helicopter, as Richard Derr leaps to the roof and boosts Mike into the copter. This is an extraordinary scene with split-second timing that it is magnificently staged and filmed, yet it appears natural, despite the technical difficulties in getting it right. This sequence is pure filmmaking at a most impressive level. *When Worlds Collide* has been dismissed by many film reviewers as being simply competent, but they have missed the amazing style and poetry in many scenes such as this rescue sequence.

REPRESENTATIVE QUOTES

"Needles in a heavenly haystack, there are more stars in the heavens than there are human beings on Earth. Through telescopes, men of science constantly search the infinitesimal corners of our solar system seeking new discoveries, hoping to better understand the laws of the universe." (Opening narration)

"The world will not end. Certainly these new bodies will pass our planet. Heavenly bodies frequently do, but we are still here. Predicting the end of the world is an annual crackpot event in our society." (Dr. Ottinger denouncing the collision theory at a UN meeting)

"Our chance of reaching the new world is as thin as your chance of ever becoming a humanitarian. If we do make it, will there be a place to land? Will the air be fit to breathe? Will there be water, vegetable life? Men and women here have been praying for God's help and guidance, not your kind of hypocritical praying but the kind that comes from deep inside a man." (Hendron's response to Stanton after hearing his suggestion to leave more people behind)

Where Have All the People Gone? (1974)

Rating: **   **Threat:** Solar flare

Metromedia. Written by Lewis Carlino & Sandor Stern; Photographed by Michael Margulies; Edited by John A. Martinelli; Music by Robert Prince; Produced by Gerald I. Isenberg & Charles Fries (executive); Directed by John Llewellyn Moxey. 73 minutes.

ANNOTATED CAST LIST

Peter Graves (*Stephen Anders*, manufacturer from Malibu); George O'Hanlon Jr. (*David Anders*, his son, a science major in college); Kathleen Quinlan (*Deborah Anders*, his daughter); Jay W. Macintosh (*Barbara Anders*, his wife, a scientist); Verna Bloom (*Jenny*, catatonic woman); Michael-James Wixted (*Michael*, young boy whose parents were shot); Nobel Willingham (*Jim Clancy*, Sierra Mountain guide); Doug Chapin (*Tom Clancy*, Jim's son); Dan Barrows (truck thief); Ken Samson (*Jack McFadden*, survivalist who settles his family at a ranch).

SYNOPSIS

This unpretentious telefilm has a narrow focus, but it is a respectable and moderately entertaining production. It was first shown by NBC as the Thursday evening feature film on October 10, 1974. Working within a modest budget, *Where Have All the People Gone* nevertheless presented a credible and effective portrait of an apocalyptic event. The inconclusive ending suggests that it may have originally been intended as a pilot for a series, with Peter Graves as Stephen Anders leading his clan of survivors through new adventures each week. It is very doubtful if a series would have been successful, since the concept seems pretty well exhausted by the end of the picture.

The story opens with the Anders family on a two-week camping trip in the High Sierras with their guide Jim Clancy. Stephen's wife, Barbara, is a scientist and has to return home early. Their guide's son drives her to the local airport. Stephen and his children explore a cave where they are digging for fossils. David is a college student with an aptitude for science. His younger sister, Deborah, is somewhat bored with their vacation adventure and asks her dad if they could spend their next holiday at a resort hotel instead. At the campfire, Jim is preparing rabbit stew for dinner when the the glow from the sun starts to increase to a blinding intensity. The guide stares at the phenomenon, which is immediately followed by earth tremors. Anders and his children run out of the cave, and Jim tells them about the strange light in the sky. David turns on the transistor radio to try to learn more about the event, but all he picks up is static. As Jim lapses suddenly into a coma, David frantically tries to raise Clancy's wife with the short-wave radio but gets no reply. Steven wonders if radiation is the cause of Jim's illness and fears that their food has been contaminated, except for the supplies they had with them in the cave. David fears that a nuclear war may have started. The next morning, they begin to hike to Rainbow, the nearest town, carrying the guide on a stretcher.

After several hours travel, the group is exhausted. While they rest, Jim dies and his body crumbles into dust. With growing panic, Anders and his children push on and manage to stumble into Rainbow the next day, but the community is completely deserted, a ghost town. Deborah keeps asking, "Where have all the people gone?" Cars are abandoned on the street. They reach Clancy's house, but the only sign of Jim's wife and his son Tom is the clothes they wore when they disintegrated into dust. David locates Clancy's Geiger counter and discovers their canned goods are free of radioactivity. He tries to start several vehicles but finds their electric generators are all burned out. By replacing the battery every few hours, he hopes they can manage to drive back home to Malibu.

Stephen and David try to understand the cause of the catastrophe, but they are unable to reach a conclusion. Down the road, they stop at a garage and load all the batteries onto Clancy's truck. When they find a dazed young woman sitting in a van, they bring her along, and Deborah takes care of her. A savage dog suddenly appears and attacks Stephen, who fights it off with a wrench. The group drives all day, and when they finally spot a man on the road, he pulls a gun on them and steals the truck. Exploring a farmhouse, they come across a young boy, Michael, whose parents have been killed by scavengers. He tells them that he and his father were bailing hay when the sun pulsated with a huge flash of light, and David concludes that a massive solar flare was the cause of the calamity. Stephen hopes that, since they survived, his wife, Barbara, may have survived as well David is almost irrational in his conviction that his mother is still alive. The survivors hitch up horses and a wagon from the farm and continue on to Los Angeles. When they arrive at a shopping center, David discovers that only cars with their motors running at the time of the solar flare have had their generators disabled. Cars that were not in use operate as normal, and they locate a new vehicle at a shopping center down the road. Now armed with a rifle from the farm, Stephen detains a stranger coming out of a supermarket. He quickly learns that he is a family man, Jack McFadden, who fled from Los Angeles with his family. Jack explains that most people died from a mysterious disease shortly after the solar flare. The dogs that survived are all vicious and many of the human survivors are also crazed. He urgers Stephen to hole up with his group at any of the nearby farms, but Stephen says he must first locate his wife.

The catatonic woman begins to talk, calling Michael "Billy," and as time passes she becomes coherent. Her name is Jenny, and she and her family were on their way to visit Disneyland when the flare struck. Her husband died and her young children were later killed by a pack of dogs when she left them to locate a car in working order. As the group gathers fresh supplies from the store, another pack of mad dogs appears. Michael is almost killed, but they fight the dogs off with gunfire. Later that day, they finally reach the empty city of Los Angeles. It is a haunting and desolate place, and they drive through as quickly as possible. As they near Malibu, they find the road blocked by the wreck of a schoolbus. While they examine the bus, another solar flare occurs, but it is less intense. They manage to get past the bus, and David rushes to search their house as soon as they arrive. He discovers a pile of dust in her bedroom, which is all that remains of his mother. She left a note for them that explains that the solar flare somehow triggered a deadly virus, which she was able to isolate. Very few people are immune to this virus, and she prays that her husband and children are among those resistant to it. All of them except for young Michael sink into a deep depression. When Stephen confesses his despair to Jenny, she is shattered, and she finally heads out to the ocean and tries to drown herself. Michael observes her, and shouts out a warning to the others, and Stephen and David swim out to rescue her.

They all embrace on the beach as Stephen says that their dead loved ones would want them to survive. The story concludes with Deborah's narration stating that they plan to seek out a farm in northern California and try to start life over again.

CRITIQUE

The most impressive element of this picture is the refreshingly different characters and the ways in which they face this crisis. Stephen Anders is an atypical hero driven on by love for his wife. He is somewhat hesitant and not an authoritarian figure, and he relies heavily on his bright son, David, for the best course of action. Peter Graves, the decisive team leader from the *Mission: Impossible* television series, is very convincing as this realistic everyman. His emotional collapse near the end of the film, which prompts Jenny's suicide attempt, is excellent acting, being low-key yet powerful. George O'Hanlon Jr. is also exceptional as David, a likable young wunderkind without a trace of arrogance or conceit. He is obviously his mother's son, and his strong attachment to her is his weak factor, as he loses his cool rationality whenever her survival is questioned. The characters of both Stephen and David are far more complex (and interesting) than the cardboard characters who usually populate disaster films, particularly one made directly for television. Deborah, played by Kathleen Quinlan, is a more typical character and an average teenager. She obviously commands far less attention from her parents, but she is neither resentful nor disheartened. Her emotions are far closer to the surface than those of her brother or father. She is the narrator of the picture, so the audience is expected to perceive events from her viewpoint. She panics after seeing the uninhabited village of Rainbow becoming somewhat numb, but when Jenny joins them, she becomes her caretaker and regains her composure from assuming this role. Jenny is also an interesting character. The affection and care she receives from the Anders family restores her sanity, and she begins to rely on Stephen as her anchor. When he expresses despair, she is completely overwhelmed. Verna Bloom is excellent in the role.

Michael is the only character who lacks credibility, largely due to the performance by Michael-James Wixted, who behaves as if on a Sunday outing.

The threat at first seems a credible one, but the concept of attributing the deaths to a mysterious virus caused by the solar flare is unconvincing. The burst of increased gamma rays would have been sufficient in terms of storyline, and the introduction of the virus angle seems extraneous. The other letdown is the abruptness of the Los Angeles segment, which should have been extended. The story appeared to be building toward their arrival in the city, and the quick passage was a missed opportunity, particularly since the Malibu scenes are a bit disappointing. After the LA scenes, the film seems to stall, and the angst of the characters debating their will to survive is dramatically unusual, but not very interesting. The very conclusion is weak, and Deborah's closing narration seems trite and unconvincing. Still, given all the positive elements, the telefilm is a modest success and worthwhile viewing.

REPRESENTATIVE QUOTES

"It was a Sunday in August. Mom, Dad, David and I were on vacation digging for fossils in the High Sierras. Mom had to go back to LA that morning. We didn't know that two and a half hours later, the world as we knew it would cease to exist." (Deborah's opening narration)

"The whole sky lit up, just like the good Lord was snapping a picture." (Jim Clancy to Anders and his children describing the spectacle caused by the sun)

"I loved her very much and I feel so lost. The only thing that kept us going was hoping that she was still alive. I never thought past this. There is nothing else now. Nothing!" (Stephen explaining his despair to Jenny after learning of his wife's death)

The World, the Flesh and the Devil (1959)

Rating: ***   **Threat:** Radioactive isotope dust

MGM. Written by Ranald MacDougall based on a story by Ferdinand Reyher; Photographed by Harold J. Mazoratis; Special effects by A. Arnold Gillespie (mechanical), Lee Le Blanc & Matthew Yuricich (photographic); Edited by Harold Kress; Music by Miklós Rózsa; Produced by George Englund; Directed by Ranald MacDougall. B & W, 95 minutes.

ANNOTATED CAST LIST

Harry Belafonte (*Ralph Burton*, mine inspector); Inger Stevens (*Sarah Crandall*, survivor who hid in a decompression chamber); Mel Ferrer (*Ben Thacker*, survivor who journeys by boat from South America).

SYNOPSIS

This film is essentially a mainstream variation of Arch Oboler's *Five* (1951). Like that problematic production, *The World, the Flesh and the Devil* has much promise but falters along the way with a weak conclusion. The real letdown is that the production came very close to being a classic but missed grabbing the brass ring. Nonetheless, there is ample quality in it to warrant repeat viewings.

Ralph Burton is a young, black safety inspector checking out a closed section of a mine in Pennsylvania. Water is a major problem in this tunnel, and without the constant use of pumps it will soon flood. A cave-in traps Ralph, but he receives a signal from above, and soon he starts to hear the sounds of rescue machinery being used to extricate him. A number of days pass, and Ralph keeps up his spirits by singing and chatting to himself. He starts to panic, however, when the water pumps stop, the lights start to flicker and the sounds of rescue cease. Fearing the rising water level, Ralph desperately tries to dig out and squeezes through a hole into one passage and then another. He finally breaks through to a higher level where he locates a ladder to the surface. When he emerges into the sunlight, he exclaims, "I'm out! I'm out!" but finds no one at the mining complex. Ralph heads to the office and is shocked to see newspaper headlines proclaiming the end of the world. Millions of people were attempting to flee from a cloud of nuclear radiation, which was slowly blanketing the entire planet.

Burton locates a Geiger counter, but the radiation level seems normal. He fires a gun into the air, but there is no response. There are no bodies anywhere, and Ralph is perplexed. He selects a new car at an auto dealership and heads off to New York City. When he reaches the George Washington Bridge, it is impassable due to the many cars abandoned on the roadway. The Holland Tunnel is equally jammed. Ralph discovers a small motorboat tied to a dock on the Hudson River, and he crosses over to Manhattan. He wanders aimlessly through the empty streets of lower Manhattan, passing Wall Street and the Federal Building. He goes to a church and tolls the bell, but again there is no response, but neither does he see any dead bodies.

In a useless gesture, Ralph begins to pick up newspapers that are blowing in the wind, crumpling them into a waste basket. He fills a small wagon with canned goods and drags it through the streets. He finally stops at a radio station powered by an electric generator. Ralph enters a studio and plays some tapes containing a jumble of emergency bulletins and news reports. One announcer speaks about loss of contact with places such as London and Chicago. Rio di Janero reports the arrival of a cloud of isotope dust. Finally, one voice provides a summary of the crisis, which began after a walkout occurred at the United Nations, and an unidentified country, in a suicidal gesture, released a fatal concoction of radioactive sodium isotopes into the upper atmosphere. This cloud of death swept relentlessly around the world, killing all human and animal life. There is no possible defense against it, but the atomic poison will dissipate after a short period of time, perhaps five days. Finally, only one voice remains on the tape, and the speaker wonders if he should continue since he is probably only speaking to himself. After this, the tape lapses into an eerie and complete silence. Ralph stoically heads back to the streets of the deserted city as a windstorm starts up.

Days pass, and Ralph sets up a luxury apartment for himself with all the latest conveniences. He stocks it with great paintings from the museum, and other artifacts. He brings a number of manikins from a department store into his building for companionship. Ralph is not really alone, however, as a beautiful young woman is discretely observing him and all his activities. Ralph eventually wires a complete block with electricity and lights it up at night. He next creates an elaborate layout of electric trains. The woman continues to keep her existence a secret until Ralph tosses one of the manikins off his balcony. At first she fears Ralph has committed suicide and screams. Hearing her, Ralph hurries down to the street and finds that the woman, Sarah Crandall, is frightened of him. She has been watching Burton since he arrived, but could never work up the courage to approach him. She explains that she hid out in a decompression chamber with two companions when the alarm was first broadcast about the atomic poison. Her friends died when they left the chamber after the second day, but Sarah waited five full days and survived. Although very reserved, Sarah tells Ralph that she needs him and then returns to her own apartment in a nearby building.

Time passes, and the two become slowly acquainted. Ralph hooks her place up to his power grid and installs a telephone between their apartments. Then he sets up a shortwave radio station, intending to broadcast a message each day at noon to hunt for any other survivors. Sarah's reticence starts to melt away as she begins to trust Ralph more and more. He, on the hand, is the one who now acts distant, and his attitude puzzles Sarah, especially when he refuses to allow her to move into the same building with him, saying, "People might talk." Her irritation begins to show. She questions his obsession with saving old books, art and other old fragments of civilization, and accuses him of caring more for things than people. Ralph then brings up the issue of race, having taken offense when Sarah says, "I'm free, white and twenty-one, and I am going to do what I please." Sarah is perplexed and tries a new approach, coaxing Ralph to give her a haircut. He bungles the job, and although Sarah tries not to show any disappointment, Ralph gets angry anyway and marches off. She tries again later to approach him, and once more he brings up race as an excuse against their romantic involvement. "Leave it the way it is," he replies when she brings up the subject of love.

Ralph heads up the Hudson River to Albany for three days without telling Sarah. Upon his return he apologizes and tries to make amends on her birthday by giving her a huge diamond brooch and preparing a special dinner. Ralph then hears a garbled message in French over the short-wave, which causes him to become depressed. He refuses to sit with Sarah at her birthday feast, acting as a waiter instead. She is delighted when she hears the news about the message, but is hurt by his pronouncement, "Civilization is back . . . and you know it makes a difference."

The next day, Sarah spots a tugboat coming up the river. The delirious man at the helm collapses moments after docking, and they bring him to Ralph's building. He falls into a coma for week, but then slowly recovers. His name is Ben Thacker and he is the sole survivor from South America. Until now he has been searching in vain for any sign of life. As Ben recovers, Ralph withdraws, leaving Ben and Sarah alone for the most part. Ben cannot understand why Ralph is leaving the way clear for a romance to develop between Sarah and himself. He also learns that Sarah is in love with Ralph but has no fellings toward him. One night Ralph runs a projector at the nearby cinema and shows the last newsreel made before the apocalypse. The program shows there was no premonition of the coming disaster. After the film ends, Ben confronts Ralph and says that he and Sarah will have no future unless Ralph clears out. Sarah is furious when she overhears their argument. Later, she challenges Ben to kiss her and make her forget Ralph. They embrace, but Sarah withdraws a moment later.

Sarah tries to talk with Ralph but encounters his usual wall of indifference. Ben visits Burton and gives him a gun. Since he refuses to leave New York City, Ben gives him notice of World War IV. When Ralph later leaves his building, Ben fires at him with a rifle. Ralph procures a rifle from a nearby store, and they begin a game of cat and mouse that lasts the entire night. Hearing the shots, Sarah attempts to follow them. At dawn, Ralph reads a hopeful message of peace inscribed outside the UN building and throws his weapon away.

Ralph appears unarmed before Ben, who raises his rifle to fire. "If you were afraid, I could do it," he says in disgust as he tosses away the gun and walks off. Sarah arrives and takes Ralph by the hand. She then calls Ben back as well, and the three of them walk off past a flock of pigeons. An overhead shot watches them proceed down the narrow city street as the closing title appears on the screen proclaiming, "The Beginning."

CRITIQUE

This atmospheric and powerful film is seriously marred by the awkward last act, starting from the moment of Ben's appearance. The ending is so trite and contrived that it tends to obscure the overall quality of the picture. In fact, the entire first half rates among the finest examples of apocalyptic cinema in spite of a few missteps. The story of the destruction of the world is given too sketchy a presentation. Videotape users can replay the explanatory snippets of the holo-caust Ralph uncovers at the radio station, but the voices overlap each other, so that viewers in a theater would only catch a fragment of the chronicle. No ex-planation is ever given about the disappearance of the bodies, and one could only assume that they disintegrated instantly after death, however, in that case, their clothes should still remain, but no remannts of clothes are present either. An apocalyptic film is always weakened when no solid foundation is provided for the events of the story. The concept of radioactive isotope dust is plausible and an interesting premise, but a more thorough exposition of the idea is needed. The five-day dissipation of the danger is an intriguing touch, but it would seem that more people could have survived with this scenario. In any case, the premise of the film is still acceptable, despite its frugal exposition.

The real problem with the film is the introduction of the race issue. Mankind has been wiped out, yet Ralph's mindset still revolves around race. Even Ben, the functional villain of the piece, seems basically free of racial prejudice. Ironi-cally, it is Ralph himself who is keeping racism alive. While in production, this picture fumbled for a title and was known for a time as *The End of the World.* MGM was somewhat concerned about the idea of an interracial couple in the film, but the picture tries too hard to ignore the obvious. With the oblitera-tion of humanity, racism is no longer an issue. Ralph's mind is stuck on a dead-end track, and he himself is the problem. Incidentally, Ben's past in the film is unresolved since he never reveals his personal survival story. If his fam-ily lived in New York on Sutton Place, what was he doing in South America? The character of Ben is largely enigmatic. Despite the name Thacker, he seems to be of Hispanic background due to his accent. (Actor Ferrer was Cuban-born, like Desi Arnaz, and their voices sound rather similar at times.) The issue of his history is never discussed. Still, the racial focus is unresolved when it is re-placed by the pointless war between Ben and Ralph. Ben believes that Sarah will love him only if he is the last man on Earth, and in a way, so does Ralph. The resolution of this confrontation does not ring true either. Nothing has changed in the final scene, unless we assume that Ralph will finally show Sarah that he returns her love. However, hat is not really indicated on screen. The ending is so disappointing that the plot seems to collapse like a house of cards. Then, there are the pigeons in the final shot. If all life was destroyed, where did they come from? The character of Ben certainly needed additional development if there was any chance for the finale of the film to work.

Unfortunately, these faults, all from the screenplay, do overshadow the strengths. The cinematography of the film is stunning, and to be fully appreciated, it must be viewed in widescreen format. Each shot is boldly and imaginatively constructed. The impressive cityscapes as Belafonte searches through New York City remain memorable long after the film is over. The editing is brilliant and impeccable. The musical score by Miklós Rózsa is very impressive, although it is somewhat reminiscent of his *Violin Concerto Op. 24*, Rózsa's greatest concert hall composition. Little criticism can be made of the direction of the film, but since the director also is the author he is principally at fault for the plot shortcomings.

Harry Belafonte gives one of the most impressive onscreen performance by an African-American in the 1950s, rivaled only by Sidney Poitier's great readings in *No Way Out* (1950) and *Edge of the City* (1956). Some critics saw Ralph as too much of a goody two-shoes, but his character is far deeper than that. If the premise is accepted that he is a man who is a pressure cooker of hidden racial animosity, then this performance is a great one indeed. By not responding to Sarah's love, Ralph seems to be hanging on to old racial scars that are meaningless in this new world. This may be different than the usual interpretation, but it reveals Belafonte's performance as a fascinating one with many shadings. One can certainly overlook that the film gives him a few moments of song. In fact, his improvised number in the cave is one of the film's highlights. Belafonte's performance stresses the absolute freedom of a person to do whatever he wishes. No doubt a few viewers have been inspired to indulge in the fantasy of having the entire city of New York as your plaything, being able to select any object from any store, museum or gallery to furnish your own living quarters. Belafonte brings this fantasy to life as Ralph, and he does it with real style and zest. Inger Stevens' also provides a more complicated performance than it appears on the surface. Her initial reserve seems natural, but she establishes herself as an distinct character rather quickly. She is also intelligent and has a knowledge of human psychology, as demonstrated by her haircut ploy. Sarah simply lacks the key to penetrate the wall of isolation that Ralph has built around himself. The scene where she challenges Ben to make her forget Ralph is unexpected. One feels sorry for Ben since it seems Sarah is using him at times to spark a reaction from Ralph. Stevens endows her reading with a mixture of warmth, longing, frustration and petulance that makes it seem far out of the ordinary. Mel Ferrer, on the other hand, is miscast. He fails to develop his character in any way and is merely a cardboard prop thrown into the mix to resolve the box in which the author trapped himself. It would have been far more interesting if the third character turned out to be more of an innocent, who was unaware of the unresolved romance of Ralph and Sarah. That would have provided a far more stimulating outcome. Instead Ben seems to be a mere adventurer with no imagination or capacity for love himself.

Finally, the plot point of the messages from France is never developed and seemingly discarded by the end of the film. With this idea dropped, we never learn if there are many or only one other survivor on Earth. By the time it was used here, ending the picture with "The Beginning" was no longer a fresh idea, and instead seemed trite.

REPRESENTATIVE QUOTES

"I don't like it, I don't like it, I don't like it here.
  You wouldn't like it. Nobody likes it. Nobody likes it here.
  Foods got moldy, I've got oldie. Nobody likes it here.
  Voices echoing, rocks are falling, I don't like it here." (Ralph's mine song)

"You think I've been acting crazy, well why not? This is a crazy world, and I thought I was all alone in it. Look, I live here. Drop me a postcard sometime." (Ralph to Sarah noticing her fear at their first meeting)

"As long as we are alive, the world is still alive. We're monuments, you and me." (Ralph's words of encouragement when Sarah says she need hope)

"It is taking you too long to accept things, Ralph. This is the world we live in. We are alone in it and we have to go on from there." (Sarah to Ralph, trying to get him to open up to her)

Zarkorr the Invader (1996)

Rating: *   Threat: Alien weapon

Monster Island Entertainment. Written by Benjamin Carr; Photographed by Joe C. Maxwell; Special effects by Michael S. Deak; Edited by Felix Chamberlain; Music by Richard Band; Produced by Albert Band (executive), Robert Talbot, Sally Clarke & Karl Edward Hansen; Directed by Aaron Osborne. 80 minutes.

ANNOTATED CAST LIST

Rhys Christian Pugh (*Tommy Ward*, postal worker and Earth's most average man); Torie Lynch (alien messenger); De'Prise Grossman (*Dr. Stephanie Martin*, zoologist from the University of Trenton); Charles Schneider (*Arthur*, wacky computer expert); Mark Hamilton (*George Ray*, policeman who helps Tommy); Ron Barncs (*Larry Bates*, George's partner); Stan Chambers (*Stan Chambers*, TV anchorman); Elizabeth Anderson (*Elizabeth Anderson*, TV anchorwoman); Robert Craighead (*Marty Karlson*, reporter killed by Zarkorr); Eileen Wesson (*Debbie Dalverson*, Newark TV reporter); William Knight (*Rocker*, Williston sheriff); Dave Richards (*Welles*, geologist in Williston).

SYNOPSIS

   Albert Band is an Italian-born film entrepreneur and producer who specialized in low-budget productions largely geared to the adolescent video market. He often worked with his sons, Charles Band and composer Richard Band. Some of their film projects, such as *Re-animator* (1985), were brilliant and creative. Most, however, were dreadful endeavors noted only for occasional flashes of wacky charm. *Zarkorr the Invader* is a typical product, unwatchable at times, but with a few moments of genuine wit.
   The picture opens in Mount Aurora, California, where a monster appears, bursting forth out of the mountain. The creature is over 180 feet tall and appears reptilian, with huge horns on its head like a bull. It launches a rampage of destruction. Meanwhile, Tommy Ward, a postal worker in Newark, New Jersey, is relaxing at his apartment when a six-inch pixie attracts his attention. She claims to be a mental image projected into his brain by an alien galactic confederation. When Tommy asks why she looks like "a teenage mall tramp," she replies her appearance was chosen to be familiar and non-threatening. She claims that he was chosen, as the most average man on Earth, to save his planet from Zarkorr, an alien weapon sent to destroy our planet. She tells him that no earthly weapon can stop Zarkorr, but the creature himself contains the key to his own destruction. Zarkorr is programmed to seek out and kill Tommy, so he cannot avoid his task. Her final suggestion is for him to act quickly. Tommy turns on his television and discovers that the attack by Zarkorr has begun. Dr. Stephanie

Martin, a scientist speaking on a local TV station, believes that Zarkorr is not a prehistoric dinosaur or a new species but is rather a creature totally contrary to all rules of science.

Tommy is bewildered as how to proceed with his incredible mission, and he decides to seek out Dr. Martin for her advice. He goes to the television studio, where he is regarded as a madman. The police are called to take him away, and he is forced to take the scientist hostage. Tommy tries to explain the situation to the cops, and one of them unexpectedly believes him. The officer, George Ray, disarms his partner and helps Tommy escape with Dr. Martin. They listen to the radio as they drive off, and Stephanie is stunned when she hears that Zarkorr is invulnerable to all weapons and shoots lightning bolts from its eyes. Tommy convinces the beautiful scientist to help him. They go to a warehouse where Stephanie's friend, Arthur, an eccentric computer wizard, has a secret electronics lab.

While Arthur tries to uncover information about Zarkorr, the others watch television, where an animal rights activist is protesting that the government keeps trying to kill the creature. Arthur's computer research reveals that Zarkorr does not eat, does not sleep and does not breathe. Tommy concludes that it must have an "off switch" that only he can activate. Further research uncovers that the at exact moment when Zarkorr was generated, another anomaly appeared in Williston, a small town fifty miles north of Yuma, Arizona. Tommy, George and Stephanie decide to travel there and investigate the alien object. Arthur hacks into an airline's computer to arrange their trip on the next flight and provide a rental car for them at the Arizona airport as well.

At Williston, they encounter a redneck sheriff who mistakes them for government agents. He turns over to them a strange, metallic capsule that has fallen out of the sky. Wells, the local geologist, claims that nothing on Earth could possibly open it. Tommy asks that they place the sphere in the trunk of their car, and when the sheriff objects, George outshouts him into compliance. As they drive off, Tommy tells George to take the most direct route to the location of Zarkorr. A policeman finally stops their car at a roadblock. As George tries to argue with the cop, Tommy jumps back in the car and drives off. The monster is tearing through a city, smashing buildings left and right. (Wildly satirizing similar scenes with Godzilla from Japanese science fiction films.) Tommy stops the car, and the capsule opens for him as he touches it. The top of the sphere appears to be a shield, and he carries it and approaches Zarkorr. The creature shoots lightning from his eyes at Tommy, but these bolts strike the shield and are reflected back to Zarkorr as Tommy passes out. At this point the creature suddenly dissolves into a small, glowing ball, which flies up and off into outer space. The evaporation of the threat posed by Zarkorr is so hasty, that none of the characters are given a chance to ponder the actual nature of the threat or consider the purpose behind it. There is no speculation about future alien hostility, or whether the alien pixie has other tribulations in store for Earth. Instead, Tommy is taken to a hospital for a leisurely recovery, without consideration of any of these issues. As soon as he awakes, a television reporter interviews him, congratulating him for saving the world. George and Stephanie join him at his bedside, and he jokes with the reporter about a rumor that he might run for president.

CRITIQUE

Zarkorr the Invader is an absurd and mindless film that combines elements of *The 27th Day* (1957), *Godzilla* (1956) and "Arena," an episode of the original *Star Trek* television series. The publicity for the film added a pointless exclamation point after the monster's name, so it actually appears as *Zarkorr! the Invader*. There is actually very little of Zarkorr in the film, and most of the action is wasted in long, dreary sequences such as the hostage stand-off at the television station. The best effects for the film are cribbed from an earlier, more successful effort called *Shrunken Heads* (1994), directed by Richard Elfman. A rather detailed model of a city had been constructed for that film, and an elaborate tracking shot was directly lifted from that picture to establish the locale of Tommy Ward's apartment. Later, Zarkorr rummaged through and destroyed this model, and these shots were repeated several times in the film. Consequently, no matter what city Zarkorr attacks, it looks the same.

The loopholes in the story are also distracting. The audience never discovers exactly what Zarkorr is. Since it does not breathe, it is most likely some sort of machine, a doomsday device of alien origin. The reason behind this test of humanity is completely ignored. The alien messenger simply states, "We are superior beings, and our moral code allows us to do whatever we wish." Added to the alien's negative view of the human spirit and the meaning of life, the backdrop of the film is amazingly nihilistic for a lightweight action film, an element that does make it stand apart from other similar features.

There is little of quality in the editing, cinematography or direction of this production. The music score by Richard Band is simply awful. Most of the cast members are bland and rather dull. Rhys Christian Pugh generates little sympathy as Tommy, and De'Prise Grossman is attractive but completely insipid as Dr. Martin. Two performers bring some real gusto and spark to their roles. Charles Schneider gives an uninhibited performance as Arthur, a giggling and loony genius, who seems like a cross between Dwight Frye as Renfield in the original *Dracula* (1931) and Jeffrey Combs (the most successful graduate from Albert Band films) in his role as Herbert West in *Re-animator*. Schneider's over-the-top wild man provides the only real fire in the film, giving it a much needed boost. Mark Hamilton is quieter in comparison as Patrolman George Ray, but he also provides some flashes of inspiration. His imitation of Jack Webb as Joe Friday when he faces down Sheriff Rocker is excellent, for instance. The scene where he is initially persuaded by Tommy that he is humankind's savior is also a gem. The only other interesting moments are provided by background bits by the television broadcasters, particularly the politically correct spokesman who complains that the army is violating Zarkorr's rights. Unfortunately, these few bright moments cannot save such an inept picture. At least the film wraps up very quickly, before the unpleasant and irritating rock song that plays over the end credits.

REPRESENTATIVE QUOTES

"You have been selected by a coalition of intelligent species in the galaxy to defend your planet against an invader. If you fail, you and your entire civilization will be destroyed." (Alien messenger to Tommy Ward)

"I thought superior beings are supposed to be morally superior. Let me tell you something, there is nothing moral about this. This is totally immoral." (Tommy's initial reaction)

Appendices

Appendix A

Filmography of Fifty Additional Examples of Apocalyptic Cinema

In analyzing the fifty films in depth, a number of additional apocalyptic titles have been mentioned. The entry on *The Day the Sky Exploded* (1958/63), for example, cited *A Fire in the Sky* (1978), *Asteroid* (1997) and *Meteorites* (1998). In addition to these supplemental examples already pointed out, this filmography provides fifty extra titles of apocalyptic cinema. The release dates and ratings are included with each entry, as well as a short annotation. Indeed, some of these titles, such as *Five Million Years to Earth* (1968) and *Twelve Monkeys* (1995), are among the finest films ever produced in this genre. This listing will further serve to illustrate the range and variety of apocalyptic films.

◇ *12 to the Moon* (1960) A lunar expedition encounters a race of superior aliens who decide to retaliate for the intrusion by freezing the surface of the earth. Ken Clark, Tom Conway, Anthony Dexter, Francis X. Bushman. Rating: **

◇ *12:01* (1993) A scientific experiment traps the entire world in a time loop that grows shorter with each cycle. Jonathan Silverman, Helen Slater, Martin Landau. Rating: ****

◇ *2010* (1984) This sequel to *2001: A Space Odyssey* has a joint American-Soviet expedition head to Jupiter to retrieve the spaceship *Discovery* and reactivate the super computer HAL. The entire mission is overshadowed by the growing possibility of nuclear war on Earth. Roy Scheider, John Lithgow, Bob Balaban, Keir Dullea. Rating: ****

◇ *Abraxas* (1991) Future governor and former wrestler Jesse Ventura stars as an intergalactic secret agent tracking down a criminal who steals a device that has the capacity to destroy a planet while opening the gateway to another dimension. The criminal hides the device on Earth, and Ventura tracks it down to save Earth from destruction. Jim Belushi, Sven-Ole Thorsen. Rating: *

◇ *Abyss* (1989) James Cameron's claustrophobic, intense thriller set in an underwater base was not apocalyptic when released to theaters, but the expanded director's cut featured a climax with an alien threat to swamp the earth with giant tidal waves. Ed Harris, Michael Biehn, Mary Elizabeth Mastrantonio, Leo Burmester. Rating: ***

◇ *Andromeda Strain* (1971) Michael Crichton's elaborate thriller of a high-tech secret lab studying a deadly virus that originated in outer space. Film was stylishly directed by Robert Wise. Arthur Hill, David Wayne, Kate Reid, James Olsen. Rating: ****

◇ *The Apocalypse (*1996) In the distant future, a computer in a spacecraft is programed to deliver and detonate a superweapon that will destroy Earth. Sandra Bernhard. Rating: *

◇ *Assignment Outer Space* (1961) This is a low-budget Italian film in which the earth is threatened by the approach of a computer-operated satellite that generates enough heat to destroy all life. Directed by Antonio Margheriti under the pseudonym Anthony Dawson. Rating: *

◇ *Battle of the Worlds* (1961) Another Margheriti production, this film benefits from the presence of Claude Rains and some fairly decent special effects. Earth is threatened by the approach of an alien planet called "The Outsider. " Rating: **

◇ *Beginning of the End* (1957) Bert I. Gordon has the planet threatened by the emergence in Illinois of a plague of giant locusts. Peter Graves, Peggy Castle, Morris Ankrum. Rating: **

◇ *The Birds* (1963) Alfred Hitchcock's deliberate, slow-paced thriller about the start of an inexplicable war on humanity launched by the birds. Based on a short story by Daphne DuMaurier, the last third of the film is remarkably intense. Pay close attention to the conversation in the diner about the end of the world. Rod Taylor, Tippi Hedron, Jessica Tandy, Suzanne Pleshette, Ethel Griffies. Rating: ****

◇ *By Dawn's Early Light* (1990) This effective nuclear war thriller is propelled by a top-notch cast. Powers Boothe, Rebecca De Mornay, James Earl Jones, Martin Landau, Darren McGavin. Rating: ***

◇ *Day of the Triffids* (1963) A double threat envelops the earth when a meteor shower causes the blindness of everyone who watches it while also seeding the earth with strange, carnivorous plants which grow overnight. The blind populace is helpless when the plants uproot themselves and feed on human victims. Howard Keel, Kieron Moore, Janette Scott, Mervyn Johns. Rating: ✳✳✳✳

◇ *Destroy All Monsters!* (1968) The only Godzilla film to turn apocalyptic. When Rodan, Gidorah, Mothra, Godzilla and six other, giant monsters are placed under control of aliens from the asteroid Kilaak in the year 1999, they set out to destroy humankind. One of the most entertaining films in the series, it was directed by Ishiro Honda, who also helmed the very first Godzilla entry in 1954. It was originally intended to conclude the series. Rating: ✳✳✳

◇ *Doomsday Rock* (1997) William Devane stars as an astronomer who seizes control of a missile base to destroy an asteroid he alone claims will strike Earth. When the asteroid changes course and veers towards the earth as he predicted, he launches nuclear warheads at the asteroid to save the planet. Connie Sellecca, Jessica Walter, Kent McCord. Rating: ✳✳

◇ *Earth Dies Screaming* (1964) Entertaining British film directed by Terence Fisher that portrays the human race overrun by robots from outer space. Willard Parker, Dennis Price. Rating: ✳✳✳

◇ *Earth vs. the Flying Saucers* (1956) An epic battle over the skies of Washington, D.C., highlights this classic film which is dominated by the special effects of Ray Harryhausen. Hugh Marlowe, Joan Taylor, Morris Ankrum. Rating: ✳✳✳

◇ *End of Days* (1999) Satan plans to take a wife in New York City on the eve of the millennium in a scheme to end the world. A broken-down cop learns about it and tries to stop him. Arnold Schwarzenegger, Gabriel Byrne, Rod Steiger, Robin Tunney. Rating: ✳✳

◇ *End of the World* (1977) Offbeat plot features aliens who pose as a priest (Christopher Lee) and six nuns while they plan to destroy the world. The last shot of the film depicts the earth blowing up as seen from space. This picture is not related to either the silent 1916 film or the Abel Gance film of the same name. Sue Lyons, Lew Ayers, Dean Jagger. Rating: ✳✳

◇ *Final Equinox* (1995) Different forces are struggling to recover the Regenerator, an alien device with the capacity to destroy all life on Earth and replace it with new life. Joe Lara, David Warner. Rating: ✳✳

◇ *Five Million Years to Earth* (1968) The best entry in England's brilliant Quatermass series, the film cleverly contains a double apocalypse, a primeval holocaust on Mars and a current threat on Earth. While excavating a London subway, workers uncover the remains of a crashed alien spacecraft. James Donald, Barbara Shelley, Julian Glover. Rating: ✳✳✳✳✳

◇ *The Flame Barrier* (1958) When a satellite crashes in the Mexican jungle, it is infested with an alien life form, which projects a field of death that will expand ever larger until it envelops the world. Arthur Franz, Kathleen Crowley. Rating: *

◇ *Flight That Disappeared* (1961) This film resembles an extended *Twilight Zone* episode, in which an airplane carrying scientists is hijacked by super-natural forces, who put them on trial before a celestial court for threatening the future of humankind. Craig Hill, Paula Raymond. Rating: **

◇ *Independence Day* (1996) This special effects extravaganza portrays the on-slaught of technically advanced aliens who want to exterminate the human race and take over the earth. Bill Pullman, Will Smith, Jeff Goldblum, Brent Spiner, Robert Loggia, Mary McDonnell, Randy Quaid, Judd Hirsh. Rating: *****

◇ *Inferno* (1998) This dramatic telefilm portrays the crisis caused by intense solar activity. James Remar, Jonathan LaPaglia. Rating: **

◇ *Invasion of the Body Snatchers* (1956) Seed pods from outer space are used to grow non-human replacements for the inhabitants of a small town. Their goal is to eliminate and supplant the entire human race. Remade in 1978 with an urban setting. Stars of the original included Kevin McCarthy, Dana Winters, King Donovan and Carolyn Jones. Rating: ****

◇ *Invisible Invaders* (1959) An unseen alien army inhabits dead bodies in a strategy to eliminate humankind and take over the earth. John Agar, Jean Byron, John Carradine. Rating: **

◇ *Last Days of Man on Earth* (1973) This bizarre British fantasy, based on the writings of Michael Moorcock, depicts the approaching end of the world. Jon Finch, Patrick Magee, Sterling Haydn. Rating: **

◇ *Last Days of Planet Earth* (1974) Set in the year 1999, this imaginative Ja-panese production presents an interpretation of the apocalypse based on the writings of Nostradamus. Tetsuro Tamba, Kenju Kobiashi. Rating: ***

◇ *Lucifer Complex* (1976) An ultra-cheap film that uses leftover footage from an earlier movie to weave a story of how the Nazis attempt to return to power in 1986 and end up destroying the world. Robert Vaughan, Aldo Rey, Keenan Wynn, Leo Gordon. Rating: *

◇ *Men in Black* (1997) This outrageous story, based on a comic series by Lowell Cunningham, finds Earth imperiled by a missing alien treasure. If the special agents, the "men in black," who oversee the aliens living among us, can not recover the object, the planet will be pulverized by the beings from whom the object was stolen. The music score by Danny Elfman is brilliant. Tommy Lee Jones, Will Smith. Rating: ****

◇ *Monolith* (1993) Two Los Angeles policemen uncover a menacing alien force with the power to annihilate mankind. Bill Paxton, Lindsay Frost, John Hurt. Rating: ✳✳

◇ *Night of the Comet* (1984) Radiation from a comet wipes out over 90 percent of the world's population, leaving most of the survivors raving lunatics. Two normal girls struggle to survive. Catherine Mary Stewart, Kelli Moroney, Mary Woronov. Rating: ✳✳

◇ *The Omega Code* (1999) Secret messages are found encoded in the *Bible*, which a powerful mogul uses to gain world domination. After he is shot, Satan takes over his body, and brings about the apocalypse. This interesting concept is awkwardly executed. Michael York, Casper Van Dien, Michael Ironside. Rating: ✳✳

◇ *Outbreak* (1995) An artificially created virus mutates and threatens global extinction when it escapes and infects the populace of a small California town. Dustin Hoffman, Rene Russo, Kevin Spacey, Donald Sutherland, Cuba Gooding Jr. Rating: ✳✳✳

◇ *Panic in Year Zero* (1962) Ray Milland directs and stars in this excellent, low-key film about an average family's vacation that turns into a nightmare when nuclear war breaks out. Rating: ✳✳✳

◇ *The Prophecy* (1995) A faction of angels in heaven revolts over the status accorded to humans by God. The angel Gabriel hopes to provoke the apocalypse by appropriating the soul of the most evil man. This is a very different interpretation of angels, harbingers of disaster with their wings "dipped in blood." Followed by two sequels. Christopher Walken. Rating: ✳✳✳

◇ *Shape of Things to Come* (1979) Combining elements of both apocalyptic and post-apocalyptic genres, this film depicts the remnants of humanity living on the moon after the destruction of the earth, where they again face extinction. Unlike the classic *Things to Come* (1936), this film relies very little on the H. G. Wells novel upon which it is supposedly based. Jack Palance, Carol Lynley. Rating: ✳✳

◇ *Spacemaster X-7* (1957) The threat is a deadly fungus from outer space, which could wipe out humankind if it gets out of control. Bill Williams, Paul Frees, Moe Howard. Rating: ✳✳

◇ *Starship Troopers* (1997) Robert E. Heinlein's novel is the basis for this gritty, dynamic and multilayered portrait of the world in peril. Overtones of World War II can be detected in the plot threads. Casper Van Dien, Denise Richards, Michael Ironside. Rating: ✳✳✳✳

◇ *Story of Mankind* (1957) Irwin Allen production portrays mankind on trial in a celestial court where the issue concerns whether the earth will be permitted to self-destruct with the test of a new weapon. The trial recounts the highs and lows of human history. (The film itself is one of the lows.) It is based on a novel by Henrik Van Loon. An all-star cast includes Ronald Colman, Vincent Price, Cedric Hardwicke, Peter Lorre, the Marx Brothers, John Carradine, Virginia Mayo, Agnes Morehead, Hedy Lamarr, Dennis Hopper, Cesar Romero and many more stars in cameo roles. Rating: *

⋄ *Teenagers from Outer Space* (1959) Entertaining "bad" movie about an alien race's plans to use the earth as a breeding ground for "gargans," which are actually lobsters the size of houses. The aliens are unconcerned that the gargans will wipe out the inhabitants of the planet. Directed by, and starring, Tom Graef. Rating: **

⋄ *Terminator II: Judgment Day* (1991) Both this film and its forerunner sequel, *Terminator* (1985), involve a future where humans battle machines that are out to exterminate them. When the machines lose, they send terminator robots back to the past (our present) to kill the leader of the human forces in his youth. Both films are directed by James Cameron. Arnold Schwarzenegger, Linda Hamilton. Rating: ****

⋄ *This Is Not a Test* (1962) Low-budget tale of nuclear paranoia as war breaks out and a state trooper in the hinterland tries to get travelers to a shelter. Instead they eventually await Armaggedon in the rear storage compartment of a truck. Rating: **

⋄ *Twelve Monkeys* (1995) One of the most complex, brilliant and accomplished examples of apocalyptic cinema, involving time travel, the nature of reality and killer viruses. There are many red herrings and false leads until the actual fanatic who wants to destroy the world is finally identified. The climax is intense and quite moving. Bruce Willis, Brad Pitt, Christopher Plummer. Rating: *****

⋄ *Until the End of the World* (1991) Wim Winders directed this lengthy, engrossing, but wayward, film centering on a camera that will permit the blind to see. The threat comes from the possible chain reaction of exploding satellites. The film also foresees the Y2K panic. William Hurt, Max von Sydow, Sam Neill. Rating: ***

⋄ *Warlock* (1991) Julian Sands plays a warlock out to destroy the world by discovering the secret name of God, which is hidden in three ancient texts. This was followed by three sequels. Rating: **

⋄ *Warning from Space* (1956) Bizarre Japanese science fiction film in which the earth is threatened by large, alien starfish, each with an oversized eye in its stomach. The actual danger is posed by collision with an alien planet. Rating: **

◇ *Within the Rock* (1998) While attempting to divert an asteroid on collision course with Earth, a team of astronauts encounters a deadly monster as they try to plant the nuclear explosives. Rating: *

◇ *World War III* (1982) Sober thriller depicts a developing nuclear war scenario and the efforts of the U.S. president (Rock Hudson) and the Soviet premier (Brian Keith) to avoid a world-ending conflict. Rating: ***

Appendix B

Sampling of Post-Apocalyptic Cinema

A number of films studied in this book combine elements of both the apocalyptic and post-apocalyptic genres. The following listing of fifty films represents works that are primarily post-apocalyptic in nature, and will be useful in categorizing some of the thematic and stylistic differences between these two similar classifications. The range of post-apocalyptic films is generally far narrower than the apocalyptic, and many of these pictures take the *Mad Max* films as their model. This type of film was particularly popular during the 1980s, and a case could be made that to some degree they adopted the characteristics of the American Western. They usually took place in a desert setting and involved a confrontation between forces of good and evil. There are also a number of quality pre-1980s titles, such as the remarkable *Soylent Green* (1973), in which Edward G. Robinson, dying in real life, had a mesmerizing death scene in a futuristic euthanasia facility, and *The Time Machine* (1960), one of the all-time finest science fiction efforts. No ratings are provided for these films, but dates and the leading cast members or directors (designated by a small "d" in parenthesis) are included.

⬦ *1990: The Bronx Warriors* (1982) Vic Morrow, Christopher Connelly

⬦ *2020 Texas Gladiators* (1982) Al Cliver

⬦ *After the Fall of New York* (1984) Michael Sopkiw, Edmund Purdom

⬦ *Aftermath* (1985) Forrest J. Ackerman, Sid Haig, Steve Barkett (d)

⬦ *America 3000* (1986) Chuck Wagner, Carmilla Sparv

⬦ *Blood of Heroes* (1989) Rutger Hauer, Joan Chen

⬦ *A Boy and His Dog* (1973) Don Johnson, Jason Robards

⬦ *Captive Women* (1952) Robert Clarke, William Schallert, Margaret Field

⬦ *Damnation Alley* (1977) Jan-Michael Vincent, George Peppard

◇ *The Day After* (1983) Jason Robards, Nicholas Meyer (d)

◇ *Defcon 4* (1983) Tim Choate, Kate Lynch

◇ *Endgame* (1983) Gordon Mitchell

◇ *Equalizer 2000* (1986) Cirio H. Santiago (d)

◇ *Escape from L.A.* (1996) Kurt Russell, Steve Buscemi, John Carpenter (d)

◇ *Final Sanctions* (1990) William Smith, Robert Z'Dar

◇ *Firebird 2015 AD* (1980) Darren McGavin, Doug McClure

◇ *The Fire Next Time* (1992) Craig T. Nelson, Bonnie Bedelia

◇ *Firepower* (1993) Gary Daniels

◇ *Future Kill* (1984) Ed Neal

◇ *Gas-s-s-s* (1970) Bud Cort, Cindy Williams, Roger Corman (d)

◇ *Glen and Randa* (1971) Jim McBride (d)

◇ *Hardware* (1990) Dylan McDermott

◇ *Interzone* (1986) Bruce Abbott

◇ *In the Aftermath* (1988) Carl Colpaert (d)

◇ *L.A. 2017* (1971) Gene Barry, Edmond O'Brien, Barry Sullivan

◇ *Lawless Land* (1988) Nick Corri

◇ *Mad Max* (1979) Mel Gibson, George Miller (d)

◇ *Mad Max Beyond Thunderdome* (1985) Mel Gibson, Tina Turner

◇ *Metalstorm: The Destruction of Jared-Syn* (1983) Charles Band (d)

◇ *Nemesis* (1992) Olivier Gruner

◇ *Planet of the Apes* (1968) Charlton Heston

◇ *The Postman* (1997) Kevin Costner

◇ *Quintet* (1979) Paul Newman, Bibi Andersson, Robert Altman (d)

◇ *Raiders of Atlantis* (1983) Christopher Connelly

◇ *Rats* (1983) Richard Raymond

◇ *Road Warrior* (1981) Mel Gibson

◇ *Robot Holocaust* (1986) Noris Culf

◇ *Rush* (1984) Conrad Nichols

◇ *Soylent Green* (1973) Charlton Heston, Edward G. Robinson

◇ *Stryker* (1983) Steve Sandor

◇ *The Time Machine* (1960) Rod Taylor, Yvette Mimieux

◇ *Ultimate Warrior* (1975) Yul Brynner, Max von Sydow

◇ *Warlords* (1988) David Carradine, Sid Haig, Robert Quarry

⋄ *Warlords of the 21st Century* (1982) Michael Beck

⋄ *Warrior of the Lost World* (1983) Robert Ginty, Persis Khambatta

⋄ *Warriors of the Wasteland* (1982) Tim Brent, Fred Williamson

⋄ *Warriors of the Wind* (1984) Hayao Miyazaki (d)

⋄ *Waterworld* (1995) Kevin Costner, Dennis Hopper

⋄ *World Without End* (1956) Hugh Marlowe, Rod Taylor

⋄ *Z.P.G.* (1972) Oliver Reed, Geraldine Chaplin

Appendix C

Apocalyptic Television

The apocalyptic genre is generally not well suited to television except for tele-films and the occasional mini-series. Still, there have been television series with genuine apocalyptic aspects. *The X Files* (1993-) has an apocalyptic un-dercurrent in which the continued existence of the human race is threatened. Other series with alien invaders instigating a possible end of the world include *The Invaders* (1967-68); *War of the Worlds* (1988-90), which linked up both the 1953 film and the Orson Welles 1938 radio broadcast; and *V* (1984-85), which actually started as two mini-series in 1984 and 1985 before being crafted into a weekly series. *Starlost* (1973) was a Canadian series created by Harlan Ellison in which Earth was destroyed and only the inhabitants of one spaceship survived to seek a new home. In an entirely different vein, the 1981 British series, *Whoops! Apocalypse*, was a satire about the ludicrous chain of events that leads to nuclear war and total destruction. John Cleese of *Monty Python* fame starred in the show, which also included Barry Morse as the president of the United States. Years later, the show was redone as a feature film with Loretta Swit as the president and a cast including Ian Richardson, Peter Cook and Herbert Lom.

The landmark science fiction series *Babylon Five* (1994-99) had a unique five-year storyline, the heart of which was an apocalyptic struggle between an ancient race known as the Shadows and an alliance of the civilized worlds of the galaxy, led by Earth and Minbari. After the defeat of the Shadows, the series concluded with several telefilms, the last of which depicted Earth becoming infected with an alien virus which, it is projected, will wipe out the planet in two years unless an antidote is discovered. Gary Cole starred in a short-lived follow-up series, *Crusade* (1999), in which he led a special team seeking a serum to save Earth.

Apocalyptic elements occasionally crept into individual episodes of numerous series such as *Voyage to the Bottom of the Sea* (1964-68), *The Man from U.N.C.L.E.* (1964-68), *Time Tunnel* (1966-67), *Planet of the Apes* (1974) and *Seaquest DSV* (1993-96). Even *The Adventures of Superman* (1951-57) had an apocalyptic episode called "Panic in the Sky," in which the earth was threatened by the approach of a giant meteor.

The truest examples of the apocalyptic genre on television, however, were anthology shows in which the threat of total extinction is a genuine possibility.
In these television dramas, anything is possible. *Tales of Tomorrow* (1951-53)
was one of the earliest and finest science fiction anthology shows. It portrayed
the end of the world in "Blunder" in which the world's leading scientist calculates
that an experiment will result in a global catastrophe. He desperately tries to
call the authorities to cancel the experiment, but his pleas are ignored and the
program ends with total destruction of the planet. In another episode, *A Child Is
Crying,* an ordinary young girl becomes the conduit for an alien intelligence who
warns Earth about approaching doom. *Alfred Hitchcock Presents* (1955-63) had
a tongue-in-cheek apocalyptic episode entitled "The Night the World Ended," in
which a practical joker, played by Harold J. Stone, convinces barfly Russell
Collins that the world is ending by showing him a phony newspaper headline
describing the approach of a large meteor. Collins spends a number of desperate
hours before learning of the deception, then returns to the bar to kill Stone, who
winds up being shot at the exact time that he had informed Collins that the
world would end.

The Twilight Zone (1959-64), perhaps the highest regarded of all anthology
shows, had numerous apocalyptic episodes. In "Time Enough at Last," book-
worm Burgess Meredith is the sole survivor of a nuclear war, having been
trapped in a bank vault at the time of the destruction. After coming to terms
with his situation, nearsighted Meredith plans a lifetime of reading enjoyment,
but then he breaks his glasses, and must spend the rest of his days with blurred
vision. In "Third from the Sun," Fritz Weaver plays a scientist who plans an
escape with several families in a spaceship when he believes an all-out nuclear
war will lead to total annihilation. In "Probe 7—Over and Out," astronaut
Richard Basehart crashes on an unknown planet, and when he calls home he
learns that a terrible war of annihilation has broken out. The surprise in both
"Third from the Sun" and "Probe 7" is that the new home planet where the survivors find refuge turns out to be Earth. In "The Midnight Sun," a delirious
woman dreams that the earth has broken out of its orbit and is heading toward
the sun. When her fever breaks, she learns that the opposite has occurred, that
Earth is heading away from the sun into the doom of remote space. In "To
Serve Man," mankind is overcome by the benevolence of a race of superior alien
giants who promise to create utopia. A language expert, Lloyd Bochner, discovers too late that the alien book *To Serve Man* is not a philanthropic plan but actually a cook book.   *The Twilight Zone* also had a number of post-apocalyptic
episodes, such as "Two," with Elizabeth Montgomery and Charles Bronson and
"The Old Man in the Cave," both which depicts survivors years after doomsday.

The Outer Limits (1963-65) was another distinguished program with apocalyptic overtones. "Demon with a Glass Hand," one of their finest episodes, is
about an elaborate ruse in which the human race averts destruction by being encoded into the interior of an android played by Robert Culp. Other apocalyptic
episodes include "Nightmare" and "The Man Who Was Never Born."

Index

About the Author

CHARLES P. MITCHELL has served as director of a number of Maine libraries and has been Chairman of the Southern Maine Library District. He is the author of *A Guide to Charlie Chan Films* (Greenwood, 1999).